AN EXEGETICAL SUMMARY OF
THE SERMON ON THE MOUNT

AN EXEGETICAL SUMMARY OF

THE SERMON
ON THE MOUNT

Second Edition

**Thomas Tehan
and
David Abernathy**

SIL International

Second Edition
© 2003, 2008 by SIL International

Library of Congress Catalog Card Number: 2008923520
ISBN: 978-155671-194-7

Printed in the United States of America

Copies of this and other publications
of SIL International may be obtained from

International Academic Bookstore
SIL International
7500 West Camp Wisdom Road
Dallas, TX 75236-5699, USA

Voice: 972-708-7404
Fax: 972-708-7363
academic_books@sil.org
www.ethnologue.com

PREFACE

Exegesis is concerned with the interpretation of a text. Exegesis of the New Testament involves determining the meaning of the Greek text. Translators must be especially careful and thorough in their exegesis of the New Testament in order to accurately communicate its message in the vocabulary, grammar, and literary devices of another language. Questions occurring to translators as they study the Greek text are answered by summarizing how scholars have interpreted the text. This is information that should be considered by translators as they make their own exegetical decisions regarding the message they will communicate in their translations.

The Semi-Literal Translation

As a basis for discussion, a semi-literal translation of the Greek text is given so that the reasons for different interpretations can best be seen. When one Greek word is translated into English by several words, these words are joined by hyphens. There are a few times when clarity requires that a string of words joined by hyphens have a separate word, such as "not" (μή), inserted in their midst. In this case, the separate word is surrounded by spaces between the hyphens. When alternate translations of a Greek word are given, these are separated by slashes.

The Text

Variations in the Greek text are noted under the heading TEXT. The base text for the summary is the text of the fourth revised edition of *The Greek New Testament,* published by the United Bible Societies, which has the same text as the twenty-sixth edition of the *Novum Testamentum Graece* (Nestle-Aland). The versions that follow different variations are listed without evaluating their choices.

The Lexicon

The meaning of a key word in context is the first question to be answered. Words marked with a raised letter in the semi-literal translation are treated separately under the heading LEXICON. First, the lexicon form of the Greek word is given. Within the parentheses following the Greek word is the location number where, in the author's judgment, this word is defined in the *Greek-English Lexicon of the New Testament Based on Semantic Domains* (Louw and Nida 1988). When a semantic domain includes a translation of the particular verse being treated, **LN** in bold type indicates that specific translation. If the specific reference for the verse is listed in *A Greek-English Lexicon of the New Testament and Other Early Christian Literature* (Bauer, Arndt, Gingrich, and Danker 1979), the outline location and page number is given. Then English equivalents of the Greek word are given to show how it is translated by commentators who offer their own translations of the whole text and, after a semicolon, all the versions in the list of abbreviations for translations. When reference is made to "all versions," it refers to only the versions in the list of translations. Sometimes further comments are made about the meaning of the word or the significance of a verb's tense, voice, or mood.

The Questions

Under the heading QUESTION, a question is asked that comes from examining the Greek text under consideration. Typical questions concern the identity of an implied actor or object of an event word, the antecedent of a pronominal reference, the connection indicated by a relational word, the meaning of a genitive construction, the meaning of figurative language, the function of a rhetorical question, the identification of an ambiguity, and the presence of implied information that is needed to understand the passage correctly. Background information is also considered for a proper understanding of a passage. Although not all implied information and background information is made explicit in a translation, it is important to consider it so that the translation will not be stated in such a way that prevents a reader from arriving at the proper interpretation. The question is answered with a summary of what commentators have said. If there are contrasting differences of opinion, the different interpretations are numbered and the commentaries that support each are listed. Differences that are not treated by many of the commentaries often are not numbered, but are introduced with a contrastive 'Or' at the beginning of the sentence. No attempt has been made to select which interpretation is best.

In listing support for various statements of interpretation, the author is often faced with the difficult task of matching the different terminologies used in commentaries with the terminology he has adopted. Sometimes he can only infer the position of a commentary from incidental remarks. This book, then, includes the author's interpretation of the views taken in the various commentaries. General statements are followed by specific statements, which indicate the author's understanding of the pertinent relationships, actors, events, and objects implied by that interpretation.

The Use of This Book

This book does not replace the commentaries that it summarizes. Commentaries contain much more information about the meaning of words and passages. They often contain arguments for the interpretations that are taken and they may have important discussions about the discourse features of the text. In addition, they have information about the historical, geographical, and cultural setting. Translators will want to refer to at least four commentaries as they exegete a passage. However, since no one commentary contains all the answers translators need, this book will be a valuable supplement. It makes more sources of exegetical help available than most translators have access to. Even if they had all the books available, few would have the time to search through all of them for the answers.

When many commentaries are studied, it soon becomes apparent that they frequently disagree in their interpretations. That is the reason why so many answers in this book are divided into two or more interpretations. The reader's initial reaction may be that all of these different interpretations complicate exegesis rather than help it. However, before translating a passage, a translator needs to know exactly where there is a problem of interpretation and what the exegetical options are.

ABBREVIATIONS

COMMENTARIES AND REFERENCE BOOKS

AAG   Black, Matthew. *An Aramaic Approach to the Gospels and Acts.* 3d ed. Peabody, MA: Hendrickson Publishers, 1967.

BAGD   Bauer, Walter. *A Greek-English Lexicon of the New Testament and Other Early Christian Literature.* Translated and adapted from the 5th ed., 1958 by William F. Arndt and F. Wilbur Gingrich. 2d English ed. revised and augmented by F. Wilbur Gingrich and Frederick W. Danker. Chicago: University of Chicago Press, 1979.

BBC   Keener, Craig S. *IVP Bible Background Commentary.* Downers Grove, IL: InterVarsity Press, 1993.

BD   Blass, F. and A. Debrunner. *A Greek Grammar of the New Testament and Other Early Christian Literature.* Translated and revised from the 9th ed. by Robert W. Funk. Chicago: University of Chicago Press, 1961.

Brc   Barclay, William. *The Gospel of Matthew: Translated with an Introduction and Interpretation,* vol. 1 (Chapters 1 to 10), Revised edition. Philadelphia: The Westminster Press. 1975.

BSC   Ridderbos, H. N. *Matthew.* Translated by Ray Togtman. Bible Student's Commentary. Grand Rapids: Regency Reference Library, Zondervan, 1987.

Dei   Deibler, Ellis W., Jr. *Exercises in Bible Translation.* Dallas: Summer Institute of Linguistics, 1988. (Answers to exercises on diskette.)

EBC   Carson, D. A. *Matthew.* In *The Expositor's Bible Commentary,* edited by Frank E. Gaebelein, vol. 8. Grand Rapids: Zondervan, 1981.

Ed   Edersheim, Alfred. *The Life and Times of Jesus the Messiah.* New American Edition. New York: E. R. Herrick & Company, 1886. pp. 524-541. Note: Talmud references are included here.

ICC   Davies, W. D. and Dale C. Allison. *A Critical and Exegetical Commentary on the Gospel According to Saint Matthew.* The International Critical Commentary on the Holy Scriptures of the Old and New Testaments, edited by J. A. Emerton, C. E. B. Cranfield, and G. N. Stanton. Edinburgh: T. and T. Clark, 1988.

LN   Louw, Johannes p. and Eugene A. Nida. *Greek-English Lexicon of the New Testament Based on Semantic Domains.* New York: United Bible Societies, 1988.

McN   McNeile, Alan Hugh. *The Gospel According to St. Matthew: The Greek Text with Introduction, Notes, and Indices.* Grand Rapids: Baker, 1980, originally 1915.

Met   Metzger, Bruce M. *A Textual Commentary on the Greek New Testament.* 2d ed. New York: United Bible Societies, 1994.

MLJ	Lloyd-Jones, D. Martyn. *Studies in the Sermon on the Mount.* Volumes 1 & 2. London: Inter-Varsity Fellowship, 1959.
Mor	Morris, Leon. *The Gospel according to Matthew.* The Pillar New Testament Commentary, edited by D. A. Carson. Grand Rapids: Eerdmans, 1992.
NAC	Blomberg, Craig L. *Matthew.* The New American Commentary, edited by David S. Dockery. Nashville, Tennessee: Broadman Press, 1992.
NCBC	Hill, David. *The Gospel of Matthew.* New Century Bible Commentary, edited by Matthew Black. Grand Rapids: Eerdmans, 1972.
NIBC	Mounce, Robert H. *Matthew.* New International Biblical Commentary, edited by W. Ward Gasque. Peabody, Massachusetts: Hendrickson Publishers, Inc., 1985, 1991.
NTC	Hendriksen, William. *Exposition of the Gospel According to Matthew.* New Testament Commentary. Grand Rapids: Baker, 1973.
Pl	Plummer, Alfred. *An Exegetical Commentary on the Gospel According to St. Matthew.* Second edition. Grand Rapids: Eerdmans, 1953, originally 1909.
TG	Bratcher, Robert. G. *A Translator's Guide to the Gospel of Matthew.* London, New York, Stuttgart: United Bible Societies, 1981.
TH	Newman, Barclay M., and Philip C. Stine. *A Translator's Handbook on the Gospel of Matthew.* Helps for Translators. London: United Bible Societies, 1988.
TNTC	Tasker, R. G. *The Gospel According to St. Matthew: An Introduction and Commentary.* The Tyndale New Testament Commentaries, edited by Leon Morris. Grand Rapids: Eerdmans, 1961.
TNTC2	France, R. T. *The Gospel According to St. Matthew: An Introduction and Commentary.* The Tyndale New Testament Commentaries, edited by Leon Morris. Grand Rapids: Eerdmans, 1985.
WBC	Hagner, Donald A. *Matthew 1-13.* Word Biblical Commentary, edited by David A. Hubbard and Glenn W. Barker. Waco: Word, 1988.
ZG	Zerwick, Max, and Mary Grosvenor. *A Grammatical Analysis of the Greek New Testament.* Unabridged, revised edition in one volume. Rome: Biblical Institute Press, 1981.

GREEK TEXT AND TRANSLATIONS

GNT	*The Greek New Testament.* Edited by B. Aland, K Aland, J. Karavidopoulos, C. Martini, and B. Metzger. 4th ed. London, New York: United Bible Societies, 1993.
HF	Hodges, Zane C. and Arthur L. Farstad. *The Greek New Testament According to the Majority Text.* Nashville: Thomas Nelson Publishers, 1982.
CEV	The Holy Bible, Contemporary English Version. New York: American Bible Society, 1995.
KJV	*The Holy Bible.* Authorized (or King James) Version, 1611.

NAB   *The New American Bible.* Iowa Falls, Iowa: World Bible Publishers, 1987.

NASB   *The New American Standard Bible.* Nashville, Tennessee: Holman, 1977.

NET   The Net Bible, New English Translation, New Testament, Version 9.206. www.netbible.com: Biblical Studies Press, 1999

NIV   *The Holy Bible: New International Version.* Grand Rapids: Zondervan, 1984.

NJB   *The New Jerusalem Bible.* Garden City, New York: Doubleday, 1985.

NLT   *The New Living Translation.* Wheaton, IL: Tyndale House Publishers. 1996.

NRSV   *The Holy Bible: New Revised Standard Version.* New York: Oxford University Press, 1989.

REB   *The Revised English Bible.* Oxford: Oxford University Press and Cambridge University Press, 1989.

TEV   *Today's English Version*, 2d ed. New York: American Bible Society, 1992.

TNT   *The Translator's New Testament.* London: British and Foreign Bible Society, 1973.

GRAMMATICAL TERMS

act.	active	mid.	middle
fut.	future	opt.	optative
impera.	imperative	pass.	passive
imperf.	imperfect	perf.	perfect
indic.	indicative	pres.	present
infin.	infinitive	subj.	subjunctive

EXEGESIS OF MATTHEW 5–7

DISCOURSE UNIT: 5:1–7:29 [BSC, EBC, McN, Mor, NAC, NCBC, NTC, Pl, TNTC2, WBC; CEV, NASB, REB]. The topic is the sermon on the mount [all except TNTC2], Jesus' teaching on discipleship [TNTC2].

DISCOURSE UNIT: 5:1–48 [NIBC]. The topic is the sermon on the mount: kingdom ethics and the law.

DISCOURSE UNIT: 5:1–16 [NAC, TNTC]. The topic is the characteristics of Christian discipleship [TNTC], introduction [NAC].

DISCOURSE UNIT: 5:1–12 [BBC; HF, NASB, NET, NIV, NJB]. The topic is the beatitudes [HF, NASB, NET, NIV, NJB], the beatitudes, or blessings [BBC].

DISCOURSE UNIT: 5:1–2 [BSC, EBC, GNT, Mor, NAC, TG, TH, TNTC2, WBC; TEV]. The topic is the sermon on the mount [GNT; TEV], Jesus on the mount [BSC], Jesus preaches on the mountain [TG, TH], setting [EBC, NAC], the setting of the sermon [WBC], introduction [Mor, TNTC2].

DISCOURSE UNIT: 5:1 [CEV, NLT]. The topic is the sermon on the mount.

5:1 Now[a] **seeing the crowds[b] he-went-up[c] on[d] the mountain/hill;[e]**
LEXICON—a. δέ: 'now' [NIV], 'and' [Mor; KJV, NASB], 'one day' [NLT], not explicit [NTC, WBC; CEV, NAB, NET, NJB, NRSV, REB, TEV, TNT].

b. ὄχλος (LN 11.1) (BAGD 1. p. 600): 'crowd' [BAGD, LN, Mor; NIV, NJB, NRSV, REB, TEV, TNT], 'crowds' [NTC, WBC; CEV, NAB, NET, NLT], 'multitude' [BAGD, LN; KJV, NASB].

c. aorist act. indic. of ἀναβαίνω (LN 15.101) (BAGD 1.a.α. p. 50): 'to go up' [BAGD, LN, Mor, NTC, WBC; all versions except NJB], 'to go' [NJB], 'to ascend' [BAGD, LN].

d. εἰς (LN 83.47); 'on' [LN; CEV, NAB, NASB, NIV], 'onto' [NJB], 'into' [Mor, NTC; KJV], 'to' [WBC], not explicit [NET, NLT, NRSV, REB, TEV, TNT].

e. ὄρος (LN 1.46) (BAGD p. 582): 'mountain' [BAGD, LN, Mor, NTC, WBC; KJV, NAB, NASB, NET, NJB, NRSV, REB], 'mountainside' [BSC; NIV, NLT], 'the side of a mountain' [CEV], 'hill' [ZG; TEV, TNT], 'hill country' [NAC]. It is an elevation that is relatively high in comparison with the surrounding landscape and the actual elevation is not the determining factor [LN].

QUESTION—What relationship is indicated by the participle ἰδών 'seeing'?

1. It indicates time [Mor, NTC, WBC; CEV, NAB, NASB, NET, NIV, NRSV, REB]: when Jesus saw the crowd, he went up onto the mountain. Although translating the relationship as 'when', it is still implied that the reason Jesus went to the mountain was to escape for a time the people who had been crowding around him for healing [WBC].

11

2. It indicates reason [ICC, TH]: because Jesus saw the crowd, he went up onto the mountain. Jesus wanted to get away from the crowd [ICC].

QUESTION—Since ὄρος is an elevation that is relatively high to its surroundings, is it here a mountain or a hill?

    1. It refers to a mountain [BSC, NTC, WBC; KJV, NAB, NASB, NIV, NJB, NRSV].

    2. It refers to a hill [ICC, LN, NAC, NIBC, Pl, TNTC2; TEV, TNT]. This term merely means that it is higher than the surrounding land, i.e., the hill country [ICC, LN, NAC, NIBC, Pl, TNTC2]. It is high ground near the lake [Pl], high ground north and west of the lake [NIBC], a plateau in a hilly area [NAC].

QUESTION—What is the significance of the article in τὸ ὄρος 'the mountain/hill'?

    1. It indicates a specific mountain or hill known to the reader [BAGD, NTC]. It refers to the only or obvious mountain nearby [BAGD (II.1.a.α. p. 552)]. It is a well-known mountain, perhaps the *Horns of Hattin*, which is four miles west of Lake Galilee, or the gentle slopes west of Tagha [NTC].

    2. It indicates an unspecified mountain or hill [BSC, EBC, Ed, McN, Mor, NCBC, Pl, TG, TH, TNTC2, ZG; KJV, NET, NIV, REB, TEV]. Perhaps it was someplace among the hills north of Capernaum [Ed], west of Lake of Galilee [EBC, McN, NCBC, TNTC2], close to Lake of Galilee [Pl]. Perhaps it was idiomatic or generic as in 'going to the hospital' [NET].

QUESTION—What is meant by ἀνέβη εἰς 'he went up onto' the mountain or hill?

The location was the side of a hill [TG, TH]. He went up to a terrace on the side of a hill [Pl]. This is the same 'level place' referred to in Luke 6:17 [EBC, LN]. He went up to a plain on the mountainside to teach his disciples [EBC, LN]. Perhaps it means he went back to the mountain top to teach his disciples after descending to a plain to heal the sick [LN].

and having-seated[a] himself his disciples came-to[b] him;

LEXICON—a. aorist act. participle of καθίζω (LN **17.12**) (BAGD 2.a.α. p. 390): 'to be seated' [LN, NTC; NJB] 'to sit down' [BAGD, **LN**, Mor, WBC; all versions except KJV, NJB], 'to sit' [LN], 'to be set' [KJV]. This participle is translated 'when he had seated himself' [NTC], 'when he was set' [KJV].

    b. aorist act. indic. of προσέρχομαι (LN 15.77) (BAGD 1. p. 713): 'to come to' [BAGD, BSC, Mor, NTC, WBC; KJV, NAB, NASB, NET, NIV, NJB, NRSV, TNT], 'to approach, to come near to' [LN], 'to gather around' [CEV], not explicit [NLT].

QUESTION—What relationship is indicated by the participle καθίσαντος 'sitting down'?

    1. It indicates time [NTC, WBC, ZG; KJV, NAB, NASB, NET, NJB, NRSV]: after or when he sat down, his disciples came to him.

2. It refers to the previous clause [REB, TEV]: he went up on a hill, where
he sat down.

QUESTION—Why did Jesus sit down?

Jesus assumed a natural position used by a rabbi when teaching [BBC, Brc,
BSC, EBC, ICC, Mor, NAC, NCBC, NIBC, TG, TH, WBC]. It indicated
that the discourse was important [McN, TNTC2] and lengthy [BSC, Pl].

QUESTION—Who are 'the disciples'?

They were a rather large group of people consisting of more people than the
four of 4:18–22 [ICC] or the Twelve [BSC, EBC, ICC, Mor, NCBC, NIBC,
TG, TH, TNTC2]. They are in contrast with the large crowd which Jesus left
behind [ICC].

DISCOURSE UNIT: 5:2–11 [CEV, NLT]. The topic is blessings [CEV], the
beatitudes [NLT].

5:2 and/then[a] opening[b] his mouth he-taught them saying,

LEXICON—a. καί (LN 89.87): 'and' [LN, Mor, NTC, WBC; CEV, KJV, NIV,
TEV], 'then' [NET, NJB, NRSV], not explicit [NAB, NASB, NLT, REB,
TNT].

b. aorist act. participle of ἀνοίγω (LN 33.29) (BAGD I.e.α. p. 71): 'to open'
[BAGD, Mor, NTC; KJV, NASB]. The phrase 'opening his mouth he
taught them saying' is translated 'he began to speak, and taught them,
saying' [NRSV], 'he began to teach them by saying' [NET], 'he began to
teach them saying' [NAB, NIV, TNT], 'he began to teach them' [TEV],
'he taught them [CEV]. This is what he taught them' [NJB], 'this is what
he taught them' [NLT], 'this is the teaching he gave' [REB]. The phrase
'opening his mouth' is a Semitic idiom [ICC, LN, McN, WBC, ZG] for
beginning to speak in a formal teaching context [LN]. It lends emphasis
by making the introduction more solemn [Brc, EBC, ICC, Mor, Pl, TH,
WBC].

QUESTION—What relationship is indicated by καί (and)?

1. It indicates simple coordination [BSC; CEV, KJV, NIV, TEV]: and.

2. It indicates time sequence [NET, NJB, NRSV]: then.

QUESTION—What is the tense of ἐδίδασκεν 'he taught'?

This is an inceptive imperfect 'he began to teach' [EBC, McN, NTC, WBC;
NAB, NET, NIV, NRSV, TEV, TNT] reflecting Semitic usage [McN].

QUESTION—What is the force of the participle λέγων 'saying'?

This participle, coupled with ἀνοίγω τὸ στόμα 'opening his mouth', reflects
a Semitic style [TH, ZG] indicating that direct discourse follows [TH].

DISCOURSE UNIT: 5:3–16 [EBC, Pl, WBC]. The topic is the kingdom of
heaven: its norms and witness [EBC], the qualifications of those who can enter
the Kingdom [Pl], introduction [WBC].

DISCOURSE UNIT: 5:3–12 [BSC, EBC, GNT, ICC, McN, Mor, NAC,
NCBC, Pl, TG, TH, WBC; NAB, TEV]. The topic is the beatitudes [BSC, GNT,
ICC, McN, Mor; NAB], nine beatitudes for the people of God [ICC], the

beatitudes, a summary of the Christian life [Pl], the foundation of righteous living: the beatitudes [WBC], the kingdom blessings [NAC], true happiness [TEV], people who are truly happy [TG, TH], the norms of the kingdom [EBC].

DISCOURSE UNIT: 5:3–10 [EBC, TNTC2]. The topic is the advantages of discipleship [TNTC2], the beatitudes [EBC].

5:3 Blessed[a] (are) the poor[b] in-spirit,[c]

LEXICON—a. μακάριος (LN **25.119**) (BAGD 1.b. p. 486): 'blessed' [BAGD, Mor, NTC; KJV, NAB, NASB, NET, NIV, NJB, NRSV, REB], 'happy' [LN, NAC, WBC; TEV, TNT], 'fortunate' [BAGD, NAC]. This noun is also translated as a verb phrase: 'God blesses' [CEV, NLT].

   b. πτωχός (LN **88.57**) (BAGD 1.c. p. 728): 'the poor' [BAGD, Mor, NTC; KJV, NAB, NASB, NET, NIV, NJB, NRSV, REB], 'the oppressed' [WBC], 'those people who depend only on him' [CEV], 'those who realize their need for him' [NLT], 'those who recognize their need of God' [LN], 'those who know they are spiritually poor' [TEV], 'those who know their spiritual need' [TNT]. It denotes absolute and abject poverty, destitution [Brc, Mor, NIBC].

   c. πνεῦμα (LN 26.9) (BAGD 3.b. p. 675): 'spirit' [BAGD, LN, Mor, NTC; KJV, NAB, NASB, NET, NIV, NJB, NRSV, REB], not explicit [WBC; CEV, NLT]. This noun is also translated as an adjective: 'spiritually (poor)' [TEV], 'spiritual (need)' [TNT].

QUESTION—Does μακάριοι refer to an objective judgment concerning such people as being blessed or to a subjective state of feeling happy?

  1. It refers to an objective judgment about such people [Pl, TH, TNTC2; KJV, NAB, NASB, NET, NIV, NJB, NRSV, REB]: they are blessed who are poor in spirit, who mourn, etc. It is God's estimate of them [Pl]. It is a condition of life, not an emotional or mental state, and it is not dependent on the circumstances of life [TNTC2]. Instead of meaning that God will bless them, it means that they are fortunate and are to be congratulated [NAC, TNTC2]. Because of what God will do for them, they in a good position, well off, or fortunate [TH]. Although they may not feel it, they are happy in the sight of God and by the standards of the kingdom; in other words they are superlatively blessed [NTC].

  2. It describes the subjective emotion of such people [Brc, NAC, NIBC, WBC; TEV, TNT]: they are happy who are poor in spirit, who mourn, etc. It means to have serene joy [Brc], deep happiness, inner joy [WBC], a joy that has its secret within itself [NIBC]. They are happy because they are beginning to experience the fulfillment of the long awaited salvation that God had promised [WBC].

QUESTION—What is meant by being οἱ πτωχοὶ τῷ πνεύματι 'the poor in spirit'?

This is the dative of respect (defining dative) 'poor with respect to their spirit'. It indicates 'in the realm of the spirit', and it is parallel to 'in heart' in 5:8 [EBC, NTC, TH, WBC, ZG]. It is an idiom meaning to be humble about one's capacity to relate to God and means to recognize one's need of God [LN (88.57)]. The emphasis is on depending on God for all things [BBC, EBC, NCBC, NIBC, TH, TNTC2]. Characteristics include humility [Brc, Ed, Pl, TG], helplessness [Brc], complete trust in God [Brc, BSC, EBC, MLJ, NTC, TH, TNTC2], piety [McN, Pl, TNTC2], suffering oppression [BSC, TNTC2], knowing personal needs [Brc, ICC, NTC, Pl, TG, TH], spiritual powerlessness [NAC], and conviction of personal spiritual poverty [NTC]. It can be contrasted on the one hand with a sense of perfectness [Ed], pride, self-reliance [MLJ], and on the other hand with diffidence, weakness, lack of courage [MLJ], poor-spiritedness [TNTC], lacking God's spirit, having no ambition [TG], and lacking spiritual gifts [Pl]. The religious connotations are not easily distinguished from πραΰς 'meek' in 5:5 [NCBC, TH]. Poverty and piety were united in Jesus' time and culture in the Hebrew word ϖαναωιμ (e.g. Isa. 6:1) [NAC]. In Hebrew ϖαναψψιν for πτωχός 'poor' and ϖαναωιν for πραΰς 'meek/humble' were used to describe 'the poor men of God, the afflicted saints'; see Psalm 35:11 [AAG (p. 156)].

for theirs is the kingdom of-the heavens.
QUESTION—What relationship is indicated by ὅτι 'for'?
　　It indicates the grounds for saying that such a person is blessed [EBC, Mor, NTC, TH, WBC; KJV, NAB, NASB, NET, NIV, NLT, NRSV]: 'because', 'for'.
QUESTION—What is the βασιλεία των οὐρανῶν 'kingdom of heaven'?
　　The βασιλεία 'kingdom' is 'the royal reign' (BAGD 3.a. p. 134). There is no practical difference between 'the kingdom of heaven' and 'the kingdom of God'; here ουρανοι 'the heavens' is used figuratively and is synonymous with God [BAGD (3. p. 599), MLJ, TG, TH]. The plural is used because of Hebrew/Aramaic influence. Out of 35 times the expression is used in Matthew, only 5 times is the singular used [ZG]. The expression is translated 'the kingdom of heaven' [all versions]. The emphasis of the expression is on the activity [TH] of complete redemption and liberation with God ruling as king [BSC] and not on a geographical territory [TH]. This includes God's rule here and now and should not imply that the rule will only take place in some future time such as the phrase 'in heaven' might imply [TG]. Matthew uses 'the kingdom of heaven' instead of 'the kingdom of God' because the Jews, who were his primary audience, avoided using God's name whenever possible [MLJ, TG].
QUESTION—What is the meaning of αὐτῶν ἐστιν 'theirs is'?
　　The phrase αὐτῶν ἐστιν 'theirs is' emphasizes the pronoun, meaning 'theirs alone' [Mor, NTC], 'precisely they among all classes' [Pl]. This emphasis is proposed for the following beatitudes also [Mor]. It could mean the kingdom 'belongs to' or 'consists of' such people [TH; NET]. However it does not mean that they own it [ICC, TG], or that they rule, since only God rules [Pl]. It does not mean 'consisting of', since as the outcome of the last judgment they will be given the kingdom [ICC]. The emphasis is on the fact that they

are already citizens who enjoy the benefits of being ruled by God [TG, TH], and are counted as God's subjects [Pl]. It is translated 'is given to them' [NLT], or 'they belong to the kingdom of heaven' [CEV].

QUESTION—What is the significance of the present tense of the verb 'is'?

The original Aramaic that Jesus spoke would have had no verb, and thus no tense indicators [ICC, McN]. The present tense of the verb 'is' indicates that this result is already taking place [BSC, EBC, ICC, Mor, NCBC, NTC, TH, TNTC2, WBC]. It emphasizes confidence and certainty [EBC, ICC, TNTC2, ZG]. This is a timeless present [McN]. Note that the second clause of the first and eighth (5:10) beatitudes are identical and both use present tense (declaring the Kingdom to be present); the other beatitudes all use future tense verbs. The future tenses serve to emphasize a future consolation with at most a partial fulfillment in this age [EBC, Mor, NAC, NCBC, NIBC, NTC, TG, WBC].

5:4 Blessed (are) those mourning,[a]

TEXT—Some manuscripts reverse the order of verses 4 and 5. GNT notes this in a footnote, but gives the present order a rating of B, indicating that this order is almost certain. Only NJB reverses the order of verses 4 and 5.

LEXICON—a. pres. act. participle of πενθέω (LN **25.142**) (BAGD 1. p. 642): 'to mourn' [BAGD, Mor, NTC, ZG; all versions except CEV, REB], 'to sorrow' [REB], 'to grieve' [BAGD, LN, WBC; CEV].

QUESTION—What rhetorical style is used in connecting the beatitudes in Mt. 5:3–17?

In this passage there is a lack of explicit connectives between the axioms, a rhetorical style called asyndeton [AAG (p. 57), BD]. This is probably not a conscious style, although it does give solemnity and weight to the discourse. It is comparable to a more conscious rhetorical asyndeton in the Epistles (e.g., 1 Cor. 7: 18, 21). In Mt. 5:3–17, asyndeton is employed both when there is no connection in thought and when there is connected thought, as in 5:17 οὐκ ἦλθον 'I came not' instead of οὐ γάρ 'for not'. [AAG (p. 57), BD (sec. 458, 462(2), pp. 239–242)]. It is obvious that Hebrew or Aramaic poetic parallelism lies behind the Beatitudes [AAG (p. 156, 276)].

QUESTION—What is meant by πενθοῦντες 'mourning'?

This is the strongest Greek word for mourning [Brc]. It means feeling utterly and sorrowfully hopeless [MLJ], having intense care and sorrow [Brc]. It is the character of one undergoing sorrow [BSC]. It is a God-centered mourning coming from the heart, changing a person and being shown in behavior [NTC]. It can be contrasted on the one hand with moroseness and misery and on the other hand with forgetting troubles, superficiality, glibness, joviality, and laughter [MLJ].

QUESTION—What are they mourning about?

People are mourning about their own sins and failings [Brc, EBC, MLJ, Mor, NAC, NTC, Pl, TG; probably BBC] and spiritual bankruptcy [NTC]. They mourn (are bereaved [BBC]) over the sins and failings of others [BAGD,

Brc, EBC, LN, McN, MLJ, Mor, NTC, Pl, TG, WBC], wickedness and oppression [BAGD, BBC, BSC, ICC, LN, NAC, NCBC, Pl], the world's suffering [Brc, MLJ], the needs of people [TG], sorrows and sins of others [McN], the plight of the downtrodden and poor [WBC]. They are lamenting that the Kingdom has been so long in coming [EBC, Pl, WBC], the slowness of God's justice [ICC, WBC], at the oppression of God's people, because the righteous suffer and the wicked prosper [ICC], at the humbling of Israel [NCBC], at both spiritual and social concerns [NAC]. They mourn because they suffer an unhappy life because of their loyalty to God [TNTC2]. It is not just mourning because of going through personal difficulties, it is mourning that comes from understanding that the world's suffering comes from the sinful tendency to ignore God [NIBC].

QUESTION—How does mourning relate to the poor in spirit in the previous verse?

Some commentators relate the cause of this mourning to the realization of being poor in spirit and thus take this group to be the same as the first [BSC, MLJ, NTC]. When one sees God, his holiness and the kind of life one should live, and then examines the reality of one's life in poverty of spirit, one mourns [MLJ]. The comfort they receive is another elaboration of the blessing about the kingdom of heaven in the previous verse [BSC].

for they will-be-comforted.[a]

LEXICON—a. fut. pass. indic. of παρακαλέω (LN 25.150) (BAGD 4. p. 617): 'to be comforted' [BAGD, LN, Mor, NTC, WBC; all versions except CEV, REB, TEV], 'to be consoled' [LN], 'to find comfort' [CEV], 'to find consolation' [REB], 'to be encouraged' [BAGD, LN]. This passive form is also translated actively: 'God will comfort' [TEV].

QUESTION—Who will comfort them?

God will comfort them [ICC, NAC, NIBC, NTC, TG, TH, TNTC, WBC, ZG; TEV]. The expression is a divine passive construction [NAC, NTC, TH, TNTC2, WBC] of Semitic character [NIBC, TH, TNTC2]. The divine passive is also used in vs. 6, 7, 9 [NAC, TNTC2, WBC]. God comforts by forgiving, delivering, strengthening, and reassuring those who mourn [NTC]. They will find in salvation a happiness that transcends the conditions that cause mourning [TNTC2].

5:5 **Blessed (are) the meek,**[a]

LEXICON—a. πραΰς (LN 88.60) (BAGD p. 699): 'meek' [BAGD, LN, Mor, NTC; KJV, NAB, NET, NIV, NRSV, TNT], 'gentle' [BAGD, LN, NAC; NASB, NJB, REB], 'gentle and lowly' [NLT], 'humble' [BAGD, NAC, WBC; CEV, TEV], 'considerate, unassuming' [BAGD], 'mild' [LN].

QUESTION—What is meant by πραΰς 'meek'?

The contrast between πραΰς 'meek' and πτωχοὶ πνεύματι 'poor in spirit' is small [BSC, EBC, NCBC, NTC, Pl, TH, TNTC2, WBC], perhaps being no more than an emphasis on waiting for God to avenge [BSC], or on one's attitude toward others [EBC, McN, MLJ, NTC], or on personal piety [ICC,

McN, NTC, Pl]. It is described with words like humble [Pl, TG, TH], gentle [EBC, TG, TH, ZG], and non-aggressive [NAC, TG, TH, TNTC2], and it contains the ideas of 'insignificant', 'lowly', and 'powerless' [ICC, TH], and willingness to suffer wrong rather than injure others [NTC]. It means God-controlled [Brc, Pl] and relying on God [Mor, TG]. It is not defensive and it allows others to be assertive [MLJ, Mor]. It can be contrasted with power, self-assurance, and aggressiveness on the one hand, and on the other with indolence, flabbiness, natural niceness [MLJ], and weakness [ICC]. It is true humility with no pride [Brc] and living a humble and sacrificial life of service [NIBC]. In the language of the day it described outward conduct between people, but in the NT it portrayed an inward quality relating primarily to God [NIBC]. This quality was not valued in the ancient Greco-Roman culture, and it would certainly not characterize those who were expected to control and inherit the earth [NAC]. It included a lack of earthly possessions [NAC].

for they will-inherit[a] the earth.[b]

LEXICON—a. fut. act. indic. of κληρονομέω (LN **57.131**) (BAGD 2. p. 434): 'to inherit' [Mor, NTC, WBC; KJV, NAB, NASB, NET, NIV, NRSV], 'to receive' [**LN**; TEV], 'to possess' [TNT], 'to have as inheritance' [NJB], 'to have for a possession' [REB], 'to acquire, obtain, come into possession of something' [BAGD], 'to be given, to gain possession of' [LN]. The whole phrase is translated 'the whole earth will belong to them' [NLT], 'the earth will belong to them' [CEV].

b. γῆ (LN 1.39) (BAGD 4. p. 157): 'earth' [LN, Mor, NTC, WBC; CEV, KJV, NASB, NET, NIV, NJB, NLT, NRSV, REB, TNT], 'land' [BAGD; NAB], 'what God has promised' [TEV]. (Both the Greek term ἡ γῆ and the Hebrew term *ha aretz* which is translated in the Septuagint by ἡ γή can mean 'the land' in a more localized sense or 'the world'.)

QUESTION—What is meant by κληρονομέω 'inherit'?

It means to receive something when the present occupants are no longer in possession [BSC, TH, TNTC]. It means to acquire or to possess, which in this case will come about at the great eschatological reversal when the present order of things will be turned upside down [ICC]. It implies possession as a right by grace, which is inalienable and unearnable [NTC]. It does not imply the death of the previous owner as English 'inherit' does [TG]. It was used to describe Israel's inheriting the promised land [EBC, McN, TG, TNTC2]. The future tense here indicates certainty also [Mor].

QUESTION—What does τὴν γῆν 'the earth' mean?

It alludes to Israel's taking possession of the Promised Land [EBC, McN, TG, TNTC2, WBC, ZG], but the meaning has been expanded [BBC, EBC]. It means the entire earth [BBC, ICC, NAC, TH, TNTC; CEV, NLT], the regenerated earth [WBC]. They will enjoy the benefits of a redeemed earth [TH]. The blessings to come will be material and physical as well as spiritual and heavenly [BSC], and the idea of an actual location is secondary [NCBC].

5:6 Blessed (are) those hungering[a] and thirsting[b] (for) righteousness,[c]

LEXICON—a. pres. act. participle of πεινάω (LN **25.17**) (BAGD 2. p. 640): 'to hunger' [BAGD, LN, Mor, NTC, WBC; all versions except CEV, TEV]. Both 'hungering' and 'thirsting' are conflated into one expression: 'who desire intensely' [LN], 'those whose greatest desire is' [TEV], and 'those who want to obey him more than eat or drink' [CEV]. To hunger and thirst is figurative for strongly desiring something [BAGD, LN].

   b. pres. act. participle of διψάω (LN **25.17**) (BAGD 3. p. 200): 'to thirst' [BAGD, LN, Mor, NTC, WBC; all versions except CEV, TEV].

   c. δικαιοσύνη (LN 88.13) (BAGD 2.b. p. 196): 'righteousness' [BAGD, LN, Mor, NTC; KJV, NAB, NASB, NET, NIV, NRSV], 'uprightness' [BAGD; NJB], 'what is right' [TNT], 'justice' [WBC; NLT]. This noun is also translated as a verb phrase: 'to do what God requires' [LN; TEV], 'to obey him' [CEV], 'to do what is right' [LN], 'to see right prevail' [REB]. See this word at 5:10.

QUESTION—What does it mean to hunger and thirst for righteousness?

The two verbs intensify each other [LN] and indicate an ardent longing [NCBC], a great desire [EBC, LN], an earnest yearning and relentless pursuit [NTC], a passionate and wholehearted concern [Mor], a desire to attain the goal of righteousness when it is currently lacking [LN]. This hunger and thirst are similar to that of a man who may starve for lack of food or die for lack of water [Brc]. Together these verbs describe deep longings and not passing feelings [ICC, MLJ]. The emphasis is not on the achievement or current possession of righteousness, but the whole-hearted longing for it [Brc, ICC, MLJ, Pl] with a consciousness of desperate need [MLJ].

QUESTION—What is meant by δικαιοσύνη 'righteousness'?

   1. It means personal righteousness, the right conduct that God requires in order to live in conformity with God's will [EBC, ICC, NCBC, NIBC, Pl, TNTC2; NJB, TEV, TNT].

   2. It means justification given by God [Mor, NTC].

   3. It means both of the above [MLJ, ZG].

   4. It means justice and vindication for all the oppressed [AAG (p. 157), BSC, EBC, McN, NAC, WBC]. They have experienced injustice and long for God to come and execute justice [WBC]. This is the spiritual food and drink that God's blessed poor long for, and vindication of their cause as in Isaiah 61:3 [AAG (p. 157)].

for they-will-be-satisfied.[a]

LEXICON—a. fut. pass. indic. of χορτάζω (LN **25.82**) (BAGD 2.b. p. 884): 'to be satisfied' [BAGD, **LN**, WBC; NAB, NASB, NET, REB, TNT], 'to be content' [LN], 'to be filled' [Mor; KJV, NIV, NRSV], 'to have one's fill' [NJB], 'to receive it in full' [NLT], 'they will be given what they want' [CEV], 'to be fully satisfied' [NTC]. The passive verb is also translated actively with God as the actor: 'God will satisfy them fully' [TEV].

QUESTION—How, when, and by whom will they be satisfied?

God will satisfy them [ICC, Mor; TEV]. Some satisfaction takes place now [MLJ], but ultimate satisfaction will happen in eternity [ICC, MLJ, WBC]. They will be satisfied by a relationship with God unclouded by disobedience [TNTC2]. They will be satisfied by a world where righteousness dwells [ICC].

5:7 Blessed (are) the merciful,[a]

LEXICON—a. ἐλεήμων (LN **88.77**) (BAGD p. 250): 'merciful' [BAGD, LN, Mor, NTC; KJV, NAB, NASB, NET, NIV, NJB, NRSV], 'those who are merciful' [CEV, NLT], 'those who are merciful to others' [TEV], 'those who show mercy' [WBC; REB, TNT], 'sympathetic' [BAGD].

QUESTION—What is meant by ἐλεήμων 'merciful'?

It describes a concern, love, and sorrow for the plight of others [BSC, NTC, TH], taking on the sufferings of others [BSC], forgiveness of the guilty [EBC, NAC, NTC, TH], intentional kindness [NIBC, TH], generosity [NAC], a focus on interpersonal relationships [NAC], and compassion for the needy [EBC, NAC]. It includes both feeling and action [NAC, NTC], not just occasional acts, but a life characterized by merciful action [Mor]. The lack of an object indicates that this is a general characteristic and not just applied to a specific situation [EBC].

QUESTION—How is this verse related to the preceding beatitudes?

Mercy is seen as flowing out of the character described here in the beatitudes [MLJ], especially out of meekness, which is acknowledging to others our sinfulness and our own need for mercy [EBC], and is a necessary reminder that our great zeal for justice/righteousness must not exclude mercy [Pl]. The emphasis of the first four beatitudes is on actions [WBC] and dependence on God [Mor]. Beatitudes 5 through 7 describe the fruit of God's work in people's hearts [Mor, NTC].

for they will-be-shown-mercy.[a]

LEXICON—a. fut. pass. indic. of ἐλεέω (LN 88.76) (BAGD p. 249): 'to be shown mercy' [BAGD, LN, Mor, WBC; NAB, NET, NLT, REB], 'to have mercy shown' [NTC; NJB], 'to obtain mercy' [KJV], 'to show mercy' [NIV], 'to receive mercy' [NASB, NRSV, TNT], 'to be treated with mercy' [CEV]. This is also translated 'God will be merciful to them' [TEV].

QUESTION—When will this mercy be shown and from whom?

The passive is used to avoid referring directly to God [LN (25.119)]; thus God, not other people, will be merciful [EBC, ICC, LN, Mor, NCBC, NTC, Pl, TH; TEV], on Judgment Day [BBC, ICC, Mor, Pl, TH].

5:8 Blessed (are) the pure[a] of-heart,[b]

LEXICON—a. καθαρός (LN 53.29) (BAGD 3.a. p. 388): 'pure' [BAGD, LN, Mor, NTC, WBC; KJV, NASB, NET, NIV, NJB, NLT, NRSV, TEV, TNT], 'clean (of heart)' [NAB], 'those whose (hearts are) pure' [CEV,

REB], 'free (from sin)' [BAGD]. It originally meant 'clean', and eventually grew to mean 'unmixed', 'unadulterated', 'unalloyed' [Brc]. It means acceptable to God [LN].

b. καρδία (LN 26.3) (BAGD 1.b.δ. p. 404): 'heart' [LN, Mor, NTC, WBC; all versions]. It is the seat of thought and will [ZG]. It is the center (core) of the personality, the innermost being, including emotions, intellect, will, and motivations [BAGD, ICC, MLJ, Mor, NTC, TH, WBC]. It refers to the motives [Brc].

QUESTION—What is meant by οἱ καθαροὶ τῇ καρδίᾳ 'the pure of heart'?

This is a dative of respect, indicating where the purity is to be practiced [McN, Pl, ZG], or a defining dative [WBC]. The expression means to be sincere, without hypocrisy [BSC, EBC, ICC, MLJ, NTC, Pl, TNTC2, ZG], single-minded not divided in heart [EBC, ICC, MLJ, NAC, NIBC, Pl, TG, TH, TNTC, TNTC2, WBC], single-minded in devotion to God [EBC, ICC, NTC, TNTC2], with inner moral purity [Brc, EBC, Pl] and moral uprightness [NAC]. It is not limited to external, ceremonial, or sexual purity [ICC, McN, NAC, NIBC, Pl, TH, TNTC2]. It means a heart that is cleansed and no longer defiled [BBC, MLJ, NAC].

for they will-see[a] God.

LEXICON—a. fut. act. indic. of ὁράω (LN 24.1) (BAGD 1.a.γ. p. 578): 'to see' [BAGD, LN, Mor, NTC, WBC; all versions].

QUESTION—How and when will they see God?

This refers to seeing God in his presence [NCBC, NIBC, TG, TH], in the future Kingdom [ICC, Mor, NCBC, NIBC, NTC, Pl, TNTC2, WBC], on Judgment Day [BBC]. There is some hint of a present, partial seeing with the eyes of faith [EBC, McN, Mor, NIBC, Pl, TNTC2], but the primary reference is not to a present mystical vision or ecstatic experience [TG].

5:9 **Blessed (are) the peacemakers,[a]**

LEXICON—a. εἰρηνοποιός (LN **40.5**) (BAGD p. 228): 'peacemaker' [BAGD, LN, Mor, NTC; KJV, NAB, NASB, NET, NIV, NJB, NRSV, REB, TNT], 'one who works for peace' [NLT, NRSV, REB, TEV], 'those who make peace' [CEV], 'those who are peacemakers' [WBC].

QUESTION—What kind of peace do they make?

It means actively promoting right relationships (reconciliation) between people [Brc, EBC, ICC, LN, Mor, NAC, NIBC, NTC, Pl, TG, TH]. It ranges from making peace in wars to resolving quarrels between individuals [Mor]. It could also mean making peace between God and man [EBC, NAC, NTC, Pl] by preaching the Gospel [EBC]. If the primary emphasis is the rich meaning of Hebrew *shalom* 'wholeness and harmony', then everything which makes for a man's highest good is intended. It would include both freedom from trouble and enjoyment of good. The general idea then would be making the world a better place [Brc, NAC].

while this describes them indirectly, in terms of what happens to them [MLJ]. The idea presented is unexpected, perhaps surprising [Mor]. It reverses the prevailing understanding that all suffering, including persecution, came from God's displeasure [NTC]. The first seven beatitudes describe character; the eighth beatitude reveals the hostile attitudes people will have toward Jesus' disciples [Pl], and which occur because godly characteristics are not welcome in the world at large [NAC]. This beatitude especially reflects the highly paradoxical language in beatitudes 1, 2, and 3 [Pl]. Verses 10–12 are the climax of the paradoxes of beatitudes [WBC]: being a peacemaker brings on persecution [EBC, MLJ], and righteousness (summarizing all the beatitudes) and loyalty to God cause further suffering [MLJ, WBC]; devotion to righteousness brings persecution [BSC, NCBC].

QUESTION—What is the force of the participle δεδιογμένοι 'having been persecuted'?

1. The perfect tense indicates a present state resulting from past action [ZG] and still continuing in effect in the present [Mor]. It refers to those who those who have suffered persecution [Mor, TH, ZG; NASB],

2. The original Aramaic saying of Jesus would be timeless, since Aramaic verbs have aspect but not tense and do not clearly specify the time of the action. The Greek perfect participle functions merely as an adjective used in place of a noun: they are 'the persecuted' or 'those who are persecuted' [EBC, McN; KJV, NAB, NIV, NJB, NRSV, REB, TEV, TNT].

QUESTION—What is meant by ἕνεκα 'because of'?

It indicates that righteous character and righteous lives are what provoke the persecution [ICC, NAC], not sin or tactlessness [NAC]. It explicitly narrows the sphere of persecution to religious persecution [McN]; other reasons are not considered [MLJ].

for theirs is the kingdom of-the heavens.

QUESTION—What is the significance of repeating the same second clause of the first beatitude?

This is a literary device called an inclusio, a statement or idea that marks the beginning and the end of a set of formally similar sentences [BBC, ICC, NIBC, TH, WBC]. These sentences form a unity [BSC, TNTC2]. It implies that possessing the Kingdom sums up all the other results listed in the second clauses of the beatitudes [ICC, Pl]. It implies that in some way the first eight beatitudes go together, and the ninth (in 5:11–12) is somehow different [BSC].

DISCOURSE UNIT: 5:11–16 [TNTC2]. The topic is the distinctiveness of the disciple.

DISCOURSE UNIT: 5:11–12 [EBC]. The topic is the norms of the kingdom: expansion [EBC].

5:11 Blessed are you(pl) when[a] they-revile[b] you(pl),

LEXICON—a. ὅταν (LN **67.31**) (BAGD 1.b. p. 588): 'when' [LN, Mor, ZG; all versions], 'whenever' [BAGD, **LN**, NTC, WBC]. It indicates not just a possibility but something that is sure to happen [BSC]. The action may be repeated [Mor].

 b. aorist act. subj. of ὀνειδίζω (LN 33.389) (BAGD 1. p. 570): 'to revile' [BAGD; KJV, NRSV, TNT], 'to cast insults at' [NASB], 'to insult' [LN, NTC; CEV, NAB, NET, NIV, TEV], 'to abuse' [NJB], 'to reproach' [BAGD, WBC], 'to heap insults upon' [BAGD, NTC], 'to mock' [NLT], 'to upbraid' [Mor]. The phrase 'when they revile you' is translated 'when you suffer insults' [REB]. It is false reproach [Pl], upbraiding or strong verbal abuse [Mor, TH].

QUESTION—What is the significance of the change in this verse from a generic third person to the second person?

Jesus makes the transition from a general reference to addressing his audience directly [BSC]. He is describing a condition that some were actually undergoing at that time [TH], and is making a transition to 5:13–18, which also uses second person plural [ICC, TH]. The second person plural applies primarily to the disciples, but it also applies to all followers of Jesus [TG]. There is also a transition to a less poetic and stylized form in 5:13–16 because 5:11–12 is irregular and longer as compared to the previous eight beatitudes [ICC]. 5:11–12 also forms a transition from the beatitudes to the commandments that follow beginning in 5:13 [BSC]. Here the prominent Semitic parallelism of the Beatitudes is absent [AAG (p. 192)].

QUESTION—What is the relation of this verse to the preceding verses?

It is different than the preceding eight verses that begin with μακάριοι 'blessed' in that it has a different character, it is put in second person, and differs from their parallel structure [BSC]. It is variously described as an elaboration [MLJ, TH, TNTC2, WBC], an explanation [Pl], a continuation in theme [ICC, NTC], an intensification [Mor], an expansion of 5:10 [NIBC], a repetition, amplification, and personalization of 5:10 [NAC] and an application of 5:10 [EBC, MLJ, NCBC, Pl, TH]. Some describe it as a separate and ninth beatitude [BSC, NTC, TH, WBC]. In practice, the righteousness of 5:10 (and all the beatitudes) is conspicuous, and thus invites persecution [TNTC2].

QUESTION—Who are the agents of ὀνειδίσωσιν 'they revile'?

They are the Jewish leaders [ICC]. It is generically translated 'men' [KJV, NASB], 'people' [NIV, NJB, NRSV, TEV, TNT], and omitted in the clause 'you suffer insults' [REB].

and persecute[a] and say[b] all-kinds-of[c] evil[d] against[e] you(pl) lying[f] because-of[g] me.

TEXT—Some manuscripts omit ψευδόμενοι 'lying'. GNT includes it in brackets with a C rating, indicating difficulty in deciding whether or not to place it in the text. It is omitted by REB and TEV. It is included in brackets by NAB. Some commentators contend that the idea 'falsely' is strongly implied even if the actual word ψευδόμενοι is not in the original Greek [EBC, McN, Mor, NAC, WBC].

LEXICON—a. aorist act. subj. of διώκω: 'to persecute'. See this word at 5:10. CEV uses 'to mistreat' here and 'are treated badly' in 5:10.

   b. aorist act. subj. of λέγω, εἶπον (LN 33.69) (BAGD 1. p. 226): 'to say' [BAGD, LN, Mor, NTC; KJV, NASB, NET, NIV], 'to tell' [LN; CEV, TEV], 'to utter' [NAB, NRSV], 'to speak' [BAGD, LN, WBC; NJB], 'to accuse' [TNT], not explicit [REB]. A Semitic idiom using Hebrew *hosi* that can be rendered 'to cause an ill name to go out' or 'to give out, publish against you an evil name' lies behind this concept; see Luke 6:22; 10:35 [AAG (p. 135)].

   c. πᾶς: 'all kinds of' [Mor, NTC, WBC; CEV, NASB, NET, NIV, NJB, NRSV, TEV], 'all manner' [KJV], 'any kind of' [ZG], 'every kind of' [NAB, REB, TNT], not explicit [NLT]. Here it is comprehensive, referring to a great variety of evil comments [Mor].

   d. πονηρός (LN **88.110**) (BAGD 2.c. p. 691): 'evil' [BAGD, LN, Mor, NTC, WBC; CEV, KJV, NAB, NASB, NIV, NRSV, TEV], 'evil things' [**LN**; NET], 'wickedness' [TNT], 'calumny' [NJB], 'calumnies' [REB], not explicit [NLT].

   e. κατά (LN **90.31**) (BAGD I.2.b.β. p. 405): 'against' [BAGD, **LN**, NTC; KJV, NAB, NASB, NIV, NJB, NRSV, TEV], 'in opposition to, in conflict with' [LN], 'about' [Mor; CEV, NET], 'concerning' [WBC], not explicit [NLT, REB, TNT].

   f. pres. act. participle of ψεύδομαι (LN 33.253) (BAGD 1. p. 891): 'to lie' [BAGD, LN, WBC], 'to tell a falsehood' [BAGD, LN]; 'to tell falsehoods' [NTC], 'to suffer calumnies' [REB]. This participle is also translated as a noun: 'lies' [CEV, TEV]; as an adverb: 'falsely' [Mor; KJV, NAB, NASB, NET, NIV, NJB, NLT, NRSV, TNT], 'lying' [WBC].

   g. ἕνεκεν: 'because of' [BAGD, LN; CEV, NIV], 'on account of' [BAGD; NET, NJB, TNT], 'for the sake of' [BAGD, Mor, NTC, WBC, ZG; KJV, NAB, NASB, NRSV, REB]. The phrase 'because of me' is translated 'because you are my followers' [NLT, TEV]. See this word at 5:10.

QUESTION—What is meant by διώκω 'persecute'?

There are various forms of persecution discussed in this verse: ὀνειδίζω in the previous clause is to revile, reproach, or insult; διώκω is persecution in deed; εἶπον πᾶν πονηρόν is to say any kind of evil against someone, slander [EBC, NTC]. These words together emphasize that the concept of persecution is extended to cover actions as well as words [Mor]. See this word at 5:10.

5:12 Rejoice[a] and be-glad[b],

LEXICON—a. pres. act. impera. of χαίρω (LN 25.125) (BAGD 1. p. 873): 'to rejoice' [BAGD, LN, Mor, NTC; KJV, NASB, NET, NIV, NJB, NRSV], 'to be happy' [CEV, NLT, TEV], 'to be glad' [BAGD, LN; NAB, TNT], 'to exult' [REB], 'to be joyful' [WBC].

b. pres. act. impera. of ἀγαλλιάω (LN 25.133) (BAGD p. 4): 'to be glad' [BAGD, WBC; NASB, NET, NIV, NJB, NRSV, REB, TEV], 'to be exceeding glad' [KJV], 'be very glad' [Mor; NLT], 'to rejoice' [NAB, TNT], 'to be excited' [CEV], 'to be extremely joyful, to rejoice greatly' [LN], 'to be overjoyed' [BAGD, LN], 'to be filled with unrestrained gladness' [NTC]. It means to be filled with deep, unrestrained, and exuberant gladness [NCBC, NTC], to experience extreme joy [TH], unbridled joy [NIBC]. An Aramaic verb *dusu*, which is associated with joyful movements and even dancing, probably lies behind this; see Is 61:3 on exultation [AAG (p. 158)].

QUESTION—Is there a difference between χαίρετε 'rejoice' and ἀγαλλιᾶσθε 'be glad'?

This is a semantic doublet, a single concept composed of synonyms with no significant difference in meaning. The two words are close in meaning and the two verbs are used for emphasis. It is possible to translate these words as one term: 'be really happy' or 'you should rejoice greatly' [TH].

for[a] your(pl) reward[b] (is) great[c] in the heavens;[d]

LEXICON—a. ὅτι: 'for' [NTC; KJV, NAB, NASB, NJB, NLT, NRSV, REB, TEV], 'because' [Mor, WBC; NET, NIV, TNT], not explicit [CEV].

b. μισθός (LN **38.14**) (BAGD 2.a. p. 523): 'reward' [BAGD, LN, Mor, NTC, WBC; all versions]. See this word at 6:1.

c. πολύς (LN 78.3) (BAGD I.1.b.α. p. 688): 'great' [LN, Mor, NTC, WBC; all versions except REB], 'rich' [REB].

d. οὐρανός (LN 1.11) (BAGD 2.d. p. 595): 'heaven' [BAGD, LN, Mor, NTC, WBC; all versions].

QUESTION—What relationship is indicated by ὅτι 'for'?

It indicates the grounds for the command to rejoice [ICC, Mor, NTC; all versions]. This introduces the first of two reasons to rejoice [Mor].

QUESTION—What does πολύς 'great' refer to?

The reward is in proportion to, but far and above what could be expected as compensation for, the suffering the disciples undergo [McN, NTC, TNTC2].

QUESTION—What is meant by μισθός 'reward'?

This is a reward that is undeserved [McN], unearned [Mor, NTC, TNTC2], and unmerited [MLJ, TH]. It is given by God's choice, out of his grace [Mor, NTC, TH, TNTC2]. It is meant as a compensation [BSC, TH, TNTC2] to be given in the future age [BSC, TG]. It is a prize given for good actions [TG]. The reward may denote good repute or glory, as opposed to the slander described in 5:11 [NCBC]. Confidence in future reward brings present joy, but the actual content of the reward is vague [WBC]. It is a future recompense for present persecution [ICC, NAC]. There is no mention of comparing those with greater or lesser amounts of reward in this passage; thus, the reward is heaven itself not something less [NAC].

QUESTION—What is meant by 'reward in heaven'?

It refers to heavenly reward in the future [WBC], a reward on judgment day [TG], the bliss of living in the consummated kingdom in eternity [WBC]. The reward is heaven itself [NAC]. 'Reward in heaven' is a circumlocution meaning 'reward with God' [ICC, McN, TH, TNTC2] or 'in God's sight' [NIBC]. God will reward them richly and God keeps the reward for them in heaven [TH].

for[a] in-the-same-way[b] they-persecuted[c] the prophets[d] before you(pl).[e]

LEXICON—a. γάρ: 'for' [Mor, NTC, WBC; KJV, NASB, NET, NIV, NRSV], 'and remember' [NLT], not explicit [CEV, NAB, NJB, REB, TEV, TNT].

b. οὕτως (LN 61.9): 'in the same way' [NTC, WBC; NET, NIV, NRSV, REB], 'in this way' [LN, Mor], 'these same things' [CEV], 'this is how' [NJB, TEV], 'that is how' [TNT], 'thus' [LN; NAB,], 'so' [LN; KJV, NASB], 'too' [NLT]. This refers to persecution, not to reward [TG].

c. aorist act. indic. of διώκω: 'to persecute'. See this word at 5:10, 11. This is a constative aorist; the meaning is not limited to a single incident [ZG].

d. προφήτης (LN 53.79) (BAGD 1. p. 723): 'prophet' [BAGD, LN, Mor, NTC, WBC; all versions]. This refers to the OT prophets [TG]. It is not a narrow definition of prophets, but refers to all of God's spokespersons [WBC].

e. πρός: 'before'. The phrase τοὺς πρὸ ὑμῶν 'those before you' is translated 'which were before you' [KJV], 'who were before you' [Mor; NASB, NIV, NRSV, TNT], 'who lived before you' [TEV], 'who lived before your time' [NTC], 'before you' [NAB, NET, NJB, REB], 'ancient' [NLT], 'who lived long ago' [CEV], 'who came before you' [WBC].

QUESTION—What relationship is indicated by ὅτι 'for'?

It indicates the second grounds for telling them to rejoice. They should rejoice because as persecuted believers they are in good company [Mor]. The argument is that persecution is the evidence they are God's servants just as the prophets were, and as a result they, like the prophets, will receive a great reward, which is a cause for rejoicing [ICC].

DISCOURSE UNIT: 5:13–7:12 [ICC]. The topic is the task of the people of God in the world.

DISCOURSE UNIT: 5:13–20 [NASB]. The topic is disciples and the world.

DISCOURSE UNIT: 5:13–16 [BBC, BSC, EBC, Ed, GNT, ICC, McN, Mor, NAC, NCBC, NTC, Pl, TG, TH, WBC; CEV, NAB, NET, NJB, NLT, NRSV, TEV]. The topic is salt and light [GNT, McN, Mor, NAC, NCBC, NTC; CEV, NET, NIV, NLT, NRSV, TEV], believers are salt and light [HF], salt for the earth and light for the world [NJB], teaching about salt and light [NLT], Jesus' followers being like salt and light [TG, TH], the Christian life as salt and light [Pl], the essence of discipleship is salt and light [WBC], the similes of salt and light [NAB], real discipleship [BBC], summary statement of the task of the people of God in the world [ICC], the starting point for the commandments

[BSC], epilog to the ten beatitudes [Ed (p. 529)], the witness of the kingdom [EBC].

5:13 You(pl) are the salt[a] of-the earth;[b]

LEXICON—a. ἄλας (LN **5.25**) (BAGD 2. p. 35): 'salt' [BAGD, LN, Mor, NTC, WBC; all versions].

    b. γῆ (LN **9.22**) (BAGD 5.b. p. 157): 'earth' [BAGD, Mor, NTC, WBC; all versions except NJB, REB, TEV], 'world' [NJB, REB], 'the whole human race' [TEV], 'everyone on the earth' [CEV], 'all mankind' [**LN**]. It refers to the inhabited globe and means the inhabitants of the earth [BAGD]. It refers to all the people living on the earth [ICC, LN], all mankind, all humanity, all people everywhere [LN, MLJ, Mor, TG, TH], the world of men [McN].

QUESTION—How is this verse related to its context?

The beatitudes which precede are a discussion of Christian character [MLJ], of blessedness [Mor, Pl, WBC], and the blessed future [ICC]. This verse is formally connected to the preceding verses by continuing the second person plural of 5:11–12 [NCBC, TH]. The switch to an emphatic 'you' points to a contrast to those who oppose God's work in the world in 5:11 [NIBC]. The Kingdom precedes the ethics; one doesn't live the way that is now commanded in order to earn a place in the Kingdom. Instead, being precedes doing (see the salt and light illustrations below) [WBC]. The last beatitude is transitional. It describes the attitude of the world to the disciples. Now in this verse the reverse is presented as the effect of the disciples on the world is discussed [NTC]. Verses 13–16 look both back and forward: they continue describing qualifications of those entering the Kingdom [Pl] and introduce the duties of those in the Kingdom [Pl]. This paragraph presents a paradox: the world is saved by those it persecutes [ICC]. Here begins a discussion of the function and purpose of Christ's followers in this world as God views them [MLJ], of responsibilities [Mor, Pl], of warnings [Pl], and of how the disciples must live [WBC]. The passage 5:13–16 is a general description that is transitional, leading to a statement of the demands of the present life (5:17–7:12). These verses also serve as the heading for 5:17–7:12 [ICC].

QUESTION—Why is the article present in τὸ ἄλας 'the salt'?

Normally predicate nouns lack articles; however, here the article indicates something well-known or alone meriting the designation [BD (sec. 273(1), pp. 143), Mor].

QUESTION—In what way were the disciples like salt for the world?

    1. The point of similarity is preservation from corruption [Brc, BSC, EBC, ICC, NAC, NIBC, NTC, TG, TNTC]. Jesus' followers are the saving element of the human race [TG]. It is a negative function [MLJ]. They have a power of preservation which counteracts corruption and decay [BSC, NAC], but they are not a source of renewal that actually causes re-creation of the present society [BSC]. As salt prevents food from spoiling, so the disciples are to prevent the corruption of morals [NAC, NIBC,

TNTC]. The presence of the disciples delays the corruption of the world and its consequent judgment [ICC].

2. The point of similarity is enhancing the taste of a substance. As salt improves the taste of food, the disciples are to improve the quality of the society in which they live [BBC, Brc, McN].

3. The similarity includes both preservation and flavoring [McN, MLJ, Mor, NCBC, NTC, Pl, TH, TNTC2]. The disciples make a purer earth and make it a better place to live [TNTC2].

4. Although it may not be possible to know exactly which aspect of the metaphor may have been intended, it is still generally true that just as salt was vitally important for life, so also are the disciples vitally important to the world in a religious sense [WBC].

but[a] if the salt becomes-tasteless,[b]

LEXICON—a. δέ: 'but' [Mor, NTC, WBC; CEV, KJV, NAB, NASB, NET, NIV, NJB, NLT, NRSV, TEV], 'and' [REB], not explicit [TNT].

b. aorist pass. subj. of μωραίνω (LN **79.44**) (BAGD 2. p. 531): 'to become tasteless' [BAGD, LN, NTC; NASB, REB], 'to lose its savor' [KJV], 'to lose its saltiness' [NIV, TEV], 'to lose its taste' [**LN**, Mor, WBC; NAB, NJB, NRSV, TNT], 'to lose its flavor' [NET, NLT], 'to no longer taste like salt' [CEV].

QUESTION—How can salt lose its saltiness?

1. The impure and highly adulterated salt of ancient times could lose its saltiness because the sodium chloride could leach out or dissolve in humid weather and leave only tasteless crystals which no longer tasted like salt [EBC, LN, Mor, NAC, NTC, Pl, TG, TNTC2]. Salt usually came from evaporating the water of the Dead Sea and it contained crystals such as gypsum that could be mistaken for salt [Mor, NTC, WBC]. The lime, etc. that was left was useless as seasoning [LN]. Salt can become so adulterated that its taste is lessened [McN]. Adulterated salt becomes useless, even dangerous [NCBC].

2. This is a metaphor that should not be pressed too far. Salt does not normally lose its saltiness, but the possibility is entertained here to emphasize that the disciples must maintain a life style radically distinct from the world [NIBC]. It is impossible for salt to become unsalty [BBC; NET] but if it did, it would be worthless [BBC]. This is a statement of the impossible, as with the camel passing through the eye of a needle in 19:24 [NET].

QUESTION—In what way might a disciple lose his saltiness?

In Rabbinic literature salt often stood for wisdom [Mor, NCBC, TNTC2] and μωραινω can mean 'to make or become foolish' [EBC, ICC, Mor, TG, TH, WBC]. Thus it is possible to interpret this verse as: disciples who lose their savor are in fact making fools of themselves [EBC, Mor, NCBC, WBC]. The Semitic term behind this Greek term contains both meanings: salt and wisdom [ICC, NCBC, WBC]. There is an Aramaic pun possible here between *tapel* 'foolish' and *tabel* 'salted' [AAG (p. 166), BBC, EBC, ICC, McN, NCBC, TNTC2].

in what-(way)[a] will-it-become-salty?[b]

LEXICON—a. τίνι (LN 92.14): an interrogative reference [LN]. The phrase ἐν τίνι 'in what way' is translated 'how' [WBC; CEV, NASB, NET, NIV, NRSV, REB], 'with what' [Mor; NAB], 'wherewith' [KJV], 'what' [NTC; NJB, NLT, TNT], 'there is no way' [TEV].

b. fut. pass. indic. of ἀλίζω (LN **5.28**) (BAGD p. 37): 'to become salty', 'to be made salty (again)' [**LN**, NTC, WBC; CEV, NASB, NET, NIV, NJB, TEV, TNT], 'to restore the flavor to salt' [LN], 'to be salted' [Mor; KJV], 'to be seasoned' [NAB], 'to restore saltiness' [NRSV, REB]; 'but what good is salt if it has lost its flavor, can you make it useful again' [NLT].

QUESTION—What relationship is indicated by ἐν τίνι 'in what way'?

Ἐν is instrumental [ZG], meaning literally 'with what' [WBC]. 'How can it be' is meant to be a question that cannot be answered [EBC], it is impossible for it to become salty again [NTC]. This rhetorical question may need to be changed to a statement so the reader will not be confused and unable to supply the right answer. Something else could then be added to convey the emphasis of the rhetorical question: 'if its saltiness *cannot* be restored' [Dei (18.c.1 p. 115)].

QUESTION—What is the force of the future tense of this verb?

Some translations translate it as a simple future e.g., 'will it be made salty (again)' [KJV, NASB, TNT]; others translate it indicating a capability, e.g., 'can it be made salty (again)' [NAB, NIV, NJB, NRSV]; still others employ infinitives, e.g., 'to make salty (again)' [REB, TEV].

it-is-good[a] for[b] nothing any-longer except[c] (for) being-thrown[d] out[e]

LEXICON—a. pres. act. indic. of ἰσχύω (BAGD 2.a. p. 383): 'to be good' [Mor, NTC; all versions except NLT, TEV], 'it is worth' [WBC]. The phrase 'it is good for nothing' is translated 'it has become worthless' [TEV]; 'it will be thrown out and trampled underfoot as worthless' [NLT], not explicit [WBC].

b. εἰς (LN 90.23) (BAGD 5. p. 230): 'for' [BAGD, Mor, NTC; all versions].

c. εἰ μή: 'except' [WBC; NASB, NET, NIV], 'but' [Mor, NTC; KJV, NAB, NRSV], 'and can only' [NJB], not explicit [CEV, NLT, REB, TEV, TNT].

d. aorist pass. participle of βάλλω (LN 15.215) (BAGD 1.b. p. 130): 'to be thrown' [BAGD, LN, Mor, NTC, WBC; all versions except KJV], 'to cast' [KJV].

e. ἔξω (LN 84.27) (BAGD 1.b. p. 279): 'out' [BAGD, LN, Mor, WBC; CEV, KJV, NAB, NASB, NET, NIV, NJB, NLT, NRSV, TEV], 'away' [NTC; REB, TNT].

QUESTION—What is the significance of being thrown out?

1. If Jesus' followers have no 'salty' influence, they have no future in the kingdom of heaven. Thus 'thrown out' is highly significant: cf., Matt

8:12; Luke 13:25; John 12:31; 15:6 [BSC]. It may hint of the last judgment; if Israel is no longer the salt of the earth, then it is also possible for the church to lose its savor and suffer rejection [ICC]. It emphasizes the uselessness of something for its primary function. If Christians are not salt (and light) they are similarly useless [MLJ, NIBC].

2. If Jesus' followers are no longer 'salty', i.e., useful as a preservative, then the present world society will respond by considering them impotent and rejecting them and their input into society [NAC].

QUESTION—What is the import of this metaphor?

Like salt, the disciples have many qualities they must demonstrate, or else they will cease to be what they should be and become useless [ICC, NIBC].

and to-be-trampled-under-foot[a] by people.

LEXICON—a. pres. pass. infin. of καταπατέω (LN 19.52) (BAGD 1.a. p. 415): 'to be trampled under foot' [BAGD, NTC; NAB, NASB, NJB, NLT, NRSV], 'to be trodden under foot' [Mor; KJV, REB], 'to be trampled' [LN; NIV], 'to trample on it' [TEV], 'to be trampled upon' [WBC], 'to tread on it' [TNT], 'and walked on' [CEV, NET]. The Aramaic ϖϖρ (resh-ayin-ayin) probably lies behind this, in which case it would be a word play on ʾarʾa (Greek γῆ) 'earth' [AAG (p. 167)].

QUESTION—What is implied by this clause?

1. The trampling is intentional; this is an infinitive of purpose [BD (sec. 390(3), pp. 197)]: to be thrown out in order to be trampled.

2. The trampling is not deliberate. It is dumped out as refuse into the street, where all refuse is dumped, and it is trampled because everything in the street is trampled [NCBC, TG, TH]. It is not a punishment [TG, TH]. The infinitive expresses the result, as it does in 7:6 [WBC]. This is a warning to count the cost [Pl].

DISCOURSE UNIT: 5:14–16 [EBC; HF]. The topic is light [EBC], disciples and the world [HF].

5:14 You(pl) are the light[a] of-the-world.[b]

LEXICON—a. φῶς (LN 14.36) (BAGD 3.b. p. 872): 'light' [BAGD, LN, Mor, NTC, WBC; all versions].

b. κόσμος (LN 9.23) (BAGD 5.a. p. 446): 'world' [BAGD, LN]. The genitive form is translated 'of the world' [Mor, NTC, WBC; KJV, NAB, NASB, NET, NIV, NLT, NRSV, TNT], 'for the world' [NJB], 'for the whole world' [CEV, TEV], 'for all the world' [REB].

QUESTION—What is implied by the presence of the pronoun ὑμεῖς 'you(pl)'?

It is emphatic [EBC, MLJ, Mor] and restrictive, suggesting 'you and you alone' [EBC, MLJ, Mor, WBC], 'you, my followers, and none others' [EBC], 'you yourselves' [WBC]. The plural emphasizes that collectively the disciples are 'the light' [NTC].

QUESTION—How is this related to the preceding verse?

The first effect of the disciples on the world as salt is general and more or less negative as a preservative; the second effect is the disciples' positive function as lights [MLJ, NTC]. Thus the metaphors complement each other [NTC], first telling what the Christian is, then what he does [MLJ]. The salt and light metaphors are not fundamentally different; both indicate the vital importance of the substance [WBC].

QUESTION—What does τὸ φῶς τοῦ κόσμου 'light of the world' mean?

It means a light to be observed by those in the darkness. It also means a light to be a guide to make the way clear to those of the world as well as to warn them [Brc]. They are a light to expose darkness and the things in darkness [MLJ]. The present world is in darkness [MLJ, Mor], and the light brings illumination through revealing God's will [NAC]. The cause of the darkness is people's estrangement from God and people's desire for the darkness [MLJ]. It means a light to be a guide to make the way clear to others [Brc, BSC]. As light shows the way to people lost in darkness, the disciples are to show the way to God [TH], and help them see God [TG]. God transmits his blessing to men by means of the disciples [NTC]. The 'light of the world' means that now they have received the Kingdom they represent salvation coming to the world [WBC]. Being a light means to give inspiration and joy to people [BSC], 'a wholesome and illuminating influence' [Pl]. Imagery in both the OT and the NT include the contrasts of purity vs. filth, truth/knowledge vs. error/ignorance, God's presence [EBC]. The light/lamp image was used at that time by Jews in speaking of Jerusalem or a rabbi, but the lamp was considered to be lit by God [Brc]. Jewish tradition considered not only the Law and God to be the light of the world, but also Israel and Jerusalem, which would perhaps be alluded to in the city on a hill [BBC].

A-city[a] set[b] on[c] a hill[d] is- not -able to-be-hidden[e]

LEXICON—a. πόλις (LN 1.88) (BAGD 1. p. 685): 'city' [BAGD, LN, Mor, NTC, WBC; all versions except REB], 'town' [REB].

b. pres. act. participle of κεῖμαι (LN **85.3**) (BAGD 1.b. p. 426): 'to lie' [BAGD, LN], 'to be (on)' [**LN**], 'to be set' [Mor; KJV, NAB, NASB, TNT], 'located' [NET], 'to be built' [CEV, NJB, NRSV, TEV], 'to stand' [REB], 'to be positioned' [WBC], 'to be situated' [NTC], not explicit [NIV, NLT].

c. ἐπάνω (LN 83.49) (BAGD 2.a. p. 283): 'on' [BAGD, LN, Mor, NTC, WBC; all versions except CEV], 'on top of' [CEV], 'over, upon' [ZG]. It signifies 'on top of' the hill [BAGD, Mor].

d. ὄρος (LN 1.46) (BAGD p. 582): 'hill' [BAGD, Mor, NTC, WBC; CEV, KJV, NASB, NET, NIV, NRSV, REB, TEV], 'hill-top' [NJB], 'mountain' [BAGD; NAB, NLT, TNT].

e. aorist pass. inf. of κρύπτω (LN 24.29) (BAGD 1.a. p. 454): 'to be hidden' [LN, Mor, NTC, WBC; CEV, NAB, NASB, NET, NIV, NJB, REB, TNT], 'to be hid' [BAGD; KJV, NRSV, TEV], 'to be concealed'

[BAGD]. This clause is translated 'like a city on a mountain glowing in the night for all to see' [NLT].

QUESTION—What is the cultural background of this image?

Ancient towns of white limestone gleamed in the sun and at night the inhabitants' lamps would shine out [EBC]. City lights illuminated a dark countryside [NAC]. Torch light at night could be seen from the surrounding countryside [BBC]. There were no trees to conceal a city on a hill at that time [EBC]. Its walls and fortresses could not be hid [NTC].

QUESTION—What is the significance of this metaphor?

Many focus on the city being easily seen because it is in a prominent place at the top of a hill [ICC, NTC, TG, TH, TNTC, WBC]. Some consider this sentence to be an intrusion into the discussion about light [ICC, TNTC]. Others keep the theme of light by referring to the lights of the city shining in the darkness from the top of a hill [BBC, NAC; NLT]. The metaphor emphasizes the idea of the disciples being conspicuously different, distinctive [TNTC2]. The application to be drawn from this is Christ's followers must be visible. The disciples cannot fail to have a positive influence on the world they live in; they cannot remain unnoticed in the world [BSC]. People cannot hide a city they set on a hill [Dei (p. 82)].

5:15 **neither do-they-light[a] a-lamp[b]**

LEXICON—a. pres. act. indic. of καίω (LN **14.65**) (BAGD 1.a. p. 396): 'to light' [BAGD, LN, Mor, NTC, WBC; all versions except NLT], not explicit [NLT]. Instead of translating this clause as coordinate with the following one, some make this subordinate: 'after lighting' [NRSV], 'when (a lamp) is lit' [REB]. It puts the emphasis less upon the act of lighting than on keeping a lamp burning [ICC, Mor]. This emphasis is obtained in one version by translating 'neither do they light a lamp and put it under the grain basket' as 'don't hide your light under a basket' [NLT]. The plural subject is indefinite and refers to people in general [NET].

    b. λύχνος (LN 6.104) (BAGD 1. p. 483): 'lamp' [BAGD, LN, Mor, NTC, WBC; all versions except KJV], 'candle' [KJV]. It is a portable lamp [ZG], a small clay bowl filled with olive oil with a wick at one end [TG], an ordinary oil burning household lamp [WBC], a small terra cotta oil lamp [ICC, NTC]. Two things are needed for the lamp: oil and wick [BSC]. No candles were in use in Palestine at this time [TH].

and[a] put[b] it under the grain-basket,[c] but-(rather)[d] on the lampstand,[e]

LEXICON—a. καί: 'and' [Mor, NTC, WBC; CEV, KJV, NASB, NET, NIV, TEV, TNT], 'and then' [NAB], not explicit [NJB, NLT, NRSV, REB].

    b. pres. act. indic. of τίθημι (LN 85.32) (BAGD I.1.a.β. p. 816): 'to put' [BAGD, LN, Mor, WBC; all versions except NLT], 'to place' [LN, NTC], 'to hide' [NLT].

    c. μόδιος (LN **6.151**) (BAGD p. 525): 'grain basket' [BAGD], 'peck-measure' (a grain measure containing 16 *sextarii* = about 8.75 liters,

almost exactly one peck) [BAGD, EBC, Mor, NTC, TH, WBC; NASB],
'basket' [LN; NET, NLT], 'bushel' [KJV], 'bowl' [NIV, TEV], 'bushel
basket' [NAB, NRSV], 'tub' [NJB], 'meal-tub' [REB], 'measuring-
vessel' [WBC; TNT], 'a clay pot' [CEV], 'the measuring bowl' [Mor].

d. ἀλλά: 'but' [Mor, NTC; KJV, NASB, NET, NRSV, REB, TNT], 'instead'
[NIV, NLT, TEV], not explicit [WBC; CEV, NAB, NJB].

e. λυχνία (LN **6.105**) (BAGD p. 483): 'lamp stand' [BAGD, LN, Mor,
NTC, WBC; CEV, NAB, NASB, NET, NJB, NRSV, REB, TEV, TNT],
'a candlestick' [KJV], 'its stand' [NIV], 'a stand' [NLT]. It was a metal
stand to support an earthenware lamp [McN], sometimes a roughly shaped
branch of wood [Brc]. Putting the lamp on a lamp stand would increase its
effectiveness [BBC]. The article 'the' is generic [ICC].

QUESTION—What is the point of what he is saying?
The light is not meant to be concealed [TNTC2]. The issue is whether the
light is seen or not seen [TNTC2, WBC]. It is absurd to deliberately conceal
one's light; our relationship to the light of the world automatically makes us
lights ourselves; having light leads to shedding light [BSC]. It is ridiculous if
we do not act as light because the Christian life cannot be hidden [MLJ].

and[a] it-gives-light[b] to-all those in the house.
LEXICON—a. καί (LN 89.87) (BAGD I.2.f. p. 392): 'and' [LN, Mor, NTC,
WBC; KJV, NASB, NET, NIV, NLT, NRSV, TNT], 'and so' [BAGD,
BD, Mor], 'where' [CEV, NAB, NJB, REB, TEV].

b. pres. act. indic. of λάμπω (LN 14.37) (BAGD 1.a. p. 466): 'to give light'
[LN, Mor, NTC; CEV, KJV, NAB, NASB, NET, NIV, NRSV, REB,
TEV], 'to shine' [LN, WBC; NJB, NLT, TNT].

QUESTION—What relationship is indicated by καί 'and'?
This is a consecutive use of καί 'and' and can be translated 'and so, so' [BD
(sec. 442(2), p. 227)]. It reflects Semitic usage of a coordinate conjunction
for a subordinate one, and indicates purpose or result [Mor, ZG].

QUESTION—What type of house was envisioned?
The house envisioned was a small, one room house common among poorer
people at the time and able to be lit sufficiently by one lamp [ICC, Mor,
NTC, TG, TH], providing light for all within the house [NAC].

5:16 **In-the-same-way[a] let-shine[b] your(pl) light before[c] the people,[d]**
LEXICON—a. οὕτως (LN 61.9) (BAGD 1.b. p. 597): 'in the same way' [NET,
NIV, NJB, NLT, NRSV, TEV, TNT], 'in such a way' [TH; NASB], 'in
this manner' [BAGD], 'in this way' [LN], 'like the lamp' [REB], 'as the
lamp on a lamp stand' [TG, TH], 'thus' [BAGD, LN, WBC], 'so'
[BAGD, LN, Mor, NTC, Pl; KJV], 'just so' [NAB], not explicit [CEV].
This particle refers to what precedes [Mor, Pl]. It is used to introduce the
moral to be applied to a figure of speech, parable, or example [BAGD].

b. aorist act. impera. of λάμπω (LN 14.37) (BAGD 2. p. 466): 'to shine'
[BAGD, LN, Mor, NTC, WBC; all versions except CEV, REB], 'to give
light' [LN], 'to make light shine' [CEV], 'to shed light' [REB]. The aorist

imperative could be inceptive, meaning 'let your light begin to shine' [ZG]. Several versions translate the imperative with 'must (shine/shed light)' [NAB, NJB, REB, TEV, TNT]. See this word in 5:15 where it is translated 'to give light' because of the slight nuance of difference in English between 'to shine' with no object and 'to give light to/for' with an indirect object.

    c. ἔμπροσθεν (LN 83.33) (BAGD 2.c. p. 257): 'before' [BAGD, LN, Mor, NTC, WBC; KJV, NAB, NASB, NET, NIV, NRSV, TEV, TNT], 'in (people's) sight' [NJB], 'among' [REB], 'for' [NLT], not explicit [CEV].

    d. ἄνθρωπος (LN 9.1) (BAGD 1.a.δ. p. 68): 'people' [LN; NET, TEV], 'men' [Mor, NTC; KJV, NASB, NIV, TNT], 'in people's sight' [NJB], 'others' [WBC; NAB, NRSV], 'your (fellows)' [REB], 'all' [NLT], not explicit [CEV].

QUESTION—How does this verse relate to the preceding one?

This verse contains the application of the light metaphor and by implication the salt metaphor [WBC]. It sums up the meaning of the paragraph 5:13–15 [ICC, MLJ, Mor, WBC]. It is the only directly hortatory line in 5:13–16 and clearly states the meaning of 5:13–15 [ICC]. This imperative is the subject of the entire Sermon on the Mount [WBC].

QUESTION—What is the focus of this command?

The disciples' conduct, or deeds, and not preaching are in focus here [McN, NTC, Pl]. 'Before men' does not mean 'in order to be seen by men'; rather, it is good influence given free play [NAC, Pl]. The motive for the good works is the glory of God and not the self-glorification condemned in 6:1 [NAC]. The people here are the Jews and Gentiles outside the church [ICC].

so-that[a] they-might-see[b] your(pl) good[c] deeds[d]

LEXICON—a. ὅπως (LN 89.59) (BAGD 2.a.α. p. 577): 'so that' [LN, WBC, ZG; CEV, NET, NJB, NLT, NRSV, REB, TEV], 'that' [BAGD, Mor, NTC; KJV, NAB, NASB, NIV, TNT], 'in order that' (as a conjunction to indicate purpose) [BAGD]. It emphasizes the goal, which is the glory of God [MLJ].

    b. aorist act. subj. of ὁράω (LN 24.1): 'to see' [LN, Mor, NTC, WBC; all versions]. The various versions try to capture the subjunctive sense in these ways: 'they may see' [WBC; KJV, NAB, NASB, NIV, NRSV, TNT], 'they can see' [NET], 'they will see' [TEV], 'seeing' [NJB], 'when they see' [REB].

    c. καλός (LN 88.4) (BAGD 2.b. p. 400): 'good' [BAGD, LN, Mor, NTC, WBC; all versions]; 'morally good, noble, praise worthy, contributing to salvation' [BAGD]. Καλός describes a work as seen by others [McN]. When compared with ἀγαθός 'good' and δικαίως 'right', καλός means the goodness that is attractive [Mor]. ἀγαθός is good in quality while καλός means good, winsome, and attractive [Brc].

    d. ἔργον (LN 42.11) (BAGD 1.c.β. p. 308): 'deed, accomplishment (of the deeds of men, characterized by an added word)' [BAGD]. The phrase τὰ καλὰ ἔργα 'the good works' is translated: 'good works' [Mor, NTC; KJV, NASB, NJB, NRSV], 'good deeds' [WBC; NAB, NET, NIV, NLT, TNT], 'the good things you do' [CEV, TEV], 'the good you do' [REB].

QUESTION—What are the good deeds Jesus is talking about?

Good deeds are the acts commanded in 5:17–7:12 [ICC]. The rest of the sermon expounds these good deeds. This verse is an indirect command for good deeds; Jesus has a greater concern for the testimony than the deeds themselves [BSC]. They include all righteousness, everything the disciples are and do that reflects God [EBC]. The good deeds result from the disciples' character; they are deeds of mercy and of reconciliation [TH]. The light is the good deeds that the disciples will do, emphasizing not an intellectual message but a way of life that other people can observe [NIBC].

and they-might-glorify[a] your(pl) father who (is) in the heavens.[b]

LEXICON—a. aorist act. subj. of δοξάζω (LN 33.357) (BAGD 1. p. 204): 'to glorify' [NTC, WBC; KJV, NAB, NASB], 'to magnify (someone)' [BAGD], 'to praise' [BAGD; CEV, NIV, NLT, TEV], 'to give praise to' [NJB, REB], 'to give glory to' [Mor; NRSV, TNT], 'to honor' [BAGD; NET].

b. οὐρανός (LN 1.11) (BAGD 2.a. p. 594): 'heaven (as the dwelling place or throne of God)' [BAGD]. The phrase ἐν τοῖς οὐρανοῖς 'in the heavens' is translated: 'in heaven' [Mor, NTC, WBC; all versions except NAB, NLT], 'heavenly (Father)' [ZG; NAB, NLT]. The plural οὐρανοῖς reflects Hebrew and Aramaic usage [WBC, ZG].

QUESTION—How and why will they glorify the Father?

The purpose of doing good works is not just to inspire people but to point them to the Father [BSC]. Glorifying God is the disciples' true goal [ICC]. The end and result of these good deeds is that God is reverenced because of his work through human lives [NTC]. The result is that people praise God. This is contrasted with the hypocrites (in later verses) who receive the praise for the good deeds [TH].

QUESTION—What is the significance of plural ὑμῶν 'your' Father and not the singular?

Jesus is emphasizing that the relationship is a privilege shared with Jesus and other believers. Although both Jesus and John the Baptist emphasized personal choice and responsibility, Jesus' repeated use of plurals indicates that he still considered the OT idea of covenant to be valid also [BSC].

QUESTION—What is the significance of τὸν πατέρα...ἐν τοῖς οὐρανοῖς 'Father in the heavens'?

This is first time the phrase is used in the Sermon on the Mount and in Matthew (contrast using the phrase one time in Mark, but many times in John) [BSC, McN, Mor, Pl]. It represents a major emphasis of Matthew; God is the Father of individuals, not just corporate Israel [NTC, TNTC2]. The understanding of God as 'Father' is central to Jesus' teaching [BSC], combining the personal 'Father' with the transcendental element 'in heaven'

[WBC] and indicating a new and special relationship between God and Jesus' followers [BSC, WBC]. Jesus gives the term 'Father' a more intimate meaning than it had in previous usage, including a certainty of salvation [BSC, WBC]. The phrase is used not only to distinguish God the Father from the disciples' earthly fathers, but it also challenges the hearers to think of their relationship with God beyond the bounds of their earthly father-child relationships [BSC].

DISCOURSE UNIT: 5:17–7:12 [ICC, Pl, WBC]. The topic is the duties of those who have entered the Kingdom [Pl], the three pillars [ICC], the main body of the sermon [WBC].

DISCOURSE UNIT: 5:17–6:18 [McN]. The topic is real and legal righteousness.

DISCOURSE UNIT: 5:17–48 [BSC, EBC, MLJ, NAC, NTC, Pl, TNTC, WBC]. The topic is Jesus and the Mosaic law [ICC, TNTC], the fulfillment of the law [BSC], the kingdom of heaven: its demands in relation to the Old Testament [EBC], the Christian life contrasted with the Jewish ideal [Pl], living the life of Christian righteousness [MLJ], the relation between the old and the new righteousness [WBC], thesis: greater righteousness [NAC], the righteousness of the kingdom [NTC].

DISCOURSE UNIT: 5:17–20 [BBC, EBC, Ed, GNT, HF, ICC, McN, MLJ, Mor, NAC, NCBC, TG, TH, TNTC2, WBC; CEV, NAB, NET, NIV, NLT, NRSV, TEV]. The topic is the law [GNT; NLT, TEV], Jesus and the law [NCBC], Jesus fulfills the law [ICC], Christ fulfills the law [HF], the fulfillment of the law [NIV], fulfilling the law [Mor], fulfillment of the law and prophets [NET], the law and the prophets [NRSV], teaching about the law [NAB], the law enforced [BBC], Jesus teaches about the law of Moses [TG, TH], the law of Moses [CEV], introduction to living a life of righteousness [MLJ], Jesus and the kingdom as fulfillment of the OT [EBC], the law not annulled but transcended [McN], Jesus' attitude toward the Old Testament [TNTC2], continuity with the old [WBC], statement [NAC], general principles [ICC].

DISCOURSE UNIT: 5:17–19 [NTC; NJB]. The topic is the fulfillment of the law [NJB], this righteousness is in full accord with the moral principles enunciated in the Old Testament [NTC].

5:17 Do- not[a] -think[b]

LEXICON—a. μή (LN 69.3) (BAGD A.III.5.a. p. 517): 'not' [BAGD, Mor, NTC, WBC; all versions]. Μή is used with the subjunctive to prohibit a specific action [BAGD, ZG].

    b. aorist act. subj. (= aorist act. impera.) of νομίζω (LN 31.29) (BAGD 2. p. 541): 'to think' [BAGD, Mor, NTC, WBC; KJV, NAB, NASB, NET, NIV, NRSV, TEV, TNT], 'to suppose' [CEV, REB], 'to imagine' [NJB], 'to believe, to hold, to consider' [BAGD]. The phrase 'do not think' is

translated 'don't misunderstand (why I have come)' [NLT]. It is an
inceptive aorist 'do not allow yourselves to suppose' [ZG].

QUESTION—What is the relation of this verse to the preceding passages?

The previous discussion of good works naturally led to consideration of the
law [BSC]. The good works performed as shining lights are in harmony with
the law [NTC]. The paragraph anticipates objections [BSC, ICC]; someone
already thinks that Jesus wants to abolish the Law [ICC, NCBC, WBC].
Jesus knew that there was a danger that people would think he had come to
abolish the law [Pl]. Jesus' ministry was beginning to give the impression to
some that he came to destroy the law [McN, NTC, TNTC2], because the
pious Jew would be suspicious of Jesus' actions such as healing on the
Sabbath and apparent laxness toward the Law [NIBC]. Jesus' teaching has
been radical enough in the preceding verses that now he must address
audience concerns about his relationship to the Law [NAC]. Twice he denies
with the greatest emphasis that he is abolishing the law [WBC]. Jesus did not
have less regard for the law and the prophets than the scribes and Pharisees
[BSC]. This is not a refutation of some widely held view but a teaching
device to clarify and remove misunderstandings; the antitheses may not be
absolute (see 3:9 and 10:34), for in some sense Jesus brings peace, and in
some sense perhaps he is abolishing the law [EBC]. Jewish thought
suggested that one 'abolished' the Law by disobeying it, thus rejecting its
authority; the one who disobeyed should be expelled from the community of
believers [BBC].

QUESTION—What is the organization and purpose of 5:17–20?

1. Verses 17–20 are the beginning of a new section which lasts until the end
of the sermon, moving from a description of the Christian to living a life
of righteousness, with first an introduction and then the details [MLJ].
Verses 17–20 explain Jesus' relationship to the law, then in 5:21–48 there
is elaboration in detail [BSC]. They constitute an introduction or preamble
to 5:21–48 [ICC]. This section is the introduction to a series of contrasts
to follow the paragraph 5:17–20, whose purpose is to prevent
misunderstanding of Jesus' teaching [TH].

2. Verses 17 to 20 relate the beatitudes with the Hebrew scriptures [Ed
(p. 530)]. Verses 17–19 are three interlocking verses in structural
similarity (parallelism) and in theme upholding the abiding authority of
the Torah; then 5:20 presents the coming theme of a better righteousness
[ICC]. The four verses of this pericope are related in theme, but not
interrelated enough to form a single coherent paragraph [WBC]. 5:17–20
has two propositions: (1) Jesus' teaching is in harmony with the OT in
5:17–18, and (2) Jesus' teaching contradicts and refutes the teachings of
the Pharisees and scribes in 5:19–20; from 5:21 on he is teaching about
the moral law [MLJ]. The purpose of this paragraph is to prevent
misunderstanding of contrasts that will follow in the sermon [NCBC]. The
purpose of the section is to explain that Christ's new ideal is
immeasurably higher than the Jewish ideal [Pl].

that I-came[a] to-abolish[b] the law[c] or[d] the prophets[e];

LEXICON—a. aorist act. indic. of ἔρχομαι (LN 15.81) (BAGD I.1.a.η. p. 311): 'to appear, to make an appearance, to come before the public' (followed by the infinitive of purpose) [BAGD]. Aspect is variously translated: 'I am come' [KJV], 'I have come' [NTC, WBC; NAB, NET, NIV, NJB, NLT, REB, TEV], 'I came' [Mor; CEV, NASB, NRSV, TNT].

   b. aorist act. infin. of καταλύω (LN 20.55) (BAGD 1.c. p. 414): 'to abolish' [BAGD, BSC, Mor, WBC; NAB, NASB, NET, NIV, NJB, NLT, NRSV, REB], 'to destroy' [WBC; KJV, TNT], 'to do away with' [BAGD, WBC; CEV, TEV]; 'to annul or repeal' [BAGD], 'to make invalid' [BAGD], 'to set aside' [NTC]. Annulling the law and the prophets would annul the social and religious order of Jewish life [McN].

   c. νόμος (LN **33.58**) (BAGD 4.a. p. 543): 'the law' [BAGD, Mor, NTC, WBC; all versions except NLT, TEV], 'the law of Moses' [NLT, TEV]. When paired with 'the prophets', 'the law' refers to the Pentateuch, the five books of Moses [BAGD, ICC], or more generally to the teachings of the Hebrew Scriptures [TG]. The phrase 'the law and the prophets' is translated 'the sacred writings' [LN].

   d. ἤ (LN **89.139**) (BAGD 1.a.β. p. 342): 'or' [BAGD, Mor, NTC, WBC; KJV, NAB, NASB, NET, NIV, NJB, NLT, NRSV, REB, TNT], 'and' [CEV, TEV].

   e. προφήτης (LN **33.58**) (BAGD 1. p. 723): 'the prophets' [BAGD, Mor, NTC, WBC; all versions except NLT, TEV], 'the teachings of the prophets' [TEV], 'the writings of the prophets' [NLT]. It refers unmistakably to the contents of the prophetic books [BAGD].

QUESTION—What is the structural function of the phrase τὸν νόμον ἢ τοὺς προφήτας 'the law and the prophets'?

The phrase is a new inclusio emphasizing the unity of 5:17–7:12; between the repetitions of the phrase is the core of the sermon [EBC, ICC]. Jesus wants to communicate his teaching and deeds in relation to the OT Scriptures [EBC].

QUESTION—What is the meaning of 'the law or the prophets'?

Together the Law and the Prophets included the whole of inspired Scriptures then in existence [EBC, ICC, McN, NTC, Pl, TNTC2], the entire Old Testament [BSC, MLJ, Mor, WBC], and everything it teaches [MLJ]. It is the law plus God's moral demands that the prophets preached [BSC]. 'The law' is the books of Moses, and 'the prophets' is the rest [BSC, ICC].

I-came not to-abolish[a] but-instead[b] to-fulfill/complete[c].

LEXICON—a. aorist act. infin. of καταλύω (LN **76.23**) (BAGD 1.c. p. 414): 'to abolish' [BAGD, BSC, Mor; NAB, NASB, NET, NIV, NJB, NLT, NRSV, REB], 'to destroy' [WBC; KJV, TNT], 'to do away with' [BAGD, **LN**; CEV, TEV], 'to make invalid' [BAGD, LN], 'to invalidate' [LN], 'to set aside' [NTC].

b. ἀλλά (LN **89.125**) (BAGD 1.a. p. 38): 'but' [BAGD, LN, Mor, NTC, WBC; all versions]. The conjunction ἀλλά marks a more emphatic contrast than δέ 'but' [LN].

c. aorist act. infin. of πληρόω (LN **33.144**) (BAGD 4.b. p. 671): 'to fulfill' [BAGD, Mor, NTC; KJV, NAB, NASB, NET, NIV, NLT, NRSV], 'to complete (them)' [NJB, REB, TNT], 'to bring them to their intended goal' [WBC], 'to give them their full meaning' [CEV], 'to make (their teachings) come true' [TEV], 'to give the true meaning to' [**LN**], 'to provide the real significance of' [LN].

QUESTION—What is the significance of Jesus' statement 'I came'?

It indicates Jesus' self-awareness and probably indicates that he came from heaven [BSC] and refers to Jesus' preexistence (Luke 12:49) [BSC, NTC, Pl]. It probably implies the Messiah's self-concept as a prophetic figure commissioned by God [ICC]. For Matthew, at least, it testifies to Jesus' divine origins [EBC].

QUESTION—How do 'annul' and 'fulfill' contrast?

There is a question about whether it is the teachings or the deeds of Jesus that are the intended object of πληρόω; some want to find both, and some choose one or the other [WBC]. Here the meaning of the verb is figurative with various possible meanings [Mor, TH, TNTC2, WBC]. Each of the various meanings points to an aspect of the truth, so Jesus may have meant that more than one meaning applied to his coming [Mor]. The various possibilities listed below are not mutually exclusive and some commentators endorse several of them.

1. Fulfill means to fully obey the laws in the OT [BSC, MLJ, Mor, TH]: I came to completely obey the Law and the Prophets. He did this by carrying out everything the Law stipulates, giving full obedience to it [MLJ]. Although Jesus' coming fulfilled the messianic promises, here Jesus is talking about the fulfilling of God's demands, which was also a Messianic expectation of the Jews [BSC]. Jesus obeys what is laid down in the OT [Mor]. The present context emphasizes how he does this in his teaching role [BSC].

2. Fulfill means to teach the true meaning and implications of the OT [McN, Mor, Pl, WBC]: I came to teach the full meaning of the Law and the Prophets. It means to bring out the full meaning of the OT [Mor]. Fulfill is to present a definitive interpretation, the intended meaning of the law, since Messiah is here with his kingdom. That is, Jesus' teaching reveals the true meaning and so brings it to fulfillment [WBC]. Jesus brings it to completeness by showing the principles underneath the letter [Pl]. He accomplishes it by pointing to its full depth of meaning and to transcend it by giving expression to the deepest principles involved in love for God and people [McN]. It means to provide the real significance or meaning of the Law and the prophets [LN; CEV]. By word and deed Jesus demonstrated the quality of life the OT was intended to produce [NIBC].

3. Fulfill means to do all those things prophesied about the Messiah in the OT [NAC, NTC; TEV]: I came to fulfill all that the Scriptures have prophesied about me. It is to complete and bring to its destined end by giving final revelations of God's will [TNTC2]. Fulfillment means bringing its completed meaning to fruition; the entire OT must be understood in light of Jesus and his ministry and the changes brought about by the new covenant he inaugurated. Jesus consciously sees himself as fulfilling all of the OT. [NAC]. Jesus' life and teaching bring the OT to its completion [Mor], in all he was and was to do: teaching, dying, and living obediently, ruling eternally [NTC], Jesus was to bring the law and prophets to their intended goal [WBC]. He came to make their teachings come true [TH; TEV].

4. Fulfill involves several aspects, including doctrinal teaching, ethical laws, and predictive prophecy. It means both to bring a new law that transcends the Mosaic law and to realize what the OT prophesied [ICC]. Fulfill means to establish the law and prophets by realizing or actualizing them completely in his life and teaching [NCBC]. Jesus is the eschatological goal of the OT, as well as being its sole authoritative interpreter. Jesus shows the direction to which the OT points [EBC].

5:18 For[a] truly[b] I-say[c] to-you(pl),

LEXICON—a. γάρ: 'for' [Mor, NTC; KJV, NASB, NRSV], not explicit [WBC; CEV, NAB, NET, NIV, NJB, NLT, REB, TEV, TNT].

b. ἀμήν (LN **72.6**) (BAGD 2. p. 45): 'truly' [BAGD, LN, Mor, WBC; NASB, NRSV], 'in truth' [NJB, TNT], '...the truth' [**LN**; NET, NIV], 'verily' [KJV], 'amen' [NAB], 'I assure you' [NLT], 'I solemnly declare' [NTC]. The phrase 'truly I say to you' is translated 'remember that' [TEV], 'I promise you that' [CEV]. This asseverative particle always occurs with λέγω 'I say' and was used by Jesus to begin a solemn declaration [BAGD]. See the phrase 'truly I say to you(pl)/(sg)' at 5:26; 6:2, 5, 16.

c. aorist act. indic. of λέγω: 'to say to' [WBC; KJV, NAB, NASB], 'to tell' [Mor; NET, NIV, NJB, NRSV, REB, TNT], 'to assure' [NLT]. See b. above for CEV, TEV.

QUESTION—What relationship is indicated by γάρ 'for'?

It indicates the reason he would not abolish the law and the prophets [EBC, MLJ, Mor; NET] or the grounds for making that statement [BSC].

QUESTION—What is the significance of the word ἀμήν 'truly'?

It has the sense of surely [EBC], verily, truly [EBC, WBC]. It is a strong affirmation of what is about to be said [LN]. It always occurs with λέγω 'I say' to begin a solemn declaration and it is used only by Jesus [BAGD]. It affirms or confirms a solemn truth or fact [NTC, Pl]; it is not an oath but it adds force and solemnity to an utterance [ICC, McN]. It is used here for the first time in the Gospel [Pl], and it is only used by Jesus [BAGD, McN, TNTC2]. It is an adverbial accusative [NTC] that also emphasizes a fact that

contradicts a popular opinion or is at least a surprise, sharply contradicting
what people have been saying [NTC].

QUESTION—What is the function of the whole clause?

The clause is an accentuated solemn introduction [BSC, WBC], a solemn
formula [Mor, TH], asserting divine truth [TH], affirming and emphasizing
[Mor], introducing a solemn and authoritative declaration [NCBC, TNTC2,
ZG]. It signals that an extremely important statement is to follow [EBC,
Mor, TNTC2], stressing the gravity of what follows [WBC]. It is similar to
the OT prophets' formula 'thus says the Lord' [ICC, Jerome in McN,
TNTC2]. It emphasizes the superior status of the speaker [ICC].

until[a] the heaven and the earth pass-away[b],

LEXICON—a. ἕως ἄν: 'until' [LN, Mor, NTC; NAB, NASB, NET, NIV, NLT,
NRSV, TNT], 'till' [KJV, NJB], not explicit [CEV]. The phrase 'until the
heaven and the earth pass away' is translated 'as long as (they) last'
[WBC; TEV], 'so long as (they) endure' [REB].

b. aorist act. subj. of παρέρχομαι (LN 13.93) (BAGD 1.b.α. p. 626): 'to
pass away' [BAGD, Mor; NAB, NASB, NET, NRSV, TNT], 'to pass'
[KJV], 'to come to an end' [BAGD], 'to disappear' [BAGD, BSC, NTC;
CEV, NIV, NJB, NLT]. See the note on the reversed meaning in the entry
on 'until': 'last' [WBC; TEV], 'endure' [REB].

QUESTION—How and when might the heaven and the earth pass away?

Heaven and earth (meaning the totality of creation [Mor]) are the most solid
and enduring things that people experience [BSC]. They will pass away at
the end of the world [TG], at the end of the age when the present world order
ends [EBC], at the end of created things [Mor], at the parousia, the end of the
present age [WBC]. This saying suggests a long time period yet to come; it
is not just hyperbole, but the actual end of heaven and earth [ICC], the end of
time [WBC] and the regeneration of the created order [ICC, WBC]. In the
new heaven and earth, a written book (the OT and NT), will no longer be
necessary, but first all will be fulfilled [NTC]. It is an idiom meaning
something inconceivable [TNTC2].

**not[a] one[b] smallest-letter[c] or one stroke-of-a-letter[d] will-disappear[e] from the
law[f]**

LEXICON—a. οὐ μή (LN **69.5**) (BAGD D.1.a. p. 517): 'not' (at the beginning
of the clause) [Mor, WBC; all versions except CEV, KJV, NLT], 'not
even' [NTC; CEV], 'in no wise' [KJV], 'by no means' [LN], 'not by any
means' [NIV], 'certainly not' [BAGD, **LN**], 'never' [BAGD]. Combined
with the negative οὐ, μή strengthens the negation [BAGD]. It is emphatic
[LN, Mor, ZG].

b. εἷς (LN 60.10) (BAGD 1.c. p. 231): (the numeral) 'one' [BAGD, Mor;
KJV, NRSV], not explicit [NAB, NASB, NIV]. With the negative
following, it is stronger than οὐδείς [BAGD]. The repetition of 'one' in
this chiastic structure emphasizes the absoluteness of what he is saying
[BD (sec. 474(1), p. 250), WBC]. The postposition of εἷς after ἰῶτα is a

Hebraism for οὐδείς 'not one' [ZG]. It is paraphrased in various ways: 'even the (smallest detail)' [NLT], 'even a (period)' [CEV], 'a (letter)' [REB]. Translations conflate εἰς with ἰῶτα 'iota' (see next entry).

c. ἰῶτα (LN **33.36**) (BAGD p. 386): 'the smallest letter' [BAGD, BSC, LN; NAB, NASB, NET, NIV], 'the tiniest letter' [NTC], 'one small letter' [**LN**; TNT], 'one letter' [NRSV], 'a letter' [REB], 'one jot' [KJV], 'one iota' [BAGD, LN, Mor], 'the least point' [TEV], 'a period' [CEV], 'one dot' [NJB]. The phrase 'one smallest letter or one stroke of a letter' is translated 'the smallest detail of God's law' [NLT]. Iota is the smallest Greek letter [BSC, NAC]. The Greek iota corresponds to Hebrew and Aramaic *yod*, the smallest letter [BAGD, BBC, EBC, McN, MLJ, Mor, NCBC, NIBC, TG, TH, TNTC2, WBC, ZG]; there are 66,420 yods in the OT [Bengel in Mor], which are often optional in Hebrew spelling [McN, TNTC2]. This word is translated 'a period' [CEV], 'small mark' [LN], 'the least point' [TEV], 'one dot' [NJB]. Together ἰῶτα and κεραία are rendered 'the slightest aspect of the law' [WBC]. See more at the third question below.

d. κεραία (LN **33.37**) (BAGD p. 428): 'stroke of a letter' [NET, NRSV], 'one little stroke' [Mor; NJB], 'the least stroke of a pen' [BSC; NIV], 'stroke' [LN; NASB, NET], 'the smallest part of a letter' [NAB], 'a part of a letter' [**LN**; TNT], 'one tittle' [KJV], 'the smallest detail' [TEV], 'a dot' [REB], 'the tiniest hook on a letter' [NTC], 'a comma' [CEV]. It is a 'serif' [BAGD; NET], a projection on letters for distinguishing one letter from another [Mor, TG]. See more at the fourth question below.

e. aorist act. subj. of παρέρχομαι (LN 13.93) (BAGD 1.b.α. p. 626): 'to disappear' [NTC; CEV, NIV, NJB, NLT, REB], 'to pass' [KJV, NAB, NET, NRSV, TNT], 'to pass away' [BAGD, Mor; NASB], 'to be done away with' [TEV], 'to fail' [WBC]. The aorist subjunctive has the sense of the future indicative [Mor]. The meaning is conflated with the 'not' resulting in: 'will remain' [NLT].

f. νόμος (LN 33.56) (BAGD 3. or 4.b. p. 542): 'law' [BAGD, Mor, NTC, WBC; all versions]. It refers especially to the Mosaic law [BAGD (3.)], or in the wider sense, the law equals the Holy Scripture generally on the principle that the most authoritative part gives its name to the whole [BAGD (4.b.)].

QUESTION—What is implied by this clause?

The importance of the OT is beyond compare [BSC]. Jesus is profoundly loyal to the Law, which remains in force in its totality [NIBC]. One must be faithful to the whole meaning of the law in order to follow the authoritative teaching of Jesus [WBC].

QUESTION—How can this figure of speech be expressed without using figurative language and making implicit information explicit?

Jot and tittle together mean the slightest aspect of the law [WBC], the smallest details of the law [LN, NIBC, TG; NLT]. The use of jot and tittle together implies that even the extent of the Scriptures cannot be reduced

[EBC]. It is not that the letters themselves could be corrupted, but that God will not drop the least of his demands [BSC]. Perhaps 'jot and tittle' is a hendiadys meaning the smallest part of the smallest letter [EBC]. No part of the Law can be considered too small to be worth keeping [BBC].

QUESTION—What precisely is meant by ἰῶτα 'smallest letter'?

Yod (or jot) was the smallest letter of the Hebrew alphabet. For instance it made the difference between Sarai and Sarah [Ed (p. 538)]. Jot (originally spelled 'iote' in the KJV) is the Greek ἰῶτα which is Hebrew ℧ the smallest letter of the Hebrew alphabet; it can often be inserted without changing the sense, when following some vowels [TNTC].

QUESTION—What precisely is meant by κεραία 'hook-on-a-letter'?

1. The meaning is unclear [McN, Mor, TG, TH], but it has the general connotation of small and insignificant [ICC].
2. The κεραία were the little hooks (small strokes) on the letters of the Hebrew alphabet that distinguished between the various characters [EBC, Ed (p. 538), Mor, NAC, NTC, TG, TH]. It was smallest point (serif) on a letter [MLJ, NIBC, NTC, ZG; NET].
3. The KJV English word 'tittle' (from Latin *titulus*) is Greek κεραία (horn), which is probably the connecting stroke sometimes placed over words in the Hebrew scriptures and which do not alter the meaning if changed.
4. The κεραία are the flourishes or 'hooks' put on Hebrew letters [BSC], purely ornamental, decorative serifs [EBC, NIBC]. They are ornamental marks; thus this is deliberate hyperbole, exaggeration to drive home the main point about preserving the law [WBC].

QUESTION—What did the Jews mean by 'the Law'?

The Law could mean several related things; only the context can distinguish among the senses. Five senses can be distinguished: (1) the Ten Commandments, (2) the Pentateuch, (3) the Law and the Prophets, where the expression meant the whole of the Hebrew scriptures, (4) the Oral or Scribal Law (the most common understanding in Jesus time) [Brc], and (5) the entire OT scriptures [EBC, NTC, TNTC2].

until[a] all[b] takes-place/is-accomplished[c].

LEXICON—a. ἕως (LN 67.119) (BAGD I.1.b. p. 334): 'until' [BAGD, Mor, NTC, WBC; NAB, NASB, NET, NIV, NJB, NLT, NRSV, REB], 'till' [BAGD; KJV, TNT], not explicit [CEV]. This temporal conjunction denotes the end of a period of time, or that the commencement of an event is dependent on circumstances [BAGD].

    b. πᾶς (LN 59.23): 'all' [Mor; KJV, NASB, NRSV, TNT], 'everything' [WBC; CEV, NET, NIV], 'all things' [NAB], 'all its purpose' [NJB], 'all that must happen' [REB], 'all (it calls for)' [NTC], 'everything written in it' [CEV].

    c. aorist act. subj. of γίνομαι (LN 13.107) (BAGD I.3.a. p. 158): 'to take place' [BAGD, Mor, NTC; NAB, NET], 'to happen' [BAGD; CEV, REB], 'to come about' [ZG], 'to be accomplished' [BSC, NAC, WBC;

NASB, NIV, NRSV], 'to be fulfilled' [KJV, TNT], 'to be achieved' [NJB]. It is paraphrased: 'must happen' [CEV], 'not until the end of all things (alt. the end of all things or all its teachings come true)' [TEV], 'it's purpose is achieved' [NLT], 'until all is past' [BAGD, Mor].

QUESTION—What relationship is indicated by ἕως ἄν 'until'?

The second ἕως ἄν phrase in this verse introduces the prophetic element and insures that it is understood as something that will definitely happen and not just as a rhetorical 'never' [ICC]. The double ἕως ἄν clause is chiastically constructed; it is an awkward structure and difficult to understand [WBC]. It repeats the idea of heaven and earth passing away, but the positions in the clauses makes the meaning obscure [Pl]. The second ἕως ἄν clause is more difficult to translate than the first [EBC].

QUESTION—What is to be fulfilled?

1. It refers to the end of the world [ICC, McN, WBC]. It refers to heaven and earth which constitute the present age [ICC, McN, WBC]. This is the implication if this clause is viewed as equivalent in meaning to the first ἕως 'until' clause. The 2nd clause is for clarifications and perhaps emphasis [ICC, NCBC, WBC]. Repetition of the ἕως clause emphasizes that the law will remain until the consummation of the age [WBC].

2. It means until the whole of divine purpose (greater than just Jesus' teachings or whole ministry and life) is accomplished [Pl]; it is best to refer to everything in the Law that concerns prophecy 'the entire divine purpose prophesied in Scripture' [EBC]. It is concerned with an aim and goal. The law points to complete accomplishment of God's will [NCBC].

3. It refers to the OT [BSC, MLJ, NAC, TG, TH, TNTC2]. It refers to Jesus' fulfillment of the OT in regard to his ministry, death, and resurrection. It means until what the Scriptures look forward to arrives, that is, the law remains valid until it reaches its intended culmination in the deeds and words of Jesus [TNTC2]. All the law and the prophets point to Jesus and will be fulfilled by him down to smallest detail [MLJ]. It is not synonymous with heaven and earth; instead it means until everything in the law is fulfilled [TH], until the law is brought to fruition in Jesus Christ [NAC]. It means until all its teachings come true [TG].

4. It means the accomplishing of God's commandments. Nothing can be suspended until it is fulfilled; however, some commandments may be fulfilled before the end of time, thus changing their significance [BSC].

5:19 Therefore[a] whoever[b] breaks/annuls[c] one[d] of the least[e] of-these commandments[f]

LEXICON—a. οὖν (LN 89.50) (BAGD 5. p. 593): 'therefore' [Mor, NTC, WBC; KJV, NAB, NJB, NRSV, REB], 'then' [NASB], 'so' [NET, NLT], 'so then' [TEV], not explicit [CEV, NIV, TNT]. Οὖν indicates a direct implication of the immense importance of the law emphasized in 5:18 [BSC], an inferential link to 5:18, an inference from what precedes [TH].

It introduces the consequence of the permanence of Scripture in the previous verse [Mor].

b. ὅς ἐάν: 'whoever' [Mor, NTC, WBC; NAB, NASB, NRSV, TEV, TNT], 'whosoever' [KJV], 'anyone who' [NET, NIV, NJB, REB], 'you' [CEV, NLT].

c. aorist act. subj. of λύω (LN **36.30**) (BAGD 4. p. 484): 'to break' [LN, WBC; KJV, NAB, NET, NIV, NLT, NRSV, TNT], 'to disobey' [TEV], 'to transgress' [**LN**], 'to willfully disregard' [NTC], 'to annul' [BAGD, Mor, NTC; NASB], 'to reject' [CEV], 'to infringe' [NJB], 'to set aside' [REB],

d. εἷς (BAGD 1.a.β. p. 230): 'one' [BAGD, Mor, NTC, WBC; KJV, NAB, NASB, NET, NIV, NJB, NRSV, TNT]. The phrase 'one of the least' is translated 'even the least' [CEV, REB, TEV], 'the smallest' [NLT].

e. ἐλάχιστος (LN **65.57**) (BAGD 2.a. p. 248): 'least' [**LN**, Mor, NTC, WBC; KJV, NAB, NASB, NET, NIV, NJB, NRSV, REB, TNT], 'least important' [LN; CEV, TEV], 'smallest' [NLT].

f. ἐντολή (LN 33.330) (BAGD 2.a.β. p. 269): 'commandment' [BAGD, Mor, NTC, WBC; KJV, NAB, NASB, NIV, NJB, NRSV, TEV, TNT], 'command' [BAGD; NET, NLT], 'command in the Law' [CEV], 'the law's demands' [REB], 'order' [BAGD]. Frequently the plural stands for the totality of legal ordinances [BAGD].

QUESTION—Does λύω refer to 'annulling' or 'breaking' a commandment?

1. It means to annul a commandment [BAGD, Mor, NCBC, TH, TNTC2]. It means to set aside as no longer applicable [NAC; REB], to repeal or abolish [Mor], to teach against as opposed to 'disobey' or 'break' [TNTC2], 'to weaken the authority of' [TH], 'to relax' [Mor]. Rather than a mere breaking of the law, it means to regard the law as nonexistent or as null and void [Mor]. It means to hold that the commandment was obsolete [NCBC]. It describes someone who says that a law is not valid [TH]. Λύω takes readers' minds back to καταλύω in 5:17 [ICC]; it is a word play on 5:17 [NAC].

2. It means to break a commandment in the sense of disobey it [NTC, WBC; KJV, NAB, NET, NIV, NJB, NLT, NRSV, TNT].

QUESTION—What is the antecedent to 'these commandments'?

It is the OT commandments [EBC, ICC, NCBC, TNTC2, WBC]. Because οὗτος 'these' in Matthew never points forward, it refers to the Law in the previous verse [EBC].

QUESTION—What is implied by 'the least of these commands'?

The Jews said there were 613 commands in the Law, some heavy (great), some light [McN, Mor, NTC]: 248 positive, 365 negative commands [Mor, NTC]. The scribes had frequent arguments about the greatest and least commandments (cf. 22:36; 23:23; Mk 7:11-13) [BSC]. Then current Jewish custom ranked the commands of the Law from greatest to least [NAC]. On the greatest see Luke 10:27–28; Matt 22:34–40; Mk 12:28-4 [TNTC2]. Later rabbis suggested the command to respect the life of a mother bird (Dt.

22:7) was the least commandment [BBC]. It refers to his statement about
'the smallest letter...the least stroke of the pen' in 5:8 [BSC, ICC]. It is used
to show Jesus upholds the entire law and imposes all of it upon his disciples;
one's position in the kingdom of heaven is dependent on one's respect for
the law [BSC], not the minutiae but the full faithful meaning as expounded
by Jesus [ICC, WBC]. It concerns God's moral law [NTC].

and teaches to people[a] (to do)-so,[b]
LEXICON—a. ἄνθρωπος (LN 9.1): 'men' [Mor, NTC; KJV]. This is translated
in the generic sense: 'people' [NET], 'others' [WBC; all versions except
KJV].
  b. οὕτως (LN **61.9**) (BAGD 1.b. p. 597): 'to do so' [NAB, TNT], 'so'
[BAGD, LN, Mor, NTC, WBC; KJV, NASB], 'to do the same' [CEV,
NIV, NJB, NLT, NRSV, REB, TEV], 'to do this' [NET], 'thus' [BAGD,
LN]. It refers to what precedes [BAGD, LN].
QUESTION—What aspect is indicated by the aorist active subjunctive of
διδάσκω?
  It is translated as 'shall teach' [KJV], 'teaches' [Mor, NTC; NAB, NASB,
NET, NIV, NJB, NLT, NRSV, REB, TEV, TNT], and 'teach' [CEV].

he-will-be-called[a] least[b] in the kingdom of-the heavens[c];
LEXICON—a. fut. pass. indic. of καλέω (LN 33.131) (BAGD 1.a.δ. p. 399): 'to
be called' [Mor, NTC, WBC; KJV, NAB, NASB, NET, NIV, NRSV,
TNT], 'to be named' [BAGD], 'to be' [BAGD, ICC, Mor; CEV, NLT,
TEV], 'to be considered' [NJB], 'to have' [REB]; 'you will be' [CEV].
The passive 'be named' approaches closely to the meaning 'to be'
[BAGD]. The person actually is what he is called [Mor]. This verb is
functionally equivalent of 'to be', since being called something by God
means to be that same thing [ICC]. See 5:9 for additional discussion.
  b. ἐλάχιστος (LN 65.57) (BAGD 2.a. p. 248): 'the least' [WBC; KJV, NJB,
NLT], 'least' [Mor, NTC; NAB, NASB, NET, NIV, NRSV, TEV, TNT],
'the least important person' [CEV], '(have) the lowest place' [REB], 'of
least importance, of very little importance' [LN]. The phrase means 'God
will consider least' [TG]. This word may not be superlative but follows
the Aramaic meaning of 'little' [NCBC].
  c. οὐρανός (LN 12.16) (BAGD 3. p. 595): 'heaven' [Mor, NTC, WBC; all
versions]. In the phrase 'kingdom of heaven', οὐρανός 'heaven' is used
figuratively to refer to God [BAGD, LN]. This is a euphemism; here
'kingdom of heaven' is equal to 'from God's viewpoint' [Dei (p. 51)].
QUESTION—What does it mean to be least in the kingdom of heaven?
  The meaning is metaphorical: the repetition of ἐλάχιστος is a stylistic
feature where the word from the earlier clause is repeated but this time in a
metaphorical sense [BD (sec. 488(1c), pp. 258–9)].
  1. It refers to one's rank in heaven [EBC, ICC, NTC, Pl]: he will be least
important. Being least in the kingdom is not exclusion from the kingdom;
instead it means low in rank in heaven and that there are degrees of

reward [ICC]. It suggests gradation of ranks in the kingdom (cf. 11:11) [EBC]. Their place in the kingdom is less glorious and secure [Pl]. Since disciples differ in degree of faithfulness in the present world, they will differ in degree of glory in heaven [NTC].

2. It refers to one's rank in the church age [BSC, NAC]: he is of least importance now. This primarily concerns their status in the kingdom that had begun with Jesus' coming [BSC]. It refers to ranking in God's honor in this present age and not in eternity, which 20:1–16 seems to rule out [NAC].

but^a whoever^b does^c and teaches^d (the commandment)

LEXICON—a. δέ: 'but' [Mor, NTC, WBC; all versions except REB, TEV], 'on the other hand' [TEV], 'whereas' [REB].

b. ὅς ἄν (BAGD 2.a. p. 48): 'whoever' [Mor, NTC, WBC; NAB, NASB, NET, NIV, NRSV, TEV, TNT], 'whosoever' [KJV], 'the person who' [NJB], 'anyone who' [NLT, REB], 'if you' [CEV]. This implies a condition 'if he does and teaches it' [BAGD].

c. aorist act. subj. of ποιέω (LN 90.45) (BAGD I.1.c.α. p. 682): 'to do' [BAGD, Mor, WBC; KJV, NET, NRSV], 'to practice' [NTC; NIV, TNT], 'to obey' [CEV, NAB, NLT, TEV], 'to keep' [BAGD; NASB, NJB, REB]. Some versions supply an object for the verb: 'them' [NTC; NET, NJB, NRSV, TNT], 'the law' [REB, TEV], 'God's laws' [NLT], 'to keep (the will or law obediently)' [BAGD].

d. aorist act. subj. of διδάσκω (LN 33.224): 'to teach' [LN]. The object for the verb is also supplied: 'to teach them' [Mor, NTC, WBC; KJV, NASB, NJB, NLT, NRSV, TNT], 'to teach these commands' [NAB, NIV], 'to teach others to do the same' [TEV], 'to teach others to do so' [NET, REB], 'to teach others its commands' [CEV]. Repeating διδάσκω stresses the disciples' responsibility to teach and not just to obey [WBC].

this-one will-be-called great^a in the kingdom of-the heavens.

LEXICON—a. μέγας (LN **87.22**) (BAGD 2.b.α. p. 498): 'great' [BAGD, **LN**, Mor, NTC, WBC; all versions except CEV, REB]. The phrase 'will be called great' is translated 'will rank high' [REB], 'will have an important place' [CEV].

DISCOURSE UNIT: 5:20–48 [NJB]. The topic is the new standard, higher than the old.

5:20 For^a I-tell^b you(pl)

LEXICON—a. γάρ: 'for' [Mor, NTC, WBC; KJV, NASB, NET, NIV, NJB, NRSV, TNT], 'then' (added at end of the verse) [TEV], 'but' [NLT], not explicit [CEV, NAB, REB].

b. pres. act. indic. of λέγω (BAGD II.1.e. p. 469): 'to tell' [Mor, NTC, WBC; NAB, NET, NIV, NJB, NRSV, REB, TEV, TNT], 'to say' [KJV, NASB], 'to promise' [CEV], 'to warn' [NLT]. It is used to introduce direct discourse after ὅτι (in next clause) [BAGD].

QUESTION—What relation is indicated by γάρ 'for'?

It forms a logical sequence with πληρόω in 5:17, but not with 5:18 and 19 [McN]. It indicates a confirmation and elucidation of the preceding topic [NTC]. It clarifies 5:18 [WBC] by dispelling any suspicion of legalism which 5:19 might have raised [TNTC2]. It is possibly an explanatory 'for, you see' [Mor]. This verse indicates a transition [TH] between 5:17–19 and 5:21–48 [ICC].

QUESTION—What is the significance of changing from the preceding third person singular verbs to second person plural here?

The switch to second person plural in 5:20 is due to the stereotyped expression 'I tell you' [ICC].

QUESTION—What is the function of the formula 'I tell you'?

It stresses the great importance of the following words [NTC, TH, WBC]. The emphasis is on the following surprising statement [Mor].

that[a] unless[b] your(pl) righteousness[c] surpasses[d] beyond (that) of-the scribes[e] and Pharisees[f],

LEXICON—a. ὅτι: 'that' [Mor, NTC, WBC; KJV, NASB, NIV, TEV, TNT], not explicit [CEV, NAB, NET, NJB, NLT, NRSV, REB].

b. ἐάν (LN 89.67) (BAGD I.3.b. p. 211): 'unless' [BAGD, Mor, NTC, WBC; NAB, NASB, NET, NIV, NLT, NRSV, REB, TNT], 'except' [KJV], 'only if' [TEV], 'if not' [BAGD; NJB], 'if you don't' [CEV].

c. δικαιοσύνη (LN 88.13) (BAGD 2.a. p. 196): 'righteousness' [BAGD, Mor, NTC, WBC; KJV, NAB, NASB, NET, NIV, NRSV, TNT], 'uprightness' [NJB]. This noun is also translated as a verb phrase: 'to obey God' [NLT], 'to obey God's commands' [CEV], 'to do what God requires' [TEV]. The phrase 'your righteousness surpasses' is translated 'show yourself far better' [REB].

d. aorist act. subj. of περισσεύω (LN **78.31**) (BAGD 1.a.β. p. 650): 'to surpass' [LN, WBC; NAB, NASB, NIV, NJB], 'to exceed' [LN, Mor; KJV, NRSV, TNT], 'to go beyond' [NET], 'to be very great' [LN], 'to be much greater than' [**LN**], 'to be better than' [CEV, NLT]. It means 'to excel' [NTC], 'to be far better (than)' [REB], 'to be more faithful than' [TEV]. This clause is translated 'you must obey God's commands better than the teachers of the Law obey them' [CEV].

e. γραμματεύς (LN 53.94) (BAGD 2. p. 165): 'scribes' [BAGD, Mor, NTC, WBC; KJV, NAB, NASB, NJB, NRSV, REB], 'teachers of the Law' [BAGD; CEV, NIV, TEV, TNT], 'teachers of religious law' [NLT], 'experts in the law' [Mor; NET], 'scholars versed in the law' [BAGD], See this word at 7:29.

f. Φαρισαῖος (LN 11.49) (BAGD p. 853): 'Pharisees' [BAGD, Mor, NTC, WBC; all versions].

QUESTION—What is the relationship of this statement to the preceding context?

This verse links to 5:19 by discussing the topic of not neglecting the smallest part of the law. Therefore it does matter what we do along with what we believe. The whole purpose of this paragraph is to emphasize the practical carrying out of the law, tying together works and the faith [MLJ]. We must keep every part of the law, and teach every part of the law; holiness means keeping and fulfilling the whole law. Were not the Pharisees and scribes the holiest people they knew? Common people thought that they could never attain to the standard of the Pharisees and scribes. Jesus wasn't going to reduce the demands of the law. Instead the demands would exceed those of the Pharisees and scribes. Jesus shows the hollowness of the teaching of the Pharisees and scribes, and then presents the new teaching [MLJ]. Jesus introduces for the first time in this sermon a category of individuals who are not within the kingdom, although the Pharisees and scribes were the greatest example of righteousness for the audience [NAC]. The concept of the kingdom of heaven binds this verse to the previous one, and functions as a bridge between what precedes and what follows [WBC].

QUESTION—Who were the scribes?

They were the trained theologians of Israel [Pl]. They expounded the Law, developed it, and administered it as assessors in courts of justice [McN]. They were men who were trained to interpret the Law of Moses and apply it to settle all kinds of disputes [TG], They were professional scholars [NTC, WBC] engaged in the detailed study of the minutiae of the law [WBC]. Like the Pharisees, they had a great knowledge of the trivia of the Law (e.g. the number of letters or words in a book) [Mor]. Not all scribes were Pharisees [McN], scribes and Pharisees were overlapping but not identical groups [TH].

QUESTION—Who were the Pharisees?

They were a sect [NTC], a party that strictly kept the law and added more regulations to it. They were popularly thought to be very pious and devoted [TG]. It was a largely lay movement that was devoted to scrupulous observance of both the OT law and of the still developing legal traditions [TNTC2]. They were among the most punctilious of that age, but Jesus said they were not good enough, not absolutely holy [EBC]. The Pharisees were followers of scribes. They took the pattern of the pious Israelite as established by the scribes, and put it into practice as nearly as possible. [BAGD].

QUESTION—What was the righteousness of the scribes and the Pharisees?

The scribes and the Pharisees represented the Jewish leaders of the time [ICC]. Their righteousness was formal and external and not of the heart. It was more concerned with the ceremonial than the moral, concerned with man-made rules based on their rationalizations, and primarily concerned about themselves and their image. They saw themselves as meeting the demands of the law and doing better than the common man, observing details rather than principles. The remainder of the Sermon expounds these attitudes [MLJ]. Their righteousness was quantitative, preoccupied with the minutiae of the law [WBC], scrupulously observing the letter of the law and assuming this is righteousness [Pl]. Pharisaic righteousness was legalism (outward conformity) and it was not sufficient [NIBC].

QUESTION—How can someone's righteousness exceed that of the scribes and the Pharisees?

Jesus wanted a newer, higher righteousness [WBC]. Jesus' standard was not more lenient than the Pharisees and scribes but perfection (cf. 5:48) [EBC]. This righteousness outstrips that of the Pharisees and scribes quantitatively and qualitatively [EBC]. Jesus was not thinking of the Pharisees and scribes at their worst but at their best, scrupulously observing the letter of the law and assuming this is righteousness [Pl]. Obedience to the law is important, but the manner of obedience is absolutely crucial, Pharisaic legalism (outward conformity) is not sufficient [NIBC]; more is required in the Kingdom to be in fellowship with God and to conform to God's will [NAC]. Jesus is simply asking for a better righteousness than the false piety of the scribes and Pharisees (see 23:23) [BSC]. In addition to keeping the external aspect of the law that deals with actions, Jesus' disciples must have a more careful regard for the spirit of the law in their motives and desires [TG].

you(pl)-will- never[a] -enter[b] into the kingdom of-the heavens.

LEXICON—a. οὐ μή: This double negative is translated 'never' [NTC; CEV, NET, NJB, NRSV], 'not' [NAB, NASB, TNT], 'certainly not' [Mor; NIV], 'not at all' [NLT], 'in no case' [KJV], 'in no way' [WBC], 'only if' [TEV]. It is an emphatic negative like in v.18; there is no question of entrance [Mor, ZG].

b. aorist act. subj. of εἰσέρχομαι (LN 15.93) (BAGD 2.a. p. 233): 'to enter' [Mor, NTC, WBC; KJV, NAB, NASB, NET, NIV, NLT, NRSV, REB, TNT], 'to be able to enter' [TEV], 'to get into' [CEV, NJB]. 'To come into something' is equivalent to 'share in something, come to enjoy something' [BAGD]. See this word at 7:21.

QUESTION—What is meant by 'entering into the kingdom of heaven'?

It does not mean 'go to heaven' but becoming one who joins the people under God's rule [TH]. The kingdom of heaven is a realm, a condition one can enter into; it is not the usual idea of heaven so 'will go to heaven' gives an incorrect impression [TG].

DISCOURSE UNIT: 5:21–48 [EBC, Ed, ICC, McN, Mor, NAC, NCBC, NTC, TNTC2, WBC; NASB]. The topic is specimens of laws which Christ fulfilled [McN], applying the law [Mor], relating the beatitudes with the Hebrew scriptures [Ed (p. 530)], personal relationships [NASB], examples of Jesus' radical ethic [TNTC2], the better righteousness [ICC], the superior righteousness [NCBC], a true account of the law in six statements [MLJ], the surpassing of the old: the six antitheses [WBC]; the six antitheses [NTC],

application: the antithesis [EBC], illustrations [NAC], two triads of specific
instruction [ICC].

DISCOURSE UNIT: 5:21–32 [ICC]. The topic is the first triad.

DISCOURSE UNIT: 5:21–26 [BBC, EBC, GNT, ICC, MLJ, Mor, NAC,
NCBC, NTC, Pl, TG, TH, TNTC2, WBC; CEV, NAB, NET, NIV, NLT, NRSV,.
REB, TEV]. The topic is anger [GNT, NCBC, TG, TH; CEV, NLT, NRSV,
TEV], teaching about anger [NAB], anger as murder [BBC], anger and murder
[TNTC2; NET], murder [ICC, Mor, NAC, WBC; NIV], thou shalt not kill
[MLJ], the first antithesis: the sixth commandment, murder [NTC], vilifying
anger and reconciliation [EBC], the first illustration [Pl].

DISCOURSE UNIT: 5:21–22 [McN]. The topic is you shall not murder.

5:21 You(pl)-have-heard[a]

LEXICON—a. aorist act. indic. of ἀκούω (LN 24.52): 'to hear' [LN].
    Throughout this discourse this aorist verb is translated in the perfect tense:
    'you have heard' [Mor, NTC, WBC; all versions except CEV]. The phrase
    'you have heard that it was said to the ancients' is translated 'you know
    that our ancestors were told' [CEV].

QUESTION—What words are repeated to give structure to this section
    5:21–48?

    In general, the overall structure throughout the six units in this section can be
    thought of as a frame consisting of an A structure followed by a clause or
    two introducing a subject, which is then followed by a B structure which
    contains Jesus' teaching on the subject.

A The A structure uses some of the words out of the clause which can be
    rendered in English: 'Again you have heard that it was said to the ancient
    people.' In verses 21, 27, 33, 38 and 43, each verse begins with
    Ἠκούσατε ὅτι ἐρρέθη 'You have heard that it was said.' In verse 31
    however, the verse begins only with ἐρρέθη δέ 'It was said.' Only in
    verses 21 and 33 is the phrase τοῖς ἀρχαίοις 'to the ancient people'
    present. Only in verse 33 is the word Πάλιν 'again' present.

B The B structure is 'But I say to you….' In verses 22, 28, 32, 34, 39 and
    44, the second half of the frame ἐγὼ δὲ λέγω ὑμῖν 'But I say to you' is
    found. (ἀμὴν λέγω σοι 'Truly I say to you' found in verse 26 is not a part
    of the overall frame although it looks similar.) In verses 22, 28 and 32, the
    phrase is followed by ὅτι πᾶς ὁ 'that all who …' In verses 34 and 39, the
    phrase is followed by negative commands. In verse 44 the phrase is
    followed by a positive command.

QUESTION—What is implied by this approach?

    Typical rabbinical style at this time was to quote a scripture verse and then
    give a full explanation of it [BBC, WBC]. Ἠκούσατε ὅτι ἐρρέθη 'you have
    heard that it was said' in verses 21, 27, 33, 38 and 43 (abbreviated to ἐρρέθη
    'it was said' in v.31) was a rabbinical device, but the second clause ἐγὼ δὲ
    λέγω ὑμῖν 'but I say to you' in verses 22, 28, 32, 34, 39 and 44 assumed

much more authority than the rabbis would dare. With the second clause, Jesus is emphasizing that he is teaching with messianic authority [WBC]. Jesus is offering himself as the 'sovereign interpreter of the law' with authority to interpret the law in a way that no one can question [NAC], with an authority equal to the giver of the Law of Moses. Jesus views his interpretation as uniquely authoritative [MLJ].

QUESTION—What is the organization of the six units of 5:21–48?

Some commentators see the organization primarily in terms of six units, while others see it as two groups of three units. Some see the units progressing with some discernable logic. The different organizational schemes do not necessarily contradict each other.

1. The rest of this chapter consists of six parts [BSC, ICC, MLJ, NAC, NTC, Pl, TG, TNTC2, WBC]. They are six examples [BSC, MLJ, TNTC2], six contrasts [MLJ, TG], six illustrations [MLJ, Pl], six units of teaching [TNTC2], six antitheses [NAC].

2. The rest of this chapter consists five antitheses. 5:1–32 on divorce does not have equal status with the other five units [NIBC]. There are only five parts and 5:31–32 is not an equal part [EBC].

3. Some commentators view the passage as divided into two triads [ICC, NIBC, Pl, TG, WBC].

   3.1 In 5:33 the second group begins with πάλιν, which indicate that a new series is starting and which functions as an editorial dividing line. This is also indicated by 5:21 and 5:33 having the full phrase 'you have heard that it was said to the men of old' [ICC]. It may be that the first triad contrasts the laws of Deuteronomy, and the second triad with the laws of Leviticus [ICC].

   3.2 In 5:21, 27, and 33 the formula: 'You have heard...but I say to you' introduces subjects in which they understood the meaning of the Law, but concerning which Jesus proceeds to deepen their understanding. In 5:31, 38 and 43 this formula introduces commands which they understood only literally, but for which Jesus must explain the real significance [NCBC].

   3.3 The first group, 5:21, 27, and 33, has quotations of one of the 10 commandments; then the discussion following in the respective paragraphs adds depth to the understanding of the command. However, the second group, 5:31, 38 and 43, has popular interpretations of other commands which Jesus invalidates [TG].

   3.4 The passage moves from the weightiest items in the 10 commandments to other Torah (i.e. Law, Pentateuch) commands, and last to implications of the Torah. The six sections represent a sampling, culminating in the last one about love [WBC].

QUESTION—What is the purpose of the six statements in the rest of Ch 5?

1. The purpose is to elaborate on and illustrate what he means by righteousness that surpasses that of the scribes and Pharisees in 5:20 [BSC, ICC, NAC]. The purpose is illustration, application and

clarification. Jesus interprets the commandments to get to the inner meaning [WBC]. These verses demonstrate that it is impossible to make a definitive list of correct actions, and that perfect obedience is an unattainable goal [NAC]. The correct approach to righteousness is spelled out [NIBC].

2. In it Jesus explains why the righteousness of the scribes and Pharisees was completely inadequate [BSC]. It is a true exposition of law contrasted with the wrong interpretation of the scribes and Pharisees [MLJ]. The purpose is to contrast Jesus' exposition of the true and ultimate meaning of the Law with common rabbinical understandings of the commandments [NTC, WBC]. It is possible that 5:21–48 describes the teachings of the scribes, and 6:1–18 describes the life of the Pharisees [McN].

3. The purpose is to expose limitations in the way a law was understood; that it is not a simple thing to keep but that a principle is involved. Jesus shows how these OT commands should be understood [Mor]. The purpose is to stress the real meaning of the word of God in the OT and to affirm that that the meaning is fulfilled in Jesus Christ [TG]. The purpose is to expound on Jesus' relationship to the Law [ICC].

4. Jesus is going above and beyond the tradition to give an entirely different teaching with a new attitude and vision [ICC].

5. The section 5:21–48 contains impractical commands which would only bring hopeless confusion if one were to try to follow them literally. They are intended rather to give a new and a challenging moral ideal about what is right and wrong [ICC].

that[a] it-was-said[b] to/by-the ancients,[c]

LEXICON—a. ὅτι: 'that' [Mor, NTC, WBC; CEV, KJV, NASB, NET, NIV, NLT, NRSV, REB, TEV, TNT], 'how' [NJB], not explicit [NAB].

b. aorist pass. indic. of λέγω (LN 33.69): 'to say' [LN, Mor, NTC, WBC; KJV, NAB, NET, NIV, NJB, NRSV, TNT], 'to tell' [CEV, NASB, REB, TEV].

c. ἀρχαῖος (LN 67.98) (BAGD 2. p. 111): 'ancient, old' [BAGD]. This word is translated 'the ancients' [NASB], 'an older generation' [NET], 'those of early times' [WBC], 'those of ancient times' [NRSV], 'men of ancient times' [LN], 'them of old time' [KJV], 'the people of old' [Mor], 'the people of long ago' [NIV], 'the men of long ago' [NTC], 'our ancestors' [CEV, NJB], 'your ancestors' [NAB] 'our forefathers' [REB], 'people in the past' [TEV], 'men in the past' [TNT], not explicit [NLT].

QUESTION—What relationship is indicated by the use of the dative form τοῖς ἀρχαίοις 'the ancients'?

1. It indicates the indirect object, meaning that someone spoke to the ancient people, whether God, Moses, or others [EBC, ICC, NAC, NCBC, TH, TNTC2, WBC; CEV, NASB, NET, NIV, NJB, NLT, NRSV, REB, TEV, TNT]: it was said to the ancient people. It is primarily or exclusively the Sinai generation, to whom God spoke through Moses [ICC, Mor, NAC,

NCBC, TH, TNTC2; NLT], though all the subsequent generations are
included [TH]. It refers to the 6th commandment (in this paragraph)
spoken by God to the people at Mt. Sinai [NAC]. It refers to the reading
of the OT in the synagogues, not to oral law or Jewish misinterpretation
[ICC]. It is a divine passive, since a human subject would be named
[ICC].

2. This is an instrumental dative, meaning 'by' [BSC, Ed, MLJ, Mor, NTC,
Pl; KJV]: it was said by the ancient people. It refers to what was taught by
the Pharisees and scribes as indicated by the fact that Jesus did not say
'You have read in the Law of Moses' [MLJ]. It refers to the generations
subsequent to the Sinai generation who passed on the law and the later
oral tradition of the Jewish teachers [BSC, Ed, Mor, NTC, Pl]. The
ancient Jewish rabbis in their oral teachings and interpretations of the law
is intended, beginning with the Babylonian exile; later the instruction
became a fixed tradition; this was the 'righteousness' that people were
taught [BSC, Ed (p. 538)]. The expounders of the law, the scribes and
Pharisees, gave incomplete teaching [NTC]. It was this tradition with
which Jesus contrasted meaning 'they said...but I say' [BSC, NTC]; he
was not contrasting his teaching with that of Moses [BSC]. The problem
was what they left unsaid as they taught [NTC]. In NT times the largely
illiterate crowd knew the law from public instruction [Pl]. This refers to
oral tradition since Jesus used εγραπται 'it is written' to quote scripture,
but here he says ἐρρέθη 'it was said' [BSC, Mor, Pl].

Do-not murder;[a]

LEXICON—a. fut. act. indic. (= aorist act. impera.) of φονεύω (LN **20.82**)
(BAGD p. 864): 'to murder' [BAGD, EBC, LN, Mor, NCBC, TNTC2,
WBC; CEV, NET, NIV, NLT, NRSV, TNT], 'to commit murder' [**LN**;
NASB, REB, TEV] 'to kill' [BAGD, NTC; KJV, NAB, NJB].

QUESTION—What meaning is intended by this verb φονεύω 'murder'?
    It means 'murder' [ICC, NAC, TH, WBC]. It refers to killing that is not
legal, not sanctioned by the community, and not accidental [LN, TH]. It is
criminal killing [TNTC2]. Killing in war and capital punishment are not
included in the prohibition [TG, TH].

QUESTION—What is the force of the future tense?
    The future tense is used for commands quoted in legal language in the OT
[Mor]. The future indicative can be used for categorical injunctions and
prohibitions (with the negative οὐ) in OT legal language, but in this chapter
it is used only in OT quotes; Jesus' injunctions never use the future
indicative [BD (sec. 362, pp. 183)]. Οὐ 'not' with the future tense indicates a
categorical prohibition [ZG].

and[a] if anyone[b] murders,

LEXICON—a. δέ: 'and' [Mor, NTC, WBC; CEV, KJV, NAB, NASB, NET,
NIV, NJB, NRSV], not explicit [NLT, REB, TEV, TNT].

b. ὅς ἄν: 'if anyone' [NJB], 'if you' [NLT], 'anyone who' [NIV, REB, TEV], 'whoever' [Mor, NTC, TH, WBC; NAB, NASB, NET, NRSV, TNT], 'whosoever' [KJV]. The phrase 'if anyone murders' is translated 'a murderer' [CEV].

he-will-be liable[a] to judgment.[b]

LEXICON—a. ἔνοχος (LN 88.312, 88.313, 37.5) (BAGD 2.a. p. 267): 'liable to' [BAGD, ICC, NAC; NAB, NASB, NRSV, TNT], 'in danger of' [KJV], 'subject to' [Mor; NET, NIV, NLT], 'brought to' [TEV], 'answerable' [BAGD, ICC], 'guilty' [BAGD, ICC, WBC], 'must be brought to' [CEV, REB], 'he must answer for it before' [NJB], 'deserves' [NTC]. This is a legal term [BAGD, ICC, Mor]. This word is also used twice in 5:22.

b. κρίσις (LN **56.1**) (BAGD 2. p. 453): 'judgment' [ZG; NAB, NET, NIV, NLT, NRSV, TNT], 'the judgment' [Mor, WBC; KJV], 'trial' [CEV, TEV], 'the court' [BAGD, **LN**; NASB, NJB], 'court of justice' [LN], 'justice' [REB]. The phrase 'will be liable to judgment' is translated 'deserves to be punished with death' [NTC]. This word is also used in 5:22.

QUESTION—What area of meaning is intended in the word κρίσις 'judgment'?

1. It refers to legal court proceedings for a person accused of murder [Brc, BSC, EBC, McN, NCBC, TG, TNTC2]; he will be subject to trial.
2. It refers to the penalty or judgment imposed upon a guilty person [NAC, NTC, TNTC]; he will be subject to condemnation.

5:22 But[a] I[b] say[c] to-you(pl)

LEXICON—a. δέ: 'but' [Mor, NTC, WBC; all versions except TEV], 'but now' [TEV]. In Matthew δέ is not always a strong contrast or antithesis, unlike ἀλλά [ICC]. The contrast is with the last clause of 5:21 and not the entire command [TH].

b. ἐγώ (LN 92.1) (BAGD p. 217): 'I' [BAGD, LN, Mor, NTC, WBC; all versions], 'I, indeed' [LN], 'I am the one telling you' [LN]. The pronoun ἐγώ 'I' is quite emphatic [BAGD, EBC, ICC, LN, Mor, NTC, TG, TH, TNTC2], both here and in each of the following six antitheses [EBC]. TEV's use of 'but *now*' tries to reflect the emphatic ἐγώ 'I' [TH].

c. pres. act. indic. of λέγω (BAGD II.1.e. p. 469): 'to say' [Mor, NTC, WBC; KJV, NAB, NASB, NET, NJB, NLT, NRSV], 'to tell' [NIV, REB, TEV, TNT], 'to promise' [CEV]. The clause is translated in a periphrastic way: 'but what I tell you is this' [REB], 'but I promise you' [CEV].

QUESTION—What is the import of this statement?

This statement opposes the tradition of the ancestors by Jesus' personal authority; the assurance of Jesus' self-authority is even greater than that of the prophets [BSC]. This is a formula emphasizing the unparalleled authority of Jesus and his emphasis on the supreme importance of the inner attitude [WBC]. Jesus is placing his authority above the Law of Moses [TG, TH], above that of the scribes [TNTC2]. This statement is Messianic because it contrasts Jesus not with the men of old but with Moses; Jesus is not just reminding his disciples of what they already know; he is passing on revelation [ICC]. Jesus is able to give a definitive declaration of God's will that ranks on a par with the Law, and which only the Messiah could do [Mor].

that[a] everyone-who[b] is-angry[c] with his brother[d] will-be liable[e] to judgment;[f]

TEXT—Some manuscripts include εἰκῇ 'without a cause' after τῷ ἀδελφῷ αὐτοῦ 'his brother'. It is omitted by GNT with a B rating, indicating that the text is almost certain. It is included by KJV only.

LEXICON—a. ὅτι: 'that' [NTC, WBC; CEV, KJV, NASB, NET, NIV, NRSV, TNT], not explicit [Mor; NAB, NJB, NLT, REB, TEV].

b. πᾶς (LN 59.24) (BAGD 1.c.g. p. 632): 'everyone who' [BAGD, Mor, WBC; NASB, TNT], 'whosoever' [KJV], 'whoever' [BAGD; NAB], 'anyone who' [NET, NIV, NJB, REB], 'if you' [CEV, NLT, NRSV, TEV], 'even anyone' [NTC]. Πᾶς followed by three 'who(ever)s' and 'the last penny' indicate this teaching is universal and uncompromising in application [ICC].

c. pres. act. participle of ὀργίζομαι (LN **88.174**) (BAGD p. 579): 'to be angry' [BAGD, LN, Mor, NTC; all versions except REB], 'to nurse anger' [REB], 'to be full of anger, to be furious' [LN]; 'to be filled with wrath against' [WBC].

d. ἀδελφός (LN **11.89**) (BAGD 4. p. 16): 'brother' [LN, Mor, NTC; all versions except CEV, NLT, NRSV], 'brother or sister' [WBC; NRSV], 'someone' [CEV, NLT]. The phrase 'his brother' is translated 'your brother' [TEV], 'a brother' [NET, NJB], 'a brother or sister' [NRSV], 'someone' [CEV, NLT]. The same word is also used in 5: 23, 24, 44; 7:7:4.

e. ἔνοχος (LN 88.312, 88.313, 37.5) (BAGD 2.a. p. 268): 'liable'. See this word at 5:21.

f. κρίσις: 'judgment' [Mor, WBC; NAB, NET, NIV, NLT, NRSV, TNT], 'the judgment' [KJV], 'justice' [REB], 'trial' [CEV, TEV], 'the court' [NASB, NJB], '(deserves) to be punished with death' [NTC]. See this word at 5:21.

QUESTION—What is meant by ἀδελφός 'brother' ?

It could be equivalent to 'countryman' or 'neighbor' [BAGD, BSC, LN], a part of group with which someone identifies ethnically and culturally [LN]. It could be a member of a common nationality or faith [LN], a member of the community of faith [BSC, NAC, NCBC, TG, WBC]. Originally 'brother' meant fellow Jews [Ed (p. 538), McN], but it was extended to every follower of Jesus [EBC, McN, NAC]. It means fellow disciple [TH, TNTC2], fellow believer [ICC], any member of God's family [Pl], the church [NCBC].

QUESTION—What is the range of meaning for ὀργίζομαι 'to be angry'?

Anger is the underlying cause of murder [EBC, NCBC, NTC]. The word ὀργίζομαι represents a 'brooding inward anger', contrasted with θυμός 'an anger that flares' [Brc, NIBC]. It is a long-lived anger, broodingly nursed and not allowed to die, seeking revenge [Brc]. It means seething with anger [EBC], unexpressed hatred [Pl]. It is not that someone who is cherishing angry feelings should be prosecuted, but that this is a kind of murder just as serious as the act which is prosecuted [Pl]. Jesus is showing that feelings and words as well as overt murder are covered by the commandment [McN].

QUESTION—What is the relation of this kind of anger and its punishment with the two following kinds and their punishments?

1. There is a neat gradation of anger and an answering gradation of punishment [Brc, NIBC, Pl, TG], but they are not to be taken literally [Brc]. The climax of penalties assume a climax of offenses [Pl]. The next offense in the next clause is more serious than the first [TG].

2. There is no gradation intended [BBC, BSC, EBC, ICC, McN, NAC, NIBC, TNTC2, WBC]. The first point is that anger is wrong, followed by two similar illustrations and all three punishments should be taken as synonyms referring to the danger of eternal punishment [NAC]. There are not three levels of sin but rather three sins that are virtually equivalent; the examples are juxtaposed with murder because they seem so insignificant as sins. There appears to be an ascending order of penalties; however, all receive the same punishment [BSC]. Gehenna is the climactic final judgment [WBC]. All three punishments were roughly equal [BBC]. Although there is a triadic structure to the verse with three assertions, there is no distinction between sins, since the punishment for anger is the same as for murder. This hyperbole emphasizes that anger and harsh words are not just failings but grievous sins. [ICC]. These are parallel statements making the same point in different ways, not different sins [TNTC2].

and if anyone says to his brother, Raka,[a] he-will-be liable to-the Sanhedrin;[b]

LEXICON—a. ῥακά (LN 32.61) (BAGD p. 733): 'Raka/Raca' [Mor, WBC; KJV, NAB, NASB, NIV], 'fool' [BAGD, LN; CEV, NJB], 'numskull' [LN], 'good for nothing' [REB], 'you good-for-nothing!' [TEV], 'you idiot!' [NLT], 'you blockhead!' [NTC], 'empty-headed one' [BAGD]. The phrase 'says...Raka' is translated 'to insult' [NET, NRSV], 'to speak contemptuously' [TNT].

b. συνέδριον (LN 11.79, 11.80) (BAGD 2. p. 786): 'the Sanhedrin' [BAGD, Mor, Pl, WBC; NAB, NIV, NJB], 'the council' [KJV, NET, NRSV, TEV], '(the) court' [CEV, NLT, REB], 'the supreme court' [NTC; NASB, TNT], 'the high council' [BAGD]. The phrase 'he will be liable to the Sanhedrin' is translated 'deserves to be condemned to death by the supreme court' [NTC].

QUESTION—What is the meaning of ῥακά 'raka'?

The word ῥακά is an Aramaic term of abuse or contempt [BAGD, Brc, BSC, LN, McN, MLJ, Mor, NAC, NIBC, Pl, TG, TH, ZG; NET], derived from the Aramaic word for 'empty' [BAGD, McN, NTC, TH, TNTC2]. It refers to one who is lacking in understanding [LN], an idiot [Brc, WBC], a blockhead [NTC, WBC], or a silly fool [Brc]. It communicates scorn and derision [MLJ] with strong emotive force [TH]. A person using this epithet could be sued [McN].

QUESTION—What was the συνέδριον 'Sanhedrin'?

1. The reference is indefinite and it may refer to the Sanhedrin or simply to a council [EBC, ICC, Mor, NCBC, TNTC2].

2. It refers to the Sanhedrin proper, the highest Jewish court in the land [NTC, TG, TH]. The Sanhedrin was composed of 70 Jewish high priests, elders, and scholars (scribes), and presided over by the ruling high Priest [BAGD, TG].

3. It refers to any local court [McN, NCBC]. It is a local court that met at a local synagogue and was a judicial body, not a governing one [McN], a body in the religious community [NCBC].

4. It is a metaphor that refers to a heavenly court or to the last judgment [BBC, TNTC2]. It is a symbol of ultimate judgment [TNTC2]; Jewish literature of the time described a heavenly supreme court that was like the earthly Sanhedrin [BBC].

and[a] whoever says, Fool,[b]

LEXICON—a. δέ: 'and' [Mor, NTC, WBC; CEV, NAB, NASB, NET, NJB, NLT, NRSV, TEV], 'but' [KJV, NIV], not explicit [REB, TNT].

b. μωρός (LN 32.55) (BAGD 1. p. 531): 'fool' [BBC, BSC, Mor, NAC, NCBC, NIBC, TNTC2, WBC, ZG; KJV, NASB, NET, NIV, NRSV, REB, TNT], 'you fool' [NAB], 'worthless fool' [TEV], 'idiot' [NTC], 'traitor' [NJB]. The phrase εἴπη Μωρέ 'says...Fool' is translated 'curse someone' [NLT], 'say that someone is worthless' [CEV].

QUESTION—What is meant by μωρός 'fool'?

1. It means 'fool' [ICC, McN, Mor, WBC]. It is probably the equivalent of, or a synonym of the preceding term ῥακά 'fool' [ICC, McN, Mor], perhaps being a translation of ῥακά [NCBC, Pl]. It was used with the meaning 'fool' in the Syriac NT and in the Talmud [Ed (p. 538)].

2. It has more of a moral emphasis than ῥακά even though it is primarily a translation [Mor]. It calls into question a person's deficient moral character as opposed to intellect incompetence [Brc, NIBC]. It implies immorality and godlessness as well as idiocy [NAC]. Μωρός expresses abuse, and may be stronger than ῥακά [NCBC, Pl, TH]. It is a transliteration of the Hebrew moreh 'rebel' [EBC, TNTC; NET].

he-will-be liable to[a] the hell[b] of-fire.

LEXICON—a. εἰς (LN 84.22) (BAGD 7. p. 230): 'to' [NAB, NET, NRSV], 'of going to' [TEV], 'to go into' [NASB], 'to be cast into' [NTC], 'of' [CEV,

KJV, NIV, NLT]. It is used to indicate motion into a thing [BAGD]. The phrase 'will be liable to' is translated 'will be sent to' [NET], 'will answer for it in' [NJB]. The reader should understand 'be cast' before εἰς 'into' [EBC]. At the entry for ἔνοχος 'liable' (BAGD 2.c. p. 267), the clause is translated 'guilty enough to go into the hell of fire' [BAGD].

b. γέεννα (LN 1.21) (BAGD p. 153): 'hell' [BAGD, LN], 'Gehenna' [BAGD, LN]. In the gospels Gehenna is the place of punishment in the next life [BAGD]. The phrase τὴν γέενναν τοῦ πυρός 'the Gehenna of the fire' is translated 'hell fire' [KJV, NJB, REB, TNT], '(the) fiery hell' [NASB, NET], 'the hell of fire' [BAGD, NTC; NRSV], 'the fire(s) of hell' [CEV, NIV, NLT, TEV], 'the fires of Gehenna' [TEV], 'the Gehenna of fire' [Brc, Mor], 'fiery Gehenna' [WBC; NAB,].

QUESTION—What is meant by τὴν γέενναν τοῦ πυρός 'the Gehenna of fire'?

It refers to the Valley of Hinnom [Brc, EBC, McN, NCBC, NIBC, TG, TH, TNTC2, WBC], southwest of Jerusalem where Ahaz had introduced heathen fire worship of Molech, including child sacrifice (2 Chr. 28:3) [Brc, EBC, McN, Mor, NAC, NCBC, NIBC, TH, WBC, ZG]. The Hebrew ge-*hinnom* can be rendered 'valley of wailing' [ZG]. Later the location became the city trash dump where fires burned regularly, smoke hung in the air, and worms abounded (Mk 9:44–48). At that time, it was associated with the accursed, useless, evil, and filthy things that were to be destroyed [Brc, EBC, McN, Mor, NAC, NIBC, Pl, TG, TH, TNTC2, WBC]. Thus it became a synonym for hell [Brc, TH, ZG], a symbol or metaphor of the place for future, ultimate, eternal punishment [EBC, Mor, NCBC, NIBC, Pl, TNTC2], a place of punishment for the dead [NET], eternal death [NTC], a place where the wicked would be burned up or eternally tortured [BBC, ICC, Mor]. It was considered to be the opposite of the heavenly paradise [BBC], an abyss in the depths of the earth [TG]. Gehenna was the abode of the wicked after judgment day as Hades was the abode before judgment day [NTC].

DISCOURSE UNIT: 5:23–26 [EBC, McN, NCBC, TNTC2]. The topic is two illustrations [TNTC2], two illustrations about the seriousness of anger [EBC], two illustrations of subduing anger by reconciliation [NCBC], two illustrations of the above principle [McN].

DISCOURSE UNIT: 5:23–24 [EBC, ICC]. The topic is the first concrete application/illustration of 5:21–22 [ICC], reconciliation with a brother [EBC].

5:23 If[a] therefore[b] you(sg)-are-bringing[c] your(sg) gift[d] to[e] the altar[f]

LEXICON—a. ἐάν (LN 89.67): 'if' [Mor, NTC, WBC; all versions except NET, NJB, NRSV], 'when' [NRSV]; not explicit [NET, NJB].

b. οὖν (LN 89.50): 'therefore' [Mor, NTC, TG, TH, WBC; KJV, NAB, NASB, NIV, TNT], 'so' [CEV, NLT, NRSV, REB, TEV], 'so then' [NET, NJB]. It indicates a positive conclusion based on the two previous

verses [BSC]. It arises from the preceding statements [Mor, NTC]. See
this word at 5:19.

c. pres. act. subj. of προσφέρω (LN 57.80) (BAGD 2.a. p. 719): 'to bring'
[BAGD, NTC; KJV, NAB, NET, NJB], 'to offer' [BAGD, Mor; NIV,
NRSV, TEV, TNT], 'to present' [BAGD; NASB, REB], 'to place' [CEV],
'to bear' [WBC], 'to stand offering' [NLT]. See this word at 5:24.

d. δῶρον (LN **57.84**) (BAGD 2. p. 211): 'gift' [BAGD, LN, Mor, WBC; all
versions except NASB, NJB, NLT], 'offering' [BAGD, NTC; NASB,
NJB], 'sacrifice' [**LN**], 'a sacrifice to God' [NLT]. God is the intended
recipient of the gift [TH].

e. ἐπί: 'to' [NTC, WBC; KJV, NAB, NASB, NET, NJB], 'at' [NIV, NRSV,
REB, TEV, TNT], 'on' [Mor; CEV], 'before' [NLT].

f. θυσιαστήριον (LN **6.114**) (BAGD 1.a. p. 366): 'altar' [BAGD, LN, Mor,
NTC, WBC; all versions], 'altar in the Temple' [NLT]. This word refers
to the literal altar of burnt offering in the temple in Jerusalem where
animal and grain were burnt as an offering to God [BAGD, Mor, TG]. It
was located in the inner court and used during solemn formal worship
[BAGD, EBC, McN, TNTC2].

QUESTION—How is the present tense of the verb interpreted?

It is translated with a continuous, progressive or incomplete aspect: 'you are
offering' [NIV, NRSV, TNT], 'you are presenting' [NASB, REB], 'you are
bringing' [NJB], 'you are about to offer' [TEV], 'on the way to offer' (an
incomplete action) [ZG], 'you are standing before' [NLT], 'you are about to
place' [CEV]. Some versions render it more simply: 'thou bring' [KJV],
'you bring' [NAB, NET].

QUESTION—Is there significance in the singular form of 'you'?

The singular form represents a shift from the general (plural) to the particular
[TG], and indicates that Jesus is speaking to each individual disciple [TH].
The shift sharpens personal application [EBC, Mor, NTC, WBC]. It is more
vivid [NTC]. The change from plural to singular is also present in 5:29, 36,
39, and 6:5.

and-there^a you(sg)-remember^b

LEXICON—a. κἀκεῖ (BAGD 1. p. 396): 'and there' [BAGD, Mor; KJV, NAB,
NASB, NET, NIV, NJB, TEV, TNT], 'and suddenly' [NLT, REB], 'and
then' [WBC], 'and' [CEV], not explicit [NRSV]. It is rendered 'while'
before the previous clause and 'there' in this clause [NTC].

b. aorist pass. (deponent = act.) subj. of μιμνῄσκομαι (LN 29.7) (BAGD
1.a.δ. p. 522): 'to remember' [BAGD, Mor, NTC, WBC; all versions
except NAB], 'to recall' [NAB].

that your(sg) brother has something^a against you(sg),

LEXICON—a. τις (sic.) (LN 92.12) (BAGD 1.b.α. p. 820): 'something'
[BAGD, Mor, WBC; NASB, NET, NIV, NJB, NLT, NRSV, TEV, TNT],
'anything' [BAGD; NAB], 'aught' [KJV], 'a grievance' [NTC; REB].

The phrase 'has something against you' is translated 'is angry with you' [CEV].

5:24 leave[a] your(sg) gift there[b] before[c] the altar,

LEXICON—a. aorist act. impera. of ἀφίημι (LN 85.45) (BAGD 3.a. p. 126): 'to leave' [Mor, NTC, WBC; all versions]. This does not mean that it is left as a sacrifice; the offering is not completed [TH].

    b. ἐκεῖ (LN 83.2) (BAGD 1. p. 239): 'there' [BAGD, Mor, NTC, WBC; all versions except NAB, REB], 'where it is' [REB], 'in that place' [BAGD], not explicit [NAB].

    c. ἔμπροσθεν (LN **83.33**) (BAGD 2.a. p. 257): 'before' [BAGD, Mor, WBC; KJV, NASB, NJB, NRSV, REB, TNT], 'in front of' [BAGD, LN, NTC; CEV, NET, NIV, TEV], 'at' [NAB], 'beside' [NLT].

QUESTION—What is Jesus intending to communicate?

Reconciliation takes precedence over sacrifice and ritual [EBC, Mor, NAC, NCBC, NIBC, TG, TNTC2, WBC]. This is hyperbole and probably is not to be taken literally [ICC].

and[a] go-away first[b] (and) be-reconciled[c] to-your(sg) brother,

LEXICON—a. καί: 'and' [Mor, NTC, WBC; KJV, NASB, NET, NRSV], not explicit [CEV, NAB, NIV, NJB, NLT, REB, TEV, TNT].

    b. πρῶτος (LN 60.46) (BAGD 2.a. p. 726): 'first' [BAGD, Mor, NTC, WBC; all versions except CEV, NLT, TEV], 'at once' [TEV], not explicit [CEV, NLT]. It is a time reference [BAGD, Mor]. See this word at 7:5.

    c. aorist pass. impera. of διαλλάσσομαι (LN **40.2**) (BAGD p. 186): 'to be reconciled (to)' [BAGD, **LN**, Mor, NTC, WBC; all versions except CEV, REB, TEV], 'to make peace (with)' [LN; CEV, REB, TEV].

and then[a] coming (back) offer[b] your(sg) gift.

LEXICON—a. (καί) τότε (LN **67.47**) (BAGD 2. p. 824): The phrase καί τότε 'and then' [BAGD, **LN**, Mor, WBC; KJV, NAB, NASB, NET, NJB, NRSV, TEV, TNT], 'and thereupon' [BAGD], 'then' [LN, NTC; CEV, NIV, NLT, REB]. 'Then make the sacrifice' implies that God will now accept it [WBC].

    b. pres. act. impera. of προσφέρω: 'to offer, to bring' See this word at 5:23.

QUESTION—How is the participle ἐλθὼν 'coming' to be interpreted?

It is used as an imperative 'come' [KJV, NAB, NASB, NET, NIV, NLT, NRSV, TNT] or 'come back' [CEV, NJB, REB, TEV].

QUESTION—What is force of the present imperative πρόσφερε 'offer'?

It has a durative force indicating that something already in existence is to continue. Here directions are given as to how offering your gift is to be carried out. It means both 'then you *may* bring/offer', and at the same time also 'resume bringing/offering' [BD (sec. 336(3), pp. 172–3)].

DISCOURSE UNIT: 5:25–26 [EBC, ICC, NIBC]. The topic is reconciliation with an adversary: temple and judicial [EBC], second concrete illustration/ application of 5:21–22 [ICC].

5:25 Make-friends-with[a] your(sg) opponent[b] quickly[c]

LEXICON—a. pres. act. participle of εὐνοέω (LN **30.23**, **31.20**, **56.3**) (BAGD
p. 323). The periphrastic verb phrase ἴσθι εὐνοῶν (using ἴσθι, the pres.
act. impera. of εἰμί 'to be, to become', with this participle) is translated:
'to make friends with' [BAGD, Mor, NTC; CEV, NASB, TNT], 'to be
well disposed to' [BAGD, WBC], 'to settle matters with' [NIV], 'to settle
the dispute' [TEV], 'to settle with' [NAB], 'to come to terms with' [NJB,
NLT, NRSV, REB], 'to reach agreement' [NET], 'to agree with' [KJV],
'to consider how to resolve (matters with)' [LN (30.23)], 'to agree with'
[LN (31.20)], 'to settle with' [LN (56.3)].

b. ἀντίδικος (LN **56.11**) (BAGD p. 74): 'opponent' [Mor, NTC; NAB,
NJB, TNT], 'adversary' [WBC; KJV], 'adversary who is taking (you) to
court' [NIV], 'opponent in a law suit' [BAGD, ZG], 'opponent at law'
[NASB], 'accuser' [LN; NET, NRSV], 'the person who has accused (you)
of doing wrong' [CEV], 'enemy' [NLT], 'plaintiff' [LN]. 'Your
opponent' is also expressed as a conditional clause: 'if someone sues you'
[REB], 'if someone brings a lawsuit against you and takes you to court'
[TEV].

c. ταχύς (LN 67.110) (BAGD 2.b. p. 807): 'quickly' [BAGD, Mor, NTC;
KJV, NAB, NASB, NET, NIV, NLT, NRSV, TNT], 'without delay, at
once' [BAGD], 'and do so quickly' [WBC], 'promptly' [REB], 'in good
time' [NJB], not explicit, combined with next clause [CEV, TEV].

QUESTION—Is this the same illustration as in the preceding verse or is it a
second one?

This is a second illustration [BSC, EBC, ICC, NAC, NIBC, WBC], a second
application [ICC], although it is closely related to the preceding illustration
following Jesus' interpretation of the sixth commandment [BSC]. It
emphasizes the urgency of reconciliation [NAC, WBC], and extends
reconciliation to those beyond the category of brother, to opponents and
enemies [ICC]. Reconciliation leads to the idea of being on continually
friendly relations even with an opponent [Mor]. Jesus is again picking up the
theme of the heavenly court (Sanhedrin) [BBC], and illustrating the urgency
of averting God's wrath on judgment day before that day arrives [NAC].

while[a] you(sg)-are (still) with him on the way[b] (to court),

LEXICON—a. ἕως (LN **67.139**) (BAGD II.1.b.γ. p. 335): 'while' [BAGD,
LN, Mor, NTC, WBC; KJV, NAB, NASB, NET, NJB, NRSV, REB,
TNT], 'while there is time' [TEV], 'do it while' [NIV], 'before it is too
late' [NLT], 'before you are dragged into court' [CEV]. The emphasis on
time is indicated by the addition of the word 'still': 'while you are still'
[Mor; NIV, NJB].

b. ὁδός (LN 1.99) (BAGD 1.b. p. 554): 'way' [BAGD]. The phrase ἐν τῇ
ὁδῷ 'on the way' [Mor; NASB, NIV] is also translated 'in the way'
[KJV], 'on the road' [WBC; TNT], 'on the way to court' [EBC, ICC, TH;
NAB, NET, NJB, NRSV], 'on your way to court' [REB], 'before you get

to court' [TEV], 'before you are dragged into court' [CEV], 'while you still have the opportunity to deal with him' [NTC], 'before it is too late and you are dragged into court' [CEV]. The phrase emphasizes urgency [WBC].

QUESTION—What is pictured in this verse about two opponents on the road to court together?

It is much easier to establish friendship in the encounter outside of court than after getting to court [Mor]. It is better to settle the dispute before a judge has to settle it; all disputes should be settled immediately because delay could cause dire circumstances [NIBC]. Jewish law did not include debt imprisonment [BBC, WBC], but the audience would have known about it from the Greek culture that surrounded them [BBC]. A defendant and plaintiff might very well meet together walking on their way to be heard by the local council of elders [Brc].

lest[a] the opponent deliver[b] you(sg) to-the judge,[c] and the judge (deliver you) to-the officer,[d]

LEXICON—a. μήποτε (LN 89.62) (BAGD 2.b.a. p. 519):, 'lest' [Mor, NTC, WBC, ZG], 'lest at any time' [KJV], 'otherwise' [NAB, REB] 'or' [NET, NIV, NJB, NRSV], 'once you are there (he will)' [TEV], 'in order that...not' [BAGD; NASB], 'if you do not' [TNT], 'if you don't' [CEV], not explicit [NLT]. Μήποτε is an emphatic form of μή that denotes purpose and possibly apprehension [BAGD].

   b. aorist act. subj. of παραδίδωμι (LN **37.111**) (BAGD 1.b. p. 614): 'to deliver' [KJV, NASB], 'to hand over' [BAGD, **LN**, Mor, NTC, WBC; NAB, NET, NIV, NJB, NRSV, REB, TNT], 'to be turned over' [BAGD, LN; CEV, TEV], 'to give up' [BAGD], 'to be dragged into court' [NLT]. Παραδίδωμι is a technical term for 'to put into custody' [Mor].

   c. κριτής (LN 56.28) (BAGD 1.a.α. p. 453): 'the judge' [BAGD, Mor, NTC, WBC; all versions except NLT], not explicit [NLT]. This refers to a person who reaches a decision and passes judgment [BAGD]

   d. ὑπηρέτης (LN 35.20) (BAGD p. 842): 'officer' [Mor, NTC; CEV, KJV, NASB, NIV, NJB, NLT, REB], '(the) police' [TEV], 'guard' [NAB, NRSV], 'jailer' [TNT], 'warden' [NET], 'servant' [BAGD, WBC], 'helper, assistant' [BAGD].

QUESTION—What is meant by the term ὑπηρέτης 'officer'?

It designates the court official who puts the guilty person in prison [Mor, TH]. He is the court officer who had the responsibility to see the debt paid and the power to imprison the defaulter [Brc]. It is possible that ὑπηρέτης designates a synagogue official [ICC], an inferior official [McN], someone designated to execute the judge's sentence [ICC]. There were two Levites assigned to each local Sanhedrin who acted as police [McN].

and you(sg) will-be-thrown[a] into the prison;[b]

LEXICON—a. fut. pass. indic. of βάλλω (LN 85.34): 'to be thrown' [Mor, NTC, WBC; all versions except CEV, KJV, TEV], 'to be cast' [KJV], 'to

be put' [CEV, TEV]. In Hellenistic Greek sometimes the future
functionally replaces the subjunctive after μήποτε [ZG], thus yielding a
translation of 'may be thrown' [NIV].

b. φυλακή (LN 7.24) (BAGD 3. p. 875): 'prison' [BAGD, Mor, NTC,
WBC; KJV, NAB, NASB, NET, NIV, NJB, NRSV, TNT], 'in jail' [CEV,
NLT, REB, TEV].

5:26 truly[a] I-say to-you(sg), you(sg)-will- not[b] -get-out[c] from-there[d]
LEXICON—a. ἀμήν (LN 72.6) (BAGD 2. p. 45): 'truly'. See the phrase 'truly I
say to you(pl)/(sg)' at 5:18; 6:2, 5, 16. When used with a detailed
allegory, it suggests that deeper meanings lie below the surface [McN,
TNTC2]. Here, literal and metaphorical elements are inextricably
combined, and the metaphor points to future judgment by God [McN].

b. οὐ μή (LN 69.3) (BAGD D.1.a. p. 517): 'not' [CEV, NAB, NASB, NET,
NIV, NJB, NLT, REB, TNT], 'never' [NTC, WBC; NRSV], 'by no
means' [KJV], 'certainly not' [Mor]. The double negative is emphatic,
meaning that performing the action of the verb will be impossible [Mor].
See this word at 5:18.

c. aorist act. subj. of ἐξέρχομαι (LN 15.40) (BAGD 1.a. p. 274): 'to get out'
[NTC, WBC; CEV, NET, NIV, NJB, NRSV], 'to come out' [BAGD,
Mor; KJV, NASB, TNT], 'to be let out' [REB], 'to be released' [BAGD;
NAB], 'to be free again' [NLT]. The whole phrase is translated 'there you
will stay' [TEV].

d. ἐκεῖθεν (LN 84.10) (BAGD p. 239): 'from there' [BAGD, Mor, WBC],
'of there' [NASB], 'of it' [TNT], 'of that place' [NTC], 'thence' [KJV],
'there' [REB, TEV], not explicit [CEV, NAB, NET, NIV, NJB, NLT,
NRSV].

until[a] you(sg)-pay[b] the last[c] penny[d].
LEXICON—a. ἕως (LN 67.119) (BAGD I.1.b. p. 334): 'until' [BAGD, LN,
ZG]. The unit ἕως ἄν is translated 'until' [Mor, NTC, WBC; all versions
except KJV, NJB], 'till' [KJV, NJB]. See this word at 5:18.

b. aorist act. subj. of ἀποδίδωμι (LN **57.153**) (BAGD 2. p. 90): 'to pay'
[LN, Mor, NTC, WBC; all versions except NASB], 'to pay up' [NASB],
'to return, to pay back (a debt)' [BAGD].

c. ἔσχατος (LN **61.13**) (BAGD 3.b. p. 314): 'last' [BAGD, LN, Mor, NTC;
all versions except KJV], 'uttermost' [KJV]. The phrase τὸν ἔσχατον
κοδράντην 'the last penny' means 'all that must be paid before you can
be set free' [TH].

d. κοδράντης (LN **6.78**) (BAGD p. 437): 'penny' [BAGD, **LN**, Mor; NAB,
NET, NIV, NJB, NLT, NRSV, REB, TEV], 'cent' [NIBC, NTC; CEV,
NASB], 'farthing' [KJV], 'small piece of money' [LN], 'quarter-penny'
[WBC], 'quadrans' [BAGD, LN; TNT]. It was 1/64 of the denarius, the
standard daily wage [LN, NAC], only a few minutes wages [BBC].

DISCOURSE UNIT: 5:27–30 [BBC, EBC, GNT, HF, ICC, MLJ, Mor, NAC, NCBC, NIBC, NTC, Pl, TG, TH, TNTC2, WBC; CEV, NET, NIV, NLT, NRSV, REB, TEV]. The topic is adultery [GNT, ICC, Mor, NAC, NCBC, TNTC2, WBC; NET, NIV, NLT, NRSV, TEV], teaching about adultery [TG; NAB], Jesus teaches about adultery [TG, TH], Jesus condemns adultery [HF], adultery and purity [EBC], the exceeding sinfulness of sin [MLJ], the second antithesis: the seventh commandment, adultery [NTC], lust as adultery [BBC], marriage [CEV].

DISCOURSE UNIT: 5:27–28 [McN]. The topic is thou shalt not commit adultery.

5:27 **You(pl)-have-heard that it-was-said,**
QUESTION—How does this clause compare with the similar one in 5:21?
   This opening phrase has the same pattern as the first antithesis 'you have heard that it was said' and it means 'you have received the following instruction in the law' [BSC]. It is a shortened formula related to the one in 5:21 [ICC]. The 'men of old' is not explicit, but it is still assumed [NCBC]. See the discussion at 5:21.

(Do) not commit-adultery.[a]
LEXICON—a. aorist act. impera. of μοιχεύω (LN 88.276) (BAGD 1. p. 526): 'to commit adultery' [BAGD, Mor, NTC, WBC; all versions except CEV]. The verb is used to refer to both sexes [BAGD]. This prohibition is also translated as a positive command: 'Be faithful in marriage' [CEV].
QUESTION—What is the relationship of this command to the preceding section?
   The previous section elaborated on one of the ten commandments [NTC, TH], the sixth commandment [BSC, NTC]. This section is related by also teaching about one of the ten commandments [NTC, TH], the seventh commandment [NTC, Pl]. This section is the second antithesis; it discusses misunderstandings of the seventh commandment [BSC], sharpening the audience's understand of the seventh commandment and presenting it in terms of the tenth commandment about desiring what is not one's own [NCBC].
QUESTION—What is the relevant cultural background to this prohibition?
   In Jewish usage the word 'adultery' referred specifically to the taking of another man's wife or betrothed. It would not mean sinful sexual intercourse in general, or a married man having sexual relations with an unmarried (or unbetrothed) woman [TH]. It was assumed that a woman would be committing adultery if she had sexual intercourse with someone other than her husband; however, a man was not bound by this and could have sexual adventures outside of marriage as long as it did not violate another man's rights to that man's wife [Mor].

QUESTION—What is the focus of this section?

This command is an exact quotation of Exodus 20:14 and Deuteronomy 5:18 [EBC, ICC, Mor, TH, WBC]. The validity of the OT command is affirmed, and thus it is still binding [ICC]. Jesus sets a new standard for purity and implies that this is the intention of the original OT command [Pl]. Men imagined that if they had not engaged in the act of adultery they were innocent and the commandment had nothing to say to them. They didn't understand that sin is ultimately a matter of the heart, not just conduct [MLJ]. Jesus contrasts his prohibition of lust with the OT command not to commit adultery. He demands more than the Ten Commandments do—he demands holiness [ICC].

5:28 But[a] I say to-you(pl) that[b] everyone[c] looking-at[d] a woman[e] in-order-to lust-after[f] her

LEXICON—a. δέ: 'but' [Mor, NTC, WBC; all versions except TNT], not explicit [TNT].

b. ὅτι: 'that' [Mor, NTC, WBC; CEV, KJV, NASB, NET, NIV, NRSV, TNT], 'if' [ICC; NJB, REB], not explicit [NAB, NLT, TEV].

c. πᾶς (LN 59.23) (BAGD 1.c.γ. p. 632): 'everyone who' [BAGD, Mor, WBC; NAB, NASB, NRSV, TNT], 'whosoever' [KJV], 'whoever' [BAGD; NET], 'anyone who' [NTC; NIV, NLT, TEV], 'a man' [NJB, REB], 'if you' [CEV]. Πᾶς grammatically unites the three paragraphs beginning at 5:21; it occurs here and in verses 22 and 32 [ICC].

d. pres. act. participle of βλέπω (LN 24.7) (BAGD 3. p. 143): 'to look at' [BAGD, Mor, NTC, WBC; all versions except KJV, NASB], 'to look on' [KJV, NASB], 'to regard' [BAGD]. This participle is translated 'even looks at' [NLT].

e. γυνή (LN 9.34 or 10.54) (BAGD 2. p. 168): 'a woman' [Mor, NTC, WBC; all versions except CEV], 'another woman' [CEV].

f. aorist act. infin. of ἐπιθυμέω (LN **25.20**) (BAGD p. 293): 'to lust after' [Mor, NTC, WBC; KJV], 'to lust for' [LN; NASB], 'to desire' [BAGD, LN, NAC; NET, TNT], 'to want' [CEV], 'to want to possess' [TEV]. The phrase 'to look at a woman in order to lust after her' is translated 'to look at a woman lustfully' [**LN**; NIV, NJB], 'to look at a woman with lust' [NAB, NRSV], 'to look at a woman with lust in his eye' [NLT], 'to look at a woman with a lustful eye' [REB]. The verb usually, but not always, refers to an evil desire [EBC, Mor].

QUESTION—What is indicated by the present participle of βλέπω 'look'?

'Anyone looking' by itself is neutral and it is actually the next clause which colors such looking negatively [NTC]. Βλέπω in this context connotes that the person goes beyond a passing glance to look continuously, not just viewing or imagining a naked body but, in view of ἐπιθυμέω 'to lust after' in the next clause, dwelling on it in lust and actually desiring to have sexual relations with someone other than one's spouse [NAC]. The sin is letting the look incite passion [ICC].

QUESTION—Who is the woman that is looked at?
1. The word γυνή 'woman' here refers to any woman [EBC, Pl, WBC].
2. The word γυνή 'woman' here refers to a married woman, the wife of another man [NCBC, NIBC, TNTC2, ZG].
QUESTION—What relationship is indicated by πρός 'in order to'?
1. It indicates the purpose of looking at a woman [Brc, BSC, Mor, NCBC, NIBC, NTC, TH, WBC; KJV, NASB, NET, TNT]: anyone looking at a woman with the intention of committing adultery with her. The clause means not just happening to see a person of the opposite sex, but gazing, staring in order to lust after her [NTC]. It is not just noticing the beauty or even briefly the sexual attractiveness of a woman. Rather, it is contemplating or intending having sex with her [TH].
2. It indicates the result of looking at a woman [BAGD (III.3.b. p. 710), BD, ICC, McN]: anyone looking at a woman with the result that he desires her. The sin is letting the look incite passion [ICC].
3. It may simply have the force of coordination and mean 'and' [CEV]: anyone looking as a woman and desiring her.

already[a] has-committed-adultery-with[b] her in his heart.[c]
LEXICON—a. ἤδη (LN 67.20) (BAGD 2. p. 344): 'already' [BAGD, Mor, NTC, WBC; all versions except TEV], not explicit [TEV].
  b. aorist act. indic. of μοιχεύω (LN 88.276) (BAGD 2.b. p. 526): 'to commit adultery with' [BAGD, Mor, NTC, WBC; all versions except CEV, TEV], 'to be unfaithful with' [CEV], 'to be guilty of committing adultery with' [TEV]. It is not 'as if' he is guilty, but that he actually is guilty of committing adultery because it is not the act that is adultery but the lust and desire to do so [TH].
  c. καρδία (LN 26.3) (BAGD 1.b.ε. p. 404): 'heart' [BAGD, Mor, NTC, WBC; all versions except CEV, TNT], 'thoughts' [CEV], 'mind' [TNT].

DISCOURSE UNIT: 5:29–30 [McN]. The topic is the right eye and hand.

5:29 **And[a] if[b] your(sg) right eye is-causing- you(sg) -to-sin,[c]**
LEXICON—a. δέ: 'and' [Mor; KJV, NASB], 'so' [NTC; NLT, TEV], 'but' [WBC], not explicit [CEV, NAB, NET, NIV, NJB, NRSV, REB, TNT].
  b. εἰ (LN 89.65) (BAGD I.1.a. p. 219): 'if' [BAGD, Mor, NTC, WBC; all versions]. Εἰ here refers to a condition thought of as real or that has actually happened [BAGD, McN, Mor, ZG]. Εἰ is also used in 5:30 with the same sense [BAGD].
  c. pres. act. indic. of σκανδαλίζω (LN 88.304) (BAGD 1.a. p. 752): 'to cause to sin' [BAGD, ICC, LN, Mor, NCBC, NTC, TG, TH, TNTC2; CEV, NAB, NET, NIV, NLT, NRSV, TEV], 'to make to sin' [Mor], 'to lure into sin' [NTC], 'to make to stumble' [NASB], 'to cause one's downfall' [REB], 'to be one's downfall' [NJB], 'to cause to fall (away)' [BAGD; TNT]. 'to cause to lust' [NLT]. The pronouns and adjectives in 5:29–30 are all singular.

QUESTION—What meanings are associated with σκανδαλίζω 'to cause to sin'?

The verb σκανδαλίζω is derived from the noun σκάνδαλον 'stumbling block, trap', referring either to a snare that will trap and hold some animal or person or to an obstacle that will cause someone to stumble. It us used as a metaphor for anything that leads someone to fall into and be trapped by sin [Mor].

1. The image is that of trapping something [Brc, Mor, NIBC, NTC]. The word comes from the noun σκανδάληθρον 'a bait-stick in a trap', or the bait on the stick that lured the animal to be caught [Brc, Mor, NIBC, NTC]. From this the verb was derived meaning 'to put a trap or snare to catch something' [Mor]. Thus in the NT it can mean 'to cause to be caught' [BAGD], or 'to ensnare' [NTC].

2. The image is that of causing someone to stumble or fall [EBC, ICC, TG, TH, WBC; NASB, NJB, REB, TNT].

3. The metaphor is dropped and the idea is then 'to cause to sin' [BAGD, ICC, LN, Mor, NCBC, NTC, TG, TH, TNTC2; CEV, NET, NIV, NLT, NRSV, TEV].

QUESTION—What is the cultural association of 'right' eye in this verse and its connection to right hand in the next verse ?

'Right eye' is in parallelism with 'right hand' in 5:30, and simply emphasizes self-sacrifice [McN, TH]. Being in parallelism to 'the right hand' in the next verse, the right eye is spoken of as being more useful [TH]. The right eye was chosen for associations with the right hand, and what was true of the right hand was true of the right eye [NCBC]. As opposed to the left hand, the right hand was viewed in antiquity as being more valuable or active than the left [ICC, NAC, NCBC, Pl], the favored hand for most people [ICC, Mor], so even the more important hand should be sacrificed to avoid eternal judgment [ICC]. The right eye was the more valuable, especially for a warrior [BAGD, EBC, Mor]. The right hand is among the most important members that can be sacrificed without dying from the loss [Pl]. The right is the preferred eye/hand and more skilled [WBC]. The right hand (and eye) corresponds to the place of honor [NIBC].

gouge- it -out[a] and throw- (it) -away[b] from you(sg);

LEXICON—a. aorist act. impera. of ἐξαιρέω (LN **85.43**) (BAGD 1. p. 271): 'to gouge out' [Mor; NIV, NLT], 'to pluck out' [NTC, WBC; KJV], 'to take out' [BAGD, LN; TEV, TNT], 'to tear out' [BAGD; NAB, NASB, NET, NJB, NRSV, REB], 'to poke out' [CEV].

b. aorist act. impera. of βάλλω (LN **15.215**) (BAGD 1.b. p. 131): 'to throw away' [BAGD, Mor; CEV, NAB, NET, NIV, NJB, NLT, NRSV, TEV, TNT], 'to cast' [WBC; KJV], 'to throw' [BAGD, LN; NASB], 'to fling away' [NTC; REB].

QUESTION—What is the intent of Jesus' statement here?

This figure uses hyperbole to make an important point memorable [TNTC2, WBC] and to communicate the seriousness of the issue [TH]. It is not commanding literal self-mutilation but drastic measures to keep oneself from sinning [EBC, ICC, NIBC, NTC, TNTC2, WBC]. This passage is meta-phoric [Pl], because obviously the loss of a hand or an eye would hardly guarantee purity [ICC, Pl, TG]. The further step of throwing the body member away adds force and vividness: 'don't keep that plucked out eye in your hand but even throw it away' [ICC].

for[a] it-is-better[b] for-you(sg) that one of your(sg) parts[c] be-lost[d]

LEXICON—a. γάρ: 'for' [Mor, WBC; KJV, NASB, NJB, TNT], not explicit [NTC; CEV, NAB, NET, NIV, NLT, NRSV, REB, TEV].

b. pres. act. indic. of συμφέρω (LN 65.44) (BAGD 2.a. p. 780): 'to be better' [BAGD, NTC, WBC; all versions except KJV, NJB, TEV], 'to be much better' [TEV], 'to be profitable' [KJV], 'to do (you) less harm' [NJB], 'to be expedient' [Mor].

c. μέλος (LN 8.9) (BAGD 1. p. 501): 'part' [BAGD], 'body part' [LN], 'member' [BAGD, LN], 'limb' [BAGD]. The phrase ἓν τῶν μελῶν σου 'one of your parts' is translated 'one part of your body' [CEV, NIV, NLT, REB, TNT], 'a part of your body' [TEV], 'one of the parts of your body' [NASB], 'one part of yourself' [NJB], 'one of your members' [Mor, NTC, WBC; KJV, NAB, NET, NRSV].

d. aorist mid. subj. of ἀπόλλυμι (LN 57.68) (BAGD 2.b. p. 95): 'to be lost' [BAGD, NTC; CEV, NET, NIV, NJB, NLT, NRSV, REB, TEV], 'to perish' [Mor, WBC; KJV, NASB, TNT], 'to lose (one of your members)' [NAB].

and-not[a] (that) your(sg) whole body be-thrown[b] into hell.[c]

LEXICON—a. καί μή: 'and not'. This phrase is translated 'and not that' [Mor; KJV], 'than that (your whole body)' [NTC, WBC; TNT], 'than for (your whole body)' [CEV, NASB, NIV, NLT, NRSV, REB], 'than to have (your whole body)' [NAB, NET, NJB, TEV].

b. aorist pass. subj. of βάλλω (LN 15.215) (BAGD 1.b. p. 130): 'to be thrown' [BAGD, Mor, NTC, WBC; NAB, NASB, NET, NIV, NJB, NLT, NRSV, REB, TEV, TNT], 'to cast' [KJV], 'to end up in' [CEV].

c. γέεννα (LN 1.21) (BAGD p. 153): 'hell' [BAGD, LN, NTC; all versions except NAB], 'Gehenna' [BAGD, LN, Mor, WBC; NAB]. In the Gospels γέεννα is the place of punishment in the next life [BAGD]. See 5:22, where γέεννα is first used [TH].

5:30 And if your(sg) right hand is-causing- you(sg) -to-sin, cut- it -off[a] it
and throw-away (it) from you(sg); for it-is-better for-you(sg), that one of
your(sg) parts be-lost than your(sg) whole body go[b] into hell.

LEXICON—a. pres. act. impera. of ἐκκόπτω (LN 19.18) (BAGD 1. p. 241): 'to
cut off' [BAGD, Mor, NTC, WBC; all versions except CEV], 'to chop
off' [CEV].

b. aorist pass. subj. of ἀπέρχομαι (LN 15.37): 'to go' [NAB, NASB, NET,
NIV, NJB, NRSV, REB, TNT], 'to go off' [Mor; TEV], 'to go down'
[NTC], 'to cast' [KJV], 'to be thrown' [CEV, NLT], 'to depart' [WBC].

QUESTION—What is the relationship to the previous verse?

There is near complete parallelism with the preceding verse, with the natural
replacement of καί 'and' for δέ 'but', χείρ 'hand' for ὀφθαλμός 'eye',
ἐκκόπτω 'to cut off' for ἐξαιρέω 'to gouge out', and ἀπέρχομαι 'to go into'
for βάλλω 'to be thrown into', as with a coordinated relationship [ICC, TH].
The small changes to the preceding verse are stylistic and not significant
[TH, WBC].

DISCOURSE UNIT: 5:31–32 [BBC, EBC, GNT, HF, ICC, McN, MLJ, Mor,
NAC, NCBC, NIBC, NTC, Pl, TNTC2, WBC; CEV, NAB, NET, NIV, NLT,
NRSV, REB, TEV]. The topic is divorce [GNT, ICC, McN, MLJ, Mor, NAC,
NCBC, TNTC2, WBC; CEV, NET, NIV, NRSV, TEV], teaching about divorce
[TG, TH; NAB, NLT], the third antithesis: the seventh commandment, divorce
[NTC], remarriage as adultery [BBC], divorce and remarriage [EBC], the third
illustration [Pl].

5:31 It-was- also[a] -said,

LEXICON—a. δέ: 'also' [NTC; NAB, NJB, NRSV, TEV], 'and' [Mor, WBC;
NASB], not explicit [CEV, KJV, NET, NIV, NLT, REB, TNT].

QUESTION—What is the relationship with the preceding passage?

There is a connection of topics [Pl]. There is logical train of thought that
sexual sin often leads to divorce [NAC, NTC].

1. This passage closes the first half of the section 5:21–48 [ICC]. Verses 31-
32 form an equal part among six parts in this section (5:21-48) of the
sermon [BSC, ICC, MLJ, NAC, NTC, Pl, TG, TNTC2, WBC].

2. There are five main parts in the sermon, but because the introductory
formula is not the same, these two verses are only a sub-point or
additional note on the preceding paragraph on adultery [NIBC]. Δέ 'also'
is a connective, indicating a continuation of the argument of the
preceding, meaning that this is not a new antithesis [EBC].

QUESTION—What is the subject of ἐρρέθη 'it was said'?

'It was said' refers to Deuteronomy 24:1-4 [EBC, NIBC, NTC, TH, TNTC2,
WBC].

Whoever[a] divorces[b] his wife,[c]

LEXICON—a. ὅς ἄν: 'whoever' [Mor, NTC, TH, WBC; NAB, NASB, NET,
NRSV], 'whosoever' [KJV], 'anyone who' [TG, TH; NIV, NJB, TEV],

'any husband who' [TG], 'any man who' [TG], 'a man' [NLT], 'a man who' [CEV, REB], 'if a man' [TNT], 'any husband who' [TH].

b. aorist act. subj. of ἀπολύω (LN **34.78**) (BAGD 2.a. p. 96): 'to divorce' [BAGD, LN, Mor, NTC, WBC; all versions except KJV], 'to put away' [KJV], 'to send away one's wife' [BAGD].

c. γυνή (LN **10.54**) (BAGD 2. p. 168): 'his wife' [BAGD, LN, Mor, NTC, WBC; all versions]. See this word at 5:28.

let-him-give[a] her a-certificate-of-divorce.[b]

LEXICON—a. aorist act. impera of δίδωμι (LN 57.71) (BAGD 2. p. 193): 'to give' [BAGD, Mor, NTC, WBC; all versions except CEV, NLT], 'to write out' [CEV], 'to merely give' [NLT].

b. ἀποστάσιον (LN **33.41**) (BAGD p. 98): 'a certificate of divorce' [BAGD, WBC; NIV, NRSV, TNT], 'a divorce certificate' [NTC], 'divorce papers' [CEV], 'a writing of divorcement' [KJV], 'a written notice of divorce' [LN; TEV], 'a bill of divorce' [NAB], 'a letter of divorce' [NLT], 'a certificate of dismissal' [NASB, REB], 'a writ of dismissal' [NJB], 'a legal document' [NET]. It was the word for relinquishing personal rights and to designate giving up rights to a wife [BAGD, Mor, WBC].

QUESTION—What Jewish custom lies behind this?

No court action was required for a man to divorce his wife; a husband could unilaterally divorce her [Mor, TNTC2]. There was a simple divorce procedure: the man wrote out a bill of divorce and presented it to his wife before witnesses [Mor, NTC]. Some rabbis taught against easy divorce, but easy divorce prevailed [ICC]. The legitimacy of and grounds for divorce and the proper procedures governing it were topics of much debate at the time [Brc, Mor, NTC]. It was maintained that the OT permitted divorce based on Deuteronomy 24:1–4 [McN, NCBC, NTC, TG, TH]. This statement by Jesus is not an exact quotation of Deuteronomy 24:1–4, but an abbreviated, summary of present scribal understanding [EBC, ICC, McN, NCBC, TH, TNTC2, WBC]. Deuteronomy 24:1–4 was actually intended as protection for a woman from a husband who might change his mind and demand that she become his wife again later [EBC, Mor, NIBC, TG, TH]. The written divorce papers limited and regulated an abusive practice already occurring at the time [Brc, BSC, EBC, ICC, McN, MLJ, NAC, NTC, Pl]. The regulation was also a discouragement of hasty divorce because of the necessity for a formal certificate [EBC]. Women could not initiate a divorce according to Jewish custom [ICC, Mor, NTC, TG, TNTC2, WBC].

5:32 But[a] I say to-you(pl)

LEXICON—a. δέ: 'but' [Mor, NTC, WBC; all versions].

QUESTION—How is this paragraph similar to and different from the other five sections?

This antithesis and the ones following deal with actions, in contrast to the previous antitheses which dealt with thoughts. Consequently the structure is simpler and does not need illustrations since it involves concrete actions. It also lacks the strong parallelism of the other antitheses [WBC]. This paragraph highlights the contrast between what the OT had written and what Jesus is saying [TH]. Jesus begins with an emphatic ἐγὼ 'I' and now discusses his own position on divorce, which is that marriage is intended to be a lifelong union that should not be lightly dissolved [Mor]. Jesus declares that divorce contradicts the true spirit of the Torah [McN]. The OT implies that not only is lust adultery but also that divorce is adultery [EBC].

that[a] everyone[b] divorcing his wife except[c] (for) (the) reason[d] of-sexual-unfaithfulness[e]

LEXICON—a. ὅτι: 'that' [Mor, NTC, WBC; KJV, NASB, NET, NIV, NLT, NRSV, TNT], 'if' [REB, TEV], not explicit [CEV, NAB, NJB].

b. πᾶς (LN 59.23) (BAGD 1.c.γ. p. 632): 'everyone who' [BAGD, Mor, WBC; NASB, NJB, TNT], 'whosoever' [KJV], 'whoever' [BAGD, NTC; NAB, NET], 'anyone who' [NIV, NRSV], 'a man' [REB, TEV], 'a man who' [NLT], not explicit [CEV]. See this word at 5:22, 28.

c. παρεκτός (LN 58.38) (BAGD 2. p. 625): 'except' [BAGD, ICC, Mor, NTC, TG, WBC; NASB, NET, NIV, NJB, NRSV, TNT], '(for any cause) other than' [REB, TEV], 'unless' [CEV, NAB, NLT], 'saving for' [KJV].

d. λόγος (LN **89.18**) (BAGD 2.d. p. 477): 'reason' [BAGD, LN], 'cause' [KJV, NASB], 'any cause' [REB, TEV], 'on account of' [TNT], 'case' [NJB], 'ground(s)' [NTC, WBC; NRSV], 'matter' [Mor], not explicit [CEV, NAB, NET, NIV, NLT].

e. πορνεία (LN 88.217) (BAGD 1. p. 693): 'marital unfaithfulness' [NTC; NIV], 'unfaithfulness' [TG; TEV], 'sexual infidelity' [WBC], 'infidelity' [NTC], 'fornication' [BAGD, Mor; KJV], 'unchastity' [BAGD; NASB, NRSV, REB], 'her unchastity' [TNT], 'immorality' [NET], 'an illicit marriage' [NJB]. This noun is also translated as a verb phrase: 'to be unfaithful' [NLT], 'to commit some terrible sexual sin' [CEV], 'unless the marriage is unlawful' [NAB]. Here the word refers to the sexual unfaithfulness of a married woman [BAGD].

QUESTION—What is the meaning of πορνεία 'sexual unfaithfulness'?

1. Context indicates that it means 'adultery' [ICC, Mor, NAC, NIBC, Pl, TH]. Because the context is a discussion of marriage, πορνεία in this passage is not a reference to fornication, that is, sexual sin prior to marriage, but to adultery [ICC, Mor, WBC]. In this context it refers to adultery by the wife [TNTC2].

2. Here πορνεία denotes any inappropriate sexual behavior before or after marriage [NCBC].

3. It means an 'unlawful marriage' [NAB, NJB].

he-makes[a] her to-commit-adultery,[b]

LEXICON—a. pres. act. indic. of ποιέω (LN 13.9) (BAGD I.1.b.θ. p. 681): 'to make' [BAGD, Mor, TG; NASB, NET, NJB, TEV], 'to cause' [BAGD, ICC, WBC; CEV, KJV, NAB, NIV, NLT, NRSV, TNT], 'to bring it about that' [BAGD], 'to expose to' [NTC], 'to involve (her) in' [REB], 'to be responsible for making' [TH].

b. aorist pass. infin. of μοιχεύω (LN **88.276**) (BAGD 2.b. p. 526): 'to commit adultery' [LN, Mor, WBC; KJV, NAB, NASB, NET, NIV, NLT, NRSV, TEV, TNT], 'to be guilty of adultery' [TH], 'to be unfaithful' [CEV]. The phrase 'he makes her commit adultery' is translated so as to show that adultery is potential and not automatic upon divorce: 'he is guilty of making her commit adultery if she marries again' [TEV], 'exposes her to adultery' [NTC]. See this word at 5:27, 28.

QUESTION—What cultural background is helpful in understanding this statement?

It was a shocking idea to the people of that time and place that someone properly divorced could be guilty of adultery by marrying a second time [WBC]. The divorced woman would still in reality be the married wife of the first husband, if the husband divorced her for any reason other than unfaithfulness; thus, when she married again, she and the man she married would be committing adultery [EBC, NTC, TG, TH]. The divorced woman would be forced to marry again, because it would be impossible for her to survive otherwise [EBC, McN, TG, TH, WBC; TEV]. So when a man divorced his wife, he compelled her to marry another and thus commit adultery [EBC, ICC, McN, Mor, WBC], or become a prostitute [WBC].

and whoever[a] marries a-divorced-woman commits-adultery.[b]

LEXICON—a. ὃς ἐάν: 'whoever' [Mor, NTC, WBC; NAB, NASB, NRSV, REB], 'whosoever' [KJV], 'anyone who' [NET, NIV, NJB, NLT], 'the man who' [TEV], 'a man' [TNT], 'any man who' [CEV].

b. pres. act. indic. of μοιχάομαι (LN 88.276) (BAGD 2. p. 526): 'to commit adultery' [WBC; KJV, NAB, NASB, NET, NIV, NJB, NLT, NRSV, REB, TEV, TNT], 'to be guilty of taking another man's wife' [CEV], 'to be made to commit adultery' [Mor], 'to involve himself in adultery' [NTC]. Μοιχάομαι is a synonym with μοιχεύω which is used in the preceding clause [ICC].

QUESTION—What cultural background is helpful in understanding this statement about men?

Jesus addressed the men because it was men who were divorcing women and not the other way around [NTC]. The blame for the adultery is put on the man who divorced, not on the woman who remarried—a radical concept for this society [TNTC2]. Jesus expected the same standard for men and women and the idea that a man could commit adultery seems to have been a new idea that his culture did not expect [McN, Mor, WBC]. The divorced woman is still in reality the married wife of the first husband, if the husband divorced her for any reason other than unfaithfulness; thus, when she marries again, she and the man she marries will be committing adultery [EBC, NTC, TG, TH]. Also the man who divorced her must bear the responsibility if the woman is forced to remarry [NTC].

DISCOURSE UNIT: 5:33–48 [ICC]. The topic is the second triad.

DISCOURSE UNIT: 5:33–37 [BBC, EBC, GNT, HF, ICC, McN, MLJ, Mor, NAC, NCBC, NIBC, NTC, Pl, TG, TH, TNTC2, WBC; CEV, Mor, NAB, NET, NIV, NLT, NRSV, REB, TEV]. The topic is vows [TEV], teaching about vows [TG, TH; NAB, NLT], oaths [GNT, ICC, McN, MLJ, Mor, NAC, WBC; NET, NIV, NRSV], swearing [NCBC, TNTC2], do not swear [ICC], promises [CEV], Jesus teaches about making vows/promises to God [TH], Jesus teaches about the commandments concerning promises before God [TH], Jesus condemns oaths [HF], integrity, not oaths [BBC], oaths and truthfulness [EBC], the fourth antithesis: the commandment concerning the oath [NTC], the fourth illustration [Pl].

5:33 **Again[a] you(pl)-have-heard that it-was-said to/by-the ancients,[b]**
LEXICON—a. πάλιν (LN 67.55) (BAGD 3. p. 607): 'again' [Mor, NTC, WBC; all versions except CEV, TEV], 'also' [TEV], not explicit [CEV].
    b. ἀρχαῖος (LN **67.98**) (BAGD 2. p. 111): 'ancients'. The phrase τοῖς ἀρχαίοις 'to/by the ancients' is the same as in 5:21.
QUESTION—What relationship is indicated by πάλιν 'again'?
    Πάλιν begins a formula used earlier in 5:21 and continues developing a theme [BAGD, Mor, TH, WBC]. The use of πάλιν confirms that the previous section on divorce was probably an added note to the antithesis on adultery and that a new theme is now introduced [EBC]. Πάλιν and the full formula indicate that a new section begins with 5:33 [ICC].

You(sg)-will- not -break-an-oath/swear-falsely,[a]
LEXICON—a. fut. act. indic. used as impera. of ἐπιορκέω (LN **33.464, 33.465**) (BAGD 1. p. 296): 'to break (your) oath' [BAGD (2.), LN (33.464), Mor; NET, NIV, NJB, REB], 'to fail to keep your oath' [**LN** (33.464)], 'to take an oath falsely' [NAB], 'to break (your) vows' [NLT, TNT], 'to break (your) promise' [TEV], 'to make false vows' [NASB], 'to swear falsely' [BAGD (1.), **LN** (33.465)], 'to perjure oneself' [BAGD (1.), LN (33.465)], 'to forswear oneself' [KJV], 'to swear falsely' [WBC; NRSV]. This command is translated 'don't use the Lord's name to make a promise unless you are going to keep it' [CEV].
QUESTION—It this a quotation from the OT?
    It is an accurate summary of the teaching of the OT [EBC, McN, Mor, NTC, TH, TNTC, WBC]. Neither this negative command 'do not take an oath falsely' nor the positive command 'you should perform what you have sworn' in the next clause is a precise quote [TH]. Jesus is no longer quoting the 10 commandments [NAC]. He is using words similar to those in the OT, but he is talking about the way in which Scripture was then understood [Mor].
QUESTION—Does ἐπιορκέω mean 'to break an oath' or 'to swear falsely'?
    This word occurs only here in the NT, and can mean either 'to break an oath' (maybe) or 'to swear falsely' [ICC, TH]. To make an oath is similar to

making a vow. Making an oath is declaring before God that something is true or making a solemn declaration that something is true and calling upon God to confirm that, whereas a vow is pledging to do something while calling upon God as witness. [TH].

1. It means to break a vow [LN, NCBC, NTC, TH, WBC; NAB, NASB, NET, NIV, NJB, REB, TEV, TNT]. It means failing to do what one promised before God or to promise to do something while intending not to do it [TH].

2. It means to swear falsely or commit perjury [ICC, Mor; KJV, NAB, NRSV]. A testimony sworn with God as witness must be truthful [Mor].

QUESTION—What is the background of this teaching about taking oaths?

In Jesus' day people used sacred language indiscriminately [Brc, BSC, McN, NTC]. Here Jesus gives a few examples of oaths that many Jews would take and then break without scruple [EBC, Pl]. There was a great emphasis on the form of the words used in the oath. [BSC, NTC, Pl]. The fine details and legal technicalities were debated in the hope of discovering the degree to which an oath would be binding and valid [BSC, EBC, McN, TNTC2]. Most important, if God's name was not used, then the oath was not considered to be binding [Brc, BSC, EBC, MLJ, Mor, NTC, Pl, TH, TNTC]. People strove to state an oath in a way that would not be considered binding and these oaths were essentially a clever way of lying [Brc, BSC, EBC, MLJ, Pl, TNTC, WBC] or of avoiding doing what was promised [WBC]. The misuse of oaths and vows implied that the speaker's words without the oath in its exact proper form could not be trusted [NIBC].

but[a] you(sg)-must-perform[b] your(sg) vow[c] to-the Lord.

LEXICON—a. δέ: 'but' [Mor, NTC, WBC; all versions except CEV, NLT, REB], 'and' [REB], not explicit [CEV, NLT].

    b. fut. act. indic. used as impera. of ἀποδίδωμι (LN **13.136**) (BAGD 1. p. 90): 'to perform' [KJV], 'to keep' [BAGD, Mor, NTC; CEV, NIV, REB], 'to do' [TEV], 'to make good' [NAB], 'to fulfill' [WBC; NASB, NET, NJB, TNT], 'to carry out' [NLT, NRSV], 'to pay what is due' [Mor]; 'you shall fulfill your oaths as unto the Lord' [WBC]. Here it means doing what was promised [LN].

    c. ὅρκος (LN 33.463) (BAGD p. 581): 'vow' [NASB, NET, NLT, NRSV, TNT], 'oath' [BAGD, Mor, NTC, WBC; KJV, NIV, NJB, REB], 'all that you vow' [NAB], 'what you have vowed to do' [TEV], 'what you have promised' [TG], 'a promise' [CEV].

QUESTION—What is the relationship of the two clauses joined by δέ 'but'?

1. The conjunction joins two parts of one quote: 'you shall not do this but you shall do that' [Mor, NTC, WBC; KJV, NAB, NASB, NET, NIV, NJB, NRSV, TEV, TNT].

2. It joins two related quotes: 'you shall not do this' and 'you shall do that' [REB].

5:34 **But I say to-you(pl) not to-swear[a] at-all;[b]**

LEXICON—a. aorist act. infin. of ὀμνύω (LN 33.463) (BAGD p. 566): 'to
swear' [BAGD, Mor; CEV, KJV, NAB, NIV, NJB, NRSV, REB], 'to
make a vow' [NLT], 'to take an oath' [BAGD, NTC, WBC; NET, TNT],
'to make an oath' [NASB]. The phrase 'not to swear at all' is translated
'do not use any vow when you make a promise' [TEV], 'not to swear by
anything when you make a promise' [CEV]. The aorist tense is a timeless
unconditional negative 'do not swear at all' as opposed to a command to
stop swearing [EBC, McN]. See this word at 5:36.

b. ὅλως (LN **78.44**) (BAGD p. 565): 'at all' [BAGD, LN, Mor, NTC, WBC;
all versions except CEV, TEV], '(do not use) any (vow)' [TEV], '(not to
swear by) anything' [CEV].

neither[a] by[b] heaven,[c] for[d] it-is (the) throne[e] of-God;

LEXICON—a. μήτε (LN 69.9) (BAGD p. 520): 'neither' [Mor; KJV], 'either'
[NTC; NASB, NIV, NJB, NRSV, TNT], 'not' [WBC; NAB, NET, REB],
'and not' [BAGD], not explicit [CEV, NLT, TEV]. Μήτε 'neither' is used
three more times in the following section to divide it into its component
parts [BAGD, Mor, TH].

b. ἐν (LN **90.30**) (BAGD IV.5. p. 261): 'by' [BAGD, LN, Mor, NTC,
WBC; all versions].

c. οὐρανός (LN 1.11) (BAGD 1.a.β. p. 593): 'heaven' [BAGD, LN, Mor,
NTC, WBC; all versions]. Here οὐρανός indicates heaven or the sky and
is not merely a Jewish way of avoiding the name of God [McN, NCBC].

d. ὅτι: 'for' [NTC; KJV, NAB, NASB, NIV, NRSV, REB, TEV], 'since'
[NJB], 'because' [Mor, WBC; NET, NLT, TNT], 'so' [CEV]. This
conjunction introduces the grounds for avoiding the particular oath in this
and the following three phrases, which is that ultimately the oath really is
about God and is therefore binding [WBC]. CEV inverts the clauses and
uses this word to introduce the conclusion to a premise: 'heaven is God's
throne, so don't swear by heaven'.

e. θρόνος (LN 6.112) (BAGD 1.b. p. 364): 'throne' [BAGD, Mor, NTC,
WBC; all versions]. The whole clause is translated: 'Heaven is God's
throne, so don't swear by heaven' [CEV], 'do not make a promise and use
the word 'heaven' to make it firm' [TG], 'if you say, 'by heaven!' it is a
sacred vow because heaven is God's throne' [NLT].

QUESTION—What is the relationship of this and the following phrases to the
previous command?

What follows were some commonly used oaths used as examples [Mor], and
the four phrases are set in the same structure to facilitate memorization
[WBC]. Some rabbis contended that an oath sworn by heaven and earth was
not binding [ICC, McN], others that swearing by one's own head was not
binding [ICC]. Each one of the following: 'heaven', 'earth', 'Jerusalem', and
'one's head' was debated in its appropriateness but Jesus contends that each
is still binding because each belongs to God in an important way [NAC].

Jesus is saying that to swear by heaven or by earth is the same as to swear by God [TG]. Jesus argues that all these oaths are binding because the objects are all linked to God [EBC, ICC, McN, Mor, NTC].

5:35 **neither by the earth, for it-is (the) footstool**[a] **of-his feet;**

LEXICON—a. ὑποπόδιον (LN **6.117**) (BAGD p. 847): 'footstool' [BAGD, LN, Mor, NTC, WBC; all versions except TEV], 'resting place' [TEV]. The clause is translated: 'The earth is God's footstool, so don't swear by the earth' [CEV], 'and if you say, 'By the earth!' it is a sacred vow because the earth is his footstool' [NLT].

neither by[a] **Jerusalem, for it-is (a/the) city of-the great king;**

LEXICON—a. εἰς (LN **90.30**) (BAGD 6.b. p. 230): 'by' [BAGD, LN, Mor, NTC; all versions], 'with reference to' [WBC].

QUESTION—What relationship is indicated by εἰς 'by'?

The phrase εἰς Ἱεροσόλυμα 'by Jerusalem' here serves as a symbolic substitute for God, who is presumed to act as guarantor for an oath [LN]. The sense is swearing in the name of, with reference to, or by Jerusalem [BAGD, LN, Mor, NTC, TH; all versions]. The preposition literally indicates that the vow was made facing towards Jerusalem [NCBC]. There was rabbinical debate about whether the words 'as Jerusalem' or 'by Jerusalem' were binding, and it was proposed that 'by Jerusalem' was not binding but 'toward Jerusalem' was binding [EBC, Mor]. A later rabbinic source required that a person must actually face in the direction of Jerusalem or the vow 'by Jerusalem' was worthless [NCBC], and this custom may have been in force in NT times [McN, TH].

QUESTION—Who is the great king?

God is the great king [ICC, McN, TG, TH, WBC]. Jerusalem is God's city, so swearing by it is swearing by God [TG]. This phrase is taken from Ps 48:1-2 where Jerusalem is called the city of God as well as the city of the great king [ICC, TG, WBC].

5:36 **neither swear**[a] **by your(sg) head**

LEXICON—a. aorist act. subj. used as aorist act. impera. of ὀμνύω (LN 33.463) (BAGD p. 566): 'to swear' [BAGD, Mor, NTC, WBC; CEV, KJV, NAB, NIV, NJB, NLT, NRSV, TEV], 'to make an oath' [NASB], 'to take an oath' [NET, TNT], not explicit [REB]. The clause is translated: 'Don't even swear "By my head!"' [NLT]. See this word at 5:34.

QUESTION—Why is the verb ὀμνύω 'to swear' added here when it was only implied in the previous three clauses?

Repeating the verb breaks the pattern of 5:34b–35 [ICC]. The verb is probably repeated here for rhetorical balance in the sentence and perhaps for emphasis [Mor].

QUESTION—Is there significance in the choice of κεφαλή 'head'?

One cannot swear by one's own head because one does not have power over it [ICC]. It might be assumed that a man at least has control over his own head, but God determines even the color of his hair [NAC, NCBC, TG, TH, WBC], so one cannot exclude God from an oath sworn by one's own head [TG, TH]. The audience would have understood this saying to emphasize that God had control over aging and its effects [BBC]. Swearing by the head would be swearing to forfeit one's life if lying because the head represented the life [BSC, Mor, NTC].

for[a] you(sg)-are- not -able[b] to-make[c] one hair[d] white or black.

LEXICON—a. ὅτι (LN 89.33): 'for' [NTC; NAB, NASB, NIV, NLT, NRSV], 'because' [Mor, WBC; KJV, NET, REB, TEV, TNT], 'since' [NJB], not explicit [CEV].

    b. pres. indic. mid/pass. (deponent = active) of δύναμαι (LN 74.5): 'to be able' [NET, TNT], 'to be (un)able' [WBC]; 'can' [Mor, NTC; all versions except NET, TNT].

    c. aorist act. infin. of ποιέω (LN 13.9) (BAGD I.1.b.ι. p. 682): 'to make' [BAGD, Mor, NTC, WBC; all versions except NJB, NLT, REB], 'to turn' [NJB, NLT, REB].

    d. θρίξ (LN 8.12) (BAGD 2. p. 364): 'hair' [BAGD, LN]. The phrase μίαν τρίχα 'one hair' [Mor, NTC, WBC; CEV, KJV, NASB, NET, NLT, NRSV, TNT], is also translated 'even one hair' [NIV], 'a single hair' [NAB, NJB, TEV], 'one hair of it' [REB].

5:37 But[a] let- your(pl) word[b] -be[c] yes yes,[d] (or) no no;[e]

LEXICON—a. δέ: 'but' [Mor, WBC; KJV, NASB], 'simply' [NIV], 'just' [NLT, TEV], not explicit [NTC; CEV, NAB, NET, NJB, NRSV, REB, TNT].

    b. λόγος (LN 33.98) (BAGD 1.b.β. p. 477): 'word' [WBC; NET, NLT, NRSV, TNT], 'communication' [KJV], 'statement' [Mor; NASB], 'promise' [CEV], 'speech' [NTC], 'what you say' [BAGD, Mor], not explicit [NAB, NIV, NJB, REB, TEV].

    c. pres. act. impera. of εἰμί: 'let be' [Mor, NTC, WBC; KJV, NASB, NET, NIV, NRSV], 'let mean' [NAB, TNT], 'say' [NJB, NLT, REB, TEV], 'is all you need to say' [NJB, REB]. The clause is translated 'all you need say is 'Yes' if you mean yes' [NJB].

    d. ναί (LN 69.1) (BAGD 5. p. 533): 'yes' [BAGD]. The phrase ναί ναί is translated: 'Yes, yes' [Mor; NASB, NET, NRSV], 'yea yea' [KJV], 'let your yes be yes' [NIV], '(let your) yes mean yes' [NAB, TEV], 'plain 'yes'' [REB], 'only 'yes'' [CEV], 'your word yes mean yes' [TNT], 'yes if you mean yes' [NJB], 'a simple, "Yes, I will"' [NLT], 'a yes is a yes' [WBC], 'such that yes is simply yes' [NTC].

    e. The phrase οὔ οὔ is translated 'No, no' [Mor], '(or) No, no' [NASB, NET, NRSV], 'nay nay' [KJV], '(and your) no no' [NIV], '(or) No' [CEV, REB, TEV], '(or) "No, I won't"' [NLT], '(and) your No mean No' [NAB, TNT], 'no if you mean no' [NJB], '(and) a no is a no' [WBC], '(and) no is simply no' [NTC].

QUESTION—What is the meaning of the phrase ναί ναί ού ού 'yes, yes, no, no'?

These represent simple statements of affirmation and negation, with a 'yes' simply meaning 'yes' and a 'no' simply meaning 'no' [ICC, TH]. The second yes and the second no are used as predicates: let your 'yes' really mean 'yes' [McN, NCBC, TNTC; NRSV]. Rabbis held that the doubled word is more significant than a single word, but it is unlikely that Jesus is engaging in such hair splitting in this context [Mor]. Jesus is actually arguing against there being any need for added emphasis [EBC, ICC, McN, NCBC, WBC], as that would be substituting one oath form for another [ICC, WBC]. The doubling of the words is a Semitic way of saying that 'yes' and 'no' are to be used alone [TNTC2]. The duplication of yes and no indicates that Jesus is being emphatic, not that the disciples must be emphatic in their yes's and no's [BAGD]. The emphasis is on telling the truth [BSC]. Full sincerity is what is expected and should be expressed by a simple and genuine yes or no [WBC]. The followers of Jesus are to stand by their word and speak the truth at all times [NIBC]. Jesus' followers are to have the integrity of character such that their word is enough without an oath [NAC].

but[a] anything beyond[b] these is from[c] the-Evil-One/evil.[d]

LEXICON—a. δέ 'but' [WBC], 'for' [KJV], 'and' [NASB], not explicit [Mor, NTC; all versions except KJV, NASB].

b. περισσός (LN 59.51) (BAGD 3. p. 651): 'anything beyond' [NTC; NASB, NIV, REB], 'anything more than' [NJB, NRSV, TNT], 'anything more' [NAB], 'anything else' [CEV], 'anything else you say' [TEV], 'whatever goes beyond' [BAGD], '(whatever/whatsoever is) more than' [BAGD, LN; KJV], 'what is more' [Mor], 'more than' [NET], 'the rest of these practices' [WBC]. The clause is translated 'to strengthen your promise with a vow shows that something is wrong' [NLT]. The phrase means 'adding to your declaration any confirmation or guarantee beyond your own word' [TH]. It refers to the oath that is prohibited; that is, an oath that goes beyond a simple yes or no is from the Evil One [ICC].

c. ἐκ (LN 90.16) (BAGD 3.c. p. 235): 'from' [BAGD, LN]. The phrase ἐκ...ἐστιν is translated 'is from' [WBC; NAB, NET], 'comes from' [NTC, TH; CEV, NIV, NJB, NRSV, REB, TEV, TNT], 'comes of' [KJV], 'is of' [Mor; NASB], 'shows that something is wrong' [NLT].

d. πονηρός (LN 12.35, 88.110) (BAGD 2.b. p. 691): 'the evil one' [BAGD, LN (12.35), Mor, NTC, WBC; NAB, NET, NIV, NJB, NRSV, REB, TEV, TNT], 'the devil' [CEV], 'evil' [BAGD, LN (88.110); KJV, NASB], not explicit [NLT].

QUESTION—Does the phrase τοῦ πονηροῦ refer to Satan or to impersonal evil?

1. The Greek is to be taken as masculine, thus referring to 'the evil one' [Brc, ICC, Mor, NTC, TG, TH, WBC; NAB, NET, NIV, NJB, NRSV, REB, TEV, TNT].

2. The Greek is to be taken as neuter and refers to evil [McN, Pl, TH]. It could be the falsehood that comes from the wickedness of the world [TNTC2], untruthfulness that is prevalent [Pl], or to evil in the human heart [McN].

DISCOURSE UNIT: 5:38–42 [BBC, EBC, GNT, HF, ICC, McN, MLJ, Mor, NAC, NCBC, NIBC, NTC, Pl, TG, TH, TNTC2, WBC; CEV, NAB, NET, NIV, NLT, NRSV, REB, TEV]. The topic is revenge [CEV, TEV], teaching about revenge [TG, TH; NLT], Jesus teaches that people should not seek revenge [TG], Jesus teaches about the commandments that are about getting revenge [TH], Jesus teaches that people should not look for revenge [TH], teaching about not getting back at people [TG], an eye for an eye [NIV], retaliation [GNT, McN, Mor, NAC, NCBC, WBC; NET, NRSV], teaching about retaliation [NAB], an eye for an eye, and a tooth for a tooth [MLJ], legal rights [TNTC2], going the second mile [HF], turning the other cheek [ICC], do not resist evil [ICC], personal injury and self-sacrifice [EBC], the fifth antithesis: the commandment concerning retaliation [NTC], nonresistance [BBC], the fifth illustration [Pl].

5:38 You(pl)-have-heard that it-was-said, An-eye for[a] an-eye and a-tooth for a-tooth.

LEXICON—a. ἀντί (LN 57.145) (BAGD 2. p. 73): 'for' [BAGD, Mor, NTC, WBC; all versions except NLT]. The clause is translated 'if an eye is injured, injure the eye of the person who did it' [NLT].

QUESTION—What is the cultural background of this verse?

'An eye for an eye, and a tooth for a tooth' (in Greek) is quoted from the Septuagint in Exodus 21:24; Leviticus 24:20; Deuteronomy 19:21 [BSC, EBC, ICC, McN, Mor, NCBC, NTC, TG, TH, TNTC2, WBC]. The quotation is referred to as the 'Lex Talionis' in the literature [Brc, EBC, ICC, Mor, NAC, NIBC, NTC], and was recognized throughout the ancient near east for millennia, including by Hammurabi in the 18th century BC [ICC, Mor].

QUESTION—What is the syntactic form of this verse?

This clause and the next are conventional formulaic ellipses, which means that a term is not expressed or it is able to be supplied from the context. Proverbial sayings like this often omit the verbs [BD (sec. 480(5), p. 254)].

QUESTION—What is the structure of this section?

Verse 38 states the basis for culturally expected retaliation [NCBC, TH], and revenge [TH]; the two sayings together represent the first half of two contrasting conduct patterns [NCBC, WBC] based on strict application of the OT code in the verses mentioned above [WBC]. Instead of this retaliation, in 5:39, Jesus introduces the new principle [NCBC], the general principle of his teaching [ICC], that one should exercise self-restraint [NCBC, TH]. The new priorities instruct disciples to be willing to relinquish their individual rights [WBC]. Verses 40-42 illuminate this principle in five figurative examples [Pl], in four situations [TH], four illustrations [EBC,

NCBC], in four scenes [ICC], in two pairs of illustrations with themes of meekness and love of enemy [ICC]. The first illustration deals with non-retaliation; the others discuss compliance with unreasonable requests [WBC]. There is strong form parallelism between 5:39b and 41, and a weaker form parallelism between 5:40 and 5:42a [WBC].

QUESTION—How can this figure of speech be expressed without using figurative language and making implicit information explicit?

The meaning is that if anyone destroys the eye or tooth of another person, his own eye should be destroyed or tooth broken [TG; NLT]. It is important to realize that this is not about some trade exchange, e.g. in order to get a tooth, you have to give a tooth [TG].

5:39 But[a] I say to-you(pl) not to-resist[b] the evil-person/evil;[c]

LEXICON—a. δέ: 'but' [Mor, NTC, WBC; all versions].

b. aorist act. infin. of ἀνθίστημι (LN 39.18) (BAGD 1. p. 67): 'to resist' [Mor, NTC, WBC; KJV, NASB, NET, NIV, NLT, NRSV, REB, TNT], 'to offer resistance to' [NAB, NJB], 'to take revenge on' [TEV], 'to try to get even with' [CEV]. The force of the infinite is imperative [Mor].

c. πονηρός (LN 88.110): 'the evil person' [Mor], 'an evil person' [NIV, NLT], 'him who is evil' [NASB], 'one who is evil' [NAB], 'a wicked (or) evil-intentioned person' [BAGD], 'an evildoer' [BAGD; NRSV], 'the evildoer' [NTC; NET], 'the wicked' [NJB], 'someone who wrongs you' [TEV], 'those who wrong you' [REB], 'anyone who would do you wrong' [TNT], 'a person who has done something to you' [CEV], 'evil' [WBC; KJV]. See this word also at 5:37.

QUESTION—What is the scope and cultural background of the phrase 'not to-resist'?

Here ἀνθίστημι is not a physical resistance but a verbal one [TH]. However there is connotation of hostility in that resistance [Mor]. It refers to actively seeking revenge [TG]. It implies a legal setting and means to oppose before a judge [EBC, NCBC, TH] or taking someone to court [NAC]. It means do not resist in a court of law [EBC]. Although there is a court background, the audience would not have limited their understanding to a court setting [BSC, ICC] but would have understood it as an example of righteous behavior [ICC]. The application is wider than 'do not retaliate' and means to be willing to accept ill-treatment and even comply willingly with it [TNTC2]. 'The spirit of revenge is forbidden' [Pl].

QUESTION—Who or what is referred to by τῷ πονηρῷ 'the evil person/evil'?

Grammatically the word is a substantive, i.e., an adjective used as a noun [BAGD, TH]. This is not a reference to Satan [EBC, Pl, WBC].

1. It is a person who is evil [BAGD, EBC, ICC, Mor, TG, TH; all versions except KJV]. It is someone who does something bad to you or causes you harm [TG, TH], who wishes to do injury [NCBC, TH].

2. It means a non-personal 'evil' [Brc, McN, Pl, WBC; KJV]. As in 5:37 it refers to the evil that is in the world [McN]. It refers to an evil deed [WBC].

but[a] whoever[b] slaps[c] you(sg) on (the) right cheek,
LEXICON—a. ἀλλά (LN 89.125): 'but' [Mor, NTC, TH, WBC; KJV, NASB, NET], 'but if' [NRSV], 'on the contrary if' [NJB], 'if' [NIV, NLT, REB, TEV, TNT], 'when' [CEV, NAB].
 b. ὅστις (LN 92.18) (BAGD 1.a. p. 586): 'whoever' [BAGD, Mor; NASB, NET], 'whosoever' [KJV], 'everyone who' [BAGD, Mor], 'anyone' [NJB, NRSV, REB, TEV, TNT], 'if someone' [NIV], 'when someone' [CEV, NAB], 'to him' [NTC], 'whenever anyone' [WBC], not explicit [NLT].
 c. pres. act. indic. of ῥαπίζω (LN **19.4**) (BAGD p. 734): 'to slap' [BAGD, LN, Mor, NTC; CEV, NASB, NLT, REB, TEV, TNT], 'to strike with the open hand' [BAGD], 'to strike' [NAB, NET, NIV, NRSV], 'to hit' [NJB], 'to insult by slapping' [WBC], 'to smite' [KJV]. This active voice is also translated as passive: 'if you are slapped on the right cheek' [NLT].
QUESTION—What is implied by the hand slap at that time in that culture?
 The slap was made from the back of the hand and was intended as an insult [Brc, BSC, EBC, Mor, NAC, NCBC, NIBC, TG, TH, WBC]. By mentioning the right cheek it makes it plain that a backhanded slap is intended [ICC]. Jews at that time considered such a calculated slap to be much more insulting than using the flat of the hand [Brc]. Culturally, this slap was a gross insult [ICC, TH] and a symbol of contempt [TNTC2] that demanded punishment [NCBC]. The ancient near east recognized this as the most grievous insult, and both Roman and Jewish law permitted retaliation for this offense [BBC].

turn[a] to-him the other (cheek) also[b];
LEXICON—a. aorist act. impera. sg. of στρέφω (LN **16.14**) (BAGD 1.a.α. p. 771): 'to turn' [BAGD, LN, Mor, NTC, WBC; CEV, KJV, NAB, NASB, NET, NIV, NLT, NRSV, TNT], 'to turn and offer' [REB], 'to offer' [NJB]. The clause is translated: 'let him slap your left cheek too' [TEV], 'turn and let that person slap your other cheek' [CEV].
 b. καί (LN **89.93**) (BAGD II.1. p. 393): 'also' [BAGD, LN, Mor, NTC; KJV, NASB, NIV, NRSV, REB, TNT], 'too' [NET, NLT, TEV], 'likewise' [BAGD], 'as well' [NAB, NJB], not explicit [WBC; CEV].

5:40 and to-the-one wanting to-sue[a] you(sg) and to-take[b] your(sg) shirt,[c]
LEXICON—a. aorist pass. infin. of κρίνω (LN 56.20) (BAGD 4.a.β. p. 451): 'to sue' [TH; CEV, NASB, NET, NIV, NRSV, REB], 'to sue at the law' [KJV], 'to take you to court to sue you' [TH; TEV], 'to take you to court' [WBC], 'to order to court' [NLT], 'to go to law' [NAB], 'to go to law with you' [Mor, NTC; NJB, TNT], 'to take you before the judge' [TG, TH], 'to make you go to be tried by a judge' [TG], 'to be judged in a

court' [WBC], 'to hale you before a court' with its forensic application [BAGD, ICC], 'to take you to court to get your garment' [WBC], 'to hand over for judicial punishment' [BAGD]. It is used as a legal technical term relating to a human court of law [BAGD]. This passive infinitive functions as a deponent [ZG].

   b. aorist act. infin. of λαμβάνω (LN **57.55**) (BAGD 1.c. p. 464): 'to take' [BAGD, LN, Mor, NTC, TH; NASB, NET, NIV, NRSV, REB, TNT], 'to take away' [KJV], 'to get' [WBC; NJB]. This infinitive is also translated 'for (your shirt)' [CEV, TEV], 'over (your tunic)' [NAB]. This is also translated passively: 'your shirt is taken from you' [NLT].

   c. χιτών (LN **6.176**) (BAGD p. 882): 'shirt' [BAGD, **LN**, NTC; CEV, NASB, NLT, REB, TEV, TNT], 'coat' [KJV, NRSV], 'tunic' [BAGD, LN, Mor; NAB, NET, NIV, NJB], 'garment' [WBC].

QUESTION—What garment is referred to by χιτών 'shirt'?

The χιτών was a close-fitting [NCBC, TH] inner garment worn next to the skin [BAGD, Brc, EBC, ICC, NCBC, NIBC, NTC, TG, TH, TNTC2, WBC; NET]. It was the long garment worn under the cloak [NET, NCBC, TH]. It had short sleeves and reached to the knees [TG]. It was a 'sack-like' [Brc] garment of comparatively little value [TH, TNTC2], made of cotton or of linen [Brc], or wool [ICC]. The χιτών was used by both sexes [BAGD, TH]. Even the poorest people usually had a change of tunics [Brc]. The χιτών could be taken as a pledge [Brc].

let- him -have[a] the coat[b] also;[c]

LEXICON—a. aorist act. impera. of ἀφίημι (LN 13.140) (BAGD 3.a. p. 126): 'to let someone have' [BAGD, Mor; KJV, NASB, NIV, NJB, REB, TEV, TNT], 'to leave an object with someone' [BAGD], 'to hand someone' [NAB], 'to give' [WBC; NET, NLT, NRSV], 'to give up' [CEV], 'to let (him) take' [NTC].

   b. ἱμάτιον (LN **6.172**) (BAGD 2. p. 376): 'coat' [**LN**, WBC; CEV, NASB, NET, NLT, TEV], 'cloak' [BAGD, LN, Mor, TH; KJV, NAB, NIV, NJB, NRSV, REB, TNT], 'robe' [BAGD, LN, NTC], 'an outer garment' [LN, Mor, NCBC].

   c. καί: 'also' [NTC; KJV, NASB, TNT], 'as well' [CEV, NAB, NET, NIV, NJB, NRSV, REB, TEV], 'too' [Mor; NLT], 'even' [WBC].

QUESTION—What garment is referred to by ἱμάτιον 'coat'?

The ἱμάτιον was an outer garment [BAGD, Brc, ICC, LN, Mor, NCBC, NIBC, TG, TH, TNTC2, WBC]. It was blanket-like [Brc], long flowing garment [TG]. It was more costly than the χιτών 'shirt' [BSC, Mor, TG, TH, TNTC2] and more essential [WBC]. The ἱμάτιον 'coat' was worn by a man as a robe by day [Brc], and used as a sleeping blanket at night [BBC, Brc, ICC, NIBC], as a covering for the night [TH]. Most men had only one [Brc]. The ἱμάτιον 'coat' was 'an inalienable possession' [EBC]; therefore, Jewish law forbade taking the cloak from the owner [BBC, Brc, TH], even as a pledge [Brc]. Exodus 22:26–27 prohibits taking it for the night [ICC]. All of a debtor's clothing could not be taken from him [ICC]. In this verse, the ἱμάτιον 'coat' could represent all of one's possessions, indicating that everything had been taken, even one's clothing [BBC].

QUESTION—To what extent does the legal background of this verse and that of 5:40 contrast?

The context is clearly legal, a court proceeding [BSC, ICC, McN, Mor, NCBC, NIBC, NTC, TG, TH, TNTC2, WBC]. However in 5:39, although ἀνθίστημι 'to resist' may have a legal background, the understanding and application seems to be wider (see the discussion under 5:39) [TG].

5:41 and whoever[a] will-force- you(sg) -to-go[b] one mile,[c] go[d] with him two.

LEXICON—a. ὅστις (LN 92.18) (BAGD 1.c. p. 586): 'whoever' [BAGD, Mor, NTC; NASB], 'whosoever' [KJV], 'everyone who' [BAGD], 'a man' [TNT], 'should anyone' [NAB], 'if anyone' [NET, NJB, NRSV], 'if someone' [NIV], 'if a soldier' [CEV, NLT], 'whenever some soldier' [WBC], 'if one of the occupation troops' [TEV], 'if someone of authority' [REB].

b. fut. act. indic. of ἀγγαρεύω (LN 37.34) (BAGD p. 6): 'to force to go' [NTC; NASB, NET, NIV, NRSV], 'to force to carry a pack' [CEV, TEV], 'to force' [BAGD], 'to compel' [BAGD], 'to compel to go' [Mor; KJV], 'to compel in public service to go' [WBC], 'to require to go' [NJB], 'to press into service for' [NAB, REB], 'to commandeer for' [TNT], 'to requisition' [Mor], 'to demand to carry his gear' [NLT]. It refers to service in bearing a load as a porter [TNTC2, WBC].

c. μίλιον (LN **81.29**) (BAGD p. 521): 'mile' [BAGD, LN, Mor, NTC, WBC; all versions]. A Roman mile is literally a thousand paces [BAGD, LN, Mor, NTC, TH]. It is about 4854 feet or 1478.5 meters [BAGD, Mor, NTC, TH], somewhat less than an American or English mile and equal to about one kilometer and a half [LN]. The exact distance is not as important as the relationship between a mile and two miles [TG, TH].

d. pres. act. impera. of ὑπάγω (LN 15.35) (BAGD 2. p. 836): 'to go' [Mor, NTC, WBC; all versions except CEV, NLT, TEV], 'to carry (it)' [CEV, NLT, TEV]. See 5:24 [BAGD].

QUESTION—What is the background of ἀγγαρεύω 'to force to go'?

It is a technical term to indicate pressing into service [NCBC, NIBC, TH] and refers to various kinds of forced labor [Brc, ICC, McN, Mor, NCBC, NIBC, NTC], or compulsory conscription [NCBC, NIBC]. A Persian word was borrowed into Greek as ἀγγαρευς meaning 'courier.' If the Persian postal system needed anything, any private person could be compelled to supply the lack. Later it came to mean any kind of forced service for the occupying power [Brc, NTC]. It refers to a Roman law that required civilians to carry equipment for a soldier [ICC, NAC, TG; NET]. It was a Roman soldier's right to commandeer civilian labor in an occupied country [TNTC2, WBC]. Roman practice was to compel civilians to carry a soldier's luggage, but it was limited to one mile [EBC]. This type of impressment always evoked outrage in the one forced to carry things, but Jesus' disciples must seek to help rather than be vengeful [EBC].

5:42 Give[a] to-the (one) asking[b] you(sg),

LEXICON—a. aorist act. impera. of δίδωμι (LN 57.71): 'to give' [Mor, NTC, WBC; all versions].

  b. pres. act. participle of αἰτέω (LN 33.163) (BAGD p. 25): 'to ask' [BAGD, Mor, NTC, WBC; all versions except NRSV], 'to beg from' [NRSV]. It is a general and unqualified term for asking [Mor] and not limited to asking for a loan [TNTC2].

and (do) not turn-away-from[a] the (one) wanting[b] to-borrow[c] from you(sg)

LEXICON—a. aorist pass. subj. used as aorist pass. imp. of ἀποστρέφω (LN **35.18**) (BAGD 3.a. p. 100): 'to turn away from someone (or) something' [BAGD, Mor, NTC; KJV, NASB, NIV, NJB, NLT, TNT], 'to turn your back on' [NAB, REB], 'to reject' [Mor; NET], 'to refuse' [NRSV], 'to refuse to help' [LN], 'to repudiate' [Mor]. The command 'do not turn away' is translated 'lend it to him' [TEV], 'lend it to them' [CEV].

  b. pres. act. participle of θέλω (LN 25.1): 'to want' [Mor, NTC; all versions except KJV], 'that would' [KJV].

  c. aorist act. infin. of δανείζομαι (LN **57.213**) (BAGD 2. p. 170): 'to borrow' [LN, Mor, NTC, TH, WBC; all versions except CEV], 'to borrow money' [CEV]. The verb usually implies that interest will be paid [LN].

DISCOURSE UNIT: 5:43–48 [BBC, EBC, GNT, HF, ICC, McN, MLJ, Mor, NAC, NCBC, NIBC, NTC, TG, TH, TNTC2, WBC; CEV, NET, NIV, NLT, NRSV, REB, TEV]. The topic is love [TNTC2; CEV], love for enemies [GNT, HF, ICC, MLJ, Mor, NAC, NCBC, TG, TH, WBC; NET, NIV, NLT, NRSV, TEV], teaching about love for enemies [NLT, TG, TH], thou shalt love thy neighbor [McN], Jesus talks about loving people who hate us [TH], hatred and love [EBC], Jesus teaches that people should love those who hate them [TG], the sixth antithesis: the summary of the second table of the Law [NTC], beyond nonresistance [BBC].

DISCOURSE UNIT: 5:43–47 [Pl]. The topic is the sixth illustration.

5:43 You(pl)-have-heard that it-was-said,

QUESTION—What is the relationship of this section to the preceding one?

  It summarizes all the ethical teaching of the previous antitheses and 5:45 gives the reason for acting in accordance with Jesus' teachings as well as the basis for doing so [WBC]. The previous paragraph presented the Christian attitude toward himself negatively; now this paragraph presents it positively [MLJ]. This section is the conclusion of the series beginning in 5:21 [NCBC].

QUESTION—What is the structure of this section?

  The structure of the antithesis is as follows: (1) The view received by the audience from their culture 5:43; (2) Jesus' correction to that view in

5:44–45a; (3) Two supporting arguments 5:45b–45c; (4) Two illustrative parallels 5:46–47; and (5) Concluding exhortation 5:48 [WBC]. Note that the language of Matthew 5:43–48 in the original Aramaic would have been rather poetic, using alliteration, assonance, parallelism and word-play [AAG (p. 179)].

You(sg)-will-love[a] your(sg) neighbor[b]

LEXICON—a. fut. act. indic. used as impera. of ἀγαπάω (LN 25.43) (BAGD 1.a.α. p. 4): 'to love' [BAGD, Mor, NTC, WBC; all versions]. Ἀγαπάω refers not just to having emotions but to having a faithful loyalty and implies care and concern for another person [TH]. Note that this future is actually an imperative in force, as in 5:21 [TH]. See this word at 5:44.

b. πλησίον (LN 11.89) (BAGD 1.b. p. 672): 'neighbor' [BAGD, Mor, NTC, WBC; all versions except CEV, TEV], 'neighbors' [CEV], 'friends' [TEV]. This term came to be applied to someone who is close by or to one's fellow man [BAGD].

QUESTION—How would the audience have understood πλησίον 'neighbor?'

This clause is a partial quote of Leviticus 19:18 [BSC, EBC, ICC, McN, NAC, NIBC, NTC, TG, TH, WBC]. The issue of debate for the audience seems to have been how small of a group they might have included in πλησίον 'neighbor.' Many contrasted neighbor with enemy, and thus allowed the scope of the commandment to be restricted to 'love only your neighbor' [ICC, Pl]. There was great debate about who one's neighbor was [BSC, Pl]. If they didn't have to love someone, they were free to hate him [Pl]. The meaning of πλησίον 'neighbor' did not include all those living close by since no Gentiles were neighbors even if they lived close by [Mor, Pl]. Gentiles living close by were not neighbors [Mor]. A neighbor included more than someone who lived near-by or in the same part of town [TH]. The meaning might refer to all fellow Jews [BSC, MLJ, Mor, TG, TH, WBC]. In Leviticus 19:18 it must mean 'fellow-Israelite' and be synonymous with 'brother' [McN]. Proselytes to Judaism could also be included (Lev. 19:34) [BSC]. The concept of 'neighbor' could be restricted to good Israelites, in whatever way a person may define that for himself [Mor].

QUESTION—Is it significant that the whole verse is not quoted?

This is the first half of a quote based on Leviticus 19:18; the second half is 'as (you love) yourself'. The rabbis left out 'as yourself' as well as adding 'hate your enemy' [BSC]. Perhaps the omission of 'as yourself' indicates that the scribes had lowered the standard from Leviticus 19:18 [Mor, NTC]. The omission is probably in order to permit parallelism [ICC, WBC].

and you(sg)-will-hate[a] your enemy.[b]

LEXICON—a. fut. act. indic. used as impera. of μισέω (LN 88.198) (BAGD 1. p. 522): 'to hate' [BAGD, Mor, NTC, WBC; all versions]. See this word at 6:24.

b. ἐχθρός (LN 39.11) (BAGD 2.b.β. p. 331): 'enemy' [BAGD, Mor, NTC, WBC; all versions except CEV, TEV], 'enemies' [CEV, TEV]. The word is used of both personal and national enemies [ICC].

QUESTION—What is the relationship of this clause to the previous one?

This addition was widely known [NAC, NTC, TH, TNTC2, WBC]. It was taught by the community at Qumran [NIBC, TH, WBC] and even by rabbis [BSC, McN, MLJ, WBC], although it was not a fair representation of the best Jewish ethics at that time [NCBC, TH]. The prevailing opinion in both Greek and Jewish thought would have considered hatred of one's enemy as legitimate, and never would have considered prayer for the well-being of that enemy as logical [BBC].

QUESTION—How was the statement 'and you will hate your enemy' understood?

1. It has an imperative force [EBC, NIBC, NTC]: you must love your neighbor and you must hate your enemy.
2. It is comparative [ICC, McN, Mor, NCBC, TNTC2]: you must love your enemy less than your neighbor.
3. It is permissive [ICC, Pl, ZG]: you need not love your enemy, and may even hate him.

QUESTION—What is the relationship of the statement 'and you will hate your enemy' to the first clause, 'you will love your neighbor'?

1. The conjunction καί 'and' joins the two clauses as two parts of one saying [Mor, NTC, WBC; all versions except NET]: 'you will love your neighbor and you will hate your enemy'.
2. The conjunction καί 'and' joins two related sayings: 'you will love your neighbor' and 'you will hate your enemy' [NET].

QUESTION—How would the audience have understood ἐχθρός 'enemy?'

To the audience, ἐχθρός meant Gentile [WBC], resulting in a wall of separation between Jew and Gentile [NTC]. Jesus' original audience would have thought of the Romans who were occupying Palestine as their enemies [ICC]. The Septuagint uses ἐχθρός for an enemy of the people of God in Psalm 31(30):8; 139(138):21 (Septuagint verse numbers differ slightly) [NCBC].

5:44 But[a] I say to-you(pl), love[b] your(pl) enemies

LEXICON—a. δέ: 'but' [Mor, NTC, WBC; all versions except TNT], not explicit [TNT].

b. pres. act. impera. of ἀγαπάω (LN 25.43) (BAGD 1.a.α. p. 4): 'to love' [Mor, NTC, WBC; all versions]. See this word at 5:43.

QUESTION—What connotations are involved the meaning of ἀγαπάω 'to love'?

The command is to love a man and treat him as if we like him [MLJ]. It is choosing to act for the benefit and well-being of others whether or not we like them [WBC]. It includes concrete action [EBC, ICC, MLJ]. Love for enemies is defined in the following verses to include praying for them, doing

good to them and greeting them [ICC]. It is not just a sentimental feeling for
persecutors but an earnest desire for their good [TNTC2]. Prayer is a
manifestation of love, and love and prayer will reinforce each other [EBC,
ICC]. Love does not necessarily include sentiment or emotion: love is not
necessarily sentiment or emotion [NCBC, WBC]. Although love includes
concrete self-giving and action, it must include concern, sentiment and
emotion [EBC]. Jesus employed a much greater scope to the concept of
'neighbor' [ICC, NIBC, Pl]. For Jesus, 'neighbor' encompassed every
human being [McN, Pl], including one's enemies [BSC, MLJ]. Jesus did not
set up a new commandment to replace the old but maintained that the new
understandings and applications are contained within the old [Pl].

and pray[a] for the (ones) persecuting[b] you(pl),

TEXT—Some manuscripts include τῶν επηρεαζόντων ὑμᾶς καί 'them which
  despitefully use you and' before τ ῶ ν διωκόντων ὑμᾶς 'the ones
  persecuting you'. It is omitted by GNT with an A rating, indicating that the
  text is certain. It is included only by KJV.
LEXICON—a. pres. act. impera. pl. of προσεύχομαι (LN 33.178) (BAGD
  p. 714): 'to pray' [BAGD, Mor, NTC, WBC; all versions]. Προσεύχομαι
  is the most general verb for prayer and a more narrow specification must
  come from context [TH]. Here the context suggests that it means to pray
  that God will bless them [TG, TH] or that God will help them [TH].
  b. διώκω (LN 39.45) (BAGD 2. p. 201): 'to persecute' [Mor, NTC, WBC;
  KJV, NASB, NET, NIV, NJB, NLT, NRSV, TEV, TNT], 'to mistreat'
  [CEV]. This verb is also translated as a noun: 'persecutors' [NAB, REB].
  In the NT διώκω usually refers to religious persecution [NCBC, TH]. See
  5:11 for more information.

5:45 that[a] you-might-be/become[b] children[c] of-your(pl) father in (the)
heavens,

LEXICON—a. ὅπως (LN 89.59) (BAGD 2.a.α. p. 576): 'that' [NTC; KJV,
  NAB, NIV, TNT], 'so that' [Mor; NET, NJB, NRSV, TEV], 'in order
  that' [BAGD, WBC; NASB], 'only so' [REB], 'then' [CEV], 'in that
  way' [NLT]. It expresses purpose [BAGD, Mor].
  b. aorist dep. subj. of γίνομαι (LN **13.48**) (BAGD I.4.a. p. 159): 'to be'
  [NTC, WBC; KJV, NAB, NASB, NIV, NJB, NRSV, REB, TNT], 'to
  become' [BAGD, LN; TEV], 'to be like' [NET], 'to act like' [CEV,
  NLT]. It refers to coming to acquire or experience a new state [LN].
  c. υἱός (LN 9.4) (BAGD 1.c.γ. p. 834): 'children' [WBC; KJV, NAB, NJB,
  NRSV, REB, TEV], 'true children' [NLT], 'sons' [BAGD, Mor, NTC;
  NASB, NIV, TNT]. The phrase 'you might be children of your Father' is
  translated 'you will be acting like your Father' [CEV], 'you may be like
  your Father' [NET]. This term includes both men and women [TH]. See
  this word at 5:9.

QUESTION—What is meant by γίνομαι 'to be/become'?
1. It is a modal form of 'to be' expressing the idea 'may be' [NTC, WBC; NAB, NASB, NIV, NJB, NRSV, TNT]: love your enemies in order that you might be your Father's children. A translation with 'to be' in English does not necessarily exclude the two following meanings.
2. It expresses a progression from where the disciple is now to where the disciple will be [EBC, ICC, LN, Mor, TG; TEV]: love your enemies in order that you might become your Father's children. It refers to a change of nature and indicates entering into the new state [BAGD]. This does not mean that they qualify for membership in the family by their deeds [EBC, Mor], but rather must grow to become increasingly like a child of God [Mor], pursuing the pattern of love laid down by the Father and continually making progress in the service of God [EBC]. If they do this they will be acting like God's children [Mor]. It refers to a spiritual and moral likeness [TG]. The desire to imitate God is the motivation [ICC].
3. It expresses the evidence that the disciple already is a child of God as demonstrated in behaving as God does [BSC, NTC, Pl, TH, WBC; CEV, NET, NLT]: love your enemies in order that you might show that you are your Father's children. The sense of 'prove yourselves to be' is found in 10:16; 24:44; Luke 6:36; 12:40; John 20:27 [Pl].

for he-causes- his sun[a] -to-rise[b] on evil-(people)[c] and good-(people)[d]

LEXICON—a. ἥλιος (LN 1.28) (BAGD p. 345): 'sun' [BAGD, Mor, NTC, WBC; all versions]. The phrase τὸν ἥλιον αὐτοῦ 'his sun' [Mor, NTC, WBC; KJV, NAB, NASB, NIV, NJB, NRSV, TEV, TNT] is also translated 'the sun' (as object) [CEV, NET, REB]. The possessive αὐτοῦ 'his' is important here [Mor, NTC, TG, TH]. The conception is not that the sun shines naturally, but that God makes *his* sun to shine [ICC, Mor, NTC].
b. pres. act. indic. of ἀνατέλλω (LN 15.104) (BAGD 1. p. 62): 'to cause to rise' [BAGD, NTC; CEV, NASB, NET, NIV, NJB, REB], 'to make to rise' [Mor, WBC; KJV, NAB, NRSV, TNT], 'to make to shine' [TEV], 'to give (sunlight) to' [NLT]. This is the causative use of the verb [BD (sec. 309(1), p. 163)]. This range of meaning reflects the Aramaic word *tsamach*, which usually means 'to rise' but may also mean 'to shine' [ICC, McN].
c. πονηρός (LN 88.110) (BAGD 2.a. p. 691): 'the wicked, evil-intentioned person, evil-doer' [BAGD], 'the evil' [KJV, NASB, NET, NIV, NLT, NRSV, TNT], 'the bad' [NAB, NJB], 'bad people' [CEV, TEV], 'bad' [REB], 'evil people' [Mor, NTC, WBC].
d. ἀγαθός (LN 88.1) (BAGD 1.b.α. p. 3): 'the good' [BAGD; all versions except CEV, REB, TEV], 'good people' [WBC; CEV, TEV], 'good ones' [Mor], 'good' [NTC; REB]. 'Good' pertains to inner moral worth [BAGD].

QUESTION—How can this figure of speech be expressed without using figurative language and making implicit information explicit?

These actions are examples that show the character and likeness of God, and if we are his sons we should be like him [TH]. God blessing both the good and the bad with sunshine and rain is an important foundation to loving one's enemies [WBC]. God also doesn't make distinctions in his love for both good and bad people [BSC]. Since God blesses all people regardless of their moral character, Jesus' disciples should be the same way [TG]. God's love for all people is demonstrated in his giving good things to all people indiscriminately [EBC, Mor]. These actions demonstrate God's favor to all people when he could justly condemn them all [EBC].

QUESTION—Why is evil mentioned first?

It is unusual to mention evil first, but the order signifies the absolutely equal treatment that both good and bad receive from God [BSC]. Mentioning evil first allows a chiastic word order [ICC, TH, WBC], as in 6:24 and 7:6 [TH]. Notice the chiasmus, a Greek oratorical device: evil–good; righteous–unrighteous [ICC, McN, NTC, WBC].

and he-sends-rain[a] on righteous-people[b] and unrighteous-people.[c]

LEXICON—a. pres. act. indic. of βρέχω (LN **14.11**) (BAGD 2.a. p. 147): 'to send rain' [BAGD, **LN**, Mor, NTC; CEV, KJV, NASB, NET, NIV, NLT, NRSV, TNT], 'to send the rain' [REB], 'to send down rain to fall' [NJB], 'to cause rain to fall' [LN; NAB], 'to give rain' [TEV] 'to cause it to rain' [BAGD, LN], 'to make it rain' [WBC].

b. δίκαιος (LN 88.12) (BAGD 1.b. p. 195): 'righteous' [NTC], 'the righteous' [BAGD; NASB, NET, NIV, NRSV, TNT], 'the just' [WBC; KJV, NAB, NLT], 'just' [BAGD, Mor], 'those who do good' [TEV], 'the upright' [BAGD; NJB], 'the innocent' [REB], 'the ones who do right' [CEV].

c. ἄδικος (LN 88.20) (BAGD 1. p. 18): 'unrighteous' [NTC], 'the unrighteous' [NASB, NET, NIV, NRSV, TNT], 'the unjust' [WBC; KJV, NAB, NLT], 'unjust' [BAGD, Mor], 'the wicked' [NJB, REB], 'those who do evil' [TEV], 'people who do evil' [TH], 'the ones who do wrong' [CEV].

QUESTION—How different are the pairs πονηρός 'evil' and ἀγαθός 'good' and δίκαιος 'righteous' and ἄδικος 'unrighteous'?

The terms are not used very precisely; instead each term has a general reference because these are the most general of blessings [BSC]. There is not much difference between good and evil vs. just and unjust [Mor]. The only differences are stylistic [WBC]. They are two pairs of synonyms that, with a different grouping, also make two pairs of antonyms [TH]. Together the terms are meant to encompass all people: God extends his favor to all people, deserving or not [NIBC]. The point is God does not limit his blessings to those who are faithful disciples; he gives even to those who oppose him [Mor]. The lack of the articles in the Greek indicates a focus on the character of the people as opposed to identifying them as particular groups [Mor, NTC]. The bad correspond to the enemies mentioned earlier [WBC]. Like wisdom literature, there are no shades of gray but only two classes of people [ICC]. Rabbis contrasted *tsaddik* and *rasa*, but they also left room for a middle group of average people [ICC].

5:46 For[a] if[b] you(pl)-love (only) the ones-loving you(pl),

LEXICON—a. γάρ (LN 89.23): 'for' [Mor, NTC, WBC; KJV, NAB, NASB, NET, NJB, NRSV, TNT], not explicit [CEV, NIV, NLT, REB, TEV]. Γάρ introduces the consequence drawn from the preceding verse [Mor].

    b. ἐάν (LN **89.67**) (BAGD I.1.b. p. 211): 'if' [BAGD, LN, Mor, NTC, WBC; all versions]. The conjunction ἐάν introduces a hypothetical condition that may or may not actually be the case [Mor].

QUESTION—What information is implied in this clause?

The word 'only' is implied in the text [ICC, TH], meaning 'if you love *only* the people who love you' [BBC, Dei (p. 101–102), ICC, TH; CEV, REB, TEV].

what reward[a] do-you(sg)-have?[b]

LEXICON—a. μισθός (LN 38.14) (BAGD 2.a. p. 523): 'reward' [BAGD, Mor, NTC, WBC; KJV, NASB, NET, NIV, NJB, NRSV, TNT], 'rewards' [REB], 'recompense' [NAB], 'what good is that' [NLT]. This noun is also translated as a verb: 'to reward' [CEV, TEV]. See this word at 5:12.

    b. pres. act. indic. of ἔχω (LN 57.1): 'to have' [Mor, WBC; KJV, NAB, NASB, NET, NRSV, TNT]. The verb and the question is translated 'can you expect' [REB], 'will you get' [NIV, NJB], 'what is your (reward)' [NTC]. This phrase is translated 'why should God reward you' [TEV], 'will God reward you for that' [CEV]. Here the present tense has a future impact as a person stores up treasure and therefore has the treasure waiting for him [EBC].

QUESTION—What is the function of this rhetorical question?

It is a rhetorical question that expresses disapproval [TG, TH] and adds force to the statement [TH]. The rhetorical question points out that a person who returns good for good has done nothing exceptional [WBC]. This rhetorical question could be translated as a statement to the effect that you have no reward from God if you only love those who love you [Dei (p. 115, 18.c.2), TG].

(Do) not[a] even[b] the tax-collectors[c] do[d] the-same-thing?[e]

LEXICON—a. οὐχί (LN **69.12**) (BAGD 3. p. 598): 'do not' [Mor, WBC; KJV, NAB, NASB, NJB, NRSV, TNT], 'are not' [NTC; NIV]. This is also added as a tag question 'don't they?' [NET], 'do they not?' [LN]. The question is translated as a positive statement that omits this word: 'Even the tax collectors do that!' [NLT, TEV], 'Even the tax collectors do as much as that' [REB], 'Even tax collectors love their friends' [CEV]. This word is used in questions that expect an emphatic affirmative answer [BAGD, LN].

b. καί (LN 89.93) (BAGD II.2. p. 393): 'even' [BAGD, Mor, WBC; all versions except NAB, NET, TNT], 'also' [TNT], 'too' [NET], not explicit [NTC; NAB]. Here and in 5:47 this is the ascensive καί meaning 'even' [BAGD, Mor].

c. τελώνης (LN 57.184) (BAGD p. 812): 'tax collectors' [BAGD, Mor, NTC, WBC; all versions except KJV, NASB, NLT], 'corrupt tax collectors' [NLT], 'the tax-gatherers' [NASB], 'revenue officer' [BAGD], 'publicans' [KJV].

d. pres. act. indic. of ποιέω (LN 90.45) (BAGD I.1.b.ε. p. 681): 'to do' [BAGD, Mor, NTC, WBC; KJV, NAB, NASB, NET, NIV, NJB, NLT, NRSV, REB, TEV, TNT], not explicit [CEV].

e. αὐτός (LN **58.31**) (BAGD 4.b. p. 123): 'the same' [BAGD, LN, Mor; KJV, NAB, NASB, NRSV, TNT], 'that' [NET, NIV, TEV], 'as much' [NJB], 'that much' [NLT], 'as much as that' [REB], 'the same thing' [NTC, WBC]. The clause is translated: 'even tax collectors love their friends' [CEV].

QUESTION—Who were the tax collectors and how were they regarded?

The τελώνης 'tax collector' collected money for the *publicani*, who in turn paid the Roman government large sums for the right to collect taxes and keep large amounts of those taxes. The KJV uses the English word 'publicans' to render τελώνης, which has caused some confusion [BAGD, EBC, ICC, McN, NTC, Pl]. The τελώνης 'tax collector' was hired from the native population, usually by someone who was a foreigner holding a tax-farming contract [BAGD]. They collected taxes on things taken in and out of towns from their fellow Jews [TG]. They were hated for dishonesty and extortion [BAGD Mor, NTC], for their rapaciousness [NCBC], and for their corruption [EBC]. The Roman tax system itself was associated with inequality and oppression [TH] and the tax-collectors were infamous for their abuse of the system [ICC]. They were viewed as Jews who oppressed their own people [McN], as apostate Jews [BBC], as traitors for serving the Romans [Brc, EBC, NTC, TG]. They were regarded as morally inferior; thus tax-collectors became almost synonymous with sinners [BSC]. By continued contact with the Romans, they were ritually unclean [BAGD, EBC, Mor]

QUESTION—Why did Jesus mention the tax-collectors and Gentiles together?

These two groups were mentioned because the scribes and Pharisees regarded them as morally inferior The term 'tax-collector' was almost synonymous with 'sinner' [BSC]. These were two groups the Jewish audience despised [TG]. Tax collectors were despised for contributing to the Roman exploitation of the Jewish people, and Gentiles were despised because they lacked true religion [NAC]. When used in a phrase like this, it was understood colloquially as equivalent to 'outsiders' or 'undesirables' [TNTC2]. It was not that Jesus had enmity toward the tax collectors or

Gentiles as a group, since, as he did with the Pharisees, Jesus could denounce their sin and still reach out to individual tax collectors [EBC, ICC].

5:47 And if you(pl)-greet[a] only your(pl) brothers,[b]

LEXICON—a. aorist mid. (deponent = act.) subj. of ἀσπάζομαι (LN 33.20) (BAGD 1.a. p. 116): 'to greet' [BAGD, Mor, WBC; CEV, NAB, NASB, NET, NIV, NRSV, REB, TNT], 'to save your greetings for' [NJB], 'to speak (only) to' [TEV], 'to salute' [KJV], 'to be kind to' [NLT], 'to approach with cordial greetings' [NTC].

b. ἀδελφός: 'brother'. The phrase τοὺς ἀδελφοὺς ὑμῶν is translated: 'your brothers' [Mor, NTC; NAB, NASB, NET, NIV, NJB, REB, TNT], 'your brethren' [KJV], 'your brothers and sisters' [NRSV], 'your friends' [CEV, NLT, TEV], 'members of your community' [WBC]. This word refers to like-minded members of a religious community [EBC, NCBC, TH, TNTC2, WBC]. See this word at 5:22.

QUESTION—What is meant by ἀσπάζομαι 'to greet'?

The meaning includes a greeting spoken toward the person being greeted [BAGD, Mor, WBC; all versions], but it indicates more than a simple greeting [BAGD, ICC, NAC]. It implies respect toward the person being greeted through a courteous greeting [EBC, NTC, TH]. It implies positives feelings toward the person being greeted [BAGD], 'to approach with cordial greetings' [NTC], 'to be kind to' [NLT]. It was not just a gesture but also a friendly spoken greeting [TG]. It suggests cherishing and being fond of someone [BAGD, NTC]. It is an expression of desire for the other person's welfare [ICC, NAC], a desire for God's peace and blessing [ICC, TH]. Since it is parallel to love in the previous verse, it carries a fuller meaning such as 'wish peace and blessing upon' or 'show favor toward' [WBC]. The Jewish greeting *shalom* 'peace' was really a prayer, wishing well and feeling warmly toward the other [Mor].

what exceptional[a] (thing) are-you(pl)-doing?

LEXICON—a. περισσός (LN **58.57**) (BAGD 1. p. 651): 'exceptional' [**LN**, NTC; NJB], 'extraordinary' [BAGD; REB], 'more than others' [Mor; KJV, NASB, NIV, NRSV], 'more' [NET], 'out of the ordinary' [TEV], 'unusual' [LN; NAB, TNT], 'outstanding' [LN], 'remarkable' [BAGD, LN], 'rewardable thing' [WBC]. This clause is translated 'what's so great about that?' [CEV], 'how are you different from anyone else?' [NLT]. It refers to doing more than what would be expected [LN]. It alludes to περισσεύω 'exceed' in 5:20 [ICC, NTC].

QUESTION—What is the function of this rhetorical question?

This is another rhetorical question and means 'you have not done anything exceptional' [TG]. The clause is a question expecting the negative answer 'nothing more!' and it can be translated as a statement: 'you are not doing anything more than what people ordinarily do' or 'you are only doing the same as everyone else' [TH].

(Do) not even[a] the Gentiles[b] do the-same-thing?[c]

TEXT—Instead of ἐθνικοί 'Gentiles', some manuscripts have τελῶναι 'tax collectors'. GNT selects the reading 'Gentiles' with a B rating, indicating that the text is almost certain. The reading 'publicans' is taken by

LEXICON—a. καί: 'even' [WBC; all versions except NAB, NET, TNT], 'also' [Mor; TNT], 'too' [NET], not explicit [NTC; NAB].

    b. ἐθνικός (LN **11.38**) (BAGD p. 218): 'Gentile' [BAGD, **LN**, Mor, NTC, WBC; NASB, NET, NJB, NRSV], 'pagan' [LN; NAB, NIV, NLT, TEV], 'heathen' [BAGD, LN; REB, TNT], 'unbeliever' [CEV], 'publican' [KJV]. See this word at 6:7.

    c. αὐτός (LN 58.31): 'the same thing' [WBC], 'the same' [Mor; NAB, NASB, NRSV, TNT], 'so' [KJV], 'that' [CEV, NET, NIV, NLT, TEV], 'as much' [NTC; NJB, REB].

QUESTION—Who were the Gentiles and why did Jesus mention them?

The racial element is indicated by some sources: 'one who is not a Jew' [LN], 'in contrast to the Jew' [BAGD, Mor]. The negative attitude toward the Gentiles reflects the Jewishness of Matthew's readers [WBC]. Gentiles were hated because of oppression and even sometimes a desire for genocide of the Jews, for idolatry, and for wanting to seduce the Jews into idolatry, and because of the Jewish hatred of them the Gentiles hated the Jews as well [NTC]. In Aramaic this may have carried the connotation of 'the rest of mankind' [AAG (p. 176)]. This word denotes more a lack of religious belief than race [EBC, TG, TH]. They are non-Christian pagans [ICC], 'those who do not know God' [TH].

DISCOURSE UNIT: 5:48 [EBC, TNTC2]. The topic is conclusion: the demand for perfection [EBC], summary [TNTC2].

5:48 Therefore[a] you(pl) will-be perfect[b] as[c] your(pl) heavenly[d] Father is perfect.

LEXICON—a. οὖν (LN 89.50) (BAGD 1.b. p. 593): 'therefore' [BAGD, Mor, NTC, WBC; KJV, NASB, NIV, NJB, NRSV], 'so then' [NET, TNT], 'so' [NAB], 'but' [CEV, NLT], 'so, consequently, accordingly, then' [BAGD], not explicit [REB, TEV].

    b. τέλειος (LN **88.36**) (BAGD 2.d. p. 809): 'perfect' [BAGD, LN, Mor, NTC, WBC; all versions except CEV, NJB, REB], 'to set no bounds to your love' [NJB], 'there must be no limit to your goodness' [REB]. The clause is translated 'you must always act like your Father in heaven' [CEV].

    c. ὡς (LN 64.12) (BAGD II.4.a. p. 897): 'as' [BAGD, NTC, WBC; NASB, NET, NIV, NRSV, REB, TNT], 'just as' [NAB, NJB, TEV], 'even as' [Mor; KJV, NLT], 'like' [CEV].

    d. οὐράνιος (LN **1.12**) (BAGD p. 593): 'heavenly' [BAGD, LN, Mor, NTC, WBC; CEV, NAB, NASB, NET, NIV, NJB, NRSV, REB, TNT], 'which is in heaven' [KJV], 'in heaven' [**LN**; NLT, TEV].

QUESTION—What relationship is indicated by οὖν 'therefore'?

1. It indicates the conclusion of 5:3–47 [BSC, NTC, TG]. It especially emphasizes 5:45, that a disciple should love like the Father does, be consistent and not partial [BSC, NTC]. Some see this verse as a conclusion of the last antithesis, which is that they should love as broadly and fully as God does [NJB, TG].
2. It indicates a summary of 5:21–48 [BBC, EBC, ICC, McN, MLJ, NCBC], as well as 5:43–47 [BBC, NAC, NCBC, TH, WBC]. This command summarizes the greater righteousness demanded in 5:20 and illustrated in 5:21–47 [TNTC2]. The verse brings the entire section and the whole teaching to a grand and glorious climax [MLJ]. Perfection has a much broader application than just love [EBC]. Οὖν indicates that this verse is the end of a major section [ICC]. Although it confirms 5:45 and concludes the shorter pericope, it is the logical conclusion to all six antitheses [WBC].

QUESTION—What is indicated by the future tense of ἔσεσθε 'you will be'?

The future indicative is used as a present imperative of εἰμί 'to be'. It is translated: 'be' [WBC; KJV, NAB, NET, NIV, NRSV], '(you) are to be' [NASB, NLT], '(you) must be' [NTC; TEV, TNT], '(you) shall be' [Mor]. The future tense has the force of a command [Mor, Pl], but it is also a promise of what the disciple will become, and the disciples can look for God's help in the fulfillment of the promise [Mor].

QUESTION—What is the significance of the pronoun ὑμεῖς 'you(pl)' used for the subject?

It emphasizes a contrast between Jesus' disciples and the tax-collectors and Gentiles [ICC, McN, Mor, Pl, TH, WBC].

QUESTION—What does it mean to be τέλειος 'perfect'?

It primarily refers to love [Brc, EBC, ICC, NAC, NCBC, NIBC, NTC, TG, WBC]. It refers to loving all people as God does [NAC, NIBC, Pl, TG; NJB]. This would especially mean being like their father in loving their enemies [NTC, WBC]. The command reflects Deuteronomy 18:13 'you must be blameless' [ICC, McN, Mor, NCBC, NTC, TG], in which the Hebrew word *tamim* 'blameless' is translated into Greek in the Septuagint by τέλειος, and to Leviticus 19:2 'be holy as I am holy' [EBC, ICC, McN, NCBC, NTC, TG, TNTC2]. It refers to all the perfection of God as exemplified in how Jesus has interpreted the law in the antitheses in this section [EBC]. This holiness is to be understood in terms of the spiritual fulfillment of the law as described in this sermon [McN]. It means to be full grown and complete with respect to the law of love [NTC]. It means to be mature and whole, growing in obedience to God and becoming more like him in loving without limits [NAC]. The emphasis is on whole-hearted commitment to imitating God and his ways in loving other people [NCBC]. Τέλειος means fulfilling an end or purpose, and human beings do this by exhibiting in their lives the characteristics of the nature of God, in whose image they are made, and which is shown in love [Brc, NIBC], in an active concern for all people everywhere regardless of whether or not they accept it [NIBC]. It is conformity to the character of God, not a matter of sinless perfection [EBC, NIBC, TNTC2]. It is a life completely integrated to the will of God and reflecting his character [TNTC2]. Love for God and others is the embodiment of ethical perfection [WBC]. It means that we must live to the highest possible standard, with all that we have and are taken up into the service of the father [Mor]. This command is an example of Jesus using hyperbole to make his teaching memorable [TG].

DISCOURSE UNIT: 6:1–34 [Mor, NIBC, NTC]. The topic is sermon on the mount: prayer and anxiety [NIBC], the essence of this righteousness with respect to man's relation to God [NTC], practicing piety [Mor].

DISCOURSE UNIT: 6:1–18 [BSC, EBC, ICC, McN, NAC, NCBC, NTC, Pl, TNTC, TNTC2, WBC]. The piety of the sons of the kingdom [TNTC], the practice of piety [NCBC], the motive for righteousness [BSC], the Christian life contrasted with faulty Jewish practice [Pl], real righteousness and pharisaic ostentation, with a digression on prayer [McN], outward and inward righteousness [WBC], the sincere devotion of the heart [NTC], teaching on religious observance [TNTC2], religious hypocrisy: its description and overthrow [EBC], the Christian cult [ICC].

DISCOURSE UNIT: 6:1–15 [NASB]. The topic is concerning alms and prayer [NASB].

DISCOURSE UNIT: 6:1–4 [BBC, GNT, HF, Mor, TG, TH, WBC; CEV, NAB, NET, NIV, NJB, NLT, NRSV, TEV]. The topic is almsgiving [GNT, Mor, WBC; NRSV], teaching about almsgiving [NAB], teaching about charity [TG, TH; TEV], Jesus teaches about helping people in need [TG, TH], Jesus teaches how needy people should be helped [TG, TH], giving to the needy [NIV, NLT], giving [CEV], almsgiving in secret [NJB], give with sincerity [HF], secret charity [BBC], pure hearted giving [NET].

DISCOURSE UNIT: 6:1 [EBC, ICC, MLJ]. The topic is the principle [EBC], general principle [ICC], living the righteous life [MLJ].

6:1 Be-careful[a] not to-do[b] your righteous-acts[c] before[d] people in-order-to[e] to-be-seen[f] by-them;

TEXT—Instead of δικαιοσύνη 'righteousness', some manuscripts have ἐλεημοσύνη 'almsgiving'. GNT does not mention this alternative. Only KJV reads 'alms'.

LEXICON—a. pres. act. impera. of προσέχω (LN **27.59**) (BAGD 1.b. p. 714): 'to be careful' [WBC; NET, NIV, NJB, REB], 'to take care' [Mor, NTC; NAB, NLT, TNT], 'to take heed' [KJV], 'to make certain' [**LN**; TEV], 'to be on guard against' [LN], 'to beware of' [NASB, NRSV], 'to be concerned about, to care for' [BAGD], 'to pay attention to' [BAGD, LN], not explicit [CEV].

b. pres. act. infin. of ποιέω (LN 42.7) (BAGD I.1.c.b. p. 682): 'to do'
[BAGD, LN; CEV, KJV, NIV, NLT], 'to perform' [LN; NAB, TEV,
TNT], 'to practice' [BAGD, NTC, WBC, ZG; NASB, NRSV], 'to parade'
[Mor; NJB, REB], 'to live' [NET]. See this word at 6:2.

c. δικαιοσύνη (LN **53.4, 57.111**) (BAGD 2.a. p. 196): 'acts of righteousness' [NIV], 'righteousness' [Mor, NTC; NASB, NJB], 'piety' [TNTC2,
WBC; NRSV], 'righteous deeds' [NAB], 'religion' [REB], 'religious
duties' [TEV, TNT], 'alms' [KJV], 'righteously' [NET], 'good deeds'
[CEV, NLT], 'practice of piety' (also in 6:2) [BAGD], 'obligations under
the Law' [ZG], 'religious observances' [**LN** (53.4)], 'religious require-
ments, or practices required by one's religion' [LN (53.4)], 'acts of
charity, alms' [LN (57.111)], 'giving to the needy' [**LN** (57.111)]. The
clause 'be careful not to do your righteous acts before people' is translated
'don't try to show off' [CEV].

d. ἔμπροσθεν (LN 83.33) (BAGD 2.c. p. 257): 'before' [BAGD, LN, Mor,
NTC, WBC; KJV, NASB, NIV, NRSV, REB], 'in front of' [BAGD, LN;
KJV, TNT]. The phrase 'before people in order to be seen by them' is
translated 'in order that people may see them' [NAB], 'in public so that
people will see what you do' [TEV], 'merely to be seen by people' [NET],
'in public to attract attention' [NJB], 'publicly to be admired' [NLT], 'to
parade your religion before others' [REB], 'don't try to show off' [CEV].

e. πρός (LN 89.60) (BAGD III.3.a. p. 710): 'in order to' [LN, Mor, WBC;
NRSV], 'in order that' [NAB, NASB], 'for the purpose of' [BAGD, LN],
'so that' [TEV, TNT], 'to (with infinitive)' [NTC; KJV, NET, NIV, NJB,
NLT], not explicit [CEV].

f. aorist pass. infin. of θεάομαι (LN 24.14) (BAGD 1.c.b. p. 353): 'to be
seen' [Mor, WBC; KJV, NASB, NET, NIV, NRSV], 'to cause to be seen'
[LN], 'to be noticed' [BAGD; NASB], 'to attract attention' [BAGD,
NTC; NJB], 'to be admired' [NLT], not explicit [CEV, REB]. The passive
voice is also translated actively with people as the subject: 'to see' [NAB,
TEV, TNT].

QUESTION—How is the term δικαιοσύνη 'righteous acts' used in this
passage?
    1. It refers to the practice of religious piety as expressed in religious
    exercises such as giving to charity, praying and fasting [ICC, NCBC,
    NTC, WBC]. It is religious observance [TG, TNTC2]. It refers to external
    conduct done in observance of the Law [Pl].
    2. It refers to righteous conduct in general as referred to in 5:20 [EBC].
QUESTION—What is the cultural background of this concern?
Almsgiving, prayer and fasting were popular components of Jewish piety
[BBC, EBC, ICC, NAC, NCBC, NIBC, Pl, TNTC2, WBC]. Jesus did not
dispute these, but was concerned about the motives involved in their
practice. [Brc, ICC, TNTC2]. The rabbis commonly used sets of three in
discussing virtues [BBC]. Both Jews and Jesus stressed that good works
should not be done for the sake of reward, but nevertheless promised a

reward given at Judgment Day [BBC]. Greek and Roman culture had no
tradition of giving to the poor out of piety; they would give in order to
increase the giver's popularity [BBC].

QUESTION—How is this statement to be understood in light of 5:16, where
Jesus commands them to let their light shine so that people might see their
good deeds?

The difference in the two passages has to do with motives. In 5:16 the
motive for one's good deeds being seen is to glorify God, whereas here the
motive for not letting good deeds be seen would be to avoid glorifying
oneself [EBC, NAC, NIBC, NTC, TNTC2]. The privacy to be avoided in
5:16 would presumably be due to a desire to avoid persecution [NIBC]. The
righteousness of the previous section, which must exceed that of the
Pharisees, is an ethical obedience, whereas here it is the religious observance
[TNTC2].

**otherwise,[a] you(pl)- do-not -have[b] reward[c] from[d] your(pl) father in the
heavens.[e]**

LEXICON—a. εἰ δὲ μή γε: 'otherwise' [NTC, WBC; KJV, NAB, NASB, NET,
NJB], 'for then' [NRSV], 'because then' [NLT], 'if you do' [Mor; CEV,
NIV, REB, TNT], 'if you do these things publicly' [TEV]. This is a
stereotyped expression meaning 'otherwise' [ZG]. The enclitic particle γέ
is appended to a word for emphasis and is often untranslatable [BAGD
(3.b.α. p. 152), LN (91.6)].

b. pres. act. indic. of ἔχω LN 57.1): 'to have (no reward)' [LN, Mor, WBC;
KJV, NAB, NASB, NET, NIV, NRSV], 'to (not) have (any reward)'
[NTC; TEV], 'to (not) get' [CEV], 'to expect (no)' [TNT]; 'to lose'
[NLT], 'to lose (all)' [NJB]. The phrase 'you do not have reward' is
translated 'no reward awaits you' [REB]. The verb ἔχω may be used to
indicate having the right of possession of something even though not
actually having it in possession at that moment [ZG].

c. μισθός (LN 38.14) (BAGD 2.a. p. 523): 'reward' [BAGD, LN, Mor,
NTC, WBC; all versions except NAB], 'recompense' [LN; NAB]; See
this word at 5:12.

d. παρά (LN 90.14) (BAGD II.1.b.g. p. 610): 'from' [LN; CEV, NAB, NIV,
NJB, NLT, NRSV, TEV, TNT], 'of' [KJV], 'with' [Mor, NTC, WBC;
NASB, NET, REB], 'with' (viewed in terms of spatial proximity)
[BAGD].

e. οὐρανός (LN 1.11) (BAGD 2.a. p. 599) 'heaven' [BAGD, LN]. The
plural form 'the heavens' is translated 'heaven' [Mor, NTC; all versions
except NAB]. The phrase 'your Father in the heavens' is translated 'your
heavenly Father' [WBC; NAB]. Heaven is the dwelling place or throne of
God [BAGD].

QUESTION—What is the significance of the present tense of ἔχετε 'you have'?
They already have their reward from men and will receive none from God
[NTC]. They will get no more than praise from men [EBC]. Good deeds

bring only one recompense, so those that have recognition from men will have none from God [McN].

QUESTION—Is it good to seek a reward?

The implication is that it is acceptable to seek God's reward; concern about rewards is encouraged in the NT as long as the desire is the reward of holiness and being with God [MLJ]. If we do not exercise such caution, then we will not receive a reward [BSC]. The rewards God gives express his character and are an integral part of his covenantal relationship with his people; however reward and punishment are not purely material, since the reward for holiness is holiness itself [NIBC]. We should primarily seek to please and glorify God, which brings a reward as a consequence [NTC]. It is highest and best to seek righteousness for its own sake, but the fact of a reward does offer a valid incentive for the less mature [Pl].

DISCOURSE UNIT: 6:2–18 [EBC, ICC]. The topic is a triad of specific instruction [ICC], three examples [EBC].

DISCOURSE UNIT: 6:2–4 [EBC, ICC, McN, NAC, NTC]. The topic is alms [EBC], almsgiving [ICC, McN, NAC], charitable giving [NTC].

6:2 Therefore[a] whenever[b] you(sg)-do[c] alms,[d]

LEXICON—a. οὖν (LN 89.50): 'therefore' [LN, WBC; KJV, NASB], 'so' [LN, NTC; NIV, NJB, NRSV, REB, TEV], 'thus' [NET], not explicit [CEV, NAB, NLT, TNT], 'then' [LN, Mor].

b. ὅταν (LN 67.31) (BAGD 1.a. p. 588): 'when' [LN, WBC; all versions except NET, NRSV], 'whenever' [BAGD, LN, Mor, NTC; NET, NRSV], 'as often as, every time that' [BAGD]. This temporal particle describes an action that is conditional, possible, and repeated and is used with a verb in the present subjunctive, in which the action of the subordinate clause is contemporaneous with that of the main clause, and usually refers to regular or repeated action [BAGD].

c. pres. act. subj. of ποιέω (LN 42.7) (BAGD I.1.c.b. p. 682): 'to do' [BAGD, LN; KJV]. This verb is conflated with 'almsgiving' (see the next entry) [Mor, NTC, WBC; all versions except KJV]. See this word at 6:1.

d. ἐλεημοσύνη (LN **57.111**) (BAGD p. 249): 'alms' [BAGD, LN; KJV], 'charitable giving' (also in 6:3) [BAGD], 'giving to the needy' [**LN**]. The phrase 'you do alms' is translated 'you give alms' [Mor, WBC; NAB, NASB, NJB, NRSV, REB, TNT], 'you do charitable giving' [NET], 'you give to the needy' [NIV], 'you give something to a needy person' [TEV], 'you give to the poor' [NTC; CEV], 'you give a gift to someone in need' [NLT]. Literally 'to do an act of mercy', the verb had become a technical term for almsgiving [WBC].

do-not sound-a-trumpet[a] before you(sg),

LEXICON—a. aorist act. subj. of σαλπίζω (LN **6.90**) (BAGD p. 741): 'to sound the/a trumpet' [BAGD, LN, Mor; KJV, NASB, NET, NRSV], 'to blow a trumpet' [NAB, TNT], 'to blow a loud horn' [CEV], 'to have it trumpeted' [NJB], 'to trumpet forth' [BAGD], 'to announce it with trumpets' [NIV], 'to announce it with a flourish of trumpets' [REB], 'to shout about it blowing trumpets' [NLT], 'to make a big show of it' [TEV]. This subjunctive form is used as an imperative [all versions].

QUESTION—What does this comment about sounding trumpets have to do with giving?

1. It is figurative language to describe trying to draw attention to oneself [BBC, BSC, ICC, NCBC, NIBC, Pl, TG, TH, TNTC2; TEV]. It is a metaphor for being a hypocrite [NTC]. It is hyperbole [TG].

2. Trumpets were blown at times of special need to call for almsgiving and fasts [EBC, NCBC]. At such a time people could be ostentatious [EBC].

3. The collection boxes in the Temple were trumpet-shaped; Jesus used this language as a figurative allusion to demonstrated piety. [BBC, Ed (p. 539)].

as[a] the hypocrites[b] do in the synagogues[c] and in[d] the streets,[e]

LEXICON—a. ὥσπερ (LN **64.13**) (BAGD 2. p. 899): 'as' [BAGD, **LN**, Mor; all versions except CEV, NJB], 'just as' [BAGD, LN], 'this is what' [CEV, NJB].

b. ὑποκριτής (LN 88.228) (BAGD p. 845): 'hypocrite' [BAGD, LN, Mor, NTC, WBC; all versions except CEV], 'show-off' [CEV], 'play-actor' [BAGD, NIBC], 'pretender' [BAGD, LN]. See this word at 6:5, 16; 7:5.

c. συναγωγή (LN 7.20) (BAGD 2.a. p. 782): 'synagogue' [BAGD, LN; all versions except TEV], 'a place of assembly' [BAGD], 'the house of worship' [TEV], 'the meeting place' [CEV].

d. ἐν (LN 83.47): 'in' [Mor; KJV, NAB, NASB, NJB, NLT, NRSV, REB, TNT], 'on' [LN; CEV, NET, NIV, TEV].

e. ῥύμη (LN 1.104) (BAGD p. 737): 'street' [all versions except CEV], 'street corner' [CEV], 'narrow street, lane, alley' [LN].

QUESTION—What is implied by ὑποκριτής 'hypocrite'?

Ὑποκριτής is the Greek word for an actor [Brc] and was used to mean pretending to be something you are not [NIBC]. Jesus had the Pharisees in mind and was continuing to illustrate 5:20. He called them hypocrites because they used the pretext of giving alms to conceal their desire to receive human praise [BSC]. They were hypocrites because their real motivation was self-glorification [WBC]. With their ostentatious displays of righteousness the Pharisees were like actors performing before an audience, though this does not mean that they were consciously insincere [NCBC, TNTC2].

in-order-that[a] they-might-be-praised[b] by-people;

LEXICON—a. ὅπως (LN **89.59**) (BAGD 2.a.a. p. 576): 'that' [BAGD; KJV, NASB], 'so that' [LN, WBC; NET, NRSV], 'they do it so that' [TEV], 'in order that' [BAGD, **LN**], 'in order to' [LN, NTC], 'for the purpose of' [LN], 'because' [CEV], not explicit [NAB, NIV, NJB, NLT, REB, TNT].

b. aorist pass. subj. of δοξάζω (LN **33.357, 87.8**): 'to be praised' [LN, Mor;
NRSV, TNT], 'to win the praise' [NAB, REB], 'to always look for praise'
[CEV], 'to have glory' [KJV], 'to be glorified' [LN (33.357), WBC], 'to
be honored' [**LN** (87.8); NASB, NIV], 'to be honored' [NASB], 'to win
admiration' [NTC; NJB], 'to be respected' [LN (87.8)], 'to call attention
to (their acts of charity)' [NLT]. The passive voice is also translated
actively with people as the subject: 'to praise' [**LN** (33.357); NET, TEV].

truly[a] I-say to-you(pl), they-are-receiving-in-full[b] their reward.[c]
LEXICON—a. ἀμήν (LN 72.6) (BAGD 2. p. 45): 'truly'. See the phrase 'truly I
say to you(pl)/(sg)' at 5:18, 26; 6: 5, 16.
  b. pres. act. indic. of ἀπέχω (LN **57.137**) (BAGD 1. p. 84): 'to have
received in full' [BAGD, LN; NIV], 'to have' [Mor; KJV, NET], 'to have
in full' [NASB], 'to have already' [CEV, REB], 'to have had' [NJB], 'to
have got' [TNT], 'to be paid in full' [**LN**], 'to have already been paid in
full' [TEV], 'to have received' [NAB, NRSV], 'to have received all one
will ever get' [NLT]. This may also be translated 'they have received all
that is coming to them' or '…all that they deserve' [LN]. The verb ἀπέχω
is a commercial technical term meaning to receive a sum in full and give a
receipt for it [BAGD], implying that all that is due has been fully paid
[LN] and that no further compensation is coming [NIBC]. This clause is
repeated at 6:5.
  c. μισθός (LN 38.14) (BAGD 2.a. p. 523): 'reward' [BAGD, LN, Mor,
NTC; all versions except TEV], 'recompense' [LN]. The phrase 'to
receive in full their reward' is translated 'to already be paid in full' [TEV].
Reward is used figuratively for the recompense God gives for the moral
quality of an action [BAGD].
QUESTION—What is the significance of the present tense ἀπέχουσιν 'they are
receiving in full'?
'They are having their reward' implies that this is all the reward they will
receive and it is in contrast with the heavenly Father's eschatological act
described in the future tense ἀποδώσει 'will reward' in 6:4, 6, 18 [WBC].
They have already received their reward and no more awaits them [NTC,
TG]. They were not giving, they were buying the praise of men, which is all
they'll have, and they can expect nothing more from God [ICC, Pl]. They
have all they will get, which is human praise [EBC, McN].

6:3 **But[a] you(sg) (when) doing[b] alms**
LEXICON—a. δέ: 'but' [Mor, NTC, WBC; NET, NIV, NLT, NRSV, REB,
TEV], not explicit [CEV, TNT].
  b. pres. act. participle of ποιέω (LN 42.7) (BAGD I.1.c.b. p. 682): 'to do'
[LN, Mor, NTC, WBC; all versions]. The phrase to do alms is translated
'to give alms' [Mor, WBC; NAB, NASB, NJB, NRSV, REB, TNT], 'to
give to the needy' [NIV], 'to give to the poor' [CEV], 'to give to
someone' [NLT], 'to help a needy person' [TEV], 'to give to charity'
[NTC], 'to do your giving' [NET].

QUESTION—What relationship is indicated by δέ (but)?

It indicates a contrast with the hypocrites' actions in the preceding verse [ICC, Mor, NTC, WBC; NET, NIV, NLT, NRSV, REB, TEV]: they sound a trumpet before them, but you must not even let your left hand know what your right hand is doing. This is a strong adversative sentence [WBC]. It introduces an antithetical corollary to the prohibition of 6:2 [ICC].

QUESTION—What relationship is indicated by the use of the participle ποιοῦντος 'doing'?

It is temporal, indicating when the command is to be carried out [Mor, NTC, WBC; all versions]: when doing alms, do not let your left hand know what your right hand is doing.

do-not let-know^a (your)(sg) left (hand)^b what your(sg) right (hand) is-doing,

LEXICON—a. aorist act. impera. of γινώσκω (LN 27.2): 'to let know' [Mor, NTC, WBC; all versions except NLT], 'to find out, to learn' [LN], 'to tell' [NLT].

b. ἀριστερά (LN **8.33**) (BAGD p. 106): 'left' (opposite to right) [BAGD, LN]. In the phrase ἡ ἀριστερά 'the left', the definite article is understood in a possessive sense 'your' and the adjective 'left' is understood as indicating the 'left hand': 'your left hand' [Mor, NTC, WBC; all versions except TEV]. The same applies for the phrase ἡ δεξιά 'the right'. The phrase 'don't let your left hand know what your right hand is doing' is translated 'do it in such a way that even your closest friend will not know about it' [TEV], 'don't let anyone know about it' [CEV].

QUESTION—What is intended by this figure of speech?

It is a hyperbole [BBC, NAC]. This is an example of Jesus' use of paradoxical statements similar to the *mashalim* or proverbs in Jewish Wisdom literature. Since the left and right hands usually work together, this is an image of deepest secrecy [BSC]. The disciple should keep almsgiving a private transaction between himself and God and let God provide the proper reward [NIBC]. Giving should be kept very secret even to the point of forgetting about it yourself so that you won't think too highly of yourself for giving [NTC]. Giving should be done with such secrecy that even we ourselves hardly know what we have given [EBC]. It means that giving should be done unselfconsciously [WBC]. He is saying that one should not think too highly of his own giving, and should not draw attention to it even to oneself [ICC].

6:4 in-order-that^a your(sg) alms^b might-be in secret;^c

LEXICON—a. ὅπως (LN 89.59) (BAGD 2.a.a. p. 577): 'in order that' [BAGD; TNT], 'so that' [LN, Mor, WBC; NAB, NET, NIV, NRSV], 'that' [BAGD, NTC; KJV, NASB], 'then' [CEV, TEV], not explicit and using imperative verb [NJB, NLT, REB]. See this word also at 6:2.

b. ἐλεημοσύνη (LN 57.111) (BAGD p. 249): 'alms' [BAGD, LN; KJV, NASB, NRSV], 'almsgiving' [Mor, WBC; NAB, NJB, TNT], 'giving' [NIV], 'giving to the needy' [LN], 'gift' [CEV, NET, NLT], 'charitable giving' [BAGD], 'deeds of charity' [NTC], 'acts of charity' [LN], 'good deed' [REB], 'it' [TEV].

c. κρυπτός (LN **28.71**) (BAGD 2.b. p. 454): 'a hidden place' [BAGD]. The phrase ἐν τῷ κρυπτῷ is translated 'in secret' [LN, Mor, NTC, WBC; CEV, KJV, NASB, NET, NIV, NLT, NRSV, TNT], 'secret' [NAB, NJB], 'a secret' [REB], 'in private' [LN], 'a private matter' [TEV]. This noun is also translated as an adverb: '(to be done) secretly' [LN]. In this verse the verb εἰμί 'be' is like its Hebrew equivalent, meaning 'remain (in secret)' [ZG].

QUESTION—What relationship is indicated by ὅπως 'in order that'?

It indicates purpose for not letting the left hand know what the right hand is doing [LN, Mor, NTC, WBC; KJV, NAB, NASB, NET, NIV, NRSV, TNT]. It introduces an emphasis on secrecy that is the main point of this and the next two sections [WBC].

and your(sg) father, the (one) seeing[a] in secret,[b]

LEXICON—a. pres. act. participle of βλέπω (LN 24.7) (BAGD 1.c. p. 143): 'to see' [BAGD, LN]. The participial phrase ὁ βλέπων 'the one seeing' is translated as a finite verb phrase: 'who sees' [Mor, NTC, WBC; all versions except CEV, NLT], 'who knows' [CEV, NLT].

b. κρυπτός (LN 28.71) (BAGD 2.b. p. 454): 'in secret' [BAGD, LN], 'in private, secretly, privately' [LN]. The phrase ἐν τῷ κρυπτῷ is translated 'in secret' [Mor, NTC, WBC; KJV, NAB, NASB, NET, NRSV, TNT], 'what is done in secret' [CEV, NIV, REB], 'all that is done in secret' [NJB], 'all secrets' [NLT], 'what you do in private' [TEV]. This whole clause is repeated in 6:6.

QUESTION—What relationship is indicated by καί 'and'?

It is consequential, introducing the consequence of something that was stated earlier [ICC].

will-reward[a] you(sg).

TEXT—Some manuscripts include αὐτός 'himself' (referring to the Father) before ἀποδώσει 'will reward'; a few others add αὐτός to the end of the verse. GNT does not mention this alternative. Only KJV reads 'himself'.

TEXT—Some manuscripts include ἐν τῷ φανερῷ 'openly' after ἀποδώσει σοι 'he will reward you'. It is omitted by GNT with a B rating, indicating that the text is almost certain. Met speculates that copyists substituted the change to make explicit the implicit parallelism in the construction of the preceding phrase ἐν τῷ κρυπτῷ. A similar process took place in 6:6 and 18 in the discussion about praying and fasting. Only KJV reads 'openly'.

LEXICON—a. fut. act. indic. of ἀποδίδωμι (LN 38.16) (BAGD 3. p. 90): 'to reward' [BAGD, LN, Mor, NTC, WBC; CEV, KJV, NET, NIV, NJB, NLT, NRSV, REB, TEV], 'to repay' [NAB, NASB], 'to recompense' [BAGD, LN; TNT]. The prefix ἀπό connotes that the restoration is due [ZG].

QUESTION—With which action is 'in secret' associated?

It goes with 'seeing' [BSC, EBC, ICC, McN, NTC, WBC]. See this same construction in 6:6 and 6:18.

DISCOURSE UNIT: 6:5–18 [NLT]. The topic is teaching about prayer and fasting [NLT].

DISCOURSE UNIT: 6:5–15 [BBC, EBC, GNT, ICC, Mor, NAC, NTC, TG, TH, WBC; CEV, NAB, NET, NIV, NRSV, TEV]. The topic is prayer [EBC, GNT, ICC, Mor, NAC, NTC; CEV, NIV, NRSV], teaching about prayer [TG, TH; NAB, TEV], prayer and the Lord's prayer [WBC], secret prayer [BBC], private prayer [NET].

DISCOURSE UNIT: 6:5–14 [NET]. The topic is private prayer.

DISCOURSE UNIT: 6:5–8 [HF]. The topic is praying with sincerity [HF].

DISCOURSE UNIT: 6:5–6 [EBC, ICC, McN, WBC; NJB]. The topic is prayer in secret [NJB], prayer [McN], the setting of prayer [WBC], how to pray: not as the 'hypocrites' in the synagogue [ICC], ostentatious prayer [EBC].

6:5 And[a] whenever[b] you(pl)-pray,[c]

LEXICON—a. καί: 'and' [Mor, WBC; KJV, NASB, NIV, NJB, NRSV], 'again' [REB], not explicit [CEV, NAB, NET, TEV, TNT], 'also' [NTC], 'and now about prayer' [NLT].

b. ὅταν (LN 67.31) (BAGD 1.a. p. 588): 'whenever' [BAGD, LN, Mor, NTC; NET, NRSV], 'when' [LN, WBC; all versions except NET, NRSV].

c. pres. act. subj. of προσεύχομαι (LN 33.178) (BAGD p. 713): 'to pray' [BAGD, LN, Mor, NTC, WBC; all versions]. This word is very broad and includes supplication as well as adoration of God [BSC].

QUESTION—Is changing from *you(pl)* in 6:1 to *you(sg)* in 6:2–4 to *you(pl)* in 6:5 to *you(sg)* in 6:6 to *you(pl)* in 6:7–14 significant?

This alteration between second person plural and second person singular takes place throughout the sermon and does not seem to have any exegetical significance. Using whichever form of second person is most natural may be used consistently throughout in translation [TH].

you(pl)-will- not -be[a] like[b] the hypocrites;[c]

LEXICON—a. future mid. (deponent = act.) indic. of εἰμί. This verb functions as an imperative: 'thou shalt not be' [KJV], 'you shall not be' [Mor], 'do not be' [NTC, WBC; NAB, NET, NIV, NLT, NRSV, REB, TEV], 'you are not to be' [NASB], 'you must not be' [TNT], 'do not imitate' [NJB], 'don't be' [CEV]. The imperative form ἔστε does not appear in the NT, so the future ἔσεσθε is used instead with the force of the imperative. [BD (sec. 98, p. 49)]. The future with οὐ expresses a categorical prohibition 'you shall not be' or 'you must not be' [ZG].

b. ὡς: 'like' [Mor, NTC, WBC; all versions except KJV, NASB, NJB], 'as' [KJV, NASB], not explicit, implied in verb [NJB].

c. ὑποκριτής (LN 88.228) (BAGD p. 845): 'hypocrites'. See this word at 6:2, 16; 7:5.

for[a] they-love[b] to-pray[c] standing[d] in the synagogues[e] and on the corners of-the main-street,[f]

LEXICON—a. ὅτι: 'for' [Mor, NTC; KJV, NASB, NIV, NRSV, TNT], 'because' [WBC; NET], not explicit [CEV, NAB, NJB, NLT, REB, TEV].

b. pres. act. indic. of φιλέω (LN **25.103**) (BAGD 1.b. p. 867): 'to love to' [BAGD, **LN**, Mor, NTC, WBC; all versions], 'to like to' [BAGD, LN].

c. pres. mid. or pass. (deponent = act.) infin. of προσεύχομαι (LN 33.178) (BAGD p. 713): 'to pray' [BAGD, LN, Mor, NTC, WBC; all versions except NJB, REB], 'to say their prayers' [NJB, REB].

d. perf. act. participle of ἵστημι (LN 17.1): 'to stand' [LN, Mor, NTC; all versions except CEV, NLT, TEV], 'to stand up' [CEV, TEV], 'to position oneself' [WBC]. This participle is also translated as an adverb modifying 'to pray': 'publicly' [NLT]. Standing was the common posture for prayer at this time [BBC]. This perfect participle has a present tense meaning [ZG]. This meaning is the intransitive use of ἵστημι, which in LN 17.1 is shown as ἵσταμαι.

e. συναγωγή (LN 7.20) (BAGD 2.a. p. 782): 'synagogue' [LN, Mor, NTC, WBC; all versions except CEV, TEV], 'house of worship' [TEV], 'the meeting place' [CEV].

f. πλατύς (BAGD a. p. 666): 'wide road, street' [BAGD], 'a square, plaza, or wide street' [ZG]. The phrase ταῖς γωνίαις τῶν πλατειῶν 'the corners of the main street' is translated 'the corners of the main roads' [WBC], 'the corners of the streets' [KJV], 'the street corners' [Mor, NTC; all versions except KJV].

QUESTION—What is implied here?

A person could time it so that he was out in public at the required times of prayer, such as noon time [BSC, NIBC, TNTC2], or situate themselves so they would be most noticed when they would pray [WBC]. If they were in a public place at the hour of prayer they liked being seen praying and were quite glad to be conspicuous about it [Pl]. The problem is not public prayer as such but ostentation [BBC, EBC, ICC, NAC, NTC].

so-that[a] they-might-be-seen[b] by people;

LEXICON—a. ὅπως (LN 89.59) (BAGD 2.a.α. p. 576): 'so that' [LN; NAB, NASB, NET, NRSV, TEV], 'that' [KJV], 'in order that' [BAGD, Mor], 'for' [NJB, REB], 'in order to' [LN], 'to' with an infinitive [NIV, TNT], 'they do this just to' [CEV], 'where' [NLT].

b. aorist pass. subj. of φαίνω (BAGD 2.c. p. 852): 'to be seen' [Mor, NTC; KJV, NASB, NIV, NRSV, TNT], 'to be observed' [WBC]. This passive verb is also translated in the active voice with people as the subject: 'to see' [NAB, NET, NJB, NLT, REB, TEV]; with 'they' as subject: 'to look good' [CEV]. See this word at 6:16, 18.

truly I-say to-you(pl), they-are-receiving-in-full their reward.

LEXICON—This whole clause is the same as in 6:2.

6:6 **But you(sg)[a] whenever you-pray, go-into[b] your(sg) private-room[c]**

LEXICON—a. σύ: 'you(sg)'. The use of the personal pronoun is understood as indicating contrast between his disciples and the hypocrites: 'but you, whenever you are praying' [Mor], 'but you, when you pray' [NASB], 'but as for you, when you pray' [WBC], 'but thou, when thou prayest' [KJV].

  b. aorist act. impera. of εἰσέρχομαι (LN 15.93) (BAGD 1.a.b. p. 232): 'to go (in/into)' [BAGD, LN, Mor, WBC; all versions except KJV, NAB], 'to go to' [NAB], 'to enter' [BAGD, LN, NTC; KJV].

  c. ταμεῖον (LN 7.28) (BAGD 2. p. 803): 'private room' [NJB], 'most private room' [NTC], 'room' [Mor; NET, NIV, NRSV, TEV], 'inner room' [LN; NAB, NASB, TNT], 'a room by yourself' [REB], 'a room alone' [CEV], 'closet' [WBC; KJV], 'innermost, hidden, or secret room' [BAGD]. The phrase 'go into your private room' is translated: 'go away by yourself' [NLT]. This room is an interior room and it normally had no windows opening to the outside [LN].

QUESTION—What was the ταμεῖον 'private room'?

  It is the storeroom where treasures were kept [TNTC], the most remote room where provisions were kept [BSC] or where the steward kept his stores and private office [ZG]. It was the most private room of a house [BBC, TNTC2, WBC; NET], usually not having windows to the outside [BBC, TNTC2; NET], and possibly the only lockable door in the house [BBC, TNTC2]. It was an inner room [EBC], or store room [EBC, ICC], or a secret room [ICC]. It was the most private and secluded room [NTC].

QUESTION—Does this imply that public prayer is inappropriate?

  Public prayer is taught and commended in the Scriptures. The principle is that we must shut out certain things when we pray [MLJ]. The emphasis is not on the place of prayer but the motive [BSC]. He is only condemning public ostentation in prayer [EBC, NIBC, Pl, TNTC2]. This is hyperbole [ICC] or figurative [McN, NCBC], his point being that prayer is for God and not for a human audience [ICC, NCBC]. Jesus does not rule out public expressions of piety but stresses its private side and the importance of right motives [NAC].

and having-closed[a] your(sg) door[b] pray to your(sg) father (who is) in secret;[c]

LEXICON—a. aorist act. participle of κλείω (LN 79.112) (BAGD 1. p. 434): 'to close' [LN; CEV, NAB, NET, NIV, TEV], 'to shut' [BAGD, LN, Mor, NTC, WBC; KJV, NASB], 'to shut yourself in' [NJB], 'to shut behind you' [NLT, NRSV, REB, TNT], 'to lock the bar' [BAGD]. This aorist participle is translated as a past participle 'having shut' [NTC]; with a temporal adverb 'when (you have shut)' [Mor; KJV, NASB]; as an imperative 'shut (the door)' [WBC; NLT, NRSV, REB, TNT], 'shut (yourself) in' [NJB], 'close (the door)' [CEV, NET, NIV, TEV].

b. θύρα (LN 7.49) (BAGD 1.a. p. 365): 'door' [BAGD, LN, Mor, NTC, WBC; all versions except NJB], not explicit [NJB].

c. ἐν τῷ κρυπτῷ: 'who is in secret' [Mor, NTC, WBC; NASB, NRSV, REB, TNT], 'which is in secret' [KJV], 'who is in that secret place' [NJB], 'who is unseen' [NIV, TEV], 'in secret' [NAB, NET], 'in private' [CEV], 'secretly' [NLT].

and your(sg) father, the-one seeing in secret will-reward you(sg).

TEXT—See text comments under verse 6:4 about the variant ἐν τῷ φανερῷ 'openly' after ἀποδώσει σοι 'he will reward you'.

LEXICON—See this same clause at 6:4.

DISCOURSE UNIT: 6:7–15 [ICC, McN, WBC; NJB]. The topic is a digression on prayer [McN], how to pray, the Lord's Prayer [NJB], on the right way to pray: 'The Lord's Prayer' [WBC], how to pray, continued [ICC].

DISCOURSE UNIT: 6:7–8 [EBC, ICC, McN]. The topic is the wrong method of praying [McN], not as the Gentiles [ICC], repetitious prayer [EBC].

6:7 And[a] **(when) praying**[b]

LEXICON—a. δέ: 'and' [Mor, WBC; NASB, NIV], 'moreover' [NTC], 'but' [KJV], not explicit [all versions except KJV, NASB, NIV].

b. pres. act. participle of προσεύχομαι (LN 33.178): 'to pray' [all versions].

QUESTION—What relationship is indicated by δέ 'and'?

1. It indicates a continuation of what he has been saying [Mor, NTC, WBC; NASB, NIV].

2. It is adversative, indicating a contrast with what he has been saying [KJV].

QUESTION—What relationship is indicated by the use of the participle προσευχόμενοι 'praying'?

It is temporal, indicating when the command is to be carried out [LN, Mor, NTC, WBC; CEV, KJV, NASB, NET, NIV, NLT, NRSV, TEV, TNT]: when praying, do not babble. It refers to whenever they pray [Mor, NTC].

do-not babble[a] **like**[b] **the Gentiles,**[c]

LEXICON—a. aorist act. subj. of βατταλογέω (LN **33.88**, **33.89**) (BAGD p. 137): 'to babble' [BAGD, Mor, WBC; NAB, NJB, TNT], 'to go babbling on' [REB], 'to babble on and on' [NTC; NLT], 'to babble repetitiously' [NET], 'to keep on babbling' [NIV], 'to talk on and on' [CEV], 'to use meaningless repetition' [NASB], 'to use vain repetition' [KJV], 'to use a lot of meaningless words' [TEV], 'to heap up empty phrases' [NRSV], 'to gabble, patter' [ZG], 'to speak without thinking' [BAGD]. It can mean 'to use many words', perhaps with the implication of using meaningless words [**LN** (33.88)], or it could mean 'to babble' by uttering senseless sounds or to speak indistinctly and incoherently [**LN** (33.89)].

b. ὥσπερ (LN 64.13) (BAGD 2. p. 899) 'like' [Mor, NTC; NAB, NET, NIV, REB, TNT], 'as' [BAGD, LN, WBC; CEV, KJV, NASB, NJB, NLT, NRSV, TEV].

c. ἐθνικός (LN 11.38) (BAGD p. 218): 'Gentile' [BAGD, LN, Mor, WBC, ZG; NASB, NET, NJB, NRSV], 'heathen' [BAGD, LN; KJV, REB, TNT], 'pagans' [LN, NTC; NAB, NIV, TEV], 'people do who don't know God' [CEV], 'people of other religions' [NLT]. See this word at 5:47.

QUESTION—What specific cultural practice is this referring to?

1. He is referring to the Gentiles' practice of using repetitive or magical phrases or meaningless syllables to try to manipulate the deity [WBC]. He is condemning the pagan practice of repeating long lists of gods' names hoping to hit the true God's name and receive a positive answer to their prayer [BBC, NIBC]. Pagan prayers also piled up long lists of the favors done for the god by the petitioner in hopes of reminding and persuading the god to grant the petition [BBC]. Pagans thought heaped up words would please the gods [BSC]. He has switched from criticism of the hypocrites to criticism of the gentiles, whose prayer was often characterized by formalized invocations and magical incantations in which performing the words exactly right was the most important thing [TNTC2]. It refers to a pagan belief about prayer that one's chances of being heard improve the longer and louder the prayer is [NTC]. This refers to the pagan practice of naming all the gods and their titles in order to be sure to address the right God by the right name [NCBC].

2. He is referring to the Jews' reciting the Eighteen Prayers once in the morning, once in the afternoon, and once in the evening. For many these became a formalized repetition. Many other repetitious prayers were required. [Brc].

3. It refers to either Jews or pagans, whoever would think that repetition and length make prayer efficacious [EBC].

for[a] they-think[b] that because-of[c] their many-words[d] they-will-be-heard.[e]

LEXICON—a. γάρ (LN 89.23): 'for' [LN, Mor, NTC, WBC; KJV, NASB, NIV, NJB, NRSV], 'because' [LN; NET], not explicit [CEV, NAB, NLT, REB, TEV, TNT].

b. pres. act. indic. of δοκέω (LN 31.29) (BAGD 1.d. p. 202): 'to think' [BAGD, LN, Mor, WBC; all versions except NASB, REB], 'to suppose' [BAGD, LN; NASB], 'to imagine' [LN, NTC; REB], 'to believe' [BAGD, LN].

c. ἐν (LN 89.26) (BAGD III.3.a. p. 261): 'because of' [BAGD, LN, NTC, WBC, ZG; NAB, NIV, NRSV], 'because' [TEV, TNT], 'on account of' [BAGD, LN], 'by' [NET, NJB, NLT], 'for' [Mor; KJV, NASB], not explicit [CEV, NLT, REB]. It here indicates the reason [BAGD]. The Semitic background makes this instance of ἐν causal 'because of' [ZG].

d. πολυλογία (LN **33.87**) (BAGD p. 687): 'many words' [**LN**, Mor; NAB, NASB, NET, NIV, NRSV], 'using many words' [NJB], 'they use many words' [TNT], 'flow of words' [NTC], 'the abundance of (their) words' [WBC], 'much speaking' [BAGD; KJV], 'wordiness' [BAGD, ZG], 'long speaking' [LN], 'long prayers' [CEV], 'the more they say' [REB], 'repeating their words again and again' [NLT], 'their prayers are long' [TEV].

e. fut. pass. indic. of εἰσακούω (LN 24.60) (BAGD 2.a. p. 232): 'to be heard' [BAGD, Mor, NTC, WBC; all versions except CEV, NLT, TEV, TNT]; making the inference explicit: 'to be answered' [NLT]. The passive voice is also translated actively: 'their gods will hear them' [TEV], 'God will listen' [TNT], 'God like to hear' [CEV].

6:8 Therefore[a] do-not be-like[b] them,

LEXICON—a. οὖν (LN 89.50) (BAGD 1.b. p. 593): 'therefore' [BAGD, LN, Mor, NTC; KJV, NASB], 'so, consequently, then' [BAGD, LN], not explicit [WBC; all versions except KJV, NASB].

b. aorist pass. subj. of ὁμοιόω (LN 64.4) (BAGD 1. p. 567): 'to be like' [BAGD, LN, Mor, NTC, WBC; all versions except REB], 'to imitate' [REB]. This passive subjunctive form has the force of an imperative [all versions].

QUESTION—What relationship is indicated by οὖν 'therefore'?

It indicates the reason for keeping prayers short, which is that they know that God knows and will grant their needs [ICC].

for[a] your(pl) Father knows[b] of-what you(pl)-have need[c] before[d] you(pl) ask[e] him.

LEXICON—a. γάρ (LN 89.23): 'for' [LN, Mor, NTC, WBC; KJV, NASB, NET, NIV, NRSV, REB, TNT], 'because' [LN; NLT], not explicit [CEV, NAB, NJB, TEV].

b. perf. act indic. of οἶδα (LN 28.1) (BAGD 1.g. p. 556): 'to know' [BAGD, LN, Mor, NTC, WBC; all versions]. This Greek verb does not have a present tense form, so where a present tense meaning is intended, the form of the perfect tense is used.

c. χρεία (LN 57.40) (BAGD 1. p. 885): 'need' [BAGD, LN], 'necessity' [BAGD], '(to have) need of' [BAGD; KJV], 'your needs are' [REB]. The phrase 'to have need' is translated 'to need' [Mor, NTC, WBC; all versions except KJV, REB].

d. πρό (LN **67.17**) (BAGD 2. p. 702): 'before' [BAGD, LN, Mor, NTC, WBC; all versions except NLT], 'even before' [NLT].

e. aorist act. infin. of αἰτέω (LN 33.163) (BAGD p. 25): 'to ask' [BAGD, LN, Mor, NTC, WBC; all versions].

QUESTION—What relationship is indicated γάρ 'for'?

It indicates the reason they should not pray like the Gentiles, which is that God already knows their needs and will grant them what they need [WBC].

DISCOURSE UNIT: 6:9–15 [HF]. The topic is Jesus teaches the model prayer [HF], the Lord's prayer [NAB].

DISCOURSE UNIT: 6:9–13 [EBC, ICC, McN, NTC]. The topic is the Lord's Prayer [ICC, McN], model prayer [EBC], the model prayer [NTC].

6:9 Therefore^a pray^b like-this;^c

LEXICON—a. οὖν (LN 89.50) (BAGD 1.b. p. 593): 'therefore' [BAGD, LN, WBC; KJV], 'then' [LN, Mor; NASB, NRSV, TEV], 'so' [BAGD, LN; NET, NJB], 'consequently' [BAGD, LN], 'then' [BAGD, LN, NTC], not explicit [CEV, NAB, NIV, NLT, REB, TNT].

   b. pres. mid./pass. (deponent = act.) impera. of προσεύχομαι (LN 33.178): 'to pray' [all versions]. The subject of the imperative verb ὑμεῖς 'you' is stated explicitly, emphasizing the contrast between the disciples 'you' and the gentiles [BD, TNTC2].

   c. οὕτως (LN 61.10) (BAGD 2. p. 598): 'like this' [Mor; CEV, NJB, NLT], 'as follows' [BAGD, LN], 'this is how' [NTC; NAB, NIV, REB, TEV, TNT], 'after this manner' [KJV], 'in this manner' [WBC], 'in this way' [BAGD; NASB, NRSV], 'this way' [NET]. Οὕτως refers to what follows [BAGD, LN].

QUESTION—What relationship is indicated by οὖν 'therefore'?

It indicates that this prayer is connected with the warning Jesus has just given [BSC]. It indicates that the following prayer is an expression of understanding God's fatherly care spoken of in 6:8, in contrast with the practice of the Gentiles [TNTC2].

QUESTION—What is the order and the structure of the prayer?

There is some disagreement regarding whether there are six petitions or seven. Some count the last pair of petitions 'do not lead us into temptation but deliver us from the Evil One' as a single petition because of the adversative conjunction ἀλλά 'but', which would indicate one petition in two parts. The order of petitions is more important than the number [MLJ].

1. The first three petitions deal with God and his glory, the second three with our needs [Brc, BSC, EBC, ICC, NAC, NTC, Pl]. The first three also look at the *telos* or end of history [ICC]. This introductory statement shows that it is undoubtedly a pattern prayer that covers everything in principle. Jesus was telling how he himself prayed [MLJ]. The first three requests relate to the future consummation of the Kingdom and the remaining requests relate to our present lives [NIBC], though each request has at least some implication for both the present and the future [NIBC, TNTC2]. It includes a concern for physical needs in the present (petition four) and spiritual needs for the past (petition five) and the future (petition six), and expresses concern for one's own needs as well as the needs of others [NTC].

2. The first three are "you" petitions which concern God and employ third person imperatives as divine passives, indicating some degree of involvement by those who pray in the fulfillment of the prayer. The next

four petitions are "we" petitions in two sets with parallel members [WBC].

QUESTION—What is the purpose and scope of use of this prayer?

It is an outline or model, giving a pattern and principles of praying [EBC, McN, NAC, NTC, Pl, WBC], for groups as well as for individuals [NTC, Pl]. It is an outline or model to be used for its content as well as a liturgical prayer to be said verbatim. [BSC]. All the pronouns are plural, so the prayer is meant to be said by the disciples as a group [NAC, TNTC2], but it is also a model for forming individual prayer as well [TNTC2].

1. It is a prayer for Christ's disciples [EBC, ICC, NAC, NTC, TNTC2], who alone have the right to call God Father [NTC, TNTC2]. It is not for everyone since being God's child occurs only through Christ [ICC].

2. It is a prayer that can be prayed by anyone who believes in God, not just Christians [Pl].

QUESTION—What is indicated by the present tense of the verb?

It indicates that praying this prayer is to be a continual, repeated act [BSC]. It indicates that it is to be used repeatedly, though that does not mean repetitiously [NTC]. It suggests a fixed or standardized form for prayer [NCBC].

DISCOURSE UNIT: 6:9b [ICC]. The topic is the address [ICC].

Our Father[a] in the heavens,[b]

LEXICON—a. πατήρ (LN 12.12) (BAGD 3.c.a. p. 636): 'father' [LN, Mor, NTC, WBC; all versions]. This is vocative [ZG].

b. οὐρανός (LN 1.11) (BAGD 2.a. p. 594): 'heaven' [BAGD, LN]. This plural noun, literally 'the heavens', is translated as singular: 'heaven' [Mor, NTC, WBC; all versions].

QUESTION—What is implied by this mode of address?

With the address 'Father' and the qualifier 'in heaven' there is a combination of intimacy and immanence as well as of God's transcendence [BSC, EBC, NAC, NTC, TNTC2]. It reveals a dramatic new relationship made possible between God and people and reminds us of the nature of our relationship to God [NIBC]. There is a mixture of confidence in God as Father and of humility and reverence as the one in heaven [Pl]. As Father, God is concerned for the needs of his children, and as the one in heaven he is all-powerful to meet those needs [WBC]. The believer prays with confidence because God as Father is willing to hear, and with humility because God is in heaven and has the right and power to answer [NTC]. 'Father' was a term of intimacy [NCBC]. The first person plural possessive noun 'our' included his disciples but not Jesus himself, who stood in such a unique relation to God that he simply called him 'Father' [McN].

DISCOURSE UNIT: 6:9c–10 [ICC]. The topic is three 'Thou' petitions [ICC].

may- your(sg) name^a -be-held-holy,^b

LEXICON—a. ὄνομα (LN 33.126) (BAGD I.4.b. p. 571): 'name' [BAGD, LN, Mor, NTC, WBC; all versions]. The noun ὄνομα 'name' is used in the Semitic sense of representing God as he reveals himself to people [TNTC2, ZG]. It refers to the person of God himself [NIBC].

b. aorist pass. impera. of ἁγιάζω (LN **88.27**) (BAGD 3. p. 9): 'to be treated as holy' [BAGD, TNTC2, ZG], 'to be treated with high and holy regard' [NIBC], 'to be hallowed' [LN], 'to be regarded as holy, to be honored as holy' [LN]. This petition is translated 'hallowed be your name' [**LN**, NTC; KJV, NAB, NASB, NIV, NRSV], 'set apart your holy name' [WBC], 'may your name be honored' [NET, NLT], 'may your name be honored as holy' [**LN**], 'may your holy name be honored' [TEV], 'may your name be held holy' [NJB], 'may your name be hallowed' [REB], 'may your name be held in reverence' [TNT], 'may your name be kept holy' [Mor], 'help us to honor your name' [CEV], 'may you be reverenced as holy' [LN], 'may you be acknowledged as God' [LN].

QUESTION—Why does he tell them to pray regarding God's name?

There is a close association between the name and the person [WBC]. In Hebrew, 'name' represents the character and personality of someone [Brc]. 'Name' means God as he has revealed himself to the world [BSC]. It represents God's character as revealed throughout time [NIBC]. God's name represents God himself as he has revealed himself [EBC, ICC, NCBC, NTC]. The name represents God's character and nature, God himself as far as he can be known [McN, Pl]. God's name refers to God's person, character, and authority, all that he stands for [NAC]. The first two clauses of this prayer more or less follow the synagogue prayer called the *Qaddish*: 'Exalted and hallowed be his great name in the world which he created according to his will. May he let his kingdom rule in your lifetime…speedily and soon' [ICC, McN, NAC, NCBC, TNTC2, WBC]. Pious Jews would referred to God indirectly as 'The Name' in order to avoid pronouncing the name YHWH [MLJ].

QUESTION—What does it mean to pray that God's name be held holy?

All that God stands for should be honored as holy because of how perfect and good he is [NAC]. It expresses the desire that all would ultimately revere and exalt him, adore and glorify him [NTC]. It expresses a deep desire for the honor and glory of God, such that the whole world would bow in adoration before God [MLJ]. It expresses the desire that God's honor and glory would shine forth undimmed throughout his entire creation world [BSC]. It represents a desire to see God truly and properly honored in the present and a longing for the time in the future when all people will honor God truly and completely [TNTC2]. God is being asked to vindicate himself [WBC]. It is a prayer for God to be honored and glorified and acknowledged by everyone [ICC], to be treated as holy and not despised by those whom he made in his image [EBC]. It means to reverence and honor God and glorify him by obeying his commands [NCBC]. It looks to the present but its fullness is only to be reached when God's kingdom comes [McN].

6:10 may- your(sg) kingdom[a] -come,[b]

LEXICON—a. βασιλεία (LN 37.64, 1.82) (BAGD 3.g. p. 135): 'kingdom' [BAGD, LN, Mor, NTC; all versions], 'eschatological kingdom' [WBC], 'rule, reign' [LN], 'the royal reign, (or) kingdom (of God)' [BAGD]. LN 37.64 focuses more on exercise of reigning authority by the ruler, whereas 1.82 focuses on the domain within which that rule is exercised.

b. aorist act. impera. of ἔρχομαι (LN 13.50) (BAGD I.2.b. p. 311): 'to come' [BAGD; all versions], 'to appear' [BAGD], 'to become' [LN]. This petition is translated 'thy kingdom come' [NTC; KJV, NASB], 'your kingdom come' [NAB, NIV, NJB, NRSV, REB], 'may your kingdom come' [Mor; NET, TEV, TNT], 'may your kingdom come soon' [NLT], 'come and set up your kingdom' [CEV], 'bring your eschatological kingdom' [WBC]. This imperative is a third person singular imperative.

QUESTION—What is meant by the petition that God's kingdom come?

In typical Hebrew parallelism the second petition explains the first, which means that God's kingdom is a society upon earth where God's will is done as perfectly as it is done in heaven [Brc]. It refers to the growth and progress of this current kingdom that began with Christ's coming in this present era. God must intervene to restore and recreate the earth which is largely ruled by Satan and characterized by sin and misery [BSC]. It is obedience to his revealed will as expressed in his law [NTC]. It is a prayer people will submit to God's rule here and now, but also that the eventual consummation of his kingdom would finally come [EBC, MLJ]. It seeks the final establishment of God's sovereign rule over people [McN, NCBC]. It looks eschatologically to the final establishment of the Kingdom of God [TNTC2], but it also realizes that there is a sense that the Kingdom has already begun in Jesus' ministry on earth and can experience progressive growth [TNTC2]. It is a request for God to establish his full and final rule on the earth [NIBC]. It is a prayer that God's rule would prevail everywhere and that men would be obedient, both as individuals and in society [Pl]. It asks the God bring the eschatological consummation of all God's purposes in history [WBC]. It looks to the eschatological culmination of God's saving work [ICC].

may- your(sg) will[a] -be-done,[b]

LEXICON—a. θέλημα (LN **30.59**) (BAGD I.a. p. 354): 'will' [BAGD, **LN**, Mor, NTC, WBC; all versions], 'intent, purpose, plan' [LN]

b. aorist pass. (deponent = act.) impera. of γίνομαι (LN 13.48) (BAGD I.2.a. p. 158): 'to be done' [Mor, NTC; all versions except CEV], 'to be fulfilled' [BAGD, WBC]. 'to be performed' [BAGD]. This petition is translated 'thy will be done' [KJV, NASB], 'your will be done' [NAB, NIV, NJB, NRSV, REB], 'may your will be done' [LN (30.59), Mor; NET, NLT, TEV, TNT], 'so that everyone will obey you' [CEV].

QUESTION—What does this petition mean?

It refers to the accomplishment of God's purposes in the world [NAC]. It applies both to people's obedience to God's will now as well as to the future ultimate establishment of God's will on earth [EBC, NCBC, TNTC2]. It looks to the eschatological realization of heaven on earth, when God's saving purposes are fully accomplished, but also includes the ethical dimension of people doing the will of God [ICC]. It is synonymous with 'may your kingdom come' and seeks that the present evil order be overturned, the earth regenerated, and God's sovereignty expressed here on earth [WBC]. It refers to God's ultimate victory concerning the moral condition of humanity such that people obey God's commandments [BSC].

as[a] in heaven also[b] on[c] earth.[d]

LEXICON—a. ὡς (LN 64.12) (BAGD II.1. p. 897): 'as' [BAGD, LN, Mor, NTC, WBC; all versions].

b. καί (LN 89.93) (BAGD II.3. p. 393): 'also' [BAGD, LN, Mor], 'likewise' [BAGD], 'so' [BAGD, NTC], 'so also' [BAGD], not explicit [all versions]. All versions reverse the order of heaven and earth: 'in earth as it is in heaven' [KJV], 'on earth as it is in heaven' [WBC; NASB, NIV, NRSV, TEV], 'here on earth as it is in heaven' [NLT], 'on earth as in heaven' [NAB, NJB, REB, TNT], 'so that everyone on earth will obey you, as you are obeyed in heaven' [CEV]. Mor and NTC have the same order as in Greek: 'as in heaven so on earth' [NTC], 'as in heaven also on earth' [Mor].

c. ἐπί (LN 83.46) (BAGD I.1.a.a. p. 286): 'on' [BAGD, LN, Mor, NTC, WBC; all versions except KJV], 'upon' [BAGD, LN], 'in' [KJV].

d. γῆ (LN 1.39) (BAGD 5.a. p. 157): 'earth' [BAGD, LN, Mor, NTC, WBC; all versions].

QUESTION—To which petition does this phrase refer?

1. It is connected with the preceding clause [EBC, ICC, NCBC, NTC, TG, WBC; CEV, KJV, NASB, NET, NIV, NLT, NRSV, TEV]: may your will be done on earth as in heaven.

2. It is connected with the two preceding clauses [NAC]: may your kingdom come and may your will be done, both of these happening on earth as in heaven.

3. It is connected with all three preceding carefully constructed clauses [McN, TNTC2; TNT]: may your name be held holy, may your kingdom come, may your will be done; all of these happening on earth as in heaven.

DISCOURSE UNIT: 6:11–13 [ICC]. The topic is three 'we' petitions.

6:11 Give[a] us today[b] our daily/today's[c] bread;[d]

LEXICON—a. aorist act. impera. of δίδωμι (LN 57.71): 'to give' [LN, Mor, NTC, WBC; all versions]. This imperative is translated 'please give' [NET].

b. σήμερον (LN 67.205) (BAGD p. 749): 'today' [BAGD, LN, Mor, WBC; NAB, NET, NIV, NJB, REB, TEV, TNT], 'this day' [NTC; KJV, NASB, NRSV], 'for today' [CEV, NLT].

c. ἐπιούσιος (LN **67.183, 67.206**) (BAGD p. 297): 'daily' [BAGD, LN (67.183), Mor, NTC; KJV, NAB, NASB, NET, NIV, NJB, NRSV, REB], 'for the day' [TNT], 'today, for today' [LN (67.206)], not explicit [CEV, NLT, TEV]. The phrase 'give us today our daily bread' is translated 'give us today the eschatological bread that will be ours in the future' [WBC]. The word can mean 'daily', i.e., recurring on a daily basis [LN (67.183)] or 'for today', i.e., what is needed for today [LN (67.206)]. The word can mean 'necessary for existence' [BAGD (1.)], 'for today' [BAGD (2.)], 'for the following day' [BAGD (3.)], 'for the future' [BAGD (4.)].

d. ἄρτος (LN **5.1**) (BAGD 2. p. 111): 'bread' [Mor, NTC; KJV, NAB, NASB, NET, NIV, NJB, NRSV, REB, TNT], 'eschatological bread' [WBC], 'food' [BAGD, LN; CEV, NLT], 'the food we need' [**LN**; TEV]. The noun ἄρτος represents food or nourishment in general [BAGD, LN].

QUESTION—What is included in the petition for bread?

It refers to food in general [ICC, TG]. It is all food, and possibly anything else we truly need [EBC]. It refers to whatever is needed for physical life [NTC], for life on earth in his service [Pl], for the things we will need today [BD (sec. 123, p. 66), Brc]. The word bread is used figuratively and is much broader in its scope than food and includes material needs, everything necessary for life in this world [MLJ]. It refers broadly to temporal and material needs for the present day [BSC]. It refers to what is needed today or for each day [TNTC2]. It refers to what is necessary for survival, a daily ration [TNTC2]. It looks forward to the final banquet of the eschaton, but also refers to regular food [WBC].

QUESTION—What is meant by ἐπιούσιος 'daily'?

The etymology of this word is uncertain, since it occurs only in the gospels and later literature derived from them. It may be derived from ἐπὶ τὴν οὖσαν ἡμέρα meaning 'for the present day'; or from ἡ ἐπιοῦσα ἡμέρα meaning 'for the coming day' or 'for the following day', either prayed the night before or in the early morning; or from ἐπὶ οὐσία meaning 'for existence' or what is required for survival; or simply from ἐπιέναι 'to come', also referring to the coming day, whether tomorrow or the coming eschatological last day [McN, NCBC, WBC].

1. It refers specifically to this day's needs, what we need for today [BSC, EBC, ICC, McN, NIBC, NTC] or for the coming day [NAC, NCBC]. It recalls Israel's experience with the manna every day in the desert [ICC, McN, NIBC].

2. It refers to the coming day of the eschatological future, and asks for the blessing of the eschaton even now [WBC]. The focus on the needs of the day does not exclude an eschatological meaning in terms of the great feast of the final consummation [ICC, NCBC].

6:12 and^a forgive^b us our debts,^c

LEXICON—a. καί: 'and' [Mor, NTC, WBC; KJV, NAB, NASB, NET, NJB, NLT, NRSV], not explicit [CEV, NIV, REB, TEV, TNT].

b. aorist act. impera. of ἀφίημι (LN **40.8**) (BAGD 2. p. 125): 'to forgive' [**LN**, Mor, NTC, WBC; all versions], 'to cancel, remit' [BAGD], 'to pardon' [BAGD, LN]. It refers to removing the guilt resulting from wrongdoing [LN]. Luke and some mss. of Matthew use the present imperative [TNTC2]. The Aramaic perfect probably lies behind this aorist Greek tense and it could be translated in either the Greek present tense or the aorist [AAG (p. 128–9), TNTC2].

c. ὀφείλημα (LN **88.299**) (BAGD 2. p. 598): 'debt' [BAGD, Mor, NTC, TNTC2; KJV, NAB, NASB, NET, NIV, NJB, NRSV, TNT], 'sin' [BAGD, **LN**; NLT], 'offenses' [WBC], 'the wrongs' [TEV], 'the wrong' [REB]. This noun is also translated as a verb phrase: 'for doing wrong' [CEV].

QUESTION—What relationship is indicated by καί 'and'?

It indicates that the last three petitions are closely linked [BSC, EBC, NTC]. This link reminds us that life requires more than food; it requires forgiveness and deliverance as well [EBC].

QUESTION—What is meant by ὀφείλημα 'debt'?

The word ὀφείλημα usually means 'what is owed' or 'debt' and here it takes on the meaning of sin because when one sins he is indebted to God. In the parallel passage in Luke 11:4, Luke made the meaning easier for his non-Jewish readers by using the ordinary word for sin, 'forgive us our sins', although he retained the idea of debt in the following phrase 'as we forgive everyone being indebted to us' [ICC]. The word 'debt' is used figuratively for 'sins', the wrongs done against God [TH]. Most take the word to refer to sins [AAG, BSC, EBC, ICC, LN, McN, MLJ, NCBC, NTC, Pl, TG, TNTC2, WBC]. The 'debt' was due to the transgression of a duty to God [Pl]. It is the debt to God that results from sin [EBC, ICC]. The word 'debt' refers to the moral debt that is incurred as the result of sin and means the guilt resulting from offenses and transgressions [LN (88.299)]. Sins are called debts because they must be punished unless payment is made by ourselves or by another. In 6:14–15 these sins are called transgressions and trespasses and must be forgiven [NTC].

just-as^a also^b we-have-forgiven^c our debtors;^d

TEXT—Instead of ἀφήκαμεν 'we have forgiven', some manuscripts have ἀφίομεν or ἀφίεμεν 'we forgive'. GNT does not mention this alternative. CEV, KJV, NAB, TEV read 'we forgive'.

LEXICON—a. ὡς (LN 64.12) (BAGD II.4.a. p. 897): 'just as' [NLT], 'as' [BAGD, LN, Mor, NTC, WBC; all versions except NLT].

b. καί: 'also' [Mor, NTC, WBC; NASB, NIV, NRSV, TNT], not explicit [CEV, KJV, NAB, NET, NJB, NLT, REB, TEV].

c. aorist act. indic. of ἀφίημι (LN 40.8): 'to forgive' [LN, Mor, NTC, WBC; all versions].

d. ὀφειλέτης (LN **88.300**) (BAGD 2.c.a. p. 598): 'one who is guilty' [BAGD], 'sinner, offender' [LN]. The phrase τοῖς ὀφειλέταις ἡμῶν 'our debtors' [BAGD, Mor, NTC; KJV, NAB, NASB, NET, NIV, NRSV, TNT] is also translated 'those who are in debt to us' [NJB], 'those who are guilty of sin against us' [BAGD], 'those who have wronged us' [REB], 'the wrongs that others have done to us' [TEV], 'those who sin against us' [LN], 'those who have sinned against us' [NLT], 'those who offend us' [WBC], 'others' [CEV]. This refers to someone who commits sin and thus incurs a moral debt [LN].

QUESTION—What relationship is indicated by ὡς 'as'?

It indicates a correlation between our forgiving others and God's forgiving us [BSC, NTC, Pl, TG, TNTC2, WBC], though not a direct one-to-one correspondence [BSC, NTC, Pl, TNTC2]. The correspondence is not exact because God forgives so much more, yet we must cultivate a forgiving spirit if we want to ask forgiveness for ourselves [Pl]. The grounds of forgiveness is not mentioned here nor the amount/degree of forgiveness; instead it is an appeal to God as his child as evidenced by the person's forgiveness of his debtors [BSC]. We do not ask God to forgive us because we have forgiven others; rather we ask God to forgive us *in the same manner* we forgive others [TH]. We do not earn forgiveness; however, there is a certain insincerity in a prayer for forgiveness from a disciple who himself will not forgive [TNTC2]. Our forgiveness is not the basis for God's forgiving us, but God's forgiveness must be received and our forgiveness is a necessary condition for that to be able to happen [EBC, ICC, NTC]. One commentary says it has the force of 'because we also forgive', meaning either that we have done so, habitually do so, or will do so [McN].

QUESTION—What is implied about forgiveness by the aorist tense of the verb ἀφίημι 'to forgive'?

1. The aorist tense indicates that forgiving others has already occurred when we ask God to forgive us [BSC, Mor, NAC, NTC, WBC; probably NASB, NET, NIV, NJB, NLT, NRSV, REB, TNT which translate the verb in the perfect tense]: as we have forgiven our debtors. Forgiveness from God is predicated on having forgiven others [NAC]. It has the sense of already having forgiven others and thus anticipates the point of 6:14–15 and also agrees with our being forgiven at God's future eschatological judgment [WBC]. There is no exact sequential relation here between having previously forgiven others and now being forgiving ourselves [EBC, NTC, WBC].

2. Forgiveness has a habitual or timeless force [McN, NCBC, TNTC2; CEV, KJV, NAB, TEV]: as we forgive our debtors. It represents an Aramaic form that would mean 'as we now forgive our debtors' [McN, NCBC, TNTC2].

6:13 and[a] do-not lead[b] us into[c] temptation/testing,[d]

LEXICON—a. καί: 'and' [Mor, NTC, WBC; all versions except CEV, NET, TEV], not explicit [CEV, NET, TEV].

  b. aorist act. subj. of εἰσφέρω (LN **90.93**) (BAGD 2. p. 233): 'to cause to, to bring in to, to lead to' [LN], 'to bring or lead someone into (temptation)' [BAGD]. It refers to causing someone to enter into a particular event or state [LN]. The phrase μὴ εἰσενέγκῃς ἡμᾶς 'do not lead us' [**LN**; NASB, NET] is also translated 'lead us not' [NTC; KJV, NIV], 'do not put us' [NJB, REB], 'do not bring us' [Mor, WBC; NRSV, TEV, TNT], 'do not subject us' [NAB], 'keep us from' [CEV], 'don't let us yield' [NLT], 'do not cause us (to be tested)' [**LN**]. This subjunctive form functions as an imperative.

  c. εἰς (LN 84.22) (BAGD 4.a. p. 229): 'into' [BAGD, LN, Mor, NTC, WBC; KJV, NASB, NET, NIV], 'to' [NAB, NJB, NLT, NRSV, REB, TEV, TNT], not explicit [CEV].

  d. πειρασμός (LN 27.46 or 88.308) (BAGD 2.b. p. 640): 'temptation' [BAGD, LN (88.308), Mor, NTC, ZG; KJV, NASB, NET, NIV, NLT], 'being tempted' [CEV], 'testing' [LN (27.46), TNTC2, WBC], 'hard testing' [TEV], 'the time of trial' [NRSV], 'the test' [NJB, REB, TNT], 'the final test' [NAB].

QUESTION—Does πειρασμός refer to 'temptation' or 'testing'?

  1. It refers to temptation to sin [Mor, NAC, NTC, TH, ZG; CEV, KJV, NASB, NET, NIV, NLT]. It refers to being tempted by Satan [MLJ], the Evil One [NTC]. It would be attacks of sin itself or circumstances where evil is hard to resist [BSC], or a trial so difficult that we would fail [NIBC], to vulnerability to fall into sin [NAC, TNTC2]. God does not tempt but he allows times of testing for his disciples, and they should pray to be spared from such because of their weakness and vulnerability to sin [TNTC2]. The petition asks that God not permit us to come into situations that might expose us to temptation and falling into sin [NTC]. It is a request that God not let them yield to temptation [NLT].

  2. It refers to testing [Brc, EBC, ICC, McN, NIBC, Pl, WBC; NAB, NJB, NRSV, REB, TEV, TNT]. Testing means to be brought into difficulty that tries one's faithfulness and this is similar to temptation except that testing can have a positive purpose, whereas temptation does not [WBC]. It is the testing of strength, loyalty, and ability to serve a process which produces stronger character [Brc]. It is primarily the fiery trial that will accompany the end of all things [McN]. Testing can result in temptation [EBC, ICC, Pl], since in any trial there exists the possibility of doing wrong [Pl]. Testing or trial may result in succumbing to the temptation of failing the test [EBC, ICC]. The request to avoid testing concerns severe testing in which the disciples' faith would not be able to survive [WBC]. It is a plea for God's support so that the disciples would not succumb to apostasy [ICC]. It is a plea that God would not put them to the test [NJB, REB] or bring them to the test [TNT], to hard testing [TEV]. It is a plea that God

would not subject them to the final test [NAB], to the time of trial [NRSV].

but[a] deliver[b] us from evil/the-Evil-one.[c]

TEXT—At the end of this verse some manuscripts include ὅτι σοῦ ἐστιν ἡ βασιλεία καὶ ἡ δύναμις καὶ ἡ δόξα εἰς τοὺς αἰῶνας. ᾿Αμήν 'for yours is the kingdom and the power and the glory forever. Amen'. It is omitted by GNT with an A rating, indicating that the text is certain. It is included only by KJV.

LEXICON—a. ἀλλά (LN 89.125): 'but' [LN, Mor, NTC, WBC; all versions except CEV], 'and' [CEV].

  b. aorist act. impera. of ῥύομαι (LN 21.23) (BAGD p. 737): 'to deliver' [BAGD, LN, Mor, NTC, WBC; KJV, NAB, NASB, NET, NIV, NLT, TNT], 'to rescue' [BAGD, LN, ZG; NRSV], 'to save' [BAGD; NJB, REB], 'to keep safe' [TEV], 'to protect' [CEV].

  c. πονηρός (LN **12.35**, 88.110) (BAGD 2.b., 2.c. p. 691): 'the Evil One' [BAGD (2.b.), **LN** (12.35), NTC, WBC; NAB, NET, NIV, NJB, NLT, NRSV, REB, TEV], 'evil' [BAGD (2.c.), LN (88.110), Mor; CEV, KJV, NASB, TNT].

QUESTION—What relationship is indicated by ἀλλά 'but'?

This conjunction indicates that this is the second part of a single petition, a petition viewed from two different angles or sides [MLJ]. It is an adversative that connects this statement with what immediately precedes it and implies that some testing will be inevitable [WBC]. Although disciples need to be aware of their weaknesses and should pray that that they be spared from experiences in which they are vulnerable, when they do find themselves in such a situation, they must pray to be delivered from committing sin [TNTC2]. It adds a second more urgent request that whatever God may do in response to the first petition, he would protect us from Satan [NTC, WBC].

QUESTION—Is τοῦ πονηροῦ here personal or impersonal?

  1. It refers to Satan, the evil one [BSC, EBC, ICC, NTC, Pl, TH, WBC; NAB, NET, NIV, NJB, NLT, NRSV, REB, TEV]. Although we are not under the power of the Evil One, if God does not preserve us we would be easy prey to him [BSC]. It is a request to not let them be conquered by the evil one [TH].

  2. It refers to evil in general [McN, Mor, NCBC; CEV, KJV, NASB, TNT].

  3. It includes not only Satan but evil in all shapes and forms which can break our fellowship with God [MLJ].

DISCOURSE UNIT: 6:14–15 [EBC, ICC]. The topic is on forgiveness [ICC], forgiveness and prayer [EBC].

6:14 For[a] if[b] you(pl)-forgive[c] people[d] their transgressions,[e]

LEXICON—a. γάρ (LN 89.23): 'for' [LN, Mor, NTC, WBC; KJV, NASB, NET, NIV, NRSV, REB, TNT], 'yes' [NJB], not explicit [CEV, NAB, NLT, TEV].

b. ἐάν (LN 89.67) (BAGD I.1.b. p. 211) 'if' [BAGD, LN, Mor, NTC, WBC; all versions]. This preposition usually takes a verb in the subjunctive.

c. aorist act. subj. of ἀφίημι (LN 40.8) (BAGD 2. p. 125): 'to forgive' [BAGD, LN, Mor, NTC, WBC; all versions], 'to cancel, remit, pardon' [BAGD]. See this word also at v.12.

d. ἄνθρωπος (LN 9.1) (BAGD 1.a.d. p. 68): 'people' [BAGD, LN], 'other people' [WBC], 'others' [CEV, NAB, NET, NJB, NRSV, REB, TEV], 'men' [Mor, NTC; KJV, NASB, NIV, TNT], 'those (who sin against you)' [NLT].

e. παράπτωμα (LN 88.297) (BAGD 1. p. 621): 'transgression' [BAGD, LN; NAB, NASB], 'sin' [BAGD, LN, WBC; NET], 'offense' [Mor; TNT], 'failing' [NJB], 'false step' [BAGD], 'trespass' [NTC, ZG; KJV, NRSV], 'a wrong' [REB, TEV], 'lapse' [ZG]. This noun is also translated as a verb phrase: 'when they sin against you' [NIV], 'who sin against you' [NLT], 'for the wrongs they do to you' [CEV].

your(pl) heavenly[a] father will-forgive[b] also[c] you(pl).

LEXICON—a. οὐράνιος (LN 1.12) (BAGD p. 593): 'heavenly' [BAGD, LN, Mor, NTC, WBC; all versions except CEV, TEV], 'in heaven' [CEV, TEV].

b. fut. act. indic. of ἀφίημι (LN 40.8) (BAGD 2. p. 125): 'to forgive' [Mor, NTC, WBC; all versions]. This forgiveness is for transgressions against God [TH].

c. καί: 'also' [NTC, WBC; KJV, NASB, NET, NIV, NRSV, REB, TEV, TNT], not explicit [CEV, NAB, NJB, NLT], 'too' [Mor]. This clause is translated 'your heavenly Father will forgive you yours' [NJB].

QUESTION—What is the relationship of this clause to the preceding context?

It states more explicitly what is implicit in the prayer. It is not that forgiveness is conditional, but that those who receive it must respond with forgiveness [NTC, TNTC2]. The point is not that God is keeping track of whom we haven't forgiven so he can withhold his forgiveness, but rather that we should have a forgiving spirit that flows from God's forgiveness of us [NIBC]. It emphasizes the point of the fifth petition and the human involvement that must be involved in that [WBC]. The right of the believing community to pray this pray depends on their willingness to live in forgiveness [ICC].

6:15 But[a] if you(pl)- do-not -forgive people, neither[b] will- your(pl) father -forgive your(pl) trespasses.

TEXT—Some manuscripts include τὰ παραπτώματα αὐτῶν 'their trespasses' after ἀνθρώποις 'people'. It is omitted by GNT with a C rating, indicating difficulty in deciding whether or not to include it in the text. It is included by KJV, NIV, TNT.

LEXICON—a. δέ (LN 89.124) (BAGD 1.a. p. 171): 'but' [BAGD, LN, Mor, NTC, WBC; all versions].

b. οὐδέ (LN 69.7) (BAGD 2. p. 591): 'neither' [BAGD, LN, Mor, NTC, WBC; KJV, NAB, NRSV, TNT], 'not' [CEV, NET, NIV, NLT], 'then …not' [NASB, REB, TEV], 'not…either' [BAGD; NJB], 'also not' [BAGD].

DISCOURSE UNIT: 6:16–24 [NASB]. The topic is fasting, true treasure, and mammon.

DISCOURSE UNIT: 6:16–18 [BBC, EBC, GNT, ICC, McN, Mor, NTC, TG, TH, WBC; CEV, NAB, NET, NIV, NJB, NRSV, TEV]. The topic is fasting [EBC, GNT, ICC, McN, Mor, NAC, NTC, WBC; NIV, NRSV], teaching about fasting [TG, TH; NAB, TEV], Jesus teaches about fasting as a religious duty [TG], Jesus teaches about how people go without food to worship God [TH], proper fasting [NET], fasting in secret [NJB], worshipping God without eating [CEV], Jesus teaches how to fast [HF], secret fasting [BBC].

6:16 And^a whenever^b you(pl) fast,^c

LEXICON—a. δέ (LN 89.94) (BAGD 1.c. p. 171): 'and' [BAGD, LN, Mor, NTC, WBC; NASB, NLT, NRSV, TEV], 'so too' [REB], 'moreover' [KJV], not explicit [CEV, NAB, NET, NIV, NJB, TNT].

b. ὅταν (LN 67.31) (BAGD 592. p. 1.a): 'whenever' [BAGD, LN, Mor, NTC, WBC, ZG; NASB, NRSV], 'when' [LN, ZG; all versions except NASB, NRSV].

c. pres. act. subj. of νηστεύω (LN 53.65) (BAGD p. 538): 'to fast' [BAGD, LN, Mor, NTC, WBC, ZG; all versions except CEV], 'to go without eating' [CEV]. Fasting was an important feature of Jewish religious life [TNTC2]. Private fasting is probably intended here [ICC]. It is to go without food as a way to honor God and may be accompanied by meditation and prayer [TH]. The purpose for fasting is implied but not stated explicitly, which is to spend time in prayer to humbly ask God's favor [Dei (p. 106)].

QUESTION—What relationship is indicated by δέ 'and'?

It is continuative, linking what follows to what has gone before [ICC, LN, Mor, NTC, WBC; KJV, NASB, NLT, NRSV, REB, TEV]. This particle is often used in relating one teaching to another [BAGD].

QUESTION—What is the relation of this statement to the previous context?

After the digression on prayer he turns to the third example of piety following the same clause structure as 6:2–4 and 5–6, using the same key words [TNTC2, WBC]. Prayer and fasting were often combined [NTC].

do-not be^a dismal^b like^c the hypocrites,^d

LEXICON—a. pres. act. impera. of γίνομαι (LN 13.3) (BAGD II.1. p. 160): 'to be' [BAGD, LN, Mor, NTC; KJV], 'to look' [WBC; NAB, NET, NIV, NRSV, REB, TNT], 'to try to look' [CEV], 'to put on' [Mor; NASB, NJB, TEV], 'to make it obvious' [NLT], 'to become, show oneself like' [BAGD].

b. σκυθρωπός (LN **25.287**) (BAGD p. 758): 'dismal' [NRSV], 'gloomy' [BAGD, **LN**; CEV, NAB, REB, TNT], 'a gloomy face' [**LN**; NASB], 'a gloomy look' [Mor; NJB], 'somber' [NIV], 'glum' [NTC], 'sad' [LN], 'of a sad countenance' [KJV], 'a sad face' [TEV], 'with a sad, (or) sullen look' [BAGD], 'sullen' [WBC; NET]. The phrase 'do not be dismal' is translated 'don't make it obvious' [NLT].

c. ὡς: 'like' [Mor, NTC; NAB, NET, NRSV, REB, TNT], 'as' [WBC; CEV, KJV, NASB, NIV, NJB, NLT, TEV].

d. ὑποκριτής (LN **88.228**) (BAGD p. 845): 'the hypocrites' [**LN**, Mor, NTC, WBC; all versions except CEV], 'those show-offs' [CEV]. See this word at 6:2, 5; 7:5.

for[a] they-disfigure[b] their faces[c]

LEXICON—a. γάρ: 'for' [Mor, NTC, WBC; KJV, NET, NIV, NRSV, TNT], not explicit [CEV, NAB, NASB, NJB, NLT, REB, TEV].

b. pres. act. indic. of ἀφανίζω (LN **79.17**) (BAGD p. 124): 'to disfigure' [LN, Mor; KJV, NIV, NRSV, TNT], 'to make unsightly' [**LN**, NTC], 'to distort' [WBC], 'to make ugly' [LN] 'to neglect' [NAB, NASB, TEV], 'to make unsightly' [REB], 'to make unattractive' [NET], 'to render unrecognizable' [BAGD, TNTC2]. This clause is translated 'who try to look pale and disheveled' [NLT], 'they go about looking unsightly' [NJB]. This whole clause is not explicit in CEV. This verb does not carry the idea of mutilation [TH; NET].

c. πρόσωπον (LN **8.18**) (BAGD 1.a. p. 720): 'face' [BAGD, LN, Mor, NTC, WBC; KJV, NET, NIV, NRSV, REB, TNT], 'appearance' [NAB, NASB, TEV], not explicit [CEV, NJB, NLT].

QUESTION—Is there a specific cultural background to this statement?

There were various types of fasts and various motivations for fasting and this practice was a part of the fast of humiliation to express sorrow for one's sins. The use of ashes on the face could become very much a performance [NTC]. It refers to the practice of making the face dirty with ashes and a generally disheveled appearance [ICC, McN, NCBC, NIBC, WBC]. They make themselves almost unrecognizable in an effort to be recognized [ICC, NIBC].

in-order-that[a] they-might-be-seen[b] fasting by-people[c]

LEXICON—a. ὅπως (LN **89.59**): 'in order that' [NTC], 'that' [KJV], 'in order to' [LN; NASB], 'so that' [Mor, WBC; NAB, NET, REB, TEV, TNT], 'so as' [NRSV], 'so' [NLT], conflated with the infinitive [NIV, NJB], the whole clause is not explicit [CEV].

b. aorist pass. subj. of φαίνω (BAGD 2.c. p. 852): 'to be seen' [WBC; NASB], 'to show' [BAGD; NIV, NRSV], 'to let know' [NJB], 'to appear' [BAGD, Mor; KJV, NAB], 'to be obvious' [TNT]. This passive verb is also translated actively with 'people/others' as the subject: 'to see' [NTC; NET, REB, TEV]. The phrase 'in order that they might be seen' is translated 'so people will admire them' [NLT]. See this word at

   c. ἄνθρωπος (LN 9.1): 'person'. [LN]. The plural form τοῖς ἀνθρώποις: is translated 'people' [NJB], 'other people' [NTC], 'unto men' [KJV], 'to men' [Mor; TNT], 'by men' [NASB], 'men' [NIV], 'others' [WBC; NAB, NRSV], 'everybody' (as subject) [REB], 'everyone' (as subject) [TEV], 'people' (as subject) [NET, NLT].

truly[a] I-say to-you(pl), they-are-receiving-in-full[b] their reward.[c]

LEXICON—a. ἀμήν (LN 72.6) (BAGD 2. p. 45): 'truly'. See the phrase 'truly I say to you(pl)/(sg)' at 5:18, 26; 6:2, 5.

   b. pres. act. indic. of ἀπέχω (LN 57.137) (BAGD 1. p. 84): 'to receive in full' [BAGD, LN, NTC; NIV], 'to receive' [WBC; NAB, NRSV], 'to be paid in full' [LN], 'to have' [Mor; KJV, NET, NJB, TNT], 'to have in full' [NASB], 'to have already' [CEV, REB], 'to have already been paid in full' [TEV]. The phrase 'they are receiving in full their reward' is translated 'that is the only reward they will ever get' [NLT].

   c. μισθός (LN 38.14) (BAGD 2.a. p. 523): 'reward' [BAGD, LN, Mor, NTC, WBC; all versions except TEV], not explicit [TEV]. See this word at 5:12.

6:17 **But[a] (when) you(sg) (are)-fasting[b]**

LEXICON—a. δέ: 'but' [Mor; all versions except CEV, NET, TEV], 'instead' [CEV], 'by contrast' [WBC], not explicit [NET, TEV]. The personal pronoun σύ is used for emphasis, to mark contrast between the hypocrites and those whom he is addressing [Mor, NTC, WBC; KJV, NASB]: the hypocrites do that, but you should do this.

   b. pres. act. participle of νηστεύω (LN 53.65) (BAGD p. 538): 'to fast' [BAGD, LN, Mor, NTC, WBC; all versions except CEV, TEV], 'to go without food' [TEV], not explicit [CEV].

QUESTION—What relationship is indicated by δέ 'but'?

   It is an adversative [Mor, WBC; CEV, KJV, NASB, NIV, NJB, NLT, NRSV, REB, TNT].

QUESTION—What relationship is indicated by the use of the participle νηστεύων 'fasting'?

   It is temporal, indicating when the command is to be carried out [Mor, NTC, WBC; all versions except CEV]: when you are fasting, anoint your head and wash your face. This is not a command to fast, it treats the occasion when the disciples think they ought to fast [NTC].

anoint[a] your(sg) head[b] and wash[c] your(sg) face

LEXICON—a. aorist mid. impera. of ἀλείφω (LN 47.14) (BAGD 1. p. 35): 'to anoint' [BAGD, LN, Mor, NTC, WBC; KJV, NAB, NASB, REB], 'to put oil on' [NET, NIV, NRSV, TNT], 'to put scent on' [NJB], 'to comb' [CEV, NLT, TEV]. Anointing with oil was a normal cosmetic and did not denote celebration [TNTC2].

b. κεφαλή (LN 8.10) (BAGD 1.a. p. 430): 'head' [BAGD, LN, Mor, NTC, WBC; all versions except CEV, NLT, TEV], 'hair' [CEV, NLT, TEV]. This pertains to grooming or combing the hair [TH].

c. aorist mid. impera. of νίπτω (LN 47.9) (BAGD 2.b. p. 540): 'to wash' [BAGD, LN, Mor, NTC, WBC; all versions].

QUESTION—What is the cultural background to the practice of anointing?

Anointing the hair and washing the face were normal behavior, so Jesus is saying that the disciple should groom himself as he normally does [Dei, EBC, ICC, MLJ, NCBC, TNTC2], but not be ostentatious about the fasting [MLJ, NIBC, TNTC2]. Jesus is urging special attention to grooming and care to the disciple's appearance in order that there would be no indication of fasting [WBC]. Jesus is saying that they must groom themselves according to the cultural norm so as to appear joyful and content [NAC].

6:18 in-order-that[a] you(sg)- not -be-seen[b] fasting by-people[c]

LEXICON—a. ὅπως: 'that' [NTC; KJV, TNT], 'so that' [Mor, WBC; NAB, NASB, NET, NIV, NJB, NRSV, REB, TEV], 'then' [CEV, NLT].

b. aorist pass. subj. of φαίνω (BAGD 2.c. p. 852): 'to be seen' [BAGD; NASB, NRSV], 'to appear' [BAGD, Mor; KJV, NAB], 'to be obvious' [NET, NIV, TNT]. This passive verb is also translated in the active voice with people as the subject: 'to see' [REB], 'to know' [CEV, NJB, TEV], 'to suspect' [NLT]. See this word at 6:5, 16.

c. ἄνθρωπος (LN 9.1): 'person'. See this word at 6:16.

QUESTION—Does he mean that no one should know that the disciple is fasting or simply that the disciple should avoid ostentation?

As a sincere act of devotion to God alone it should be as inconspicuous as possible [NTC]. The intent is to avoid drawing attention to oneself [NCBC]. He is saying that no one should know that the disciple is fasting [EBC, NIBC, WBC].

but[a] by-your(sg) father the (one) in secret[b]

LEXICON—a. ἀλλά: 'but' [Mor; CEV, KJV, NASB, NRSV], 'but only' [NET, NIV, REB], 'only' [TEV, TNT], 'but only' [NTC, WBC], 'except' [NAB, NJB, NLT]. This whole clause is left implicit [CEV].

b. κρυφαῖος (LN **28.72**) (BAGD p. 454): 'secret' [BAGD, LN], 'hidden' [BAGD]. The phrase τῷ ἐν τῷ κρυφαίῳ 'the one in secret' is translated 'who is in secret' [Mor, WBC; NASB, NRSV, REB, TNT], 'which is in secret' [KJV], 'who is hidden' [NAB], 'who is unseen' [NIV], 'who is unseen will know' [TEV], 'who sees all that is done in secret' [NJB], 'who sees in secret' [LN, NTC; NET], 'who knows what you do in secret' [NLT].

QUESTION—What relationship is indicated by ἀλλά 'instead'?

It indicates a contrast with people [Mor, NTC, WBC; CEV, KJV, NASB, NET, NIV, NRSV, REB]: you will be seen fasting not by people but by God. It is a strong adversative; fasting is for God alone, not for other men [NTC].

and your(sg) father the-one seeing in secret will-reward[a] you(sg).

TEXT—Some manuscripts include ἐν τῷ φανερῷ 'openly' after ἀποδώσει σοι 'he will reward you' (as in 6:4). It is omitted by GNT with a B rating, indicating that the text is almost certain.

LEXICON—a. fut. act. indic. of ἀποδίδωμι (LN 38.16) (BAGD 3. p. 90): 'to reward' [NTC, WBC; CEV, KJV, NET, NIV, NJB, NLT, NRSV, TEV], 'to repay' [NAB, NASB], 'to recompense' [BAGD, LN, Mor; TNT], 'to give (you your) reward' [REB].

DISCOURSE UNIT: 6:19–7:12 [ICC, Pl]. The topic is the Christian life in its own working [Pl], social issues [ICC].

DISCOURSE UNIT: 6:19–34 [BSC, EBC, ICC, McN, NAC, NCBC, NTC, TNTC, TNTC2, WBC; NLT]. The topic God and mammon [ICC], teaching about money and possessions [NLT], wealth and worry [NCBC], single-mindedness [TNTC], the kingdom comes first [BSC], true righteousness in its attitude to wealth [McN], wealth and worry: money versus real riches [NAC], the disciple's attitude to material possessions [TNTC2], dependence on God [WBC], unlimited trust [NTC], kingdom perspectives [EBC], more on the good works Jesus demands from his followers [BSC].

DISCOURSE UNIT: 6:19–24 [BBC, EBC, ICC, Mor, NAC, WBC; NET, NIV]. The topic is treasures in heaven [NIV], lasting treasure [NET], a triad on true treasure [ICC], love of the world [MLJ], two masters [NAC], serving God rather than wealth [WBC], possessions [Mor], don't seek possessions [BBC], metaphors for unswerving loyalty to kingdom values [EBC].

DISCOURSE UNIT: 6:19–21 [EBC, GNT, HF, ICC, McN, TG, TH; CEV, NAB, NJB, NRSV, TEV]. The topic is treasure(s) in heaven [GNT; CEV, NAB], riches in heaven [TG, TH; TEV], Jesus teaches about riches in heaven [TG, TH], Jesus teaches about how people can have riches in heaven [TG], Jesus teaches about the kinds of riches we should store up [TH], true treasures [NJB], treasure(s) [EBC, McN; NRSV], lay up treasures in heaven [HF], store up treasure in heaven [ICC].

6:19 Do-not store-up[a] for-yourselves treasures[b] on[c] earth,[d]

LEXICON—a. pres. act. impera. of θησαυρίζω (LN 65.11) (BAGD 1. p. 361): 'to store up' [BAGD, WBC; all versions except KJV, NASB, NET], 'to lay up' [Mor; KJV, NASB], 'to accumulate' [NET], 'to gather' [BAGD, NTC], 'to treasure up, to keep safe' [LN].

b. θησαυρός (LN 65.10) (BAGD 2.a. p. 361): 'treasures' [Mor, NTC, WBC; all versions except REB, TEV], 'treasure' [BAGD, LN; REB], 'riches' [LN; TEV]. Expensive clothes and grain in storehouses were among the main signs of wealth during this period [BSC]. See this word at 6:20, 21.

c. ἐπί (BAGD I.1.a.a. p. 286): 'on' [BAGD, Mor, NTC; all versions except KJV, NASB], 'upon' [BAGD; KJV, NASB], 'in (this world)' [WBC].

d. γῆ (BAGD 5.a. p. 157): 'earth' [BAGD, Mor, NTC; all versions], 'this world' [WBC]. Earth is contrasted with heaven [BAGD].

QUESTION—Does the present negative imperative μὴ θησαυρίζετε imply that they should shop something that they are already doing?

1. It is a simple prohibition of the activity, not a command for the cessation of it [NTC, WBC].
2. It is a command to stop storing up treasures and make a decisive break with that practice [EBC].

where[a] clothes-moth[b] and rust[c] destroy,[d]

LEXICON—a. ὅπου (LN 83.5) (BAGD 1.a.a. p. 576): 'where' [BAGD, LN, Mor, NTC, WBC; all versions except CEV], not explicit [CEV]. This denotes a place [BAGD].

b. σής (LN **4.49**) (BAGD p. 749): 'moth' [BAGD, LN, Mor, NTC, WBC; all versions except CEV, NLT, TEV], 'moths' [CEV, NLT, TEV]. It is the larvae of the moths that eat clothing [BAGD]. The moth deposits its eggs in wool clothing and the larvae feed on the cloth [NTC].

c. βρῶσις (LN **2.62**) (BAGD 2. p. 148): 'rust' [BAGD, Mor, NTC; CEV, KJV, NASB, NET, NIV, NRSV, REB, TEV], 'rusting, tarnishing' [LN], 'decay' [NAB], 'corrosion' [BAGD, **LN**, WBC; TNT], 'woodworm' [NJB]. This noun is also translated as a verb: 'to get rusty' [NLT]. The word is literally 'eating'. Almost all take it to refer to the process of producing rust or tarnish by oxidation [LN]. However, since it is linked with 'moth', it might actually refer to a type of insect, as it does in the Septuagint of Malachi 3:11 [LN] and one version understands it to refer to an insect such as a locust, or 'woodworm' [NJB].

d. pres. act. indic. of ἀφανίζω (LN **20.46**) (BAGD p. 124): 'to destroy' [BAGD, **LN**, Mor; all versions except KJV, NLT, NRSV], 'to ruin' [BAGD, LN], 'to completely ruin' [LN], 'to corrupt' [KJV], 'to consume' [NTC; NRSV], 'to be subject to the ravages of' [WBC], 'to be eaten (by moths) and to get rusty' [NLT].

QUESTION—Why are moths and rust mentioned as the agents of destruction?

These are only two examples to show that treasures stored away on earth are insecure [WBC]. Probably moth and rust are used to represent all the agencies and processes that diminish the value of various kinds of possessions [NTC]. Although here βρῶσις has been generally understood to mean rust or corrosion, it might actually refer to anything that consumes [BAGD, EBC, ICC, LN, McN, NCBC, NIBC, TH, TNTC2, WBC]. The destruction could come from a variety of causes such as rodents, mildew, insects, decay, or even wear from use [NTC].

and where thieves[a] break-in[b] and steal;[c]

LEXICON—a. κλέπτης (LN **57.232**) (BAGD p. 434): 'thief' [BAGD, LN, Mor, NTC, WBC; all versions except TEV], 'robbers' [TEV]. Also in 6:20 [BAGD].

b. pres. act. indic. of διορύσσω (LN 19.41) (BAGD p. 199): 'to break in' [BAGD, LN, Mor, WBC; all versions except KJV], 'to break through' [BAGD, LN; KJV], 'to dig through' [BAGD, NTC]. At that time many houses had walls of dried mud or clay that could be dug through by thieves [Brc, ICC, LN, NCBC, NIBC, NTC, TH].

c. pres. act. indic. of κλέπτω (LN 57.232) (BAGD p. 434): 'to steal' [BAGD, LN, Mor, NTC, WBC; all versions].

6:20 but[a] store-up[b] for-yourselves treasures[c] in heaven,

LEXICON—a. δέ: 'but' [Mor, NTC, WBC; KJV, NAB, NASB, NET, NIV, NJB, NRSV, REB, TNT], 'instead' [CEV, TEV], not explicit [NLT].

b. pres. act. impera. of θησαυρίζω (LN **65.11**) (BAGD 2.a. p. 361): 'to store up'. See this word at 6:19.

c. θησαυρός (LN 65.10) (BAGD 2.b.a. p. 361): 'treasures'. See this word at 6:19.

QUESTION—What are the treasures in heaven?

The treasures are whatever rewards God will give for deeds of kindness on earth [EBC]. It is good works stored up before God [WBC]. Jewish people believed that kind deeds and generosity would be rewarded by treasures in heaven [Brc]. Here it refers especially to the use of material wealth to help meet the needs of other people, whether spiritual or physical [NAC]. Treasures in heaven would be actions that gain God's approval and which he will reward in the coming kingdom [NCBC]. The treasures are all the spiritual blessings promised in Scripture, including pardon, answered prayer, the hope of heaven, Christ's peace and joy, and the indwelling Holy Spirit [NTC]. It is the kingdom of God and its blessings [BSC]. It is the kingdom of God and all its blessings [ICC].

where neither clothes-moths nor rust destroy, and where thieves do-not break-in and steal;

LEXICON—The words repeat the words used in 6:19.

6:21 for[a] where[b] your(sg) treasure[c] is, there[d] will-be also your heart.[e]

LEXICON—a. γάρ: 'for' [Mor, NTC, WBC; all versions except CEV, NLT], not explicit [CEV, NLT].

b. ὅπου (LN 83.5) (BAGD 1.a.a. p. 576): 'where' [BAGD, LN, Mor, NTC; all versions except NJB, NLT], 'wherever' [LN, WBC; NJB, NLT].

c. θησαυρός (LN 65.10) (BAGD 2. p. 361) 'treasure' [BAGD, LN, Mor, NTC, WBC; all versions except TEV], 'riches' [TEV]. See this word at 6:19, 20.

d. ἐκεῖ (LN 83.2) (BAGD 1. p. 239): 'there' [BAGD, LN, Mor, NTC, WBC; all versions except CEV, TEV]. This relation is translated 'your heart will be where' [CEV, TEV].

e. καρδία (LN 26.3) (BAGD 1.b.e. p. 404): 'heart' [LN, Mor, NTC, WBC; all versions except NLT], 'heart and thoughts' [NLT]. This verse is

translated 'for your heart will always be where your riches are' [TEV],
'your heart will always be where your treasure is' [CEV].

QUESTION—What relationship is indicated by γάρ 'for'?

It introduces the reason for preferring heavenly treasure to the earthly, which
is that our hearts will then be drawn upwards [Pl].

QUESTION—What is Jesus' primary concern in this teaching?

He is concerned about what a man values and sets his heart upon the most
[Brc]. Jesus is not so much concerned about the wealth of the disciples as
with how materialism will compromise their loyalty to him [TNTC2]. What
a man ultimately aims for in his striving is his real treasure, and Christ wants
them to have the joyful recognition of God's sovereignty in their lives as
their first priority [NTC]. Jesus is concerned that a person's attention and
commitment be turned toward the will of God more than toward earthly
matters [WBC]. Allegiance to what one counts as most important determines
the direction of one's life [NAC]. He wants them to set their hearts or minds
on heaven and on fulfilling heaven's will [ICC].

QUESTION—What is meant by the figurative term 'heart'?

It is the seat of a person's thoughts and desires [BSC]. The heart is the very
center of a person's life [NTC]. It is the center of the affections and
commitments [NAC]. It is a metaphor for the center of a person's inner
being and therefore of that person's attention and commitment [WBC]. It is a
person's mind, the seat of knowledge and self-direction [ICC]. It is the
center of personality, encompassing mind, emotions and will [EBC]. It
represents the feelings, concerns, interests [TH].

DISCOURSE UNIT: 6:22–23 [EBC, GNT, HF, ICC, McN, TG, TH; CEV,
NAB, NJB, NRSV, TEV]. The topic is the light of the body [GNT, TG, TH;
NAB, TEV], Jesus teaches about the light of the body [TG], Jesus teaches about
what gives light to the body [TH], Jesus tells people about what gives them light
[TH], Jesus teaches how the eyes are like lamps for us [TH], the eyes as the
Light for the body [TG], light [EBC; CEV], the eye, the lamp of the body [NJB],
the lamp of the body [HF], the sound eye [NRSV], the single eye [McN], the
parable of the good eye [ICC].

6:22 The lamp[a] of-the body[b] is the eye.[c]

LEXICON—a. λύχνος (LN 6.104) (BAGD 2. p. 483): 'lamp' [BAGD, LN,
NTC; all versions except CEV, KJV], 'light' [Mor, WBC; KJV],
'window' [CEV]. This sentence is translated 'the eye enables a person to
see light' [WBC], 'your eyes are like a window for your body' [CEV].

b. σομα (LN 8.1): 'body' [LN]. The phrase τοῦ σώματος 'of the body'
[LN, Mor; all versions except CEV, NLT, TEV] is also translated 'for the
body' [TEV], 'for your body' [CEV, NLT], not explicit [WBC].

c. ὀφθαλμός (LN 8.23) (BAGD 1. p. 599): 'the eye' [LN, Mor, NTC,
WBC; all versions except CEV, TEV]. This singular noun is also
translated as plural: 'the eyes' [TEV], 'your eyes' [CEV].

QUESTION—What is meant by calling the eye ὁ λύχνος τοῦ σώματος 'the lamp of the body'?

1. The eye is that organ which allows light into the body [EBC, McN, NAC, NIBC, NTC, Pl, TH], and therefore the critical organ for illumination and direction [McN, NTC]. 'Light' is a metonymy for the eye itself, as it is the eye that allows light into the body; so also a person's outlook will determine the ethical or moral condition of his life [WBC]. This does not mean that the eye is the source of the light, but that it is the means by which the body receives illumination and direction [NTC]. The eye is like a window that lets light into the body [CEV]. A generous spirit enables a person to morally healthy, whereas a mean spirit blinds him to what is important [NIBC].

2. The eye is that organ which sends forth light, in keeping with the ancient understanding of vision [ICC, TNTC2]. Therefore in the next sentence the causal condition is stated in the apodosis and the effect is stated in the protasis, which is the opposite of how it is normally understood; that is, if your eye is sound it is because your whole body is full of light. The application of this teaching is that one's moral disposition depends on his spiritual state: singleness of purpose or generosity (the good eye, which sends forth light as it should) requires inner illumination (being full of light) [ICC]. The lamp enables the body (person) to find his way to a purposeful life [TNTC2].

If[a] therefore[b] your(sg) eye[c] is sound,[d]

LEXICON—a. ἐάν (LN 89.67): 'if' [LN, Mor, NTC, WBC; all versions except CEV, NLT], not explicit [CEV, NLT].

b. οὖν (LN 89.50): 'therefore' [LN, Mor, NTC, WBC; KJV, NASB], 'then' [LN; NET], 'it follows that....' [NJB], 'so' [LN; NRSV], 'when' [CEV], not explicit [NAB, NIV, NLT, REB, TEV, TNT].

c. ὀφθαλμός (LN 8.23): 'eye' [LN, Mor, NTC, WBC; NAB, NASB, NET, NJB, NLT, NRSV, TNT], not explicit [CEV]. This singular noun is also translated as plural: 'eyes' [NIV, REB, TEV]

d. ἁπλοῦς (LN **23.132, 57.107**) (BAGD p. 86): 'sound' [BAGD, **LN** (23.132), NTC, TNTC2; NAB, NET, REB, TEV], 'single' [KJV], 'good' [CEV, NIV], 'clear' [BAGD; NASB, NJB], 'healthy' [BAGD, LN (23.132), Mor; NRSV], 'pure' [NLT], 'in good condition' [TNT], 'generous' [BAGD, **LN** (57.107), WBC].

QUESTION—What is meant by the term ἁπλοῦς 'sound'?

The eye in the metaphor is medically in good condition, that is, it is clear and healthy so that it works properly. But this physical condition has a figurative application here [TH].

1. It refers to generosity [Brc, LN (57.107), McN, WBC]. It is a Semitic metaphor for not having a greedy, grudging spirit, and means that a generous spirit leads to moral health and wholeness, but a stingy spirit

keeps a person from seeing what is really important [NIBC]. A grudging and ungenerous spirit distorts a person's view of life and of others [Brc],

2. It refers to the mind's capacity to guide a person morally and spiritually [BSC, NTC; NET]. The word ἀπλοῦς means 'sound in functioning' and emphasizes the importance of setting the heart on one thing alone [BSC]. It means that the disciple must be careful as to what he pays attention to [NET].

3. It carries both meanings [ICC, MLJ, NAC, NCBC, Pl, TNTC2, WBC]. It refers to generosity, but also carries the connotation of devotion to one purpose [NCBC, WBC]. Having a good eye is parallel to storing up treasure in heaven, and having a bad eye is parallel to storing up treasure on earth, so it refers to how a person's heart condition is expressed through generosity [NAC]. The statement contains a double-entendre with the meaning of both loyalty to God and freedom from materialism resulting in generosity. It reinforces the message of undivided loyalty to God. A person whose life is well-illuminated can see his direction in life sufficiently to live a life with purpose [TNTC2]. It contrasts clear vision that sees things the way they really are with double or blurred vision, and emphasizes the fact that the treasures of this world can grip the mind and hearts of believers [MLJ]. The eye of the soul is that moral quality that enables a person to see and understand the true value of things, and if the 'eye' is free from distortion there will be liberality [Pl].

your(sg) whole[a] body[b] will-be full-of-light;[c]

LEXICON—a. ὅλος (LN 63.1) (BAGD 2.a. p. 564): 'whole' [LN, Mor, NTC, WBC; all versions except CEV, NLT], not explicit [CEV, NLT].

b. σῶμα (LN 8.1) (BAGD 1.b. p. 799): 'body' [LN, Mor, NTC; all versions except CEV, NLT], 'soul' [NLT], 'person' [WBC]. The phrase ὅλον τὸ σῶμά σου 'your whole body' is translated 'you' [CEV].

c. φωτεινός (LN **14.51**) (BAGD p. 872): 'full of light' [BAGD, **LN**, WBC; KJV, NASB, NET, NIV, NRSV, TEV, TNT], 'filled with light' [KJV, NAB, NJB], 'illuminated' [BAGD, Mor], 'illumined' [NTC], 'well lighted' [LN]. This adjective is also translated as a verb phrase: 'to have light' [REB]. The whole clause is translated 'you have all the light you need' [CEV], 'a pure eye lets sunshine into your soul' [NLT].

QUESTION—How can this figure of speech be expressed without using figurative language and making implicit information explicit?

It may be necessary to speak of 'having light inside' or to indicate the absence of darkness, 'your whole body will have no darkness in it' [LN (14.51)]. Here he means the person will be able to move about freely and without suffering an accident [BSC]. It means that the person will be guided both morally and spiritually to keep in contact with God [NTC]. It means knowing clearly what one is doing in every aspect of life [TH].

6:23 but[a] if[b] your(sg) eye[c] is bad,[d]

LEXICON—a. δέ: 'but' [Mor, NTC, WBC; all versions except REB], not explicit [REB].

b. ἐάν: 'if' [Mor, NTC, WBC; all versions except CEV, NLT], 'when' [CEV], not explicit [NLT].

c. ὀφθαλμός (LN 8.23) (BAGD 1. p. 599): 'eye' [BAGD, LN, Mor, NTC, WBC; KJV, NASB, NJB, NRSV, TNT], 'eyes' [CEV, NIV, REB, TEV], 'an evil eye' [BAGD; NLT]; 'one that looks with envy or jealousy upon other people' [BAGD].

d. πονηρός (LN 88.110, 23.149, 65.27) (BAGD 1.a.α. p. 690): 'bad' [LN (65.27); CEV, NAB, NASB, NET, NIV, REB], 'no good' [TEV], 'in bad condition' [TNT], 'in poor condition' [BAGD, NTC], 'sick' (in the physical sense of the eye) [BAGD], 'diseased' [LN (23.149); NJB], 'unhealthy' [NRSV], 'evil' [LN (88.110), Mor; KJV, NLT], 'covetous' [WBC].

your(sg) whole[a] body will-be full-of-darkness.[b]

LEXICON—a. ὅλον: 'whole' [Mor, NTC, WBC; all versions except CEV, NLT, TEV], 'everything' [CEV], not explicit [NLT, TEV]. The phrase ὅλον τὸ σῶμά σου 'your whole body' is translated 'you' [NLT].

b. σκοτεινός (LN 14.54) (BAGD p. 757) 'full of darkness' [WBC; KJV, NASB, NET, NIV, NRSV, TNT], 'dark' [BAGD, LN, NTC; CEV], 'darkened' [Mor]. This adjective is translated as a prepositional phrase: 'in darkness' [LN; NAB, TEV], 'into darkness' [NLT]; as a noun: 'darkness' [NJB, REB].

QUESTION—What is the meaning of this figure of speech?

Covetousness is the source of moral or ethical darkness or evil [WBC]. Inordinate yearning for earthly wealth will cause a person to fail to promote God's glory, which is what his goal should have been [NTC]. It means not what one is doing in any aspect of life [TH]. If a man's moral self-awareness or conscience has gone bad, the resulting darkness in his life is great [McN]. The presence of divine illumination within a person will be evidenced outwardly by generosity, and a lack of such illumination within will show itself outwardly through stinginess [ICC]. Avarice can result in distortion of moral perspective, as can prejudice or superstition [Pl].

If[a] therefore[b] the light[c] in[d] you(sg) is darkness,[e]

LEXICON—a. εἰ (LN 89.65) (BAGD I.1.a., VI.10. p. 219): 'if' [BAGD (I.1.a.), LN, Mor, NTC, WBC; all versions]. 'if, therefore' [BAGD (VI.10.)].

b. οὖν (LN 89.50): 'therefore' [LN, Mor, WBC; KJV, NASB], 'then' [LN, NTC; NET, NIV, NJB, REB], 'so' [LN; TEV], 'and' [TNT], not explicit [CEV, NAB, NLT].

c. φῶς (LN 14.36) (BAGD 1.b.a. p. 872): 'light' [BAGD, LN, Mor; all versions], 'the very light' [NTC], 'the very organ that should bring you light' [WBC], 'the only light' [REB].

d. ἐν: 'in'. The phrase τὸ ἐν σοί 'the (light) in you' is translated 'that is in you' [Mor; KJV, NASB], 'in you' [Mor, NTC; NAB, NET, NRSV, TEV, TNT], 'within you' [NIV], 'inside you' [CEV, NJB], 'you have' [REB], 'the light you think you have' [NLT], not explicit [WBC].

e. σκότος (LN 14.53) (BAGD 2.b. p. 758): 'darkness' [BAGD, LN, Mor, NTC; all versions except CEV, NJB], 'dark' [CEV], 'the source of darkness' [WBC]. Instead of saying that 'the light is darkness', some translate to show that the light is not literally equated with darkness: 'if then, the light inside you is darkened' [NJB], 'if the light you think you have is really darkness' [NLT], 'if then the only light you have is darkness' [REB]. This word is used of religious and moral darkness resulting from sin [BAGD].

QUESTION—What is meant by the image of light being darkness?

It is describing the condition of having darkness where there should be light [TH]. If that moral capacity within a person that should lead him to good actually leads him to evil, he is truly perverse [NAC]. If the inner moral capacity for generosity becomes affected by covetousness the result is a personal inner darkness or evil [WBC]. If the moral and spiritual capacity to bring the inner life into contact with the heavenly Father is obscured by sin, the disciple will fail to achieve what should be his chief goal, which is to glorify God [NTC]. If one's direction in life is not fixed on obedience to God, that person will be plunged into spiritual darkness or evil [NCBC]. It is a way of saying that a person's inner character is bad [ICC]. If the opportunity for inner illumination has gone without effect the soul will truly be in moral darkness [Pl]. Being morally darkened is made even more terrible by failing to recognize the condition for what it is [EBC].

how-great[a] (is) the darkness.[b]

LEXICON—a. πόσος (LN **78.13**) (BAGD 1. p. 694): 'how great' [BAGD, **LN**, Mor, NTC, WBC; KJV, NAB, NASB, NET, NIV, NRSV, TNT], 'how deep (will be)' [NLT], 'what (darkness that will be)' [NJB], 'how great (a darkness that will be)' [REB], 'how terribly (dark it will be)' [TEV] 'how, very, how much, intense, severe' [LN].

b. σκότος (LN 14.53) (BAGD 2.b. p. 758): 'darkness' [BAGD, LN, Mor, NTC, WBC; all versions except CEV, TEV], 'dark' [TEV]. This phrase is translated 'you surely are in the dark' [CEV]. This word is used here figuratively of religious and moral darkness [BAGD].

DISCOURSE UNIT: 6:24–34 [TG, TH; TEV]. The topic is God and possessions [TG, TH; TEV], Jesus teaches about God and money [TG, TH], people cannot serve God and riches [TG], Jesus teaches about God and the things we can own [TH], people cannot serve God and money too [TH].

DISCOURSE UNIT: 6:24 [EBC, GNT, HF, ICC, McN; CEV, NAB, NJB, NRSV]. The topic is God and Mammon [GNT], God and money [NAB, NJB], money [CEV], serving two masters [NRSV], you cannot serve God and mammon [HF], the single service [McN], second parable: the two masters [ICC], slavery [EBC].

6:24 No-one[a] is-able[b] to-serve[c] two masters;[d]

LEXICON—a. οὐδείς (LN **92.23**) (BAGD 2.a. p. 591): 'no one' [BAGD, LN, Mor, NTC; all versions except CEV, KJV, TEV], 'no man' [KJV], 'nobody' [BAGD], '(impossible for) anyone' [WBC], 'you cannot' [CEV, TEV].

b. pres. act. indic. of δύναμαι (LN **74.5**): 'is able to' [LN; NET], 'can' [**LN**, Mor, NTC; all versions except NET]. The phrase 'no one is able' is translated 'it is impossible' [WBC].

c. pres. act. infin. of δουλεύω (LN **35.27**) (BAGD p. 205): 'to serve' [LN, NTC; all versions except CEV, NJB, TEV], 'to be the slave of' [Mor, TNTC2, WBC; CEV, NJB, TEV].

d. κύριος (LN **37.51**) (BAGD 1.a.β. p. 459): 'master' [BAGD, **LN**, NTC, WBC; all versions], 'owner' [BAGD, Mor] 'ruler, lord' [LN].

QUESTION—What is the cultural background of this statement?

To be a slave to a master meant to be absolutely owned by the master, the slave having no personal rights or any time that was his own [Brc]. Serving one person implies not being available for the other [BSC]. While it is not impossible to have two employers, it is impossible to have two owners [TNTC2]. Here the verb 'serve' indicates the realm of the will and action [MLJ]. Although unusual, it was possible for a slave to be owned by two masters, as in the case of two brothers, but in such a case he could not do justice to either one [WBC].

for[a] either[b] he-will-hate[c] the one[d] and he-will-love[e] the other,[f]

LEXICON—a. γάρ 'for' [Mor, NTC, WBC; KJV, NASB, NET, NLT, NRSV, REB, TNT], not explicit [CEV, NAB, NIV, NJB, TEV].

b. ἤ...ἤ (LN **89.140**) (BAGD 1.b. p. 342): '(disjunctive, ἤ...ἤ) either...or' [BAGD]; 'either' [Mor, NTC, WBC; all versions except CEV, NLT, TEV], not explicit [CEV, NLT, TEV]. The repetition of ἤ indicates a double alternative 'either...or' [LN].

c. fut. act. indic. of μισέω (LN **88.198**) (BAGD 1. p. 522): 'to hate' [BAGD, LN, Mor, NTC; all versions except CEV], 'to neglect' [WBC], not explicit [CEV]. This word is used here in a comparative sense to indicate displacement by a higher loyalty [TNTC2]. See this word also at 5:43.

d. εἷς (LN **92.22**) (BAGD 5.d. p. 232): 'one' [BAGD, LN, Mor, NTC, WBC; all versions except NJB, REB], 'the first' [NJB, REB].

e. fut. act. indic. of ἀγαπάω (LN **25.43**) (BAGD 1.a.α. p. 4): 'to love' [BAGD, LN, Mor, NTC; all versions except CEV], 'to like' [CEV], 'to prefer' [WBC].

f. ἕτερος (LN **58.37**) (BAGD 1.a. p. 315): 'the other' [BAGD, LN, Mor, NTC, WBC; all versions except KJV], 'the second' [NJB, REB].

QUESTION—What does he mean by the term μισέω 'hate'?

1. It is used comparatively [ICC, McN, NAC, NCBC, TH, WBC; CEV].
   'You will like one more than the other' [CEV]. As in Luke 14:26, Jesus is
   describing a disciple's need for undivided and absolute commitment
   [NCBC, WBC]. In Semitic usage 'love' and 'hate' often mean 'to choose'
   or 'not choose' [NAC]. 'Love' and 'hate' refer not so much to emotions
   but to faithful serving: to love means to serve [ICC]. Hate is not an
   emotion but refers to a decision to be more loyal to one [TH]. Here 'to
   hate' means to be indifferent toward or not concerned for [NCBC].
2. It is used absolutely. In times of crisis a person will choose what matters
   most; the allegiance that wins will be the master and object of worship,
   and the other will be hated and even betrayed just as Judas betrayed Jesus
   [NTC].

or he-will-be-devoted-to^a one^b and he-will-despise^c the other;^d

LEXICON—a. fut. mid. indic. of αντέχω (LN **34.24**) (BAGD 1. p. 7): 'to be
   devoted to' [BAGD, NTC; NAB, NET, NIV, NLT, NRSV, REB], 'to be
   attached to' [NJB, TNT], 'to be loyal to' [CEV, TEV], 'to pay attention
   to' [WBC], 'to hold to' [Mor; KJV, NASB], 'to adhere to' [LN].
   b. εἷς (LN 92.22): 'the one' [LN, Mor, WBC; KJV, NET, NIV, NRSV],
   'one' [NTC; CEV, NAB, NASB, NLT, TEV, TNT], 'the first' [NJB,
   REB].
   c. fut. act. indic. of καταφρονέω (LN 88.192) (BAGD 1. p. 420): 'to
   despise' [BAGD, LN, Mor; all versions except CEV], 'to look down on'
   [BAGD, LN, NTC], 'to scorn, to treat with contempt' [BAGD], 'to
   disregard' [WBC], not explicit [CEV].
   d. ἕτερος (LN 58.37): 'the other' [LN, Mor, NTC, WBC; all versions except
   NJB, REB], 'the second' [NJB, REB].

QUESTION—What is meant by the verb καταφρονέω 'despise'?

1. It has the sense of 'disregard', which is milder than true hatred [WBC].
2. Love and loyalty toward one object of supreme devotion will lead to
   hatred and even betrayal of other contenders [NTC]. It is translated
   comparatively: 'You will be more loyal to one than the other' [CEV].

you(pl)-are- not -able^a to-serve^b God and^c money.^d

LEXICON—a. pres. act. indic. of δύναμαι (LN 74.5) (BAGD 1.a. p. 207):
   'can' [BAGD, LN, Mor, NTC, WBC; all versions except NET], 'to be
   able to' [BAGD, LN; NET], 'to be able to do or to experience something'
   [LN].
   b. pres. act. infin. of δουλεύω (LN 35.27) (BAGD 2.a. p. 205): 'to serve'
   [BAGD, LN, NTC; CEV, KJV, NAB, NASB, NET, NIV, NLT, NRSV,
   REB, TEV, TNT], 'to be the slave (both) of' [NJB], 'to be a slave to'
   [Mor, WBC].
   c. καί: 'and' The phrase 'God and' is translated 'both God and' [CEV, NIV,
   NLT, TEV], 'to God and to' [Mor, WBC]. The phrase 'you are not able to

serve God and money' is translated 'You must serve God or money; you
cannot serve both' [Knox (in NIBC)].
  d. μαμωνᾶς (LN 57.34) (BAGD p. 490): 'money' [WBC; CEV, NIV, NJB,
  NLT, REB, TEV], 'mammon' [BAGD, Mor, NTC; KJV, NAB, NASB],
  'wealth' [BAGD; NRSV, TNT], 'worldly wealth' [LN], 'riches' [LN],
  'possessions' [NET].
QUESTION—What is meant by μαμωνᾶς 'money'?
  This Aramaic term for wealth or property is personified as a potential master
  [EBC, ICC, McN, NTC, TH, WBC]. This Aramaic word has senses of
  'profit' and 'money' [AAG (p. 139), TH] and 'wealth' [TH]. In the Aramaic
  Targums μαμωνᾶς implied dishonesty and the selfish exploitation of another
  person, and hence it came to have a derogatory sense [NIBC]. It can refer to
  any material possession, even legitimate ones, which can rival our loyalty to
  God, thus implies the principle of materialism [TNTC2].

DISCOURSE UNIT: 6:25–34 [BBC, EBC, GNT, HF, ICC, McN, MLJ, Mor,
NAC, NIBC, TNTC2, WBC; CEV, NASB, NET, NIV, NJB, NRSV, REB]. The
topic is care and anxiety [GNT], earthly anxiety [McN], anxiety and trust [Mor],
worry [CEV], do not worry [HF, NET, NIV, NRSV], the cure for anxiety
[NASB], trust in Providence [NJB], anxiety [TNTC2], anxiety and care with
respect to the world and affairs [MLJ], the futility of worry [NAC], the disciple
and anxiety [WBC], don't worry about possessions [BBC], encouragement: 'do
not worry' [ICC], uncompromised trust [EBC].

DISCOURSE UNIT: 6:25 [EBC; NAB]. The topic is uncompromised trust
[EBC], dependence on God [NAB].

6:25 Therefore[a] I-say[b] to-you(pl),
LEXICON—a. διά τοῦτο (LN 89.26) (BAGD B.II.2. p. 181): 'therefore'
  [BAGD, NTC; KJV, NAB, NIV, NRSV, TNT], 'for this reason' [Mor;
  NASB], 'that is why' [NJB], 'this is why' [REB, TEV], 'because of this'
  [LN; NET], 'so' [NLT], 'with this in view' [WBC], not explicit [CEV].
  b. pres. act. indic. of λέγω (LN 33.69) (BAGD II.1.c. p. 469): 'to say to'
  [LN, Mor; KJV, NASB, NET], 'to tell' [LN; all versions except KJV,
  NASB, NET].
QUESTION—What relationship is indicated by διά τοῦτο 'therefore'?
  He is continuing and expanding his previous theme of not depending on
  earthly goods [BSC]. It introduces a logical conclusion based on the premise
  in 6:24 that serving God rules out serving money [NIBC, Pl], that followers
  of Christ should not be anxiously concerned about food and clothing [EBC,
  NIBC], or that they should stop worrying about worldly wealth and devote
  their affections and energies to God [Pl]. It draws a conclusion from
  6:19–24, and especially 6:24, which is that total allegiance to God means
  that one should not be worried about material needs [WBC]. Since earthly
  treasures do not satisfy and valuing them implies that the pleasures of heaven
  will be lost (6:19–24), and since earthly wealth blinds one's vision

(6:22–23), and since one must choose between God and wealth (6:24), disciples should therefore not set their hearts on earthly things [NTC]. It draws a conclusion from 6:19–24 and introduces the answer to a potential question about how a disciple is to be provided for if he does not seek after material things [ICC]. It draws a conclusion from the previous passage, especially 6:21 [TH].

do-not worry[a] (about) your(pl) life[b]

LEXICON—a. pres. act. impera. of μεριμνάω (LN 25.225) (BAGD 1. p. 505): 'to worry (about)' [CEV, NAB, NET, NIV, NLT, NRSV, TEV], 'to have anxiety, to be (unduly) concerned' [BAGD], 'to be filled with anxiety' [WBC], 'to be anxious (about/for)' [BAGD, LN, Mor, NTC; NASB, REB, TNT], 'to take thought (for)' [KJV]. See this word at 6:27, 28, 31, 34.

   b. ψυχή (LN 23.88) (BAGD 1.a.b. p. 893): 'life' [LN, Mor, NTC, WBC; CEV, KJV, NAB, NASB, NET, NIV, NRSV]. It has the connotation of earthly life as prolonged by nourishment [BAGD]: '(food and drink) to keep you alive' [REB, TNT], '(food and drink) you need in order to stay alive' [TEV], 'everyday life' [NLT].

QUESTION—Why is this imperative in the present tense?

   It is a prohibition against worry as well as a command to stop worrying if they are doing so [NTC].

QUESTION—What is the intent of this prohibition against worry?

   This is not meant as comfort for the poor but continues the theme of not depending on earthly goods [BSC]. He is concerned about their state of mind and their priorities, but he is not ruling out wise concern and provision for the future [TNTC2]. He is concerned that a life consumed by anxiety would distract from their absolute discipleship [WBC]. He does not want confused priorities to distract the [NTC]. They should give up trying to serve wealth because it only causes anxiety [McN]. Just as one must chose to serve either God or money, one must choose to be sustained by anxiety or faith [ICC].

what you(pl)-might-eat,[a] or what you(pl)-might-drink[b]

TEXT—The words ἢ τί πίητε 'or what you might drink' are included in brackets by GNT with a C rating, indicating difficulty in deciding whether or not to include them in the text. They are omitted only by NJB. They are included in brackets by Mor, WBC; NAB, TNT.

LEXICON—a. aorist act. subj. of ἐσθίω (LN 23.1) (BAGD 1.a. p. 312): 'to eat' [BAGD, LN, Mor, NTC, WBC; KJV, NAB, NASB, NET, NIV, NJB, NRSV]. The phrase 'what you might eat' is translated 'about having something to eat' [CEV], 'whether you have enough food' [NLT], 'about food' [REB, TEV, TNT].

   b. aorist act. subj. of πίνω (LN 23.34) (BAGD 1. p. 658): 'to drink' [BAGD, LN, Mor, NTC, WBC; KJV, NAB, NASB, NET, NIV, NRSV], not explicit [NJB]. The phrase 'what you might drink' is translated 'about having something to drink' [CEV], 'whether you have enough drink' [NLT], 'about drink' [REB, TEV, TNT].

nor[a] (about) your(sg) body[b], what you(pl)-might-wear.[c]

LEXICON—a. μηδέ (LN 69.7, 69.8) (BAGD 1.a. p. 517): 'nor yet' [KJV], 'or' [CEV, NAB, NET, NIV, NRSV, TEV], 'nor' [LN, Mor, NTC; NASB, NJB, TNT], 'and' [REB], 'or' [WBC], 'and not, but not, nor' [BAGD].

  b. σῶμα (LN 8.1) (BAGD 1.b. p. 799): 'body' [LN], 'the living body (with and in contrast to ψυχή)' [BAGD]. The dative phrase τῷ σώματι 'the body' is translated 'for your body' [Mor; KJV, NASB], 'about your body' [NTC; NAB, NIV, NJB, NRSV], 'your body' [WBC; REB, TEV, TNT], not explicit [CEV, NLT].

  c. aorist mid. subj. of ἐνδύω (LN 49.1) (BAGD 2.a. p. 264): 'to wear' [BAGD, NTC; NAB, NET, NIV, NJB, NRSV], 'to put on' [BAGD, LN, Mor; KJV, NASB], 'to put on, to clothe' [LN], 'to clothe oneself in' [BAGD, WBC]. The phrase 'what you might wear' is translated 'about having something to wear' [CEV], 'whether you have enough clothes' [NLT]. 'about clothes to cover' [REB], 'about clothes for' [TEV, TNT].

Is not[a] life[b] more-than[c] food[d]

LEXICON—a. οὐχί (LN 69.12) (BAGD 3. p. 598): 'not' [Mor, NTC, WBC; CEV, KJV, NAB, NASB, NET, NIV, NRSV, TNT]. This word marks an affirmative response that is more emphatic than is expected with οὐ [LN, TH]. The phrase οὐχὶ...ἐστιν is translated 'isn't there' [NET], 'doesn't life consist of' [NLT], 'after all, isn't (life more)' [TEV]. This clause translated as statement rather than as a rhetorical question: 'surely life is more than food' [NJB, REB].

  b. ψυχή (LN 23.88): 'life' [LN; all versions except KJV], 'the life' [Mor, NTC, WBC; KJV].

  c. πλείων (LN 78.28) (BAGD II.2.c. p. 689): 'more than' [BAGD, LN, Mor; all versions except NET, NIV, TEV], 'more important than' [BAGD, NTC; NIV], 'more significant than' [WBC], 'worth more than' [TEV], 'more to (life) than' [NET].

  d. τροφή (LN 5.1) (BAGD 1. p. 827): 'food' [BAGD, LN, Mor, NTC; all versions except KJV], 'meat' [KJV], 'nourishment' [BAGD, WBC].

and[a] the body[b] (more-than)[c] clothing?[d]

LEXICON—a. καί 'and' [Mor, NTC, WBC; KJV, NAB, NASB, NET, NIV, NJB, NLT, NRSV], 'and isn't' [TEV], 'or' [CEV], not explicit [REB, TNT].

  b. τὸ σῶμα: 'the body' [Mor, NTC, WBC; all versions except CEV, NLT], not explicit [CEV, NLT]

  c. There is no lexical entry for 'more than' in the Greek text, it is implied, being carried forward from the previous phrase. It is represented in translation as 'than' [Mor; KJV, NASB, NET], 'more than' [NAB, NJB,

NRSV, REB, TNT], 'more important than' [NTC; NIV], 'more significant than' [WBC], 'worth more than' [TEV], not explicit [CEV, NLT].
  d. ἔνδυμα (LN 6.162) (BAGD 1. p. 263): 'clothing' [BAGD, LN, Mor, WBC; CEV, NAB, NASB, NET, NJB, NRSV], 'clothes' [NTC; NIV, NLT, REB, TEV, TNT], 'raiment' [KJV]. See this word at 6:28.
QUESTION—What is the point of this rhetorical question?
  It makes an emphatic statement comparing the greater value of life and the body to food and clothing [TH]. Many people live life only concerned about eating, drinking, the body, and clothing [MLJ]. Jesus is saying that sufficient food and clothing are not enough for life, because you can die even with enough food and clothes [BSC]. It is an argument from lesser to greater: life is greater and more important than those things which sustain it, and since God provides the greater, he will certainly provide the lesser also [EBC, ICC, NTC, Pl, WBC].

DISCOURSE UNIT: 6:26–30 [EBC]. The topic is the examples of uncompromised trust.

DISCOURSE UNIT: 6:26–27 [EBC]. The topic is life and food.

6:26 **Look[a] at the birds[b] of-the air[c]**
LEXICON—a. aorist act. impera. of ἐμβλέπω (LN 30.1) (BAGD 1., 2. p. 254): 'to look at' [BAGD (1.), Mor, NTC; all versions except KJV], 'to behold' [KJV], 'to think about' [LN], 'to consider' [BAGD (2.), **LN**], 'to consider well' [WBC]. It is possible to regard ἐμβλέπω in Matthew 6:26 as involving a combination of seeing (see LN 24.9) plus intellectual activity [LN]. This is not a command to look up at the birds, but it is a way of drawing attention to the subject of birds to be used in an illustration [TH].
  b. πετεινός (LN 4.38) (BAGD p. 654): 'bird' [BAGD, LN, Mor, NTC, WBC; all versions except KJV], 'fowl' [KJV].
  c. οὐρανός (LN 1.5, **4.41**) (BAGD p. 654): 'sky' [LN]. The phrase τοῦ οὐρανοῦ is translated 'of the air' [Mor, NTC; KJV, NASB, NIV, NRSV, TNT], 'in the sky' [CEV, NAB, NJB, REB], 'of the sky' [WBC; NET], 'wild (birds)' [**LN**] not explicit [NLT, TEV]. The Greek expression τὰ πετεινὰ τοῦ οὐρανοῦ 'the birds of the sky' designates wild birds in contrast with domestic fowl, such as chickens. In translating 'the birds of the sky', one may wish to use a general designation for 'all wild birds' [LN].

that/for[a] they- do-not -sow[b] nor[c] do-they-reap[d]
LEXICON—a. ὅτι: 'that' [Mor; NASB], 'for' [KJV], not explicit [NTC, WBC; all versions except KJV, NASB].
  b. pres. act. indic. of σπείρω (LN 43.6) (BAGD 1.a.α. p. 761): 'to sow' [BAGD, LN, Mor, NTC, WBC; all versions except CEV, NLT, TEV], 'to plant' [CEV, NLT, TEV]. The implied object is 'seeds' [TH].

c. οὐδέ (LN 69.7) (BAGD 1. p. 591): 'nor' [LN, Mor, NTC, WBC; NRSV], 'neither' [LN; KJV, NASB], 'or' [CEV, NAB, NET, NIV, NJB, NLT, TNT], 'and' [REB], 'and not' [LN], not explicit [TEV].

d. pres. act. indic. of θερίζω (LN 43.14) (BAGD 1. p. 359): 'to reap' [BAGD, LN, Mor, NTC, WBC; KJV, NAB, NASB, NIV, NJB, NRSV, REB, TNT], 'to harvest' [BAGD, LN; CEV, NET, NLT], 'to gather a harvest' [TEV]. The implied object is 'crops' [TH].

nor^a do-they-gather^b into barns,^c

LEXICON—a. οὐδέ (LN **69.7**): 'nor' [LN, Mor; KJV, NASB, NRSV, TNT], 'nothing' [NAB], 'or' [NET, NIV, NJB, NLT], 'and' [REB, TEV], 'even' [CEV].

b. pres. act. indic. of συνάγω (LN 15.125) (BAGD 1. p. 782): 'to gather' [BAGD, LN, Mor, NTC, WBC; KJV, NAB, NASB, NET, NJB, NRSV, TNT], 'to store away' [NIV], 'to store' [REB], 'to store grain' [CEV], 'to put it' [TEV], 'to put food into' [NLT]. The implied object is 'crops' or 'what has been reaped' [TH].

c. ἀποθήκη (LN 7.25) (BAGD p. 91): 'barn' [BAGD, LN, Mor, NTC; all versions], 'storehouse' [BAGD, LN, WBC].

and-yet^a your(pl) heavenly father feeds^b them.

LEXICON—a. καί (LN 91.12) (BAGD I.2.g. p. 392): 'and yet' [BAGD, Mor; NASB, NET, NIV, NRSV], 'yet' [LN, NTC, WBC; CEV, KJV, NAB, NJB, REB, TEV, TNT], 'and in spite of that, nevertheless' [BAGD], 'because' [NLT].

b. pres. act. indic. of τρέφω (LN 23.6) (BAGD 1. p. 825): 'to feed' [BAGD, Mor, NTC; all versions except CEV, TEV], 'to provide with food' [BAGD, LN, WBC], 'to nourish, support' [BAGD], 'to take care of' [CEV, TEV].

Are- not^a you(pl)-worth^b much-more-than^c they?^d

LEXICON—a. οὐ (LN 69.11) (BAGD 4.c. p. 590): 'not' [BAGD; all versions except NLT]. This word is used in questions expecting an affirmative answer [BAGD, LN]: 'are ye not' [KJV], 'are not you' [CEV, NAB], 'are you not' [Mor, WBC; NASB, NIV, NJB, NRSV, REB, TNT], 'you are...are you not' [NTC], 'aren't you' [NET, TEV], 'and you are far more valuable to him than they are' [NLT].

b. pres. act. indic. of διαφέρω (LN **65.6**) (BAGD 2.b. p. 190): 'to be worth (more than)' [BAGD, LN, Mor, WBC; CEV, NASB, NJB, REB, TEV], 'to be superior to' [BAGD], 'to be better (than)' [KJV], 'to be (more) important (than)' [NAB], 'to be (more) valuable (than)' [**LN**; NET, NIV, NLT, TNT], 'to be of (more) value (than)' [NTC; NRSV].

c. μᾶλλον (LN 78.28) (BAGD 1. p. 489): 'much' [ZG; KJV, NASB, NIV, NJB, TEV, TNT], 'more' [BAGD, LN], not explicit [Mor, WBC; CEV, NAB, NET, NRSV, REB]. Μᾶλλον here is pleonastic 'greatly', rather than comparative [McN].

d. αὐτῶν: 'they' [NTC, WBC; KJV, NAB, NASB, NIV, NRSV, TNT], 'they are' [Mor; NET, NJB, NLT], 'the birds' [REB], 'birds' [CEV, TEV].

QUESTION—What is the implied answer to this rhetorical question?

It makes a statement, which is that they are worth much more than birds [TH]. The point is that God will surely supply food and clothing for you [Dei (p. 105)]. The point is that if birds don't have to worry, an even more valuable disciple certainly doesn't have to worry [TNTC2, WBC]. The birds have to expend a lot of energy to get the provided food, so the point of comparison is not the amount of work that will be expected. The details of the illustration should not be pressed too far, since people still need to grow and harvest food [TNTC2]. If God provides for lesser creatures, he will provide much more so for those made in his image [NAC, NTC]. If God provides for creatures that don't labor, he will much more provide for those who do [ICC].

6:27 And[a] which[b] of-you(pl) (by) worrying[c]

LEXICON—a. δέ: 'and' [Mor, NTC; NASB, NRSV], 'for' [TNT], 'besides' [WBC], not explicit [all versions except NASB, NRSV, TNT].

b. τίς (LN 92.14) (BAGD 1.a.α. p. 819): The phrase τίς ἐξ ὑμῶν 'which of you' [Mor; KJV, NASB, TNT] is also translated 'who of you' [WBC; NIV], 'who among you' [NTC]. This rhetorical question is also phrased as a rhetorical question expecting a yes or no answer: 'can any of you' [CEV, NAB, NET, NJB, NRSV, REB, TEV], 'can worry make you live longer' [CEV], 'can anxious thought add a single day to your life' [REB]. The implied expected response is made explicit: 'of course not' [NLT].

c. pres. act. participle of μεριμνάω (LN 25.225) (BAGD 1. p. 505): 'to worry' [CEV, NAB, NET, NIV, NJB, NRSV, TEV], 'to be anxious' [LN, Mor, NTC, WBC; NASB, TNT], 'to take thought' [KJV]. The phrase τίς δὲ ἐξ ὑμῶν μεριμνῶν 'and which of you by worrying' is translated in connection with the following clause: 'can any of you, however much you worry' [NJB], 'can anxious thought' [REB], 'can any of you...by worrying about it' [TEV], 'can all your worries' [NLT], 'can worry' [CEV]. See this word at 6:25, 28, 31, 34.

is-able[a] to-add[b] to his life-span[c]/stature[c] one cubit?[d]

LEXICON—a. pres. act. indic. of δύναμαι (LN 74.5): 'to be able' [LN, NTC], 'can' [LN, Mor, WBC; all versions].

b. aorist act. infin. of προστίθημι (LN 59.72) (BAGD 1.a. p. 719): 'to add' [BAGD, LN, Mor, NTC, WBC; KJV, NAB, NASB, NET, NIV, NJB, NLT, NRSV, REB, TNT], not explicit [CEV, TEV]. This entire clause is translated 'can...make you live longer' [CEV, TEV], 'can...you live a bit longer' [TEV].

c. ἡλικία (LN **67.151**) (BAGD 1.a., 2. p. 345): 'span of life' [LN; NJB, NRSV], 'life time' [**LN**], 'life span' [NTC; NAB, NASB], 'life' [WBC; NET, NIV, NLT, REB], 'the length of his life' [TNT], 'age, time of life' (generally of time that is passed) [BAGD (1.)]. This noun is also translated as a verb phrase: 'to live longer' [CEV, TEV], For many languages the most appropriate term is one which means 'day', but it would also be possible to use some other unit of length if this would clearly imply an impossibility [LN]. This could also refer to bodily stature [BAGD (2.)]: 'stature' [KJV], 'height' [Mor].

  d. πῆχυς (LN **81.25**, 67.151) (BAGD p. 657): 'cubit' [BAGD, LN]. The phrase πῆχυν ἕνα is translated 'one cubit' [Mor, NTC; KJV], 'one single cubit' [NJB], 'a half meter' [**LN**], 'a bit' [TEV], 'a single moment' [NAB, NLT], 'a single hour' [NASB, NIV, NRSV], 'even one hour' [WBC], 'a single day' [LN (67.151); REB], 'even one hour' [NET], not explicit [CEV, TNT]. Although 'cubit' is normally used in reference to distance, it can also be used of time, here a brief span [TH].

QUESTION—Is the basic illustration here one of height or of length of life?

  1. It is duration of life [BSC, EBC, ICC, MLJ, NAC, NCBC, NIBC, NTC, Pl, TNTC2, WBC; CEV, NAB, NASB, NET, NIV, NJB, NLT, NRSV, REB, TEV, TNT]. Because no one could add 18 inches to his height, and because if one were to do so it would be only a 'small thing' as he says in Luke 12:26, the analogy has to do with length of life [MLJ, NAC, NTC, Pl, WBC].

  2. It is height [McN, Mor; KJV]. Because adding 18 inches to one's height would be a tremendous miracle, one which only God could perform, is it not much more likely that he will do a much smaller thing such as provide clothing? [McN].

DISCOURSE UNIT: 6:28–30 [EBC]. The topic is the body and clothes [EBC].

6:28 **And about clothing,[a] why do-you(pl)-worry?[b]**

LEXICON—a. ἔνδυμα (LN **6.162**) (BAGD 1. p. 263): 'clothing' [**LN**, Mor, WBC; NASB, NET, NJB, NRSV], 'clothes' [NTC; CEV, NAB, NIV, NLT, REB, TEV, TNT], 'apparel' [LN], 'raiment' [KJV]. See this word at 6:25.

  b. pres. act. indic. of μεριμνάω (LN 25.225) (BAGD 1. p. 505): 'to worry' [LN; CEV, NAB, NET, NIV, NJB, NLT, NRSV, TEV], 'to be anxious' [BAGD, LN, Mor, NTC, WBC; NASB, REB, TNT], 'to have anxiety' [BAGD], 'to take thought' [KJV], 'to be (unduly) concerned' [BAGD]. See this word at 6:25, 27, 31, 34.

Consider[a] the lilies[b] of-the field[c] how[d] they-grow.[e]

LEXICON—a. aorist act. impera. of καταμανθάνω (LN 30.30) (BAGD p. 414): 'to consider' [**LN**, Mor, NTC; KJV, NRSV, REB, TNT], 'to observe' [BAGD, LN; NASB], 'to see' [NIV], 'to look (how)' [CEV, TEV], 'to look (at)' [NLT], 'to think of' [NJB], 'to think about' [LN; NET], 'to notice, to learn something' [BAGD], 'to learn from' [NAB], 'to learn a lesson from' [WBC], 'to examine with care' [NIBC]. This verb is slightly stronger than 'look at' in 6:26. He is inviting them to meditate on these things and consider their deeper significance [MLJ]

    b. κρίνον (**LN 3.32**) (BAGD p. 451): 'lily' [BAGD, **LN**, NTC; KJV, NASB, NIV, NLT, NRSV, REB], 'wild lily' [TNT], 'wild flower' [LN; CEV, NAB, TEV], 'flower' [Mor, WBC; NET, NJB].

    c. ἀγρός (LN 1.87 or 1.95) (BAGD 1. p. 13): 'field' [BAGD, LN (1.95)], 'fields, countryside, rural area' [LN (1.87)], 'of the field' [Mor, NTC, WBC; KJV, NASB, NET, NIV, NRSV], 'in the field' [NJB], 'in the fields' [REB], 'wild (flowers)' [CEV, NAB, TEV, TNT], not explicit [NLT].

    d. πῶς (BAGD 2.a. p. 732): 'how' [BAGD, Mor, NTC, WBC; all versions except NAB, NJB], 'and how' [NLT], not explicit [NAB, NJB]. 'How' means growing without toil on their part [NTC].

    e. pres. act. indic. of αὐξάνω (LN 23.188) (BAGD 3. p. 121): 'to grow' [BAGD, LN, Mor, NTC, WBC; all versions].

QUESTION—What plant is he speaking of when he mentions the lilies of the field?

He was probably referring to wild flowers in general [EBC, ICC, NAC, NCBC, NTC, TH, WBC]. It refers to the natural wild flowers and grass, something common and familiar [MLJ]. It is wild vegetation in general, which testifies to the abundant provision of God [TNTC2]. It was perhaps the purple anemone, purple leading to comparison with the royal purple of Solomon's clothing [NIBC].

They- (do) not -work[a] nor[b] do-they-spin[c] (thread).

TEXT—There are a variety of textual variations regarding the last two verbs in 6:28. GNT takes the reading οὐ κοπιῶσιν οὐδὲ νήθουσιν 'they do not work nor do they spin' with a B rating, indicating that the text is almost certain. Only WBC has 'they neither labor nor toil'.

LEXICON—a. pres. act. indic. of κοπιάω (LN 42.47) (BAGD 2. p. 443): 'to work' [Mor; CEV, NAB, NET, NJB, NLT, REB, TEV, TNT], 'to work hard' [BAGD, LN], 'to toil' [BAGD, LN, NTC; KJV, NASB, NRSV], 'to labor' [LN, WBC; NIV].

    b. οὐδέ (LN 69.7) (BAGD 1. p. 591): 'nor' [LN, Mor, NTC, WBC; NASB, NRSV], 'or' [NAB, NET, NIV, NJB, NLT, TEV], 'neither' [KJV], (not explicit, uses negated verb) [CEV, REB, TNT].

    c. pres. act. indic. of νήθω (LN 48.2) (BAGD p. 537): 'to spin' [BAGD, LN, Mor, NTC; all versions except CEV, NLT, TEV], 'to make clothes for themselves' [TEV], 'to make their clothing' [NLT], 'to make their clothes' [CEV], 'toil' (another text) [WBC]. The reference is to spinning fiber to make clothes [TH].

QUESTION—What significance is there in the two activities represented by the verbs κοπιάω 'work' and νήθω 'spin'?

The two activities represent men's work in the fields and women's work in the home respectively [ICC, McN, NAC, NIBC]. Another interpretation is that the toil concerns making clothes [TH, WBC]. They don't work to make cloth for clothing themselves [TH]. They do not do the woman's work of drawing out some fiber and twisting it into thread [WBC].

6:29 **But I-say to-you(pl) that not-even[a] Solomon[b] in all his glory[c]**

LEXICON—a. οὐδέ (LN **69.8**) (BAGD 3. p. 591): 'not even' [BAGD, LN, Mor, WBC; NAB, NIV, NJB, TEV, TNT], 'even' ('not' in next clause) [NTC; KJV, NASB, NRSV, REB], ('not' in next clause) [CEV, NET, NLT].

  b. Σολομών (LN 93.344) (BAGD p. 759): 'Solomon' [BAGD, LN, Mor, NTC, WBC; all versions except TEV], 'King Solomon' [TEV],

  c. δόξα (LN **79.18**) (BAGD 2. p. 204): 'glory' [LN, Mor; KJV, NASB, NET, NLT, NRSV, TNT], 'splendor' [BAGD, **LN**, NTC, WBC; NAB, NIV, REB], 'magnificence' [BAGD], 'royal robes' [NJB], 'wealth' [CEV, TEV].

clothed-himself[a] like one of-these.[b]

LEXICON—a. aorist mid. indic. of περιβάλλω (LN **49.3**) (BAGD 1.b.e. p. 646): 'to clothe (oneself)' [LN, Mor; NASB], 'to have clothes' [TEV], 'could match (such) clothing' [WBC]. This middle verb is also translated as passive: 'to be arrayed' [KJV], 'to be dressed' [NIV, NLT, TNT], 'to be clothed' [CEV, NAB, NET, NJB, NRSV], 'to be attired' [NTC; REB]. See this word at 6:31.

  b. ὡς ἓν τούτων: 'like one of these' [Mor; KJV, NASB, NET, NIV, NJB, NRSV, TNT], 'like one of them' [NAB, REB], 'as one of them' [CEV], 'as beautifully as they are' [NLT], 'as beautiful as one of these flowers' [TEV], 'such (clothing)' [WBC].

6:30 **Now/but[a] if[b] the grass[c] of-the field[d] existing[e] today[f]**

LEXICON—a. δέ: 'now' [Mor, NTC, WBC; NJB], 'and' [NET, NLT], 'wherefore' [KJV], 'but' [NASB, NRSV], not explicit [CEV, NAB, NIV, REB, TEV, TNT].

  b. εἰ (LN **89.30**) (BAGD III. p. 219): 'if' [Mor, NTC; all versions except CEV, TEV], 'even though' [CEV], 'since' [BAGD, **LN**, WBC]. Εἰ may be used where an actual case is taken as a supposition [BAGD, LN]. In a number of languages the use of the word 'if' would imply doubt as to whether God actually does perform such an activity, so it may be necessary to translate this word as 'because' or 'since' [LN].

  c. χόρτος (LN 3.15) (BAGD p. 884): 'grass' [BAGD, LN, Mor, NTC, WBC; all versions except CEV, NJB, NLT], 'wildflowers' [NJB], 'flowers' [NLT], 'everything that grows' [CEV], 'hay (of wild grass in contrast to cultivated plants)' [BAGD].

  d. ἀγρός: 'field'. See this word at 6:28.

  e. pres. act. participle of εἰμί (LN 13.69): 'to exist' [LN], 'to be' [LN, Mor; KJV], 'to be (here)' [CEV, NET, NIV, NLT, TEV, TNT], 'to be (there)' [NJB, REB], 'to be alive' [NTC, WBC; NASB, NRSV], 'to grow' [NAB].

f. σήμερον (LN 67.205) (BAGD p. 749): 'today' [BAGD, LN, Mor, NTC; all versions], 'one day' [WBC], 'now' [BAGD].

and tomorrow[a] is-being-thrown[b] into an-oven[c]

LEXICON—a. αὔριον (LN 67.207) (BAGD 2. p. 122): 'tomorrow' [BAGD, LN, Mor, NTC; all versions except TEV], 'the next (day)' [Mor], 'gone tomorrow' [TEV]. It has the sense of 'soon, in a short time' [BAGD].

b. pres. pass. participle βάλλω (LN 15.215) (BAGD 1.b. p. 131): 'to be thrown' [BAGD, LN, Mor, NTC; all versions except KJV, NLT, TEV], 'to be cast' [KJV], 'to burned up' [TEV]. The phrase 'is being thrown into an oven' is translated 'is used as fuel for the oven' [WBC], 'to be gone' [NLT].

c. κλίβανος (LN 7.74) (BAGD p. 436): 'oven' [BAGD, LN, WBC; KJV, NAB, NRSV, TEV], 'stove' [REB], 'furnace' [Mor, NTC; NASB, NJB, TNT], 'fire' [CEV, NIV], 'into the fire to heat the oven' [NET], not explicit [NLT].

QUESTION—What practice does this refer to?

The κλίβανος was a dome-like structure made of clay, in which wood and dried grass were burned, and then after being heated in this way, was used for baking bread [LN, TH]. Clay oven temperatures were quickly raised to bake bread by throwing dried grasses and flowers inside to burn [Brc, MLJ, NAC].

God thus[a] clothes,[b]

LEXICON—a. οὕτως (LN 61.9) (BAGD 1.b. p. 597): 'so' [LN, Mor, NTC; KJV, NAB, NASB, NRSV], '(if) that is how' [NIV, NJB], 'that is how' [REB], 'in this way' [LN; TNT], 'this way' [NET], 'surely' [CEV], not explicit [WBC].

b. pres. act. indic. of ἀμφιέννυμι (LN 49.3) (BAGD p. 47): 'to clothe' [BAGD, LN, Mor, NTC, WBC; KJV, NAB, NET, NIV, NJB, NRSV, REB, TEV, TNT], 'to dress' [BAGD], 'to array' [NASB], 'to do' [CEV]. All versions begin with the 3rd clause first, e.g. 'if God thus clothes'.

(will he) not much more[a] (do so for) you(pl),(you) of-little-faith?[b]

LEXICON—a. μᾶλλον (LN 78.28) (BAGD 2.b. p. 489): 'more, even more, more than, to a greater degree' [LN], 'more (surely), more (certainly)' (following a conditional clause) [BAGD]. The phrase πολλῷ μᾶλλον 'much more' [Mor, WBC; KJV, NAB, NASB, NIV, NJB, NRSV, TNT] is also translated 'all the more' [REB, TEV], 'even more' [CEV, NET], 'much more surely' [NTC]. This means God will much more surely clothe you [TH].

b. ὀλιγόπιστος (LN 31.96) (BAGD p. 563): 'of little faith' [BAGD, LN]. This vocative is translated 'O ye of little faith' [KJV], 'O you of little faith' [NAB, NIV, NRSV], 'you people of little faith' [Mor], 'O men of little faith' [NTC; NASB], 'men of little faith' [TNT], 'you who have so little faith' [WBC; NJB], 'you people of little faith' [Mor; NET], 'you

have so little faith' [NLT], 'how little faith you have' [REB], 'what little
faith you have' [TEV], 'Why do you have such little faith' [CEV].

QUESTION—What is the expected reply to this rhetorical question?

It is because you are much more important to him than grass that he will do
this for you [BSC, Dei, TH, WBC]. If God provides for short-lived grass, he
will certainly provide for his children who are destined for eternal glory
[NTC].

QUESTION—What is meant by the term ὀλιγόπιστοι 'you of little faith'?

Having little faith is a failure to apply what one knows [MLJ]. 'Little faith'
means those who worry about these things [BSC]. It is a failure to trust God
for material needs [TNTC2]. It refers to people whose faith has fallen short
of what could normally be expected [NIBC]. It describes their proneness to
anxiety and failure to trust God completely [WBC]. They did not sufficiently
take to heart the comfort that they should have had from Christ's love,
promises and power [NTC]. Worry can only indicate lack of confidence in
God's goodness and mercy [NAC], or his care and provision [NCBC]. It
refers to insufficient faith but not a complete lack of faith [ICC]. This is a
statement of surprise and rebuke at the fact that they did not trust God as
they should [TH].

DISCOURSE UNIT: 6:31–32 [EBC]. The topic is distinctive living.

6:31 Therefore[a] do-not-worry,[b] saying,[c]

LEXICON—a. οὖν (LN 89.50) (BAGD 1.b. p. 593): 'therefore' [BAGD, LN,
Mor, WBC; KJV, NRSV], 'then' [BAGD, LN; NASB], 'so' [BAGD, LN,
NTC; NAB, NIV, NJB, NLT, TEV, TNT], 'so then' [LN; NET],
'consequently, accordingly, then' [BAGD, LN], not explicit [CEV, REB].

    b. aorist subj. indic. of μεριμνάω (LN 25.225) (BAGD 1. p. 505): 'to be
worried, to be anxious' [LN], 'to have anxiety, to be anxious, to be
(unduly) concerned' [BAGD]. This negated imperative is translated 'do
not worry' [CEV, NAB, NET, NIV, NJB, NLT, NRSV], 'do not start
worrying' [TEV], 'do not (ask) anxiously' [REB], 'do not be anxious'
[Mor; NASB, TNT], 'do not become anxious' [NTC], 'do not be full of
anxiety' [WBC], 'take no thought' [KJV]. See this word at 6:25, 27, 28,
34.

    c. pres. act. participle of λέγω: 'saying' [Mor, NTC, WBC; KJV, NASB,
NET, NIV, NRSV, TNT], 'and say' [NAB]. This negated imperative is
translated 'do not say' [NJB], 'don't ask (anxiously)' [REB], 'don't...ask
yourselves' [CEV], not explicit [NLT, TEV].

QUESTION—What relationship is indicated by οὖν 'therefore'?

It introduces a summary and restatement of what he has said in 6:25–30
[NTC, WBC]. It introduces a conclusion based on the discussion of God's
bountiful care, which is that the disciple must live differently than those who
don't know God [EBC].

What will-we-eat?[a] or, What will-we-drink?[b] or, What will-we-wear?[c]

LEXICON—a. aorist act. subj. of ἐσθίω (LN 23.1) (BAGD 1.a. p. 312): 'to eat' [BAGD, LN; all versions except TEV]. The question is translated 'what will we eat' [NET, NRSV], 'what shall we eat' [Mor; KJV, NASB, NIV], 'what are we to eat' [WBC; NAB, NJB, REB, TNT], 'what are we going to eat' [NTC], 'where will my food come from' [TEV], 'will we have anything to eat?' [CEV]. See this word at 6:25.

b. aorist act. subj. of πίνω (LN 23.34) (BAGD 1. p. 658): 'drink' [BAGD, LN, NTC, WBC; all versions]; 'shall we drink' [Mor; KJV, NASB, NIV], 'will we drink' [NET, NRSV], 'are we to drink' [WBC; NAB, NJB, REB, TNT], 'what are we going to drink' [WBC], 'my drink' [TEV], 'will we have anything to drink' [CEV]. See this word at 6:25.

c. aorist mid. subj. of περιβάλλω (LN 49.3) (BAGD 1.b.α. p. 646): 'to wear' [NTC, WBC; NAB, NET, NIV, NJB, NRSV, REB, TNT], 'to clothe ourselves' [LN, Mor; NASB], 'my clothes' [TEV], 'will we have any clothes to wear?' [CEV]. This verb in the middle voice is translated as passive: 'to be clothed' [KJV]. See this word at 6:29.

6:32 for[a] the Gentiles[b] run-after[c] all these-things;

LEXICON—a. γάρ: 'for' [Mor, NTC, WBC; KJV, NET, NIV, NRSV], not explicit [NAB, NASB, NJB, REB, TEV, TNT]; 'why be like' [NLT], 'only' [CEV].

b. ἔθνος (LN 11.37) (BAGD 2. p. 218): 'the Gentiles' [BAGD, Mor, NTC, WBC; KJV, NASB, NJB, NRSV], 'the pagans' [BAGD, LN; NAB, NIV, NLT, TEV], '(the) heathen(s)' [BAGD, LN; REB, TNT], 'the unconverted' [NET], 'people who don't know God' [CEV].

c. pres. act. indic. of ἐπιζητέω (LN 25.9) (BAGD 2.a. p. 292): 'to run after' [NIV], 'to strive for' [NRSV], 'to occupy the minds of' [REB, TNT], 'to set their hearts on' [NJB], 'to be concerned about' [NLT, TEV], 'to pursue' [NET], 'to wish, wish for' [BAGD], 'to desire, to want' [LN], 'to seek' [Mor; KJV, NAB], 'to earnestly seek after' [WBC], 'to eagerly seek for' [NASB], 'to worry about' [CEV], 'to crave' [NTC]. The present tense is expressed as ongoing action by use of the temporal adverb 'always' [CEV, NAB, TEV].

QUESTION—What relationship is indicated by γάρ 'for'?

It introduces the first of two reasons that the disciples should not be anxious [McN, NTC], the first being that they are different from the Gentiles and must not sink to their level, and the second being that God already knows their needs [NTC].

QUESTION—What is implied by the term 'Gentiles'?

It refers to Gentiles as distinct from the Jews [McN]. It refers to non-Jewish pagans who are misguided and ignorant of God [ICC]. This word is not a racial distinction but a religious one, meaning men without God [TH, TNTC2], unbelievers outside the circle of disciples [NIBC], heathen who have no revelation or knowledge of God [MLJ]. To the Jews it implies religious and moral inferiority [BAGD]. It has a negative connotation and refers to those outside the family of faith [WBC]. They are people who do not know or acknowledge a heavenly Father and are ignorant of the higher spiritual realities [NTC]. They are pagans who don't know God's fatherly care and have no goals beyond gaining material things [EBC]. They are those who don't believe in God and who are always concerned about material needs [TH]. See additional notes at 5:47 and 6:7.

for[a] your(pl) heavenly father knows[b] that you(pl)-need[c] all these-things.[d]

LEXICON—a. γάρ: 'for' [Mor; KJV, NASB, NET], 'and' [NIV], 'and indeed' [NRSV], 'but' [WBC; REB], 'besides' [NTC], not explicit [CEV, NAB, NJB, NLT, TEV, TNT].

b. pref. act. indic. of οἶδα (LN 28.1) (BAGD 1.e. p. 556): 'to know' [BAGD, LN; all versions except KJV]; 'to already know' [NLT]. This Greek verb does not have a present tense form, so where a present tense meaning is intended, the form of the perfect tense is used.

c. pres. act. indic. of χρήζω (LN **57.39**) (BAGD p. 885): 'to need' [BAGD, LN, Mor, NTC, WBC; all versions except KJV], '(to have) need (of).' [BAGD; KJV], 'all of your needs' [NLT].

d. τούτων ἁπάντων: 'all these things' [Mor; KJV, NASB, NRSV, TEV], 'all of these' [CEV], 'all of these things' [WBC], 'them all' [NTC; NAB, NJB, REB, TNT], 'them' [NET, NIV].

QUESTION—What relationship is indicated by γάρ 'for'?

It introduces the second of two reasons they should not have anxiety, which is the fact that God knows their needs and will provide [NTC].

DISCOURSE UNIT: 6:33 [EBC]. The topic is the heart of the matter.

6:33 But[a] seek[b] first[c] the kingdom[d] of God and his righteousness,[e]

TEXT—There are several textual variants in this clause. GNT takes the reading τὴν βασιλείαν [τοῦ θεοῦ] καὶ τὴν δικαιοσύνην αὐτοῦ, 'the kingdom [of God] and his righteousness' (with 'of God' included in brackets) with a C rating, indicating difficulty in deciding which variant to place in the text. The reading taken by GNT is followed by WBC; KJV, NAB, NRSV, REB, TEV, and TNT (with WBC and NAB including 'of God' in brackets). The reading τὴν βασιλείαν καὶ τὴν δικαιοσύνην αὐτοῦ 'his kingdom and his righteousness' is taken by Mor, NTC; NASB, NET, and NIV.

LEXICON—a. δέ (LN 89.124) (BAGD 1.d. p. 171): 'but' [LN, Mor, NTC; CEV, KJV, NAB, NASB, NET, NIV, NRSV], 'instead' [TEV], 'and' [NLT] 'rather' [BAGD], 'so' [WBC], not explicit [NJB, REB, TNT].

b. pres. act. impera. of ζητέω (LN 57.59) (BAGD 2.a. p. 339): 'to seek' [LN, Mor, NTC; KJV, NAB, NASB, NET, NIV, TNT], 'to keep seeking' [WBC], 'to strive for' [NRSV], 'to set your hearts on' [NJB], 'to set your mind on' [REB], 'to be concerned with' [TEV], 'to make your concern' [NLT], 'to put (God's work) first' [CEV], 'to try to obtain' [BAGD, LN], 'to desire to possess something' [BAGD]. The present imperative implies a continuing obligation [TNTC2, WBC].

c. πρῶτος (LN 60.46) (BAGD 2.c. p. 726): 'first' [LN, Mor, NTC; KJV, NAB, NASB, NET, NIV, NJB, NRSV, TNT], 'before everything else' [REB], 'above everything else' [TEV], 'above all else' [WBC], 'more than anything else' [CEV], 'in the first place, above all, especially' (of degree) [BAGD]. The phrase 'seek first the kingdom of God' is translated 'make the kingdom of God your primary concern' [NLT].

d. βασιλεία (LN 37.64) (BAGD 3.b., 3.g. p. 135): 'the royal reign (or) kingdom (of God)' [BAGD], 'rule, reign' [LN]. The phrase τὴν βασιλείαν [τοῦ θεοῦ] is translated: 'his kingdom' [Mor, NTC; NASB, NET, NIV, NJB], 'the kingdom of God' [WBC; KJV, NAB, NLT, NRSV, TEV], 'God's kingdom' [REB, TNT], 'God's work' [CEV].

e. δικαιοσύνη (LN 88.13) (BAGD 2.b. p. 196): 'righteousness' [LN, Mor, NTC; KJV, NAB, NASB, NET, NIV, NRSV, TNT], 'the righteousness he demands' [WBC], 'justice' [REB], '(God's) saving justice' [NJB], 'what he requires of you' [TEV]. This noun is also translated as a verb phrase: 'to do what God requires' [LN], 'to live for him' [NLT], 'to do what he wants' [CEV].

QUESTION—What relationship is indicated by δέ 'but'?

It introduces the contrast between how pagans live and how disciples should live as people over whom God rules [TH]. It emphasizes the contrast between this positive command and the negative warnings that have just been made [ICC]. Here Jesus turns to the positive side of this issue. God's kingdom and righteousness is not put up to contrast with life and body [BSC]. It introduces the conclusion to be drawn from what has been said, which is that the kingdom of God must be the sole priority of the disciple [WBC]. It introduces the command that is the climax of what he has just been saying [NTC].

QUESTION—What is meant by the term πρῶτος 'first'?

It indicates that the kingdom is to be of first importance in the life of the disciple [WBC]. It is not a question of the exclusion of life and body, but a question of priority of the kingdom and righteousness, in which life and body have an eternal place [BSC]. They must give God the priority that is due him [NTC]. As in the model prayer, God's name, kingdom, and will take precedence over concern for food [McN].

QUESTION—What is meant by δικαιοσύνη 'righteousness'?

Jesus is saying to set your affections not only on things above, that is, God's kingdom, but also to be anxious about your spiritual condition, your nearness to God and your relationship to Him [MLJ]. It is a demand to find and do the will of God out of total loyalty and commitment to God's purposes [TNTC2]. Righteousness is that which is the will of God as defined in Jesus' teaching [EBC, WBC]. It is the righteousness that God requires, which is the law of God's kingdom [ICC]. 'Kingdom' and 'righteousness' go together [ICC, NAC, NTC]; to seek God's righteousness and God's kingdom is

essentially the same thing [ICC]. They are to make God king in their own
lives and seek for him to be king in the hearts and lives of others and in
every sphere of living; when this happens righteousness will prevail [NTC].
Seeking the righteousness of the kingdom means obedience to what Jesus
has commanded [NAC]. It is a life lived in obedience to God [NCBC].

and[a] all these-things[b] will-be-added[c] to-you(pl).

LEXICON—a. καί: 'and' [Mor, NTC, WBC; all versions except CEV], 'then'
   [CEV]. Some versions supply an additional word or phrase to amplify the
   meaning of καί: 'in addition' [TNT], 'as well' [Mor; CEV, NIV, NJB,
   NRSV, REB], 'also' [WBC], 'besides' [NAB], 'as an extra gift' [NTC]. It
   implies 'if you do that, then this will happen' [TH].

   b. ταῦτα πάντα (BAGD 1.e.b. p. 638): 'all these things' [Mor, NTC, WBC;
   KJV, NAB, NASB, NET, NIV, NRSV], 'all these other things' [NJB,
   TEV], 'the other things' [CEV], 'all the rest' [REB], 'these' [TNT], 'all
   you need' [NLT].

   c. fut. pass. indic. of προστίθημι (LN 59.72) (BAGD 2. p. 719): 'to be
   added' [LN; KJV, NASB], 'to be given' [BAGD, Mor; NAB, NET, NIV,
   NJB, NLT, NRSV, TNT], 'to be provided' [BAGD], 'to be granted'
   [BAGD, NTC]; 'will come to you' [REB], 'will be yours' [WBC; CEV],
   'he will provide you with' [TEV]. This is a divine passive, indicating that
   God is the actor [WBC]. These do not come as a matter of course; it is
   God who provides them [TH].

QUESTION—What is referred to by the phrase ταῦτα πάντα 'all these things'?
   It is food, drink and clothing [ICC, NTC]. It means those things necessary
   for life and the body [BSC, NCBC]. It is the fullness of God's provision
   [WBC]. It refers to fundamental human needs, which God will provide for
   believers through the Christian community if its priorities are right [NAC].

DISCOURSE UNIT: 6:34 [EBC]. The topic is abolishing worry.

6:34 **Therefore[a] don't worry[b] about tomorrow,**

LEXICON—a. οὖν (LN 89.50): 'therefore' [LN, Mor, NTC; KJV, NASB, NIV,
   TNT], 'then' [LN, WBC], 'so' [LN; NJB, NLT, NRSV, REB, TEV], 'so
   then' [LN; NET], not explicit [CEV, NAB].

   b. aorist act. subj. of μεριμνάω (LN 25.225) (BAGD 1. p. 505): 'to worry'
   [LN; CEV, NAB, NET, NIV, NJB, NLT, NRSV, TEV], 'to be anxious'
   [BAGD, LN, Mor; NASB, REB, TNT], 'to become anxious' [NTC], 'to
   be filled with anxiety' [WBC], 'to be (unduly) concerned' [BAGD], 'to
   take thought' [KJV]. See this word at 6:25, 27, 28, 31.

QUESTION—What is the background of this saying?
   It comes from a rabbinic proverb 'don't worry about tomorrow because you
   don't know what a day may bring forth' [Ed, ICC, McN]. The second clause
   of this proverb is not used but that implies the person may not even be alive
   tomorrow [Ed (p. 539)].

QUESTION—What relationship is indicated by οὖν 'therefore'?

This is the conclusion of this section (ch. 6) about our relationship to the world and its things. Verse 6:33 is the climax, and 6:34 is an extension, not just a summary or repetition as might be expected. Before he was looking at the present, now he looks to the future as well [MLJ]. It introduces the conclusion from what has just been said that worrying about tomorrow is useless [NTC].

for[a] tomorrow will-worry[b] for-itself.[c]

LEXICON—a. γάρ: 'for' [Mor, NTC, WBC; KJV, NASB, NET, NIV, NLT, NRSV, TNT], not explicit [CEV, NAB, NJB, REB, TEV],

b. fut. act. indic. of μεριμνάω (LN 25.225) (BAGD 2. p. 505): 'to worry about' [LN; NET, NIV], 'to bring worries' [NLT, NRSV], 'to have enough worries' [TEV], 'to be concerned about something' [BAGD], 'to be anxious about' [Mor; TNT], 'to be anxious for' [NTC], 'to have its (own share) of anxiety' [WBC], 'to look after' [REB], 'to take thought for' [KJV], 'to take care of' [CEV, NAB, NJB], 'to care for' [BAGD; NASB].

c. ἑαυτῆς: 'itself' [Mor, NTC; CEV, NAB, NASB, NET, NIV, NJB, REB, TNT], 'the things of itself' [KJV], 'of its own' [NRSV, TEV], 'its own' [WBC; NLT].

QUESTION—What did he mean by this?

Since every day has its own share of troubles, let tomorrow worry about itself; that is, the disciple should live in the present, not in the future or the past either [WBC]. This is said with a touch of humor [EBC, NTC]. Don't add tomorrow's worries to today's worries [TH].

Sufficient[a] to the day[b] (is) its-own trouble.[c]

LEXICON—a. ἀρκετός (LN **59.45**) (BAGD p. 107): 'sufficient' [BAGD, **LN**, Mor; KJV, NAB, TNT], 'quite sufficient' [WBC], 'enough' [BAGD, NTC; CEV, NASB, NET, NIV, NJB, NLT, NRSV, REB], 'sufficient unto…is' [KJV]. This pertains to what is sufficient for some purpose [LN].

b. ἡμέρα (LN 67.178) (BAGD 2. p. 346): 'the day' [LN, Mor; KJV], 'today' [CEV, NET], 'each day' [NTC, WBC; NASB, NIV, NJB, REB, TEV], 'today's' [NLT, NRSV], 'the day's' [TNT], 'a day' [NAB].

c. κακία (LN **22.5**) (BAGD 2. p. 397): 'trouble(s)' [BAGD, Mor, NTC; NASB, NET, NIV, NJB, NLT, NRSV, REB, TNT], 'evil' [LN, WBC; KJV, NAB], 'hardships' [LN]. This clause is translated 'you have enough to worry about today' [CEV], 'there is no need to add to the troubles each day brings' [TEV], 'today's trouble is enough for today' [NLT], 'each day has enough trouble all by itself' [NTC].

QUESTION—What does he mean by this?

It is as though there is a daily quota of problems and difficulties [MLJ]. Jesus was acknowledging that from a strictly human perspective there is plenty of cause for worry [BSC]. He is using irony; since each day has its share of anxieties; why add tomorrow's problems to today's? [NIBC]. Every day has its own share of trouble or evil [NTC, WBC]. He is acknowledging that the promise of 6:33 will never be totally implemented in this age [NAC]. Don't add to the trouble that happens each day by worrying about what the next day might bring [TH].

DISCOURSE UNIT: 7:1–29 [MLJ, NIBC]. The topic is by their fruits [NIBC], judgment [MLJ].

DISCOURSE UNIT: 7:1–12 [BSC, EBC, ICC, NAC, NCBC, NTC, WBC]. The topic is one's neighbor [ICC], righteousness and the relationship to one's neighbor [BSC], how to treat others [NAC], judgments and requests [NCBC], the essence of this righteousness with respect to man's relation to man [NTC], various teachings and the golden rule [WBC], balance and perfection [EBC].

DISCOURSE UNIT: 7:1–6 [GNT, HF, ICC, Mor, NAC, TG, TH, TNTC, TNTC2; CEV, NAB, NASB, NET, NIV, NLT, TEV]. The topic is judging other people [GNT, NAC, TH; CEV, NAB, NASB, NIV, TEV], judging [Mor], judging and discriminating [TNTC], do not judge [HF, NET], Jesus teaches about people judging other people [TG], don't condemn others [NLT], Jesus teaches about condemning other people [TG], the disciples' attitude to one another [TNTC2], a triad on attitude toward others [ICC].

DISCOURSE UNIT: 7:1–5 [BBC, McN, NCBC, Pl, WBC; NJB, NRSV]. The topic is do not judge [NJB], judging others [NCBC; NRSV], reasons for not judging others [MLJ, WBC], against judging [McN], warning against criticizing others [Pl], reciprocal judgment [BBC].

7:1 (Do) not[a] judge,[b]

LEXICON—a. μή (LN 69.3) (BAGD A.I.2. p. 516): 'not'. See 5:29 and 6:16 for more information.

b. pres. act. impera. of κρίνω (LN 56.30) (BAGD 6.a. p. 452): 'to judge' [BAGD, Mor, WBC; all versions except CEV], 'to judge as guilty' [LN], 'to condemn' [LN; CEV], 'to pass judgment upon/on others' [BAGD, NTC]. This verb connotes condemnation and fault-finding [TNTC2], having a harsh and judgmental spirit [NIBC], condemning or avenging [NAC]. Here Jesus' command means to avoid judgmentalism and censoriousness [EBC]. In this context κρίνω is almost synonymous with κατακρίνω 'to condemn, to pass judgment on' (as in Matt 12:41) [ICC].

QUESTION—What is the relationship of this section to the preceding passages?

1. There is no connection in thought to what immediately precedes in chapter 6 [McN, NCBC, TH], but there is a better connection with 5:48 [NCBC, TH].
2. There is a thematic connection.
2.1 There is a relatively abrupt break between chapters 6 and 7, but there is a general relationship to the themes of mercy and forgiveness that Jesus mentioned earlier [WBC]. 7:1–12 is not connected to what precedes by

explicit connectors, but by certain similar themes such as the demand for a higher righteousness (5:17–20), warnings against hypocrisy (6:1–18), and new perspectives demanded by the Kingdom (6:19–34). These flow naturally into warnings against judgmentalism (vv.1–5) and lack of discernment (v.6) [EBC]. As these warnings are heeded, the disciples will recognize their inadequacy and be forced to turn to prayer (vv.7–11) [EBC].

2.2 Chapter 6 is about a negative attitude regarding your own business, which is worry, and chapter 7 is about a negative attitude regarding other people, which is judging [Mor]. Chapter 6 described people's duty toward God, and now chapter 7 describes people's duty toward people [NTC]; both are related to humans being created in the image of God (Gen 1:27) [NTC].

2.3 Both this and the preceding chapter concern social issues, moving from our relationship to mammon to our relationship to our neighbors. This statement also is the reverse of the Lex Talionis 'an eye for an eye' in 5:38 [ICC].

2.4 In 7:1–5 and in 6:19–34 Jesus is probably criticizing faults common among the Pharisees, but these faults are also condemned in all people and not just them [Pl]. Earlier he discussed the love of money; here it is the love of passing judgment on others [Pl]. Perhaps since so much of the Sermon criticizes the Pharisees' behavior, then this is (in part) a condemnation of the Pharisees' characteristic judgmental attitude [ICC].

QUESTION—What are the implications of the present imperative verb form κρίνετε 'do not judge'?

The present imperative here can indicate a general rule of conduct [Mor, Pl], or it can prohibit continuation of a habitual practice [ZG]. Most versions render the command in a simple verb form such as 'do not judge'. The negative particle μή plus the present imperative indicates a command to stop doing something [Mor, NIBC, Pl; NAB, NLT] as well as the general prohibition against doing it [Mor]. The pres. imperative contrasts with the aorist imperatives in 7:6 [Pl].

QUESTION—What kind of judgment is Jesus prohibiting?

He is prohibiting the condemning of others [MLJ, NAC, NCBC, NIBC, TNTC2], with a spirit that is unfair, unloving [WBC], harsh [NTC], and overly critical [BSC, McN, Mor, NCBC, NTC]. It concerns speaking harshly to others [ICC, NIBC, WBC], with traits that are opposite to the virtues of mercy [ICC, NTC], love [NTC], humility, tolerance [ICC] and generosity [EBC]. He is talking about proud and hard-hearted criticism [BSC], about being censorious [NCBC, NTC], unfair or uncharitable [WBC]. He is not just addressing unjust judgment, but the habit of judgmentalism [McN]. He is addressing self-righteous judgment [MLJ, NTC]. He is warning against hasty judgments and a readiness to find fault [Mor, NTC], especially while being blind to one's own faults [TNTC2]. It does not preclude exercising moral judgment [BSC, ICC, MLJ, NIBC, WBC] or critical thinking [ICC,

MLJ, Mor, NAC, NIBC, NTC, WBC], or urge being blind to important issues [EBC, Mor].

so-that[a] you(pl)- not -be-judged;[b]

LEXICON—a. ἵνα (LN 89.59) (BAGD I.1.c. p. 377): 'so that' [LN; NRSV, TEV], 'in order that' [BAGD, Mor], 'that' [BAGD, NTC; KJV, NAB, TNT], 'lest' [WBC, ZG; NASB], 'or' [NIV], 'and' [CEV, NET, NJB, NLT, REB]. This indicates the first reason for not judging [MLJ].

    b. aorist pass. subj. of κρίνω (LN 56.30) (BAGD 4.b.α. p. 452): 'to be judged' [BAGD, LN, Mor, WBC; KJV, NAB, NASB, NET, NIV, NJB, NLT, NRSV, REB, TEV, TNT], 'to be condemned' [LN], 'to have judgment passed on oneself' [NTC]. This passive verb is also translated as an active verb with God as the agent of the judging: 'and God won't condemn you' [CEV], 'so that God will not judge you' [TEV].

QUESTION—By whom would they be judged?

    1. Judgmental people will be judged by God at the final judgment [BSC, EBC, McN, MLJ, Mor, NCBC, NTC, TG, TH, TNTC2, WBC, ZG; CEV, TEV]: do not judge people and you will not be judged by God. This is the 'divine passive' [TNTC2, WBC], and God alone has the prerogative to judge [WBC]. Jesus was not warning against them about the danger of reciprocal criticism since this solemn sermon indicates that he is talking about God's judgment [TH].

    2. Critical people get criticized by other people during this age [BSC, McN, MLJ, NCBC; NLT]: do not judge people and other people will not judge you.

    3. Judgmental people will be judged by others as well as by God [NTC]: do not judge people so that you will not be judged by anyone. Such a self-righteous faultfinder will be condemned by other people as well as by God [NTC].

7:2 for[a] with[b] what judgment[c] you(pl)-judge[d]

LEXICON—a. γάρ: 'for' [Mor, NTC, TH, WBC; all versions except CEV, NJB], 'because' [TH; NJB], not explicit [CEV].

    b. ἐν (LN 89.84): 'with' [LN, Mor, WBC; KJV, NRSV], 'in accordance with' [NTC], 'by' [NET], not explicit [all versions except KJV, NET, NRSV]. This pertains to the severity in which judgment is made [TH].

    c. κρίμα (LN 30.110) (BAGD 6. p. 451): 'judgment' [BAGD, LN, Mor, WBC; KJV, NJB, NRSV], 'the judgment' [NTC], 'standard' [NET], not explicit [CEV, NAB, NASB, NIV, NLT, REB, TEV, TNT]. Κρίμα points to the sentence resulting from the judgment [Mor]. It refers to the standard of judgment that is applied [NTC].

    d. pres. act. indic. of κρίνω (LN 56.30): 'to judge' [LN]. The phrase ἐν ᾧ κρίματι κρίνετε 'with what judgment you judge' [KJV] is also translated 'in the way you judge' [NASB], 'in the same way you judge others' [NIV, TEV], 'by the standard you judge' [NET], 'as you judge' [NAB], 'as you judge others' [REB, TNT], 'the judgments you give' [NJB], 'with the judgment you make' [NRSV], 'in accordance with the judgment whereby you pass judgment' [NTC]. The whole clause is translated 'God will be as hard on you as you are on others' [CEV]. Combining the clause about judgment with the clause about measure, it is translated 'whatever measure you use in judging others' [NLT].

QUESTION—What relation is indicated by γάρ 'for'?

It introduces the second reason for not judging—because we set the standard of our own judgment [MLJ, Mor]. This time the warning against judgment is said with even stronger words [BSC]. This verse answers the question about why Jesus' followers should not judge others [TG]. The thought of 7:1b is expressed again here for emphasis with different phraseology [NTC]. Repetition reinforces the lesson [Mor].

you(pl)-will-be-judged,[a]

LEXICON—a. fut. pass. indic. of κρίνω (LN 56.30): 'to be judged' [Mor, NTC, WBC; KJV, NAB, NASB, NET, NIV, NRSV, REB, TNT] '(the judgments) you will get' [NJB], not explicit [CEV, NLT]. This passive is also translated actively: 'God will judge you' [TEV].

and[a] with what measure[b] you(pl)-measure[c]

LEXICON—a. καί: 'and' [Mor, NTC, WBC; all versions except CEV, NLT], not explicit [CEV, NLT]. Καί indicates synonymous parallelism, so the first half of the verse means the same as the second half [ICC].

b. μέτρον (LN 81.1) (BAGD 1.a. p. 515): 'measure' [BAGD, LN, Mor, NTC, WBC; KJV, NAB, NET, NIV, NJB, NLT, NRSV, REB, TNT], 'standard of measure' [NASB], 'standard' [NJB], 'rules' [TEV], not explicit [CEV]. This is a unit of measure used in connection with length or volume [LN].

c. pres. act. indic. of μετρέω (LN **57.92**) (BAGD 2. p. 514): 'to measure' [BAGD, Mor, NTC, WBC, ZG; NAB, NJB], 'to mete' [KJV], not explicit [CEV, NASB]. In conjunction with the noun 'measure' it is translated '(measure) you use' [NET, NIV], '(standard) you use' [NJB], '(measure) you use for others' [TNT], '(measure) you use in judging others' [NLT], '(rules) you apply' [TEV], '(measure) you give' [BAGD, **LN**; NRSV], '(measure) you deal out' [ZG; REB]. Ancient Judaism often associated 'measure for measure' with the final judgment day [ICC].

it-will-be-measured[a] to-you(pl).

LEXICON—a. fut. pass. indic. of μετρέω (LN 57.92): 'to be measured' [LN, Mor, WBC; KJV, NASB, NIV], 'to be measured out' [NAB], 'to be measured back' [NTC]. The clause is translated: 'will be the standard used for you' [NJB], 'will be the measure you receive' [NET], 'will be the measure you get' [NRSV], 'will be dealt to you' [REB], 'will be used for you also' [TNT], 'it will be used to measure how you are judged' [NLT], 'he will apply to you' [TEV].

QUESTION—What is the background of this saying about being measured?
Jesus may be quoting a proverb then in circulation [EBC, McN, NCBC].
Perhaps it alludes to the Jewish idea of God having two measures, one for
mercy and one for judgment, so the disciples should make sure that they
were dealing from the mercy container [EBC, NCBC, TNTC2].

DISCOURSE UNIT: 7:3–5 [EBC, ICC]. The topic is a parable about the log in
the eye; the splinter, and the log [ICC], an example [EBC].

7:3 And^a why do-you(sg)-look-at^b the speck^c

LEXICON—a. δέ: 'and' [Mor, NTC; KJV, NASB, NLT], 'then' [TEV], not
    explicit [WBC; CEV, NAB, NET, NIV, NJB, NRSV, REB, TNT].
    b. pres. act. indic. of βλέπω (LN 24.7) (BAGD 1.a. p. 143): 'to look at'
    [BAGD, Mor, TG; NASB, NIV, REB, TEV, TNT], 'to see' [BAGD, LN,
    WBC; CEV, NET, NRSV], 'to behold' [KJV], 'to observe' [NJB], 'to
    gaze at' [NTC], 'to worry about' [NLT], 'to see so well' [WBC], 'to
    notice' [LN; NAB]. The present probably has a continuative force 'keep
    looking at' [NTC]. Notice that the verbs here and through 7:5 are singular
    [TG].
    c. κάρφος (LN **3.66**) (BAGD p. 405): 'speck' [BAGD, LN, Mor, NTC,
    WBC; CEV, NASB, NET, NLT, NRSV, TEV, TNT], 'speck of saw dust'
    [NIV, REB], 'splinter' [LN; NAB, NJB], 'mote' [KJV]. This refers to a
    small piece of wood, chaff, or even straw [BAGD, LN, NTC; NET],

QUESTION—What is the function of this rhetorical question?
Jesus employs the rhetorical question to attack the hasty judgment of others
from a different angle [Mor]. The rhetorical questions in 7:3–4 are preparing
the audience for the exhortation to the hypocrite in 7:5 [ICC]. The questions
could be represented as a negative statement 'You should not, therefore'
[TG].

QUESTION—What figure of speech is Jesus employing here?
The verse uses hyperbole [EBC, Mor, NAC, NCBC, NIBC, Pl] and
exaggeration for vividness [TG, WBC]. It is purposely ridiculous to
highlight the contrast between the insignificant and the enormous in the
moral realm [TH]. Hyperbole silences the critic with ridicule [Mor], and
illustrates the foolishness of judgmentalism [NAC]. It is an image of how
incomparably greater God's judgment is than man's, and consequently how
foolish it is to criticize one's neighbor too much [BSC]. The verse uses
sarcasm and irony [MLJ]. It perhaps has a sarcastic meaning that when you
remove the log from your eye you will find that there is no speck in the
brother's eye [TNTC2]. This is sarcasm at its highest; our own condition
precludes us from helping others [MLJ]. The point is not that the person
judging will always be wrong, but that it is insignificant for him compared to
the sin God sees in him [Mor]. This may have been a common proverbial
statement at that time [McN, Pl].

that (is) in your(sg) brother's[a] eye,

LEXICON—a. ἀδελφός (LN 11.23) (BAGD 4. p. 16): 'brother' [Mor, NTC; all versions except CEV, NLT, NRSV], 'neighbor' [NRSV], 'friend' [CEV, NLT], 'brother or sister' [WBC]. This word signifies the community of believers [EBC, WBC].

but[a] the log[b] which (is) in your(sg)-own[c] eye

LEXICON—a. δέ: 'but' [WBC; CEV, KJV, NAB, NASB, NET, NRSV], 'when' [NLT], 'and' [Mor; NIV, NJB, TEV, TNT], 'while' [NTC], not explicit [REB].

b. δοκός (LN **7.78**) (BAGD p. 203): 'log' [WBC; CEV, NASB, NLT, NRSV, TEV], 'the great log' [NJB], 'beam' [**LN**, NTC; KJV], 'the beam of timber' [NET], 'wooden beam' [NAB], 'beam of wood' [BAGD, LN], 'the plank of wood' [TNT], 'plank' [Mor; NIV, REB].

c. σός (LN **92.8**) (BAGD 1. p. 759): 'your own' [**LN**, Mor, NTC, WBC; all versions except NAB], 'your' [BAGD, LN; NAB]. 'Your own' focuses on the contrast between the brother's eyes and your own eyes [Mor].

you(sg)- don't -notice?[a]

LEXICON—a. pres. act. indic. of κατανοέω (LN 24.51) (BAGD 1. p. 415): 'to notice' [BAGD, LN, Mor; CEV, NASB, NJB, NRSV, TNT], 'to observe' [NTC], 'to perceive' [NAB], 'to consider' [KJV], 'to pay attention to' [NIV, TEV], not explicit [NLT]. With the negating particle οὐ this verb is translated 'with never a thought for' [REB], 'to fail to see' [NET], 'to fail to regard' [WBC]. The verb κατανοέω 'notice' is used instead of βλέπω 'to see' because we perceive or notice but not see what is in our eye [ICC, Pl].

7:4 **Or[a] how[b] will/can-you-say-to[c] your(sg) brother, Let[d] (me) take-out the speck from your(sg) eye,**

LEXICON—a. ἤ (LN 89.139) (BAGD 1.d.δ. p. 342): 'or' [BAGD, LN, Mor, NTC, WBC; KJV, NASB, NET, NRSV, TNT], not explicit [CEV, NAB, NIV, NJB, NLT, REB, TEV]. The conjunction ἤ often occurs in an interrogative sentence which follows another interrogative sentence. While its seems to imply another possible behavior, the action of the question is really an impossibility [Mor].

b. πῶς (LN 92.16) (BAGD 1.c. p. 732): 'how' [BAGD, LN, Mor, NTC, WBC, ZG; all versions except NET], 'why' [NET], 'in what way?' (in direct questions denoting disapproval or rejection), 'with what right?, how dare you?' [BAGD, Mor]. Semitic influence would allow a modal interpretation 'can you say' [EBC, ZG].

c. fut. act. indic. of λέγω: 'to say.' The verb is translated: 'wilt thou say' [KJV], 'will you say' [Mor, WBC], 'can you say' [NTC; CEV, NAB, NASB, NIV, NRSV, REB, TNT], 'dare you say' [NJB, TEV], 'do you say' [NET], 'can you think of saying' [NLT]. 'How can you say' is the

modal use of the future tense [ZG]. Aramaic usage would lend support to
interpreting this future with the sense of 'can' [AAG].

d. aorist act. impera. of ἀφίημι (LN **13.140**) (BAGD 4. p. 126): 'to let'
[BAGD, LN, Mor, NTC, WBC; all versions except NLT, TEV], 'to allow'
[LN]. This is also translated with an accompanying verb: 'please let me'
[TEV], 'let me help you' [NLT].

QUESTION—What is the structure of 7:4 and 5?

The structure is a chiasm giving the order speck, log, log, speck [ICC,
WBC].

and[a] look,[b] a log (is) in your(sg) eye?

LEXICON—a. καί (LN 91.12): 'and' [NTC; KJV, NASB], 'while' [Mor, WBC;
NAB, NET, NRSV], 'when all the time' [NIV, REB], 'when' [NJB, NLT,
TEV, TNT], 'when you don't see' [CEV], 'then, indeed' [LN].

b. ἰδού (LN 91.13) (BAGD 1.b.β. p. 371): 'look' [BAGD, LN, Mor, NTC;
NJB], 'behold' [BAGD, WBC; KJV, NASB], not explicit [CEV, NAB,
NET, NIV, NLT, NRSV, TEV, TNT]. The particle ἰδού is used for
emphasis [Mor, WBC].

7:5 Hypocrite,[a] first[b] throw-out the log out-of your(sg) eye,

LEXICON—a. ὑποκριτής (LN 88.228) (BAGD p. 845): vocative case:
'you/thou hypocrite' [NTC; KJV, NAB, NASB, NIV, NRSV, REB,
TEV], 'hypocrite' [LN, Mor, NTC; all versions except CEV], 'show-off'
[CEV]. See this word at 6:2, 5, 16.

b. πρῶτος (LN 60.46) (BAGD 2.a. p. 726) 'first' [LN, Mor, WBC; all
versions]. See this word at 5:24.

and then[a] you(sg)-will-see-clearly[b] (enough) to-take-out[c] the speck out-of your(sg) brother's eye.

LEXICON—a. καὶ τότε (LN 67.47) (BAGD 2. p. 824): 'and then' [Mor, NTC,
WBC; all versions except CEV, NAB, NLT], 'then' [LN; CEV, NAB],
'then perhaps' [NLT]. The words καὶ τότε 'and then' indicate that this
action is secondary in priority [Mor]. See 5:24.

b. fut. act. indic. of διαβλέπω (LN **24.35**) (BAGD 2. p. 181): 'to see clearly'
[BAGD, LN, Mor, NTC; KJV, NAB, NASB, NIV, NRSV, REB, TNT],
'to be able to see clearly' [LN; TEV], 'can see clearly' [NET], 'to see
clearly enough' [NTC, WBC; NJB], 'to see well enough' [NLT], 'can see
how' [CEV], 'to be able to see plainly, to be able to distinguish clearly'
[LN]. Notice v.3 has βλέπω not διαβλέπω as here [ICC, Mor].
διαβλέπω is more intense, and is thus often translated 'see clearly'
[WBC]; the δια- intensifies the verb stem βλέπω: 'see clearly enough'
[ZG]. Notice the occurrence of 'enough' in the versions above and refer to
the note on the verb in the next clause for more information about the
sense 'enough'.

c. aorist act. infin. of ἐκβάλλω (LN 15.220): 'to take (out)' [Mor, NTC,
WBC; CEV, NASB, NJB, NRSV, REB, TEV, TNT], 'to cast out' [KJV],

'to remove' [NAB, NET, NIV], 'to deal with' [NLT]. This is a consecutive infinitive (a consequence meaning 'so as to') with the previous verb resulting in 'will see clearly enough to throw out' [ZG].

QUESTION—What does this illustration indicate about judging others?

This last instruction indicates that there really was a fault in the brother's life [TNTC2]. Jesus did not intend to forbid mutual discipline in which a brother would be restored in a spirit of gentleness. In fact, this addition encourages both self-discipline and mutual discipline [NTC]. After one's own faults have been remedied, a person may turn to help with the shortcomings of another. There is the implication that being aware of one's own faults will make a more charitable judgment of others [WBC].

DISCOURSE UNIT: 7:6–12 [BBC]. The topic is imitating God's gifts.

DISCOURSE UNIT: 7:6 [EBC, Ed, ICC, McN, Mor, NCBC, NIBC, Pl, WBC; NAB, NJB, NRSV]. The topic is profaning the holy [NRSV], a prohibition to profaning sacred things [NJB], spiritual judgment and discrimination (this is the conclusion of the discussion in 7:1–5) [MLJ], dogs and swine [McN], pearls before swine [NAB], a second parable about pearls before swine [ICC], discrimination [NCBC], discernment in proclaiming the Gospel [WBC], the danger of being undiscerning [EBC], that the Kingdom of Heaven cannot be externally extended [Ed (p. 531)].

7:6 (Do) not give[a] the holy[b] (thing) to-dogs,[c]

LEXICON—a. aorist act. subj. used as aorist act. impera. of δίδωμι (LN 57.71) (BAGD 1.a. p. 191): 'to give' [BAGD, LN, Mor, NTC, WBC; all versions]. The command is emphatic [BD (sec. 337(3), p. 173–4), Mor, TNTC]. The aorist subj. plus μή prohibits future action [ZG].

  b. ἅγιος (LN 88.24) (BAGD 2.a.α. p. 9): 'holy' [BAGD, LN]. The phrase τὸ ἅγιον 'the holy (thing)' is translated 'what is holy' [BAGD, Mor, NTC, WBC; NAB, NASB, NET, NJB, NLT, NRSV, REB, TEV], 'that which is holy' [KJV], 'what is sacred' [NIV, TNT], 'what belongs to God' [CEV].

  c. κύων (LN 4.34) (BAGD 1. p. 461): 'dog' [BAGD, LN, Mor, NTC, WBC; all versions except NLT], 'unholy people' [NLT]. This word is used figuratively of unclean persons [BAGD].

QUESTION—What is the relationship of this verse to what precedes it?

  1. There is little or no relation to the preceding section, or the connection is unclear [Pl, TG, TH, WBC]. The transition is abrupt [TH]. It is an unrelated proverbial saying of Jesus [WBC].

  2. There is some thematic connection, which is that Jesus' followers should show discernment in thinking critically. It balances Jesus' command not to judge others by warning that they should not extend the range of that command too far [BSC, ICC, McN, MLJ, Mor, NAC, NCBC, NTC, TNTC2]. Jesus is showing that although he does not want them to be hypocrites, he also does not expect them to be so endlessly patient such

that they lose discernment [NTC]. In sacred matters some critical thinking must still be exercised [ICC]. They should attain a balance between being too severe in judgment and too lax in discernment [ICC]. Avoiding haughty judgment shouldn't lead to throwing sacred things to dogs. [BSC].

QUESTION—What does τὸ ἅγιον 'the holy thing' refer to?

In the image, the holy thing would refer to consecrated food which only priests and their families could eat, and consecrated food would never be given to dogs which were fed only unclean food [TNTC2]. In its application, the holy thing refers to the gospel or to spiritual truth, which should not be shared indiscriminately with those who are not willing to accept it [EBC, Mor, NCBC, NIBC, NTC, Pl, TNTC2, WBC]. It is the holiness of the gospel, which the followers of Jesus should not offer continually to obstinate rejecters [Mor, NTC]. This statement offers a balance to Jesus' statement about not judging; while the disciples must not be judgmental, they must be discerning [EBC, McN, NCBC, Pl, TNTC2].

QUESTION—How is the term κύων 'dog' to be understood?

The term κύων 'dog' was a term of contempt or reproach [ICC]. Dogs and swine were ritually unclean, animals [Mor, NAC, Pl] and are natural contrasts to holy and valuable things [NAC]. They represent those who cannot understand sacred things [TG], or who would disdain sacred things [BSC]. Dogs are not household pets but despised wild and unclean animals [EBC, NTC, WBC], wild scavengers [ICC, MLJ, NAC]. Dogs and pigs together represent those who are vicious, unclean, and abominable [EBC], wicked, vicious, and despicable [NTC]. The dogs referred to here are stray dogs, and in this case represent profane men [BD (sec. 111(3), p. 60)]. 'Dogs' are obstinate rejecters [Mor], those who are irresponsible and unappreciative [NCBC], who are scornful of God [EBC, Mor], who ridicule the Gospel [NTC], the ungodly who scorn Jesus' message [NAC]. The focus is not on their unworthiness but on their lack of receptivity [WBC].

nor[a] throw[b] your(pl) pearls[c] before[d] pigs,[e]

LEXICON—a. μηδέ (LN 69.7) (BAGD 1.b. p. 517): 'nor' [BAGD, LN], 'neither' [KJV], 'or' [NAB, NET], 'not' [CEV, NIV, NLT, REB, TEV], 'and not' [BAGD, Mor, NTC, WBC; NASB, NJB, NRSV, TNT]. With μηδέ an imperative can be replaced by equivalent subjunctive forms [BAGD].

b. aorist act. subj. used as aorist act. impera. of βάλλω (LN 15.215) (BAGD 1.b. p. 130): 'to throw' [BAGD, Mor; all versions except KJV, NLT], 'to fling' [NTC], 'to cast' [KJV], 'to give' [NLT], 'to set' [WBC].

c. μαργαρίτης (LN **2.43**) (BAGD 2. p. 491): 'pearl' [BAGD, LN, Mor, NTC, WBC; all versions].

d. ἔμπροσθεν (LN 83.33) (BAGD 2.a. p. 257): 'before' [LN, NTC; KJV, NAB, NASB, NET, NRSV, TNT], 'to' [NIV, NLT, REB], 'in front of' [LN, Mor; CEV, NJB, TEV].

e. χοῖρος (LN 4.36) (BAGD p. 883): 'pig' [LN, Mor, WBC; CEV, NET, NIV, NJB, REB, TEV, TNT], 'swine' [BAGD; KJV, NAB, NASB, NLT, NRSV], 'hog' [NTC].

QUESTION—What is the cultural background associated with pigs?

Pigs were classified as being ritually unclean [EBC, MLJ, NAC, Pl], as were dogs [NAC, Pl]. Both animals are natural contrasts to holy and valuable things [NAC]. Therefore, they should not be given holy things [Mor]. Pigs and dogs could not appreciate the true value of these sacred things [TG] and in fact would trample the sacred things under their feet [BSC]. Pigs were to be avoided [MLJ]. Pigs were characterized by wildness and viciousness, whose savageness can endanger a person [EBC]. Pigs and dogs are derogatory terms for Gentiles, perhaps referring to all people not following Jesus [NIBC]. Here they represent Jews and Gentiles who are unreceptive to spiritual truth [WBC]. Pigs were unclean for Jews but the focus here is on pigs not being able to appreciate valuable and beautiful things or to treat them appropriately [Mor]. Apparently Jesus is making a distinction between the brothers of 7:3–5 and the dogs and hogs of this verse [NTC].

lest[a] they will-trample[b] them with their feet[c] and having-turned,[d] they-tear-you(pl) -in-pieces.[e]

LEXICON—a. μήποτε (LN **89.62**) (BAGD 2.b.γ. p. 519): 'lest' [LN, Mor, NTC, WBC; KJV, NAB, NASB], '(in order) that...not' [BAGD, **LN**], 'if you do' [NIV, TNT], 'or' [NJB, NRSV], '(they will) only' [REB, TEV], 'otherwise' [NET], not explicit [CEV, NLT]. Μήποτε is a marker of negative purpose, 'so that...not' [BAGD, LN, Mor]. It is a more emphatic form of μή [BAGD]. It is often used to express apprehension [BAGD, LN].

b. fut. act. indic. of καταπατέω (LN **19.52**) (BAGD 1.a. p. 415): 'to trample' [BAGD, **LN**, Mor, NTC; all versions], 'to trample down' [WBC], 'to trample on' [LN]. Καταπατέω means 'to treat with utter disdain' [NTC], 'to step down forcibly upon, often with the implication of destruction or ruin' [LN]. This is a final purpose clause; the future tense was not used in classical Greek and is unusual in the NT [BD (sec. 369(2), p. 186-7)]. NT Greek does allow such a construction after μήποτε when it is in a context of fear [WBC].

c. πούς (LN 8.49) (BAGD 1.a. p. 696): 'foot' [BAGD, LN, Mor, NTC; KJV, NASB, NET, NIV], 'hoof' [WBC], not explicit [CEV, NJB, NLT, REB]. The phrase 'with their feet' is translated 'underfoot' [NAB, NRSV, TEV, TNT].

d. aorist pass. participle of στρέφω (LN 16.14) (BAGD 2.a.α. p. 771): 'to turn' [LN, Mor, NTC, WBC; all versions except KJV, NET, NJB], 'to turn again' [KJV], 'to turn on you' [NJB], 'to turn around' [BAGD; NET].

e. aorist act. subj. of ῥήγνυμι (LN 19.31) (BAGD 1. p. 735): 'to tear to pieces' [BAGD, Mor, NTC; NAB, NASB, NET, NIV, NJB, REB, TNT], 'to tear' [LN], 'to rend' [KJV], 'to attack' [CEV, NLT, TEV], 'to maul' [NRSV], 'to slash with their teeth' [WBC].

QUESTION—What is the structure of this verse and what are the subjects or pronoun referents of these last two clauses?

    1. The structure is a chiasm, a kind of reverse parallelism or crossing over in which the thought is organized topically in an a-b-b-a pattern. The structure of dogs, pigs, trample, and turn-and-tear, would associate the outside elements 'dogs' and 'turn and tear', and the inside elements 'pigs' and 'trample' [EBC, ICC, Mor, NIBC, TG, TH; CEV, TEV]: lest the pigs trample them with their feet and the dogs turn and tear you in pieces. The dogs will turn on those that feed them and attack [NIBC]. The dogs expect to be fed, and when they are disappointed they turn to attack the one pretending to feed them [TG]. Dogs are disgusted with the sacred things and turn on the giver [EBC]. Both CEV and TEV rearrange the clause order in their translations to reflect a chiastic understanding of the verse, for example, 'Don't give to dogs what belongs to God. They will only turn and attack you. Don't throw pearls down in front of pigs. They will trample all over them' [CEV].

    2. It is the pigs who both trample and turn to tear to pieces [NTC, TNTC; probably NIV, NJB, NLT which connect the last clause with 'and then']: lest the pigs trample them with their feet and then turn and tear you in pieces. The pigs would find that they couldn't eat the pearls they had thought to be peas or acorns, and so they would angrily trample the pearls underfoot and turn to attack those who had flung such non-edible objects before them [NTC].

DISCOURSE UNIT: 7:7–12 [Ed, GNT, HF, TG, TH; CEV, NASB, NET, NIV, TEV]. The topic is ask, seek, knock [GNT, TG, TH; CEV, NET, NIV, TEV], keep asking, seeking, knocking [HF], Jesus teaches people to ask for things from God [TH], Jesus teaches that we should ask God for what we need [TH], encouragement to pray [NASB], the Kingdom comes to us from God [Ed (p. 531)].

DISCOURSE UNIT: 7:7–11 [EBC, ICC, McN, Mor, NAC, NCBC, NIBC, Pl, TNTC, TNTC2, WBC; CEV, NAB, NJB, NLT, NRSV, TEV]. The topic is prayer [Mor, NCBC], the answer to prayers [NAB], effective prayer [NJB, NLT], exhortation to earnest prayer [Pl], ask, search, knock [CEV, NRSV], ask, seek, knock [TEV], perseverance in prayer [TNTC], the value of prayer [McN], encouragement to ask [ICC], God's generosity [NAC], the answering Father [WBC], the disciple's attitude to God [TNTC2], source and means of power [EBC].

7:7 Ask[a] and[b] it-will-be-given[c] to-you(pl),

LEXICON—a. pres. act. impera. of αἰτέω (LN 33.163) (BAGD p. 26): 'to ask' [BAGD, LN, Mor, NTC, WBC; all versions]. The asking is a request for something and not asking a question [TG]. Αἰτέω is asking is general while the context tells us it pertains to prayer and no particular kind of prayer is singled out [Mor]. If implied information must be supplied, the clause could be translated 'ask God for what you need' [TG, TH].

b. καί (LN 89.87) (BAGD I.2.f. p. 392): 'and' [LN, Mor, NTC, WBC; all versions], 'and then' [BAGD, LN], 'and so' (to introduce a result, which comes from what precedes) [BAGD].

c. fut. pass. indic. of δίδωμι (LN 57.71): 'to be given' [LN, Mor, NTC, WBC; all versions except CEV, REB, TEV], 'to receive' [CEV, REB, TEV]. This is a theological/divine passive construction [ICC, NAC, WBC] with God is the agent: 'he will give' [NAC, TG, TH, WBC]. Δίδωμι 'give' is used five times and is the key word of this passage 7:7–11 [NAC].

QUESTION—What is the force of the present imperative(s) in this verse?

The present imperative of αἰτέω 'ask' implies ongoing or continuous asking [Brc, ICC, MLJ, Mor, NIBC, NTC, Pl, TH, TNTC2, WBC, ZG; NLT], persistence in asking [Brc, MLJ, Mor, NAC, NIBC, NLT, TH, TNTC2, WBC], or perseverance [Pl]. It gives added emphasis [NCBC, TH]. These are positive commands that follow a section with many negative commands in which μή 'no/not' is used 14 times in 6:1–7:6 [ICC]. Also note that no objects for the three imperatives in this verse or the three participles in the next verse are given so that one is not told what to ask for. There is a broad application, as the 'good things' of 7:11 seem to imply [WBC].

QUESTION—What is the relationship of this verse to its context?

1. There is little direct connection with what precedes or follows [McN, NCBC, WBC]. This section is a contrast with its context. The sections 6:25–34 and 7:7–11 are given as encouragement and as a relief from the harsh demands of the rest of the sermon [ICC]. Anticipating the golden rule, Jesus demonstrates how generously God treats people, often better than they treat each other [NAC].

2. Although explicit connection words are not present [EBC], there is a thematic connection with what precedes. Now that the disciples know the difficulties of discipleship, Jesus exhorts them to pray and gives them assurance of answers [BSC, EBC, MLJ, Mor, NTC]. This section may link backwards by showing how people can get the help they need to practice the new righteousness that Jesus is teaching [NAC].

QUESTION—Is there a significant difference between αἰτέω 'ask', ζητέω 'seek', and κρούω 'knock'?

Jesus is emphasizing that we need persistence, perseverance and importunity [MLJ]. Together the three verbs emphasize the effectiveness of prayer—it gets things done, even if we do not understand it [Mor]. The verse is a threefold expression to emphasize prayer [Pl]. Jesus is demanding persistence in prayer; the three-fold repetition emphasizes assurance of answered prayer if it is persistent [BSC]. The verse contains three syntactically balanced clauses strongly exhorting prayer [TNTC2].

1. The three verbs are synonyms; seeking and knocking are pictures to illustrate asking [McN]. Here seeking and knocking are activities that occur within prayer, and are thus more or less equivalent with asking [ICC]. 'Seek' and 'knock' are not separate commands but would have been recognized by the audience as metaphors for prayer [TNTC2].
2. The three words represent three different modes or ways of prayer [BSC]. There is a progression from general to particular: asking is the most general, seeking is trying to find a particular thing, and knocking is going to the place where that where the sought thing can be found [TG]. There is a rising scale of intensity and a cumulative relationship: asking is coming with humility before a personal God with faith and awareness of need, seeking is earnestly asking plus acting in ways consistent with having the prayer answered, knocking is seeking plus persevering, knocking again and again until the door is opened. Perseverance is probably implied for all three because of the present tense, but it is certain in the last because of the inherent connotation of the word [NTC]. Asking is prayer, seeking is earnest sincerity, and knocking is an active and diligent pursuit of God's way [EBC]

seek[a] and you(pl)-will-find,[b]

LEXICON—a. pres. act. impera. of ζητέω (LN 27.41) (BAGD 1.a.β. p. 338): 'to seek' [BAGD, Mor, NTC, WBC; KJV, NAB, NASB, NET, NIV, REB, TEV, TNT], 'to search' [CEV, NJB, NRSV], 'to look (for)' [LN; NLT].

b. fut. act. indic. of εὑρίσκω (LN 27.27) (BAGD 1.a. p. 324): 'to find' [LN, Mor, NTC, WBC; all versions]. Εὑρίσκω is not finding accidentally but on purpose [TG, TH].

QUESTION—What additional insights have commentators given into ζητέω 'to seek'?

This word indicates that a person must not only ask but also act in a way to obtain what is prayed for [Mor, NTC]. He must put forth much effort to find what he seeks [BSC]. It is implied that the person here is not seeking God, but seeking from God something he is looking for [TG, TH]. It may imply that the person praying is not sure what he should ask for, though he knows that what he seeks is a gift of God. Seeking may also be more intensive than just asking [Mor].

knock[a] and it-will-be-opened[b] to-you(pl).

LEXICON—a. pres. act. impera. of κρούω (LN **19.12**) (BAGD p. 454): 'to knock' [BAGD, LN, Mor, NTC, WBC; all versions]. In the NT, κρούω is used only of knocking at a door [BAGD].

b. fut. pass. indic. of ἀνοίγω (LN **79.110**) (BAGD 1.a. p. 71): 'to be opened' [BAGD, LN, Mor, NTC, WBC; all versions]. This is a theological passive [ICC], God is the one who will open the door [TG, TH]. The phrase 'it will be opened' is translated 'the door will be opened' [all versions except KJV, NASB].

QUESTION—What may be implied in the use of the verb κρούω 'knock'?
'Knock' evokes the image of a closed door that must be opened, that one must press God insistently in prayer [BSC]. Although there is no explicit mention of what the person is knocking at, the image is knocking at a door that the person cannot open himself, which means that prayer will result in opening doors that would be closed otherwise [Mor]. This is not knocking to enter heaven [McN, Mor, NCBC, TG], but to enter the place where something being sought can be found [NCBC, TG].

7:8 **For^a everyone^b asking receives,^c and the one-seeking finds, and to-the one-knocking it-will-be-opened.**

LEXICON—a. γάρ (LN 89.23) (BAGD 1.d. p. 152): 'for' [BAGD, LN, Mor, NTC, WBC; all versions except CEV, NJB], not explicit [CEV, NJB].
   b. πᾶς (LN 59.23) (BAGD 1.c.γ. p. 632): 'everyone' [Mor, WBC; all versions], 'all' [LN], 'whoever' [NTC]. Πᾶς 'all' does not mean every person but every son of the kingdom [ICC], everyone participating in the Kingdom that Jesus inaugurated [WBC].
   c. pres. act. indic. of λαμβάνω (LN 57.125) (BAGD 2. p. 465): 'to receive' [LN, Mor, NTC, WBC; all versions].

7:9 **Or^a is (there) some man^b among you(pl),**

LEXICON—a. ἤ (LN 89.139) (BAGD 1.d.δ. p. 342): 'or' [BAGD, LN, Mor, NTC; KJV], not explicit [WBC; CEV, NAB, NET, NIV, NJB, NLT, NRSV, REB, TEV, TNT]. Here and in v.10 ἤ 'or' probably indicates 'or to put the matter another way' [EBC]. ἤ is used to connect questions [BAGD, Mor]. See also 7:4.
   b. ἄνθρωπος (LN 9.24) (BAGD 3.a.ζ. p. 69): 'man' [BAGD, LN]. The phrase τίς...ἄνθρωπος is translated 'what man' [NTC; KJV], 'which man' [Mor], 'which one (of you)' [NAB], 'which (of you)' [NIV], 'anyone' [NET, NJB, NRSV], 'any (of you)' [CEV, REB], 'any (of you who are fathers)' [TEV], 'any one (of you)' [TNT], 'no one (among you)' [WBC]. The word ἄνθρωπος serves to emphasize the contrast between a typical human being and God, the heavenly Father [BSC, Mor], or to accentuate the contrast between Jesus and humankind [NAC].

who^a (when) his son^b will-ask-for bread,^c he-will-not-give to-him a-stone (will-he)?

LEXICON—a. ὅς: 'who...when' [NTC, WBC; NJB], 'when' [NAB, NASB, REB, TEV], 'who if' [KJV, NET, NRSV], 'who....if' [TNT], 'if' [CEV, NIV, NLT], 'whom' [Mor].
   b. υἱός (LN 10.42) (BAGD 1.a.α. p. 833): 'son' [BAGD, LN, Mor, NTC; KJV, NAB, NASB, NET, NIV, REB, TEV, TNT], 'child' [CEV, NLT, NRSV], 'a son or daughter' [WBC].
   c. ἄρτος (LN 5.8) (BAGD 1.a. p. 110): 'bread' [BAGD, Mor, NTC, WBC; all versions except NAB, NASB, NLT], 'a loaf of bread' [LN; NAB, NLT], 'a loaf' [NASB]. This is a small round loaf of ordinary bread, not

luxury food [TG]. Some versions reverse the order of the clauses [TEV, TNT]: will he give the son a stone when he asks for bread.

QUESTION—What are the implications of this rhetorical question?

These rhetorical questions expect a negative answer [ICC, NAC, WBC], one which is obvious to all [ICC]. Rhetorical questions beginning with μή amount to affirmations: 'when a child asks, no parent would give' [WBC]. Rhetorical questions can be translated as affirmative statements: 'no father would give his son a stone when he asks for bread' [TH].

7:10 Or[a] also-(if)[b] he-will-ask-for a-fish[c] —

LEXICON—a. ἤ (LN 89.139) (BAGD 1.d.β. p. 342): 'or' [BAGD, LN, Mor, NTC; all versions except CEV], 'and' [WBC], not explicit [CEV]. The conjunction ἤ ties the questions together, substituting fish for bread and again expecting a negative answer [Mor]. It often occurs in interrogative sentences to introduce a question which is parallel to or supplemental to a preceding question [BAGD].

　　b. καί: 'also if' [NTC], 'if' [Mor; KJV, NASB, NET, NIV, NLT, NRSV, TNT], 'when' [NAB, NJB, REB, TEV], not explicit [WBC; CEV].

　　c. ἰχθύς (LN **4.59**) (BAGD p. 384): 'a fish' [LN, Mor, NTC, WBC; all versions]. Some versions reverse the order of the two clauses [NAB, NJB, REB, TEV, TNT].

he-will- not -give to-him a snake[a] (will-he)?

LEXICON—a. ὄφις (LN 4.52) (BAGD 1. p. 600): 'snake' [BAGD, LN, Mor, WBC; all versions except KJV], 'serpent' [BAGD, NTC; KJV].

QUESTION—In these two examples of fathers not refusing requests, what is the point of similarity?

The primary lesson is that prayer is in the context of a father-son relationship with God [NCBC]. The reason for assurance that God answers continuous, persistent prayers lies in his fatherhood [TNTC2]. God will not refuse our requests and he certainly won't mock them [Brc, ICC, Pl]. A parent might refuse, but he certainly should not mock the requests of his children with useless or even dangerous substitutions [Pl]. A stone would be meant to deceive the child [BSC], which is unthinkable [NTC]. No parent would try to trick his child into thinking that the child's request had been granted [EBC, NAC]. Just as a human father would not refuse a request for food from his son and substitute useless or harmful things instead, so God the Father will not refuse his children [TNTC2]. It is not just an issue of parents being willing to give gifts, but being willing to give good gifts even though they are evil [EBC]. The repetition of the previous verse emphasizes that even sinful humans do not give unsatisfying or harmful things to the ones they love when those whom they love are asking for something they need [Mor].

QUESTION—Why does he talk about bread and fish?

They would have been the most common food around Lake Galilee [McN, NCBC, TH, TNTC2]. They are staple foods [BSC, ICC, NIBC, NTC], and these are requests for necessities, not the miraculous [WBC].

QUESTION—Why does he talk about a stone and a snake?

There is a resemblance between bread and a stone and between a fish and a snake [Brc, ICC, Mor, NTC, TH, WBC]. Rough resemblance is the point of comparison [McN, NAC, Pl, TH, WBC]. The typical small loaf of bread resembles a stone in shape [ICC, Mor, NTC, TH, TNTC2, WBC]. A father won't mock a son by giving something that looks like bread (a stone) and yet is inedible [Brc]. The snake here may resemble an eel-like fish that lives in Lake Galilee [NTC, TNTC, TNTC2]. A snake might resembles certain fish [NIBC]. Snakes were not eaten by the Jews [TG, TH].

7:11 Therefore[a] if[b] you(pl) being[c] evil[d]

LEXICON—a. οὖν: 'therefore' [Mor, NTC], 'then' [KJV, NASB, NJB, NRSV, TEV, TNT], 'then though' [NIV], 'so then' [NET], 'well, then' [WBC], not explicit [CEV, NAB, NLT, REB].

b. εἰ (LN 89.65) (BAGD III. p. 219): 'if' [LN, Mor, NTC, WBC; all versions except CEV, TEV], 'if even' [WBC]. It is a condition [ZG] that assumes the supposition to be correct [Mor]. This assumption is shown in some versions which translated this as a statement: 'you know how' [TEV], 'you still know how' [CEV]

c. pres. act. participle of εἰμί (LN 13.1) (BAGD II.8. p. 224): 'to be' [BAGD, LN, Mor, NTC, TH, WBC, ZG; all versions except NLT], not explicit [NLT]. The participle ὄντες 'being' is concessive [TG, WBC, ZG; NET]: although you are evil.

d. πονηρός (LN 88.110) (BAGD 1.b.α. p. 691): 'evil' [BAGD, LN, Mor, NTC; KJV, NASB, NET, NIV, NJB, NRSV, TNT], 'wicked' [LN; NAB], 'bad' [BAGD, TH; CEV, REB, TEV], 'sinful' [WBC], 'sinful people' [NLT].

QUESTION—What is the significance of Jesus' using 'you' and not 'we' in this statement?

Jesus separates himself from 'you' (the disciples, men and women) who are evil [EBC, ICC, Mor, Pl]. 'You' also focuses attention on the hearers knowledge of giving good gifts [Mor]. If Jesus has said '*we* being evil' it would have implied that Jesus considered himself to be sinful like those in the audience. We not only do evil things, we are evil [MLJ].

QUESTION—Why did Jesus call his audience πονηρός 'evil'?

Jesus inserted the word πονηρός 'evil' even when the illustration works without it, thus indicating a particular emphasis on this word [Mor]. It is also stated without any justification, so Jesus assumes the proposition should be taken for granted. Also it is assumed that the word applies to all human beings as a universal characteristic [Mor]. Πονηρός is an intentionally 'strong word that Jesus chose to employ when he could have chosen a weaker and less offensive word [TNTC2]. Jesus is setting up a 'how much more is God' argument in this verse, making a contrast with God who has no shadow of evil [EBC]. 'Evil' refers to the innate sinfulness of human nature [BSC, EBC, Mor, TNTC2]. Because people are self-centered and not God-centered everything they do is tainted with evil. This does not mean that Jesus thinks that humans are as evil as they can be or that everything they do is evil [EBC]. The essential sinfulness of man is assumed, but even the normal emotions of human fatherhood can prevail in cases like this [TNTC2]. It invites a comparison between parents' natural acts of kindness toward their children and the perfection of God's generosity toward those who seek his favor [NIBC]. Even those who are grudging are likely to be generous to their own children [Pl]. The important point is the contrast between a holy God and evil humans: people are evil in contrast to God [BAGD, EBC, TH, WBC]. It is not a reference to original sin [McN], or about human nature [TH]. All humans are morally degraded, especially when compared to the righteous and holy Father [WBC]. Jesus, like in Mk 10:18, is asking how good we (even as kind parents) really are when compared to God [McN, NCBC].

know-how[a] to-give your(pl) children good[b] gifts,[c]

LEXICON—a. perf. act. indic. of οἶδα (LN **28.7**) (BAGD 3. p. 558): 'to know how' [BAGD, LN, Mor, NTC, WBC; all versions]. This Greek verb does not have a present tense form, so where a present tense meaning is intended the form of the perfect tense is used.

b. ἀγαθός (LN 65.20) (BAGD 1.a.β. p. 2): 'good' [LN, Mor, NTC, WBC; all versions], 'beneficial' [BAGD, Mor].

c. δόμα (LN 57.73) (BAGD p. 203): 'gift' [BAGD, LN, Mor, NTC, WBC; all versions except NJB, REB, TEV], 'what is (good)' [NJB], 'things' [REB, TEV].

how-much[a] more[b] your(pl) father, the-one in the heavens,[c] will-give good[d] (things) to-the (ones) asking him.

LEXICON—a. πόσος (LN 78.13) (BAGD 1. p. 694): 'how much' [LN, Mor, NTC, WBC; all versions except CEV], not explicit [CEV]. This interrogative particle is used in exclamations [ZG].

b. μᾶλλον (LN 78.28) (BAGD 2.b. p. 489): 'more' [LN]. The phrase πόσῳ μᾶλλον is translated '(how) much more' [BAGD, Mor, NTC; all versions except CEV], 'is even more ready (to give)' [CEV], 'how much more is it true that' [WBC].

c. ὁ πατὴρ ὑμῶν ὁ ἐν τοῖς οὐρανοῖς: 'your father which is in heaven' [KJV], 'your Father who is in heaven' [Mor; NASB], 'your Father in heaven' [NTC; NET, NIV, NJB, NRSV, TEV, TNT], 'your heavenly Father' [WBC; NAB, NLT, REB]. See 5:16 [TG], see 5:45 [EBC] for more information.

d. ἀγαθός (LN 65.20): 'good' [LN]. This adjective is translated 'good things' [Mor, NTC, WBC; CEV, KJV, NAB, NJB, NRSV, REB, TEV, TNT], 'what is good' [NASB], 'good gifts' [NET, NIV, NLT]. In this clause the adjective functions as a noun and is thus considered a substantive.

QUESTION—What relationship is indicated by πόσῳμᾶλλον 'how much more?'

This is the conclusion of this section with a lesser to greater argument. It was used here to emphasize the certainty of God giving good gifts [EBC, ICC, Mor, NAC, NCBC, NTC, TH, WBC]. This passage emphasizes that God is not reluctant to grant our requests, which we might have inferred from the earlier call for persistence in prayer [TNTC2]. This is the point of 7:7–11: the Father cares and hears prayers [ICC].

QUESTION—What are the ἀγαθά 'good (things)'?

It refers to both material and spiritual blessings [McN]. For Matthew the good things include the Holy Spirit, as in Luke, and are even broader, including the material provision of 6:25–34 [NTC, TNTC2]. The ἀγαθά 'good (things)' are the things necessary to live as a child of God, just as bread and fish are necessary for a man's children to live [BSC]. The ἀγαθά represents all that the disciple needs in order to follow the instructions in the Sermon [ICC], things that related to seeking God and his righteousness as mentioned in 6:33 [NAC], the qualities of character demanded by the sermon [WBC], the Holy Spirit as that which is necessary for understanding and obeying God's will [BSC]. This is not a broad promise of answered prayer: the disciple will not necessarily receive everything he asks for [NAC, NTC]. Parents don't always give exactly what the children ask for because children ask for many useless, unwise and even harmful things; however, our heavenly Father, like human parents, will give good things to his children [Pl].

QUESTION—How is this verse punctuated?

This verse is punctuated as a statement ending in a period [GNT; CEV, NLT], as an exclamation [Mor, NTC, ZG; NASB, NET, NIV, NJB, NRSV, REB, TEV, TNT], as a rhetorical question [WBC; KJV], as a rhetorical question expecting a negative answer 'will your father do any less?' [ICC].

DISCOURSE UNIT: 7:12–29 [TNTC]. The topic is the golden rule; the two ways; false prophets, and the two builders.

DISCOURSE UNIT: 7:12 [EBC, ICC, McN, MLJ, Mor, NAC, NCBC, NIBC, NTC, Pl, TG, TNTC2, WBC; NAB, NJB, NLT, NRSV]. The topic is the golden rule [McN, MLJ, Mor, NAC, NCBC, NTC, Pl, WBC; NAB, NJB, NLT, NRSV], a summary of Jesus' ethic [TNTC2], balance and perfection [EBC], a concluding statement—the golden rule, the law and the prophets [ICC].

7:12 Therefore[a] all-things whatsoever[b] you(pl)-might-wish[c]

LEXICON—a. οὖν: 'therefore' [Mor, NTC, WBC; KJV, NASB], 'so' [NIV, NJB], not explicit [all versions except KJV, NASB, NIV, NJB].

    b. ὅσος (LN 59.19) (BAGD 2. p. 586): 'as much as' [BAGD, LN]. The phrase πάντα ὅσα 'all things whatsoever' [Mor; KJV] is also translated 'whatever' [NTC; NAB, NASB, TNT], 'what' [NLT, TEV], 'everything' [WBC], 'in everything' [NET, NIV, NRSV], 'always' [NJB, REB], not

explicit [CEV]. The phrase πάντα ὅσα 'all things whatsoever' indicates
unlimited scope [WBC]. The adjective πάντα stresses the quantity of the
action as well as the quality [EBC, NCBC].

c. pres. act. subj. of θέλω (LN 25.1) (BAGD 1. p. 355): 'to wish' [LN, Mor],
'to want' [BAGD, LN, NTC; CEV, NASB, TEV, TNT]. This verb is
translated 'ye would' [KJV], 'you would have' [NAB, NIV], 'as you
would have' [NRSV], 'as you would like' [NJB, REB], 'you would like'
[WBC], 'as you would want' [NET], 'what you would like' [NLT]. The
following versions begin the verse with an imperative clause: e.g., 'treat
others...' [CEV, NAB, NET, NIV, NJB, NLT, NRSV, REB, TEV].

QUESTION—What relationship is indicated by οὖν 'therefore'?

It summarizes the whole sermon [BSC, EBC, McN, Mor, NAC, TNTC2,
WBC], or the sermon beginning at 5:17 [EBC, ICC, NTC, Pl], as evidenced
by the repetition of the phrase 'the law and the prophets' [EBC, ICC, Pl], or
to the whole sermon beginning at 5:20 [NCBC]. This verse is the highpoint
or climax of the sermon [Brc, NIBC, Pl]. This verse is the nutshell version of
the greater righteousness [TNTC2]. It sums up the good works expected of
Jesus' followers as described in 5:20–7:11 [NCBC]. it sums up 5:17–7:11
[ICC, NTC]. It is a general conclusion to the whole sermon to this point, thus
making 7:13–27 an epilogue [McN]. 7:12 summarizes 7:1–11 and possibly
the whole sermon with a statement on ideal interpersonal behavior [NAC]. It
is the conclusion not only of 7:1–12 but also of the main section of the whole
sermon on good works (5:16) and righteousness (5:20). It also refers to the
immediately preceding verses, suggesting that the disciple should act out of
gratitude for all God's good gifts [Mor, NTC]. It appears to signal a
summation of the preceding verses [McN, TH], but there is a switch in focus
here from a relationship to God in the preceding verses to a relationship to
other people [TG, TH]. For this reason, some versions (such as TEV) do not
put in a transition word here [TH]. Οὖν indicates that a separate paragraph
should be made because there is not a close relationship to the preceding
verses [TG].

that[a] people[b] would-do[c] (to/for)[d] you(pl), so[e] also[f] do (to/for) them;

LEXICON—a. ἵνα (LN 90.22) (BAGD II.1.a.α. p. 377): 'that' [LN, Mor; KJV],
not explicit [all versions except CEV, KJV]. The conjunction ἵνα does not
indicate purpose, as 'in order to make something happen' [EBC, Mor,
NAC], but states the content of the wish [Mor].

b. ἄνθρωπος (LN 9.1) (BAGD 1.a.δ. p. 68): 'people' [LN, NTC; NASB],
'men' [Mor; KJV, TNT], 'them' [CEV, NAB, NET, NJB, NLT, NRSV,
REB, TEV], 'others' [WBC]. Here ἄνθρωπος refers to people in general,
not just men [TH].

c. pres. act. subj. of ποιέω (LN **41.7**) (BAGD I.1.d.β. p. 682): 'to do
(to/for)' [BAGD, **LN**, Mor, NTC, WBC; KJV, NAB, NET, NIV, NLT,
NRSV, TEV, TNT], 'to treat' [CEV, NASB, NJB, REB], 'to behave
toward, to deal with, to act' [LN].

d. There is no lexical entry for this preposition indicating the relationship between the verb 'do' and its object 'you'. It is implied in the Greek by the use of the dative case of the pronoun ὑμῖν 'you'. This relation is translated 'to you' [Mor, WBC; KJV, NAB, NIV, NRSV, TNT], 'for you' [NTC; NASB, NLT, TEV], '(to treat) you' [CEV, NET, NJB, REB]. It should be noted that when used with the verb 'do' the English preposition 'to' has a generally negative connotation, whereas the preposition 'for' has a generally positive connotation. The Greek construction ποιῶσιν ὑμῖν 'that people would do to/for you' is probably neutral, as reflected in the rendering 'treat you' by several versions.

e. οὕτως (LN 61.9): 'so' [LN, Mor, NTC; KJV, NASB], not explicit [WBC; all versions except KJV, NASB].

f. καί (LN 89.93): 'also' [LN, Mor, NTC; TNT], 'as' [CEV], 'even' [KJV], not explicit [WBC; all versions except CEV, KJV, TNT].

for[a] this is[b] the law and the prophets.

LEXICON—a. γάρ: 'for' [Mor, NTC, WBC; KJV, NASB, NET, NIV, NRSV, TNT], not explicit [CEV, NAB, NJB, NLT, REB, TEV].

b. pres. act. indic. of εἰμί (LN 13.4): 'to be' [LN, Mor, NTC, WBC; CEV, KJV, NAB, NASB, NJB, NRSV, REB], 'to sum up' [EBC, Mor, NAC; NIV], 'to fulfill' [EBC, NAC; NET], 'to be the essence of' [WBC], 'to be the meaning of' [TEV, TNT], 'to be a summary of' [NLT].

QUESTION—What is meant by ὁ νόμος καὶ οἱ προφῆται 'the law and the prophets'?

This concerns 'the meaning of the law of Moses and of the teachings of the prophets' [TEV], 'what the Law and the Prophets are all about' [CEV]. This was a customary way of referring to the whole OT [Mor, NTC]. By mentioning the same phrase as in 5:17, this phrase functions as an inclusio and summary of everything between 5:17 and 7:11 [ICC, NAC]. See this phrase at 5:17.

DISCOURSE UNIT: 7:13–29 [NCBC]. The topic is the two ways.

DISCOURSE UNIT: 7:13–27 [BBC, BSC, EBC, ICC, McN, Mor, NAC, NTC, Pl, TNTC2, WBC]. The topic is righteousness and the entrance into the kingdom [BSC], exhortation to enter the kingdom [NTC], warning of the judgments which await the members of the kingdom [Pl], warnings against spurious discipleship [TNTC2], three warnings, the prospect of eschatological judgment [ICC], conclusion [WBC], the two ways [BBC], true and false discipleship [Mor], conclusion: only two ways [NAC], conclusion: call to decision and commitment [EBC], epilogue [McN].

DISCOURSE UNIT: 7:13–23 [Pl; NASB]. The topic is a contrast of ways and of fruits [NASB], exhortation to enter the Christian life, avoiding false guides and false professions [Pl].

DISCOURSE UNIT: 7:13–14 [EBC, Ed, GNT, HF, ICC, McN, NAC, NCBC, NIBC, NTC, TG, TH, WBC; CEV, NAB, NET, NIV, NJB, NLT, NRSV, TEV]. The topic is enter the narrow gate [NET], the narrow gate [GNT, TG, TH; CEV, NAB, NLT, NRSV, TEV], the narrow way [TG; HF], the narrow and wide gates [NIV], the two ways [EBC, ICC, WBC; NJB], two gates, two ways [NCBC], the narrow gate, the two ways [McN], the narrow versus the wide gate/road [NAC], the narrow entrance to life [TG], the gate to real life is narrow [TH], the path to life is a narrow one [TH], the beginning of the way: the narrow gate and the constricted way versus the wide gate and the broad way [NTC], we enter the Kingdom by choice and personal separation [Ed (p. 531)].

7:13 **Enter**[a] **through**[b] **the narrow**[c] **gate;**[d]

LEXICON—a. aorist act. impera. of εἰσέρχομαι (LN 15.93) (BAGD 1.f. p. 233): 'to enter' [BAGD, LN, Mor, NTC; all versions except CEV, TEV, TNT], 'to go in(to)' [BAGD, LN, WBC; CEV, TEV, TNT].

    b. διά (LN 84.29) (BAGD A.I.1. p. 179): 'through' [LN, Mor, WBC; CEV, NAB, NET, NIV, NLT, NRSV, TEV], 'only through' [NLT], 'by' [NTC; NASB, NJB, REB, TNT], 'at' [KJV].

    c. στενός (LN **81.19**) (BAGD p. 766): 'narrow' [BAGD, **LN**, Mor, NTC, WBC; all versions except KJV], 'strait' [KJV], 'restricted' [LN].

    d. πύλη (LN 7.48) (BAGD 2. p. 729): 'gate' [BAGD, LN, Mor, NTC, WBC; all versions]. This kind of gate is a main entrance into something [Mor], such as a city [Mor, Pl] or a temple or prison [Mor]. Instead of a gate as an object, this seems to refer to the space of the gateway [LN (81.16)].

QUESTION—What is the relationship of this passage to the context?

This verse is a major turning point in the sermon [WBC]. It begins the conclusion [BSC, Mor, TNTC2]. The passage 7:13–27 is a general conclusion on the demands of discipleship, following on the ethical climax of 7:12 [TNTC2]. These verses begin the concluding section [Mor]. There is no more ethical teaching [WBC]. It is the end of explication [BSC]. In the rest of this chapter no new commands are issued [NAC]. Instead, there is a climactic admonition [WBC], with this verse beginning a set of exhortations to obey the commandments of this sermon [BSC].

for[a] **the gate (is) wide**[b]

TEXT—The word πύλη 'gate' does not occur here in some manuscripts. It is included by GNT with a B rating, indicating that the text is almost certain. It is omitted only by NJB.

LEXICON—a. ὅτι (LN 89.33) (BAGD 3.b. p. 589): 'for' [BAGD, LN, Mor, NTC, WBC; KJV, NAB, NASB, NIV, NRSV], 'because' [LN; NET, TEV, TNT], 'since' [NJB], not explicit [CEV, NLT, REB]. This conjunction indicates the reason for seeking the narrow gate, which is that it is not as easily found as the wide gate [Mor].

    b. πλατύς (LN **81.16**) (BAGD p. 667): 'wide' [BAGD, LN, NTC, WBC; all versions except TNT], 'broad' [BAGD, LN, Mor; TNT].

QUESTION—How are the gates and the roads related in this illustration?
The idea of the two ways was current in contemporary Jewish thought of that time [McN, Mor, NAC, NCBC, Pl, TNTC2]. The image of the two gates is less common [ICC, Mor]. The general picture here is clear; there are two gates, two roads, two crowds, and two destinations [EBC]. The narrow road of discipleship is contrasted with the broad and easy road representing the self-centered life that most people live [NIBC]. The emphasis is on the fact that that there are two, and only two, roads in life and people must choose one or the other [Mor]. True discipleship is chosen only by a minority [TNTC2].

1. The road and the gate are different metaphors for the same thing [BSC, ICC, TNTC2, WBC]. The narrow gate and the difficult road represent the rigors of discipleship [WBC], or obedience [BSC]. The metaphor mans that they must avoid all obstacles and diversions that would hinder entering the kingdom [ICC]. If life is viewed as a unity, it is a gate; if life is viewed as a series of choices, then it is a road [BSC]. The images coalesce; the difficult road is through the narrow gate [TNTC2]. One cannot put the gate before the road or the road before the gate; they are set side by side and are synonymous [ICC].

2. The road leads to the gate, which opens to the final destination [Mor, TNTC; TEV]. The splendid gate is obvious and easily seen, but the narrow, inconspicuous gate can only be seen by those who search carefully for it [Mor].

3. The two gates open to two roads, which lead in turn to two different destinations [EBC, NTC, TG]. The gate is the present choice that Jesus is talking about now and the road is the subsequent life. The right initial choice leads to sanctification, but the wrong initial choice is followed by gradual hardening [NTC]. Entrance begins now on the road of persecution but ends in the consummated kingdom [EBC, NTC]. The gate is necessary in the illustration because it indicates that even at the beginning of the disciple's journey the entrance is restrictive and a decisive break is needed [EBC].

and[a] the road[b] (is) spacious[c] leading[d] into destruction,[e]

LEXICON—a. καί: 'and' [Mor; all versions except NJB], 'since' [NJB].

b. ὁδός (LN 1.99) (BAGD 2.a. p. 554): 'road' [LN, Mor; NAB, NIV, NJB, NRSV, REB, TNT], 'the road to it' [TEV], 'the road that leads there' [CEV], 'way' [BAGD, LN, NTC; KJV, NASB, NET], 'highway' [LN; NLT], 'the path' [WBC].

c. εὐρύχωρος (LN 81.18) (BAGD p. 326): 'broad' [BAGD, **LN**, NTC, WBC; KJV, NASB, NIV, NLT, REB], 'spacious' [BAGD, **LN**, Mor; NAB, NET, NJB], 'roomy' [BAGD], 'wide' [TNT], 'easy' [NRSV, TEV], 'easy to follow' [CEV].

d. pres. act. participle of ἀπάγω (LN 84.33) (BAGD 3. p. 79): 'to lead' [BAGD, LN, Mor, NTC, WBC; CEV, NAB, NASB, NET, NIV, NJB,

NRSV, REB, TEV]. This participle is translated 'the way to' [TNT], 'the highway to' [NLT].

e. ἀπώλεια (LN 20.31) (BAGD 2. p. 103): 'destruction' [BAGD, LN, Mor, NTC; all versions except NLT, TEV], 'final ruin' [WBC], 'hell' [NLT, TEV]. This means eternal destruction, the equivalent of hell [TH].

QUESTION—What is implied in the term εὐρύχωρος 'spacious'?

1. The image of the road is described as being spacious [EBC, LN, Mor, NCBC, NTC, TNTC2, WBC; all versions except CEV, NRSV, TEV]. It is spacious and able to accommodate larger crowds [EBC, Mor]. It is more readily available and more used [TNTC2].

2. Since the road is spacious, some focus on the implication that it is easy to travel on [NAC, NIBC, Pl, TG, TH, WBC; CEV, NRSV, TEV]. It is the path of ease and comfort [WBC]. It is popular because it requires no self-discipline [Pl, WBC]. It is the path of self-centeredness and which offers the least resistance [NIBC]. It connotes a lack of striving or work [ICC].

and those entering[a] through it are many.[b]

LEXICON—a. pres. act. participle εἰσέρχομαι (LN 15.93) (BAGD 2.a. p. 233): 'to enter' [LN, NTC; NAB, NASB, NET, NIV, REB], 'to go' [CEV] 'to go in' [LN, Mor; KJV], 'to go (that way)' [WBC; TNT], 'to come' [BAGD], 'to travel (it)' [TG; TEV], 'to take (it)' [NJB, NRSV], 'to walk on (it)' [TG], 'to choose (the easy way)' [NLT].

b. πολύς (LN 59.1) (BAGD I.1.a.α. p. 687): 'many' [BAGD, Mor, NTC, WBC; all versions except CEV], 'a lot of people' [CEV].

7:14 How narrow[a] (is) the gate

TEXT—Instead of τί 'how', some manuscripts have ὅτι 'for'. GNT selects the reading 'how' with a B rating, indicating that the text is almost certain. The reading ὅτι is taken and translated 'for' by NTC; NASB, NRSV. It is translated 'because' by KJV. It is not translated by NET, NIV, NJB, NLT, REB, TEV.

LEXICON—a. στενός (LN 81.19) (BAGD p. 766): 'narrow' [LN, Mor, NTC, WBC; CEV, NAB, NET, NJB, NRSV, REB, TEV, TNT], 'small' [NASB, NIV, NLT], 'strait' [KJV]. The phrase 'how narrow' is translated 'very narrow' [CEV], 'so narrow' [TNT];

QUESTION—What is implied by the term στενός 'narrow'?

It implies restriction; the idea here has more to do with popularity or availability than with ease of travel [TNTC2]. Wide and narrow refer to levels of difficulty in traveling the road as well as the number of people accommodated [NAC]. The 'strait' of the KJV is from the Latin *strictum* and does not connote 'straight' in the sense of not bending or curving [EBC]. The spatial terminology is used to connote the difficulty of radical discipleship [WBC].

and difficult^a the road leading into life,^b

LEXICON—a. perf. pass. participle of θλίβω (LN **22.21**) (BAGD 2.b. p. 362): 'difficult' [LN; NET], 'hard' [TG; CEV, NJB, NRSV, TEV, TNT], 'so hard' [TNT], 'so hard to follow that' [CEV], 'narrow' [BAGD; KJV, NASB, NIV, NLT], 'restricted' [BAGD], 'confined' [BAGD, WBC], 'constricted' [Mor, NTC; NAB, REB]. Literally it means 'pressed together' [NCBC, TH], thus not spacious and roomy, able to accommodate only a few people in comparison [NCBC].

b. ζωή (LN 23.88) (BAGD 2.b.β. p. 341): 'life' [BAGD, LN, Mor, NTC, WBC; all versions except TEV], not explicit [TEV]. This refers to eternal life [ICC, Mor, NAC, Pl, TG, TH, TNTC2, WBC], and is parallel to entering heaven in v.21 [TG, TNTC2]. It is life in the final consummation [BAGD, EBC].

and few^a are those finding^b it.

LEXICON—a. ὀλίγος (LN 59.3) (BAGD 1.b. p. 563): 'few' [BAGD, LN, Mor, NTC, WBC; KJV, NAB, NASB, NET, NRSV, REB, TNT], 'only a few' [NIV, NJB, NLT], 'only a few people' [CEV], 'few people' [TEV].

b. pres. act. participle εὑρίσκω (LN 27.27) (BAGD 1.a. p. 324): 'to find' [LN, Mor, NTC, WBC; all versions except TNT], 'to discover' [TNT].

QUESTION—To what does αὐτήν 'it' refer?

It refers to 'the road' [NCBC, NIBC, TG, TH, WBC]. It is parallel to 'it' in 7:13.

DISCOURSE UNIT: 7:15–23 [ICC, McN, NAC, WBC; NIV]. The topic is a tree and its fruit [NIV], profession and real fruit [McN], good versus bad fruit [NAC], the false and the genuine [WBC], beware of false prophets [ICC].

DISCOURSE UNIT: 7:15–20 [EBC, GNT, HF, NTC, NCBC, NIBC, Pl, TG, TH, TNTC2, WBC; CEV, NAB, NET, NIV, NJB, NLT, NRSV, TEV]. The topic is two trees [EBC], a tree known by its fruit [GNT], a the tree and its fruit [TG, TH; CEV, NET, NIV, NLT, NRSV, TEV], the kind of fruit a tree produces [TG, TH], good fruit and bad fruit [TG], by their fruits you shall know them [HF], Jesus warns about false prophets [TH], false prophets [NCBC, TNTC2; NAB, NJB], untrustworthy guides [Pl], warning against/concerning false prophets [TG, WBC], warning with respect to the believers' progress on the way [NTC].

DISCOURSE UNIT: 7:15–16 [Ed]. The topic is that the Kingdom must be preached with more than external thoughts. [Ed (p. 531)].

7:15 **Beware^a of the false-prophets,^b**

LEXICON—a. pres. act. impera. of προσέχω (LN 27.59) (BAGD 1.b. p. 714): 'to beware (of)' [Mor, NTC, WBC; KJV, NAB, NASB, NJB, NLT, NRSV, REB, TNT], 'to be on your guard (against)' [LN; TEV], 'to watch out (for)' [CEV, NET, NIV].

b. ψευδοπροφήτης (LN 53.81) (BAGD p. 892): 'false prophet' [BAGD, LN, Mor, NTC, WBC; all versions]. This term can refer to those who claim to be prophets of God but are not [NAC, TG, TH], or to those who prophesy what is false [TG].

QUESTION—What is the relationship of this section to what precedes it?

This is a second warning unit [ICC]. After talking about the paths, Jesus now talks about the teachers that will help or hinder those walking on the narrow path [McN, Mor]. Those who want to find the right way that leads to life must make sure that their guides are trustworthy [Pl]. The false prophets hinder others from entering the narrow gate by standing in front of the broad gate and beckoning others to enter it [ICC, MLJ]. Jesus is now addressing the situation where a greater number of people profess to follow him than actually do [NAC]. The focus seems to be on criteria for judging who is a false prophet in the community of faith [NCBC]. They reject the narrow gate and the restricted way to life. Verses 7:21–23 show that they do not function under Jesus Christ's authority, and since there are only two roads, if the false prophets divert the disciples from the true path, they are endangering the disciples with destruction [EBC].

who come[a] to you(pl) in sheep's[b] clothing,[c]

LEXICON—a. pres. mid./pass. (deponent = act.) indic. of ἔρχομαι (LN 15.81) (BAGD I.1.a.β. p. 310): 'to come' [BAGD, LN, Mor, NTC, WBC; all versions except CEV]; 'they dress up like' [CEV].

b. πρόβατον (LN 4.22) (BAGD 1. p. 703): 'sheep' [BAGD, LN; all versions].

c. ἔνδυμα (LN 6.162) (BAGD 2. p. 263): 'clothing' [BAGD, LN]. The phrase ἐνἐνδύμασινπροβάτων 'in sheep's clothing' [LN (88.233), NTC; KJV, NAB, NASB, NET, NIV, NRSV] is also translated 'disguised as sheep' [TG; NJB, NLT, TNT], 'disguised as harmless sheep' [NLT], 'dressed up as sheep' [Mor; REB], 'dressed to look like sheep' [TG], 'dressed as if they were sheep' [NTC], 'looking like sheep' [WBC], 'looking like sheep on the outside' [TG; TEV].

QUESTION—What qualities are emphasized by the figure of a wolf in sheep's clothing?

They are deceptive and are pretenders [LN, NAC, Pl, WBC]. They are not what they appear to be [McN, NIBC, TNTC2, WBC]. Inwardly they are strong and cruel [TG]. They are the opposite of sheep, who are harmless [Mor, TH], innocent [LN, Pl], guileless [TH], weak and meek [TG, TH].

but[a] inside[b] they-are ravenous[c] wolves.[d]

LEXICON—a. δέ: 'but' [Mor, NTC; all versions except REB], 'while' [WBC; REB].

b. ἔσωθεν (LN 26.2) (BAGD 2. p. 314): 'inside' [BAGD; CEV], 'on the inside' [TEV], 'within' [BAGD, WBC], 'inwardly' [Mor, NTC; KJV, NASB, NET, NIV, NRSV, TNT], 'in the inner being' [LN], 'underneath' [NAB, NJB, REB], not explicit [NLT].

c. ἅρπαξ (LN **20.4**) (BAGD 1. p. 109): 'ravenous' [BAGD, Mor, NTC; NAB, NASB, NJB, NRSV, TNT], 'ravening' [KJV], 'rapacious' [BAGD], 'vicious, destructive' [LN], 'ferocious' [NIV], 'savage' [REB], 'wild' [TEV], 'voracious' [NET], 'predatory' [WBC], 'who have come to attack you' [CEV], 'that will tear you apart' [NLT].

d. λύκος (LN 4.11, 88.121) (BAGD 2. p. 481): 'wolf' [BAGD, LN (4.11), Mor, NTC, WBC; all versions]. Wolf is a figurative extension of meaning for a person who is vicious, fierce, and dangerous [LN].

QUESTION—What quality of the false prophets is like wolves?

This is a metaphor illustrating that they appear to be one thing, but in reality they are something completely different and quite dangerous [NET]. The difference between what they seem to be and what they really are is emphasized [TG]. The false prophets and the followers of Jesus are natural mortal enemies just as wolves and sheep are [WBC]. The false prophets are really interested in their own profit [Mor], in furthering their own interests at the expense of the flock [Mor]. They are prompted by personal greed, and will destroy others for their own gain [NIBC]. In that culture destructiveness and greediness were associated with wolves, so one of those attributes may need to be made explicit in the translation: 'they are destructive like wolves' [TH].

DISCOURSE UNIT: 7:16–20 [McN]. The topic is good and bad trees.

7:16 By[a] their fruits[b] you(pl)-will-know[c] them;

LEXICON—a. ἀπό: 'by' [NCBC, NTC, WBC; all versions], 'from' [Mor].

b. καρπός (LN **42.13**) (BAGD 2.a. p. 405): 'fruit' [BAGD, LN, Mor, NTC; all versions except CEV, NLT, TEV], 'deed' [**LN**, WBC], 'what they do' [CEV, TEV], 'the way they act' [NLT], 'their conduct' [NCBC]. This is a figurative extension of the meaning of fruit and means the natural result of what has been done. This word refers to deeds in general [BSC, ICC, NCBC, NIBC, Pl, TH, TNTC2], or to character, actions and words [EBC, MLJ, Mor, NTC]. The prepositional phrase is in an emphatic prominent position at the beginning of the sentence [TH, WBC].

c. future mid. (deponent = act.) indic. of ἐπιγινώσκω (LN 27.61) (BAGD 2.a. p. 291): 'to know' [BAGD, Mor, TG; KJV, NAB, NASB, NRSV, TEV], 'to recognize' [LN, NTC, TG, TH, WBC; NET, NIV, REB, TNT], 'to detect' [NLT], 'to be able to tell them' [NJB], 'to tell what they are' [CEV]. See this word at 7:20.

(people do) not[a] gather[b] grapes[c] from thorn-bushes[d] or figs[e] from thistle,[f] (do they)?

LEXICON—a. μήτι (LN **69.16**) (BAGD p. 520): (negation plus tag question) 'not...are they' [NTC; NASB], '...does one?' [WBC], 'do they' [NET], not explicit [KJV, NIV, NJB, REB, TEV]. This is an interrogative particle used in questions that expect a negative answer [BAGD]. It marks a somewhat more emphatic negative response than μή [LN]. This rhetorical

question is translated as a statement [CEV, NLT], 'no one…' [CEV].
Μήτι introduces a rhetorical question that expects a negative answer
[ICC, McN, TH].

b. pres. act. indic. συλλέγω (LN 18.10) (BAGD p. 777): 'to gather' [BAGD,
Mor; KJV, NASB, NET, NRSV, TNT], 'to pick (something)' [BAGD,
LN, NTC, WBC; CEV, NAB, NIV, NJB, NLT, REB], not explicit [TEV].
The subject of this plural verb is indefinite, referring to people in general
[NET].

c. σταφυλή (LN 3.38) (BAGD p. 765): 'grapes' [LN, Mor, NTC, WBC; all
versions].

d. ἄκανθα (LN **3.17**) (BAGD p. 29): 'thorn bushes' [**LN**, Mor, WBC; CEV,
NAB, NASB, NIV, NLT, TEV], 'thorns' [NTC; KJV, NET, NJB, NRSV,
TNT], 'briars' [LN; REB], 'thistle' [LN]. It refers to any kind of thorny
plant [LN, TH]. It is a thorn-plant in contrast to useful plants [BAGD].

e. σῦκον (LN 3.36) (BAGD p. 776): 'figs' [BAGD, LN, Mor, NTC, WBC;
all versions].

f. τρίβολος (LN 3.17) (BAGD p. 826): 'thistles' [BAGD, LN, Mor, NTC,
WBC; KJV, NAB, NASB, NET, NIV, NJB, NLT, NRSV, REB, TNT],
'briars' [TEV], not explicit [CEV]. This noun and ἄκανθα 'thorn bush'
are both included in the same semantic domain [LN]. It refers to various
types of prickly plants [TH].

QUESTION—How much detail is needed about the types of plants here?
These are illustrations from nature that would be familiar to the audience
[Mor], but the details not important; in the broad understanding any child
would understand [ICC]. There are many kinds of thorny and prickly plants
in the area and precise identification is not necessary; what is important is
that prickly weeds do not yield desirable fruit [TH]. The point is that
superficial resemblances between true and false prophets should not fool us
[Brc]. The main emphasis is on the difference between plants either being
weeds or bearing choice fruit [BSC].

7:17 Thus[a] every[b] good[c] tree[d] produces[e] good[f] fruit,[g]

LEXICON—a. οὕτως (LN 61.9) (BAGD p. 597): 'thus' [BAGD, LN, WBC],
'even so' [KJV, NASB], 'just so' [NAB], 'so' [BAGD, LN, NTC],
'likewise' [Mor; NIV], 'in the same way' [NET, NJB, NRSV], not
explicit [CEV, NLT, REB, TEV, TNT].

b. πᾶς: 'every' [Mor, NTC, WBC; KJV, NAB, NASB, NET, NIV, NRSV,
TNT], 'a' [CEV, NJB, NLT, TEV], 'a (good tree) always' [REB].

c. ἀγαθός (LN **65.20**) (BAGD 1.a.β. p. 2): 'good' [LN, WBC; CEV, KJV,
NAB, NASB, NET, NIV, NRSV, REB], 'sound' [Mor; NJB, TNT],
'healthy' [NTC; NLT, TEV].

d. δένδρον (LN **3.2**) (BAGD p. 174): 'tree' [BAGD, LN, Mor, NTC, WBC;
all versions]. The implication is that these are trees planted in an orchard
and are not wild trees [TH].

e. pres. act. indic. of ποιέω (LN 23.199) (BAGD I.1.b. p. 681): 'to produce'
   [BAGD, LN, WBC; CEV, NJB, NLT, TNT], 'to bring forth' [KJV], 'to
   bear' [BAGD, LN, Mor, NTC; NAB, NASB, NET, NIV, NRSV, TEV],
   'to yield' [BAGD; REB].

f. καλός (LN **65.22**) (BAGD 2.a. p. 400): 'good' [LN, Mor, NTC, WBC; all
   versions except REB], 'fine' [**LN**], 'sound' [REB]. The meaning is similar
   to ἀγαθός but with more emphasis on the outward appearance [Mor].

g. καρπός (LN **3.33**) (BAGD 1.a. p. 404): 'fruit' [BAGD, LN, Mor, NTC,
   WBC; all versions]. In the previous verse the emphasis was on the kind of
   fruit [Mor]; now it shifts to the quality of fruit and the trees that bear it
   [Mor].

but/and[a] the unhealthy/worthless[b] tree produces bad[c] fruit.

LEXICON—a. δέ: 'but' [Mor, NTC, WBC; KJV, NASB, NET, NIV, NJB,
   NRSV, TEV], 'and' [CEV, NAB, NLT, REB, TNT].

b. σαπρός (LN 65.28) (BAGD 1. p. 742): 'unhealthy' [NLT], 'decayed'
   [BAGD, WBC], 'unsound' [TNT], 'diseased' [LN], 'sickly' [NTC],
   'rotten' [BAGD; NAB, NJB], 'poor' [REB, TEV], 'worthless' [ICC,
   Mor], 'corrupt' [KJV], 'bad' [LN; CEV, NASB, NET, NIV, NRSV].

c. πονηρός (LN 65.27) (BAGD 1.a.γ. p. 690): 'bad' [BAGD, LN, Mor,
   WBC; all versions except KJV], 'evil' [KJV], 'spoiled, worthless'
   [BAGD], 'worthless' [NTC]. Σαπρός and πονηρός are synonyms,
   having no substantial difference in this context and being used only for
   sake of variety [McN]. See also in v.18.

QUESTION—What is the quality σαπρός associated with the tree?

The following senses are not necessarily exclusive of each other.

1. The focus is on the tree's health: 'unhealthy' [NLT], 'decayed' [BAGD,
   ICC, WBC], 'corrupt' [KJV], 'rotten' [BAGD, ICC; NAB, NJB],
   'unsound' [TNT], 'not healthy' [Mor, TH], 'not growing properly' [TH],
   'diseased' [LN], 'seriously diseased' [LN], 'sickly' [NTC], 'a tree that
   isn't healthy' [TG], 'a tree that isn't growing well' [TG], 'old and worn
   out' [ICC]. It is the diseased nature of the tree that makes evil fruit the
   only possible fruit [Mor].

2. The focus is on the quality of the tree: 'bad' [LN; CEV, NASB, NET,
   NIV, NRSV], 'poor' [TG; REB, TEV]. It is more a general and
   unspecified condition of the tree [Mor]. It refers to poor or bad quality and
   hence of little or no value [LN].

3. The focus is on the tree's productivity: 'worthless' [ICC].

QUESTION—What is the quality πονηρός associated with the bad fruit?

Different aspects of the word are brought into focus. The following senses
   are not necessarily exclusive of each other.

1. The focus is on the quality of the fruit: 'spoiled, worthless' [BAGD],
   'worthless' [NTC], 'evil' [KJV], 'bad' [BAGD, LN, Mor, TG, WBC; all
   versions except KJV]. Here it indicates bad or worthless fruit [Mor]. The

different kinds of fruit here resemble each other, but as you judge the fruit, one is poor in quality [MLJ].

2. The focus is on the taste of the fruit. It is fruit that tastes bad or that no one wants to eat [TG, TH].

7:18 A good tree is- not -able[a] to-produce bad fruit, nor[b] an unhealthy/ worthless tree to-produce good fruit.

LEXICON—a. pres. act. indic. of δύναμαι (LN 74.5): 'to be able' [LN, WBC; NET], 'can' [LN, Mor, NTC; all versions except NET, TNT], 'to be possible' [TNT].

b. οὐδέ (LN 69.7) (BAGD 1. p. 591): 'nor' [LN, WBC; NAB, NASB, NET, NJB, NRSV], 'neither' [LN, Mor, NTC; KJV], 'or' [REB, TNT], 'and' [CEV, NLT, TEV].

QUESTION—How is this verse connected with the previous one?

The Semitic style of emphasis is to state something negatively after stating it positively [EBC, McN, NCBC, TG].

7:19 Every[a] tree not producing good fruit is-cut-down[b] and is-thrown[c] into (the) fire.

LEXICON—a. πᾶς: 'every' [Mor, NTC, WBC; CEV, KJV, NAB, NASB, NET, NIV, NLT, NRSV, TNT], 'any' [NJB], 'a' [REB], 'and any' [TEV]. The previous verse talked of the tree's fruit; this verse now talks about the fate of the tree itself [Mor].

b. pres. pass. indic. of ἐκκόπτω (LN 19.18) (BAGD 1. p. 241): 'to be cut down' [BAGD, LN, Mor, NTC, WBC; all versions except CEV, KJV, NLT], 'to be hewn down' [KJV], 'to be chopped down' [CEV, NLT].

c. pres. pass. indic. of βαλλω: 'to be thrown' [Mor, NTC, WBC; all versions except CEV, KJV], 'to be cast' [KJV], 'to be burned' [CEV]. There is a connotation of violence and decisive rejection [Mor].

QUESTION—What is the image in this verse?

People who operate orchards do not tolerate trees that do not produce the quality of fruit desired because the trees take up space and may spread their corruption to other healthy trees. Thus there is no justification for permitting the tree to exist [Mor]. The image is of a person (not God) cutting down the tree, even though the ultimate intent is to provide a picture for God's judgment [TG]. For the basic image, the fire is literal and necessary in order to contain the disease of the unhealthy tree, but the fire will also bring to mind the fire of hell [Mor]. The images tie it to the final judgment when God will be the one acting [WBC]. This verse is exactly like 3:10b, with the same words as John the Baptist [BSC, EBC, ICC, McN, Mor, NAC, NCBC, TG, TNTC2].

7:20 So[a] then you(pl)-will-know[b] them[c] from their fruits.

LEXICON—a. ἄρα (LN 89.46) (BAGD 4. p. 104): 'then, then indeed' [LN], 'so, as a result, consequently' [BAGD, LN, Mor, ZG]. The phrase ἄρα γέ is translated 'so then' [Mor; NASB, NET, TEV, TNT], 'so' [NAB], 'thus'

[NIV, NRSV], 'that is why I say' [REB], 'I repeat' [NJB], 'yes' [NLT], 'therefore' [NTC], 'wherefore' [KJV], 'clearly then' [WBC], not explicit [CEV]. Γέ strengthens and emphasizes the meaning of ἄρα [Mor, ZG].

 b. future mid. (deponent = act.) indic. of ἐπιγινώσκω (LN 27.61) (BAGD 2.a. p. 291): 'to know'. See this word at 7:16.

 c. αὐτός: 'them' [Mor, NTC; KJV, NAB, NASB, NET, NIV, NJB, NRSV, REB, TNT], 'a tree' [NLT], 'a tree or a person' [NLT], 'the false prophets' [TG, WBC; TEV], 'who the false prophets are' [CEV]. There is a more direct connection with 'the false prophets' of 7:16–18 than to 7:19; this verse has the same meaning as v.16a [TG]. The pronouns refer to the false prophets and not the trees [TH, WBC].

QUESTION—What relationship is indicated by ἄρα γέ 'so then'?
It picks up the thought from 7:16 and infers from 7:17-19: 'so then you see that...' [McN]. It indicates that this verse is the logical conclusion of the previous argument [Mor]. It introduces a strong inferential conclusion [WBC], and 'indicates that as trees are recognized by their fruit, so are men' [TH].

DISCOURSE UNIT: 7:21–27 [NTC; NJB]. The topic is the true disciple [NJB], the end of the way: sayers versus doers [NTC].

DISCOURSE UNIT: 7:21–23 [EBC, Ed, GNT, HF, McN, NCBC, NIBC, NTC, Pl, TG, TH, TNTC2, WBC; CEV, NAB, NET, NJB, NLT, NRSV, TEV]. The topic is Jesus' statement 'I never knew you' [GNT, TG, TH; HF, TEV], Jesus says who he will not recognize as being his people [TH], the true disciple [NAB, NJB], true disciples [NLT], a warning [CEV], concerning self-deception [NRSV], warning against self-deception [McN], pretenders judged [NET], the day of judgment [TG, TH], the day when God will judge people [TH], Jesus says who will enter the Kingdom of Heaven [TG, TH], those who will be under God's rule/reign [TH], the insufficiency of the charismata [WBC], the end of the way: sayers versus doers [NTC], two claims [EBC], true and false service [NCBC], the kingdom contrasts with the common life of religionists.[Ed (p. 531)].

7:21 Not everyone[a] saying[b] to-me, Lord[c] Lord,
LEXICON—a. πᾶς: 'everyone' [Mor, NTC, TG, WBC; all versions except NJB, NLT], 'all people who sound religious' [NLT], '(it is not) anyone' [NJB].

 b. pres. act. participle of λέγω: 'to say' [Mor, NTC, TG; all versions except CEV, NLT, TEV], 'to call' [CEV, TEV], 'to acknowledge' [WBC], 'to refer' [NLT]. Semitic *amar* 'to speak' can also have the meaning 'to designate, name' (Luke 6:46 uses καλέω 'call') [AAG (p. 193)].

 c. Κύριος (LN 12.9) (BAGD 2.c.β. p. 459): 'Lord' (in reference to Jesus) [BAGD, LN]. The repeated vocative is translated 'Lord Lord' [Mor, NTC, WBC; all versions except CEV, NLT], 'Lord' [NLT], '(their) Lord' [CEV].

QUESTION—What is meant by the title 'Lord'?

It was used generally as a term of polite address, but is used in this context as a reverential title [NIBC]. It is more than polite address since it occurs in the context of a discussion of what will happen on judgment day [ICC, McN, Mor]. It has overtones of divinity [Mor]. Jesus sometimes referred to himself in such veiled terms as 'son of Man' or 'Lord' of which the disciples only understood the true significance after the Resurrection. Whatever their initial understanding of the term may have been, in the following verses he stretches their understanding of it as he portrays himself as the center of Kingdom activity and as the final judge [EBC]. It indicates Jesus' authority and exalted status, especially as Jesus presents himself and not God as the judge on the great judgment day [TNTC2]. It means more than 'rabbi' or 'master' because it indicated a dependent relationship between servant and lord [BSC]. Calling someone 'Lord' was a polite way of saying that one was available to serve that person [TG]. To the original audience Κύριος would have meant 'master' or 'teacher', implying that Jesus had the right to lead and to teach [NCBC].

QUESTION—What is implied by the repetition of the title 'Lord' in this verse?

Repetition of the word emphasizes the lordship, that they are regarding Jesus as their Lord [Mor]. The doubled 'Lord, Lord' reflects fervency [EBC] and earnestness [ICC]. The repetition means that the person is in the habit of saying that Jesus is his Lord [TH].

will-enter[a] into the kingdom[b] of-the heavens,

LEXICON—a. future mid. (deponent = act.) indic. of εἰσέρχομαι (LN 15.93) (BAGD 2.a. p. 233): 'to enter' [LN, Mor, NTC, WBC; all versions except CEV], 'to get into' [CEV]. It is translated: 'they still won't enter' [NLT]. See this word at 5:20.

b. εἰς τὴν βασιλείαν: 'the kingdom' [Mor, NTC, WBC; all versions].

QUESTION—What is meant by entering the kingdom of heaven?

The kingdom is pictured as a future event and indicates eternal life with God [TG]. Entering the kingdom refers to salvation at the last judgment [WBC].

but[a] the (one) doing[b] the will[c] my father, who (is) in the heavens (will enter).

LEXICON—a. ἀλλά (LN 89.125) (BAGD 1.a. p. 38): 'but' [LN, Mor, NTC; KJV, NASB, NJB], 'but only' [WBC; NAB, NIV, NRSV, REB, TEV], 'only' [CEV, NET, TNT], 'only' [CEV], not explicit [NLT]. The conjunction ἀλλά points to the contrast between just using the title and obeying the Father [BSC].

b. pres. act. participle of ποιέω (LN 42.7) (BAGD I.1.c.α. p. 682): 'to do' [LN, Mor, WBC; all versions except CEV, NLT], 'to obey' [CEV, NLT], 'to put into practice' [NTC].

c. θέλημα (LN 25.2, 30.59) (BAGD 1.c.γ. p. 354): 'will' [BAGD, LN (30.59), Mor, NTC, WBC; all versions except CEV, NLT, TEV], 'wish,

desire' [LN (25.2)], 'what my Father in heaven wants them to do' [TEV],
not explicit [CEV, NLT].
QUESTION—What is the significance of the possessive pronoun 'my' in this
verse?
  This is the first instance of 'my Father' in Matthew and supports Jesus'
  claim to be the sole revealer and interpreter of the Father's will [EBC] and
  the authorized representative of the Father [ICC]. It implies a unique, close
  relationship between Jesus and the Father [Mor].

7:22 Many (people) will-say[a] to-me on that day,[b]
LEXICON—a. fut. act. indic. of λεγω: 'to say(to me)' [Mor, NTC, WBC; all
    versions except CEV, NLT], 'to call (me)' [CEV], 'to tell (me)' [NLT].
  b. ἡμέρα (LN 67.178) (BAGD 3.b.β. p. 347): 'day' [BAGD, LN; all
    versions]. The phrase 'that day' is translated: 'when the day comes' [NJB,
    REB], 'when the Judgment Day comes' [TG; TEV], 'on the day of
    judgment' [WBC; CEV], 'on judgment day' [NLT], 'in that day' [Mor,
    NTC].
QUESTION—In what sense is ἐν ἐκείνῃ τῇ ἡμέρᾳ 'on that day' used?
  'Day' stands for the event of God's judgment. 'When I start to judge
  everyone, many will say...' [Die (p. 48)]. It is the day of judgment when
  Jesus will be the judge [MLJ]. It is the final judgment (cf. Isa. 2:11, 17;
  Zech. 14:6-9) [BSC], the final day of judgment [TNTC2], the day of
  judgment [EBC, NIBC], the Last Judgment [NCBC, NTC], the last day
  [ICC]. It is a technical eschatological term [NCBC]. This is the Judgment
  Day when Jesus will be the Judge [Mor, Pl]. It is the day of the Lord [WBC].

Lord, Lord, in-your(sg) name did-we- not -prophesy,[a]
  LEXICON—a. aorist act. indic. of προφητεύω (LN 33.459) (BAGD 1.
    p. 723): 'to prophesy' [LN, Mor, NTC, WBC; KJV, NAB, NASB, NET,
    NIV, NJB, NLT, NRSV, REB, TNT], 'to speak God's message' [TEV],
    'to preach' [CEV], 'to proclaim a divine revelation' [BAGD].
    Προφητεύω 'to prophesy' means to deliver a spiritual message [MLJ],
    not just to tell the future but to proclaim truth in all ways [WBC]. It is
    proclaiming divine revelation as opposed to predicting the future [TH].
    The aorist is constative or global, summarizing action in its entirety [ZG].
QUESTION—What is the significance of the phrase τῷ σῷ ὀνόματι 'in your
name'?
  There is no lexical entry for the preposition 'in', the dative case being used
  to express the fact that the name of Jesus was used to cast the demons out
  [McN, ZG]. It means by the power and authority of his name [ICC, Mor,
  TG, WBC, ZG]. It means claiming to act for Jesus and with his authority
  [NCBC, NIBC]. It is a claim that fellowship with Jesus is the source of their
  power, but in reality they have only used his name as a magic formula
  [NTC]. It means that they professed homage to Jesus Christ [Pl]. The phrase
  'in your name' is repeated three times and placed first in each clause for
  emphasis [Mor, Pl, WBC].

QUESTION—What is implied by the rhetorical question?
These questions expect the affirmative answer 'yes you did' [Mor, NIBC, TH]. and the context indicates they did do these things [Brc, EBC, ICC, Mor, NCBC, NIBC, WBC]. Their argument is that they could not have done these things if they did not belong to Jesus [EBC, ICC, McN, Mor, NCBC, NIBC, Pl, WBC]. The question expresses surprise as well as the recognition that the answer they will get will be negative [NTC].

and in-your(sg) name we-cast-out[a] demons,[b]
LEXICON—a. aorist act. indic. of ἐκβάλλω (LN 15.44, 53.102) (BAGD 1. p. 237): 'to cast out' [Mor, NTC, WBC; KJV, NASB, NET, NLT, NRSV], 'to drive out' [BAGD, LN; NAB, NIV, NJB, REB, TEV, TNT], 'to force out' [CEV], 'to expel' [BAGD, LN]. This word conveys the notion of force [TH].
  b. δαιμόνιον (LN 12.37) (BAGD 2. p. 169): 'demon' [BAGD, LN, Mor, NTC, WBC; all versions except KJV], 'devil' [KJV], 'evil spirit' [BAGD]. In the NT demons are personal beings that do evil and are associated with Satan [Mor].

and in-your(sg) name we-did[a] many miracles?[b]
LEXICON—a. aorist act. indic. of ποιέω (LN **90.45**) (BAGD I.1.b.β. p. 681): 'to do' [BAGD, **LN**; KJV, NAB, NET, NRSV, TNT], 'to perform' [BAGD, LN, Mor, NTC, TG, WBC; NASB, NIV, NLT, REB, TEV], 'to work' [CEV, NJB].
  b. δύναμις (LN 76.7) (BAGD 4. p. 208): 'miracle' [BAGD, LN, WBC; CEV, NASB, NIV, NJB, NLT, REB, TEV], 'wonderful work' [KJV], 'deed of power' [BAGD; NRSV], 'powerful deed' [NET], 'work of power' [TNT], 'mighty deeds' [LN; NAB], 'mighty work' [Mor, NTC], 'wonder' [BAGD]. The miracles were probably miraculous healings [WBC].

7:23 **And then[a] I-will-declare[b] to-them that[c]**
LEXICON—a. τότε (LN 67.47) (BAGD 2. p. 824): 'then' [BAGD, LN, Mor]. The phrase καὶ τότε 'and then' [Mor, NTC, WBC; KJV, NASB] is also translated 'then' [NAB, NET, NIV, NJB, NRSV, REB, TEV, TNT], 'but' [CEV, NLT].
  b. fut. act. indic. of ὁμολογέω (LN **33.221**) (BAGD 4. p. 568): 'to declare' [BAGD, LN, Mor, WBC; NAB, NASB, NET, NRSV, TNT], 'to declare plainly' [WBC], 'to profess' [KJV], 'to tell' [CEV, NIV, NJB, REB], 'to say' [Mor, NTC; TEV], 'to say openly' [NTC], 'to reply' [NLT]. An adverb or adverbial phrase is used to show that this is a strong statement: 'solemnly' [NAB], 'plainly' [Mor, WBC; NIV, REB], 'to their faces' [NJB].
  c. ὅτι (LN **90.21**) (BAGD 2. p. 589): This word marks direct discourse to follow and is represented in translation by quotation marks [Mor, NTC, WBC; all versions].

I- never^a -knew^b you(pl);

LEXICON—a. οὐδέποτε (LN 67.10) (BAGD p. 592): 'never' [BAGD, LN, Mor, NTC, WBC; all versions except CEV], not explicit [CEV].

b. aorist act. indic. of γινώσκω (LN 28.1, 31.27) (BAGD 7. p. 161): 'to know' [LN (28.1), Mor, NTC; all versions except CEV], 'to acknowledge' [BAGD, LN (31.27), WBC]. This clause is translated: 'I will have nothing to do with you!' [CEV].

QUESTION—What is the force of the clause 'I never knew you'?

'I never knew you' means that Jesus would never recognize or acknowledge them as what they claimed to be [BAGD, BSC, ICC, McN, Mor, WBC]. It means that he had never had any dealings or personal relationship with them [BSC]. He wasn't even acquainted with them [Pl], they were complete strangers to him [Brc]. They never really were his followers [TG], they meant nothing to him [NCBC, TH], and they never had participated in the Kingdom of God [WBC]. It was not that Jesus was ignorant of them or their deeds [Mor, NTC], for he obviously knew about them [BSC]. This statement is not to be understood literally, but is formulaic, and means that Jesus will not recognize that they are his own [ICC]. In the Semitic sense γινώσκω 'to know' implies election, and not just knowledge [WBC].

go-away^a from me

LEXICON—a. pres. act. impera. of ἀποχωρέω (LN 15.51) (BAGD p. 102): 'to go away, leave, depart from' [BAGD, LN]. The clause ἀποχωρεῖτε ἀπ' ἐμοῦ 'go away from me' [Mor, NTC; NET, NRSV, TNT] is also translated: 'depart from me' [BAGD, LN, WBC; KJV, NAB, NASB], 'out of my sight' [REB], 'away from me' [NIV, NJB], 'get away from me' [TEV], 'get out of my sight' [TH; CEV], 'go away' [NLT].

QUESTION—What is the force of the clause 'go away from me'?

The rabbis used a statement such as this one to ban people from their presence and fellowship [NCBC, TH]. It was a formula of repudiation as in Peter's denial [TNTC2]. In this context it is obviously final and drastic [EBC], a solemn and final judgment, the ultimate anathema [BSC], a verdict of complete rejection [Mor]. It is a way of saying 'I will have nothing to do with you' [EBC, NCBC, TG, TH]. Their punishment is being banned from Christ's presence [Pl]. The price of masquerading as a follower of Christ is to be eternally separated from him [NAC]. The verse is a quotation of Psalm 6:8, the words that a pious sufferer speaks to his persecutors [EBC, Mor, TH, TNTC2].

you^a doers (of) lawlessness.^b

LEXICON—a. ὁ (LN 92.24) (BAGD II.1.i. p. 551): The definite article with this participle in the nominative case is vocative: 'you' [BAGD, Mor, NTC, WBC; CEV, KJV, NAB, NASB, NIV, NRSV, TEV, TNT], not explicit [NET, NJB, REB].

b. ἀνομία (LN 88.139) (BAGD 2. p. 72): 'lawlessness' [LN, Mor; NASB], 'lawless deed' [BAGD], 'iniquity' [WBC; KJV], 'evil' [NJB]. The phrase οἱ ἐργαζόμενοι τὴν ἀνομίαν is translated 'you evil doers' [NAB, NIV, NRSV], 'you who practice lawlessness' [NASB], 'you who work lawlessness' [Mor], 'you who work against God's law' [TNT], 'ye that work iniquity' [KJV], 'you wicked people' [TEV], 'you evil people' [CEV], 'all evil doers' [NJB], 'lawbreakers' [NET], 'law-despisers' [NTC], 'doers of iniquity' [WBC], 'the things you did were unauthorized' [NLT], 'your deeds are evil' [REB].

QUESTION—What is meant by ἀνομία 'lawlessness'?

It is not just doing wrong but rejecting the law of God, an inner state where the will has decided against obedience [Mor]. It is a violation of the Father's will [WBC]. It means that one's ways are contrary to God [TH]. Since they had no relationship to Jesus their life had never been deeply touched by God's law [BSC]. It is behavior contrary to God's law as Jesus has interpreted it in the Sermon on the Mount [NCBC]. Matthew preserves the Septuagint wording of Psalm 6:8 for 'workers of lawlessness' (ἀνομία), whereas Luke has 'workers of unrighteousness' (ἀδικία) [ICC, McN, NCBC, Pl]. Matthew's choice of wording reflects the point of view of his Jewish audience and Luke's reflects that of the Greek audience [Pl].

DISCOURSE UNIT: 7:24–29 [GNT, HF, NAC, Pl; CEV, NAB, NASB, NET, NIV, NLT, NRSV]. The topic is the two foundations [GNT; NAB, NASB], the wise and foolish builders [NAC; NIV], two builders [CEV], building on a solid foundation [NLT], hearers and doers [NRSV], hearing and doing [NET], building on the rock [HF], the judgments which await the members of the kingdom [Pl].

DISCOURSE UNIT: 7:24–27 [EBC, Ed, ICC, McN, MLJ, NAC, NCBC, NTC, TG, TH, WBC; NET, NIV, NLT, NRSV, TEV]. The topic is the two house builders [EBC, ICC, TG, TH; TEV], the two men and the two houses [MLJ], two men build houses [TH], two different kinds of houses [TH], the two foundations [McN], two different kinds of foundations [TG], building on a solid foundation [NLT], the parable of the two builders [WBC], the parable of the two house builders [NCBC], two built houses [TH], the parable of the wise and foolish builders [Pl], wise versus foolish builders [NAC], the wise and foolish builders [NIV], the end of the way: doers versus hearers: the parable of the two builders [NCBC, NTC], hearers and doers [NRSV], hearers and doers of the word [ICC], hearing and doing [NET], what hearing really means [TH], a house on rock and a house on sand [TG], the house on the sand and the house on the rock [TH], the received kingdom is like a house on a solid foundation which cannot be destroyed [Ed (p. 531)].

7:24 Therefore[a] everyone[b] who hears these words[c] of-mine and does[d] them,
LEXICON—a. οὖν (LN **89.50**) (BAGD 1.a. p. 593): 'therefore' [BAGD, LN, Mor, WBC; KJV, NASB, NIV, NJB], 'consequently' [BAGD, LN], 'accordingly' [BAGD, LN], 'then' [BAGD, LN, NTC; NRSV], 'so then'

[LN; TEV], 'so' [BAGD, LN; REB], not explicit [CEV, NAB, NET, NLT, TNT].

b. πᾶς (LN 59.23, 59.24) (BAGD 1.c.γ. p. 632): See 5:22, or 1.c.g. p. 637. 'everyone' [BAGD, Mor, NTC, WBC; NAB, NASB, NET, NIV, NJB, NRSV, TNT], 'all' [LN (59.23)], 'anyone' [LN (59.24); CEV, NLT, TEV], 'whoever' [BAGD; REB], 'whosoever' [KJV].

c. λόγος (LN 33.98) (BAGD 1.a.δ. p. 477): 'words' [LN, Mor, NTC, WBC; all versions except CEV, KJV, NLT], 'sayings' [LN; KJV], 'teachings' [CEV, NLT].

d. pres. act. indic. of ποιέω (LN 42.7) (BAGD I.1.c.α. p. 682): 'to do' [LN, Mor, WBC; KJV, NET], 'to put into practice' [NTC; NIV], 'to act on/upon' [NAB, NASB, NJB, NRSV, REB, TNT], 'to obey' [CEV, NLT, TEV]. Ποιέω repeats a key word in each of the sections 7:15–20, 21–23 and 24–27 [ICC, NCBC, TNTC2]. It emphasizes that a practical response is needed, not a merely superficial one [TNTC2]. It is the equivalent of 'obeys' in 7:26 [TH]. For the disciple there is an intimate connection between the teaching and how life is lived [NCBC].

QUESTION—What is referred to by the phrase 'these words of mine'?

It refers to all the things Jesus said in the Sermon on the Mount [EBC, ICC, McN, NCBC, TG, TH]. Μου 'of mine' is in an emphatic position, emphasizing the personal element; that is, everyone who hears me [ICC, Mor, NCBC, NTC, TH, WBC]. 'These' and 'mine' together also add force to each other [ICC].

he-will-be-like[a] (a) wise[b] man,[c]

TEXT—Instead of ὁμοιωθήσεται 'he will be like', some manuscripts have ὁμοιώσω αὐτόν 'I will liken him'. GNT selects the reading 'he will be like' with a B rating, indicating that the text is almost certain. The reading 'I will liken him' is taken only by KJV.

LEXICON—a. fut. pass. indic. of ὁμοιόω (LN 64.4, 64.5) (BAGD 1. p. 567): 'to be like' [LN (64.4), NTC, WBC; CEV, NAB, NET, NIV, NJB, NRSV, REB, TEV], 'to be likened to' [Mor] 'to be compared to' [LN (64.5); NASB, TNT]. This future passive verb is translated as a present active verb 'is like' [CEV, NET, NIV, REB, TEV], 'is wise' [NLT]; as a present passive 'may be compared' [NASB]; as future active 'will be like' [NTC, WBC; NAB, NJB, NRSV]. The future tense is used here to describe a true condition or circumstance regardless of when it occurs [TH]. See this word at 6:8.

b. φρόνιμος (LN **32.31**) (BAGD p. 866): 'wise' [BAGD, LN, Mor, WBC; CEV, KJV, NAB, NASB, NET, NIV, NLT, NRSV, TEV], 'sensible' [BAGD, NTC, ZG; NJB], 'to have sense' [REB], 'prudent' [BAGD, WBC; TNT]. For Matthew the wise person is the obedient person, as with the wise and foolish maidens in 25:1–13 [WBC]. Φρόνιμος is a favorite word of Matthew's (10:16; 24:46; 25:2, 4, 8, 9) [NCBC, TH].

c. ἀνήρ (LN 9.1) (BAGD 4. p. 66): 'man' [BAGD, Mor, NTC; all versions
except CEV, NLT], 'person' [LN, WBC; CEV, NLT].

who builds[a] his house upon the rock.[b]
LEXICON—a. aorist act. indic. of οἰκοδομέω (LN **45.1**) (BAGD 1.a. p. 558):
'to build' [BAGD, LN, Mor, NTC, WBC; all versions].
   b. πέτρα (LN 2.21) (BAGD 1.a. p. 654): 'rock' [BAGD, LN, Mor, NTC; all
versions except CEV, NLT], 'solid rock' [CEV, NLT], 'a foundation of
rock' [WBC], 'bedrock' [LN]. This term refers the underlying bedrock
and not just to stones or stony ground [TG, TH]. Note that 'these words of
mine', 'them', and 'rock' all refer to the same thing in this illustration,
which is the words in this sermon [NTC],

7:25 **And[a] the rain[b] came-down[c]**
LEXICON—a. καί: 'and' [Mor; KJV, NASB], 'when' [WBC], 'though' [NLT],
not explicit [NTC; all versions except KJV, NASB, NLT].
   b. βροχή (LN **14.10**) (BAGD p. 147): 'rain' [BAGD, LN, Mor, NTC, WBC;
all versions].
   c. aorist act. indic. of καταβαίνω (LN **15.107**) (BAGD 1.b. p. 408): 'to
come down' [BAGD, LN, Mor; NIV, NJB, REB], 'to fall' [BAGD, WBC;
NAB, NET, NRSV, TNT], 'to descend' [LN; KJV, NASB] 'to pour
down' [NTC; CEV, TEV], 'to come in torrents' [NLT].
QUESTION—What is the structure of the next verses?
   The pattern of this verse is: conjunction + verb + article + element. That
   pattern is repeated three times in perfect parallelism and then followed by the
   climax 'and hit upon that house' [ICC]. There is an almost exact symmetry
   in parallelism [WBC], a strict parallelism of 7:24–25 with 7:26–27,
   indicating that there is much in common in the two approaches to how
   people build their lives and the risks they encounter [BSC].
QUESTION—What kind of rainfall is this?
   The picture is based on winter cloudbursts in Palestine [BSC], when
   torrential rains bringing flash floods through the wadis [EBC, WBC]. The
   picture is of a tempest, a large storm [NCBC, WBC]. This is a heavy
   torrential rain, not an ordinary gentle one [Mor].
QUESTION—What is the meaning of the storm imagery here?
   In the OT a large storm is often an indication of the wrath and judgment of
   God [NCBC, WBC]. Rains and rivers are often symbols of God's judgment
   [ICC]. They stand for tests that search and try us to the very depths [MLJ].
   The ultimate test comes at the judgment day, but there are tests in life before
   then [EBC, NTC]. Only storms will reveal the true differences in work
   quality between apparently identical houses. The point is that the wise man
   has built a house that can withstand anything [EBC]. This is an image of the
   coming judgment when all men will be examined down to their very roots,
   and a warning not to deceive themselves about their relationship to Jesus
   [BSC]. The combination of rain falling, rivers rising, and winds beating
   against the house make for the severest test a house can endure [Mor]. The

test at the last day of judgment cannot be avoided, it will come no matter
what and it may come suddenly and allow no further preparation [NTC]. The
natural association for Matthew and his readers would have been the test at
the last Judgment [ICC].

and^a the floods/rivers^b came^c

LEXICON—a. καί: 'and' [Mor, NTC, WBC; KJV, NASB, NLT], not explicit
[all versions except KJV, NASB, NLT].
  b. ποταμός (LN 1.76) (BAGD 1. p. 694): 'flood' [NTC; KJV, NAB, NASB,
    NET, NJB, NRSV, REB], 'floodwaters' [NLT], 'river' [BAGD, LN, Mor,
    WBC; CEV, TEV, TNT], 'stream' [BAGD, LN; NIV]. These are torrents
    which arise in ravines after a heavy rain and sweep all things away before
    them [BAGD, ICC, McN, Mor, ZG].
  c. aorist act. indic. of ἔρχομαι (LN 15.7) (BAGD I.1.c.α. p. 311): 'to come'
    [BAGD, NTC; KJV, NAB, NASB, NET, NRSV], 'to rise' [Mor; NIV,
    NJB, NLT, REB, TNT], 'to flood' [CEV], 'to overflow' [WBC], 'to flood
    over' [TEV].
QUESTION—What is the image portrayed in 'the floods/rivers came'?
  Flash floods overflowing the riverbanks and hitting the houses are a natural
  occurrence in autumn in Palestine; the otherwise dry ravines suddenly turn
  into torrents after autumn rains [NIBC]. A solid foundation in the Palestinian
  desert must be able to withstand the flash floods resulting from sudden
  storms [NAC]. The rivers/floods represent the world beating against us
  (sometimes hard, sometimes just seeping in) [MLJ]; the floods and winds
  probably stand for the pressures of life in this world [TNTC2]. Like a flood,
  the day of judgment will disclose which spiritual structures will last, but
  other crises before that day can also reveal which structures were wisely
  built [NAC].

and^a the winds^b blew^c

LEXICON—a. καί: 'and' [Mor; CEV, KJV, NAB, NASB, NIV, NLT, NRSV,
    TEV], 'while' [NTC], 'and while' [WBC], not explicit [NET, NJB, REB,
    TNT].
  b. ἄνεμος (LN 14.4) (BAGD 1.a. p. 64): 'wind' [BAGD, LN, Mor, NTC; all
    versions except NJB], 'gale' [WBC; NJB], 'strong winds' [Mor].
  c. aorist act. indic. of πνέω (LN 14.4) (BAGD 1.a. p. 679): 'to blow'
    [BAGD, LN, Mor, NTC, WBC; all versions except CEV, NET, NLT,
    TEV], 'to blow hard' [TEV], not explicit [CEV, NET, NLT].

and^a beat-against^b that house,

LEXICON—a. καί: 'and' [Mor, NTC; CEV, KJV, NAB, NASB, NIV, NJB,
    NRSV, REB], 'and these together' [WBC], not explicit [NET, NLT, TEV,
    TNT].
  b. aorist act. indic. of προσπίπτω (LN 19.11) (BAGD 2. p. 718): 'to beat
    against' [Mor; CEV, NET, NIV, NLT], 'to strike against' [LN], 'to burst
    against' [NASB], 'to hurl against' [NJB], 'to buffet' [NAB], 'to fall upon'

[BAGD, NTC], 'to beat upon' [BAGD; KJV, REB, TNT], 'to beat on' [NRSV], 'to assail' [WBC], 'against' (no new verb) [TEV].

QUESTION—What is the subject of the verb 'beat against'?

1. The winds are the subject [TH; CEV, NAB, NASB, NET, NIV, NLT, NRSV, REB, TEV]: the winds blew and beat against that house. There were strong winds that blew against the house [TH].

2. The rain, the rivers, and the winds are the subject [WBC; TNT]: and they all beat against that house. All three nouns (rain, rivers, and winds) are the subject of this verb and of προσκόπτω 'beat against' in 7:27 [WBC].

and[a] it- (did)-not -fall,[b]

LEXICON—a. καί: 'and' [KJV, NJB], 'yet' [NASB, NIV], 'but' [Mor, NTC; CEV, NAB, NET, NRSV, REB, TEV], not explicit [WBC; NLT, TNT].

b. aorist act. indic. of πίπτω (LN 15.119) (BAGD 1.b.β. p. 659): 'to fall' [BAGD, LN, Mor, NTC, WBC; CEV, KJV, NASB, NIV, NJB, NRSV, REB, TEV], 'to fall down' [LN], 'to collapse' [BAGD; NAB, NET, NLT, TNT].

for it-was-founded[a] upon the rock.[b]

LEXICON—a. pluperfect pass. indic. of θεμελιόω (LN **7.42**) (BAGD 1. p. 356): 'to be founded' [BAGD, LN, Mor, NTC, WBC; KJV, NASB, NET, NJB, NRSV], 'to have its foundation' [NIV], 'to be built' [CEV, NLT, TEV], 'to be set solidly' [NAB], 'its foundation was' [TNT], 'its foundations were' [REB]. This pluperfect verb is translated as a pluperfect (past perfect): 'had been founded' [Mor; NASB, NET, NRSV], 'had been set solidly' [NAB]; as a simple aorist: 'was founded' [NTC, WBC; NJB], 'was built' [CEV, KJV, TEV]; as a present tense: 'it is built' [NLT].

b. πέτρα (LN **2.21**) (BAGD 1. p. 356): 'rock' [LN, Mor, NTC, WBC; all versions]. See 7:24.

7:26 And[a] everyone hearing[b] these words of-mine and[c] not doing[d] them

LEXICON—a. καί: 'and' [Mor, NTC, WBC; KJV, NAB, NRSV, REB], 'but' [NASB, NIV, NJB, NLT, TEV], not explicit [CEV, NET, TNT].

b. pres. act. participle of ἀκούω: 'to hear' [Mor, NTC, WBC; CEV, KJV, NASB, NET, NIV, NLT, NRSV, REB, TEV, TNT], 'to listen to' [NAB, NJB].

c. καί: 'and' [Mor, NTC, WBC; all versions except NAB], 'but' [NAB].

d. pres. act. participle of ποιέω (LN 42.7) (BAGD I.1.c.a. p. 682): 'to do' [LN, Mor, WBC; KJV, NET], 'to put into practice' [NTC; NIV], 'to act upon/on' [NAB, NASB, NJB, NRSV, REB, TNT], 'to obey' [CEV, TEV]. The phrase 'not doing them' is translated 'ignores it' [NLT].

he-will-be-like a-foolish[a] man, who builds his house upon the sand.[b]

LEXICON—a. μωρός (LN **32.55**) (BAGD 1. p. 531): 'foolish' [LN, Mor, NTC, TG, WBC; all versions except NAB, NJB, REB], 'stupid' [Mor; NJB], 'who was foolish enough' [REB]. The phrase 'foolish man' is translated 'fool' [NAB]. See 5:22.

b. ἄμμος (LN **2.28**) (BAGD p. 46): 'sand' [LN, Mor, NTC, TG, WBC; all
versions]. This is not a deliberate choice of sand but a lack of diligence to
lay a sound foundation [Mor], the result of shortsightedness [ICC]. The
only important characteristic of sand here is that it is not suitable for a
foundation [WBC]. The foolish man has no foresight and presumes that
the present dry and pleasant weather will continue forever so he takes no
thought about preparing for different conditions [NTC].

7:27 And[a] the rain fell and[b] the floods came

LEXICON—a. καί: 'and' [Mor; KJV, NASB], 'when' [WBC; NLT], not
explicit [NTC; all versions except KJV, NASB, NLT]. The repetitive
vocabulary stresses that it is the same test for this house as for the wise
man's house [Mor].
  b. καί: 'and' [Mor, NTC, WBC; KJV, NASB, NLT, NRSV], not explicit
[CEV, NAB, NET, NIV, NJB, REB, TEV, TNT].

and[a] the winds blew and[b] beat-against[c] that house,

LEXICON—a. καί: 'and' [Mor, WBC; CEV, KJV, NASB, NET, NIV, NLT,
NRSV], 'while' [NTC], not explicit [NAB, NJB, REB, TEV, TNT].
  b. καί: 'and' [Mor, NTC, WBC; CEV, KJV, NAB, NASB, NIV, NJB,
NRSV, REB], not explicit [NET, NLT, TEV, TNT].
  c. aorist act. indic. of προσκόπτω (LN 19.5) (BAGD 1.b. p. 716): 'to beat
against' [BAGD, NTC; CEV, NET, NIV, NLT, NRSV], 'to beat upon'
[KJV], 'to strike against' [LN; TNT], 'assailed' [WBC], '(blew hard)
against' [TEV], 'to buffet' [NAB], 'to burst against' [NASB], 'to batter
against' [REB], 'to strike' [Mor; NJB].

and[a] it-fell,[b]

LEXICON—a. καί: 'and' [Mor, NTC, WBC; all versions except NLT, TNT],
not explicit [NLT, TNT].
  b. aorist act. indic. of πίπτω (LN 15.119): 'to fall' [LN, Mor, NTC; all
versions except NAB, NET, TNT], 'to collapse' [Mor, WBC; NAB, NET,
TNT], 'to fall down' [LN].

and[a] its crash[b] was great.[c]

LEXICON—a. καί: 'and' [NTC, WBC; KJV, NAB, NASB, NJB, NRSV, TEV,
TNT], 'with' [Mor; NLT], not explicit [CEV, NET, NIV, REB].
  b. πτῶσις (LN 20.50) (BAGD p. 728): 'crash' [Mor, NTC; CEV, NIV,
REB], 'fall' [BAGD; KJV, NASB, NET, NJB, NRSV, TEV], 'downfall'
[TNT], 'destruction' [LN], 'falling, collapse' [BAGD], 'damage' [WBC].
  c. μέγας (LN 78.2): 'great' [LN, Mor, WBC; KJV, NASB, NIV, NRSV,
REB, TNT], 'terrible' [LN; TEV], 'tremendous' [NTC; NET], 'a mighty
crash' [NLT], not explicit [CEV]. This phrase is translated 'what a fall it
had' [NJB], 'was completely ruined' [NAB]. That the extent of the ruin
was great means that much of the house fell [McN], the ruin was complete
[Pl], a total ruin [ICC, NTC, TH], a total collapse [TNTC2], a complete
collapse [ICC], a disaster [WBC]. The rhythm of the extended parallelism

is broken here, lending great emphasis to the fall [WBC]. The use of μέγας 'great' as the last word gives additional emphasis [Pl, WBC].

DISCOURSE UNIT: 7:28–8:1 [ICC]. The topic is the conclusion: the crowds and the mountain [ICC].

DISCOURSE UNIT: 7:28–29 [BBC, BSC, EBC, ICC, McN, Mor, NAC, NCBC, NIBC, NTC, TG, TH, TNTC2, WBC; NJB, TEV]. The topic is the authority of Jesus [TG, TH; TEV], Jesus teaches with authority [TG, TH], Jesus has authority when he teaches [TH], the teaching of Jesus has authority [TG], the amazement of the crowds [NJB], the impact of the sermon on the mount [BSC], conclusion of the inaugural sermon [ICC], editorial conclusion [McN, NCBC], conclusion [Mor, TNTC2], response [NAC], response of the masses [BBC], the astonishment of the crowds [WBC], transitional conclusion: Jesus authority [EBC].

7:28 **And it-happened**[a] **(that) when**[b]

LEXICON—a. aorist mid. (deponent = act.) indic. of γίνομαι (LN 13.107) (BAGD I.3.f. p. 159): 'to happen' [BAGD, LN, WBC], 'take place' [BAGD], 'to come to pass' [Mor; KJV], not explicit [NTC; all versions except KJV].

    b. ὅτε (LN **67.30**) (BAGD 1.b. p. 588): 'that when' [Mor, WBC], 'when' [BAGD, LN; CEV, KJV, NAB, NET, NIV, REB, TEV], 'now when' [NTC; NRSV, TNT], 'the result was that' [NASB], 'after' [NLT], not explicit [NJB]. It is a phrase that echoes the Septuagint Greek rendering of a typical Hebrew expression [Mor]. In this gospel it is repeated at the end of each major discourse, indicating transition to the next section and indicating that the significance of the discourse [Mor].

QUESTION—What is the relationship of this section to the preceding passage?

    This is a transitional conclusion [EBC], demonstrating the effect of the preceding teaching [Mor, NTC]. Verse 7:28 describes the impact on the hearers and 7:29 gives the reason for that impact [WBC]. Verses 7:28–8:1 form an inclusio with 4:23–5:2 [ICC, WBC]. This paragraph signals that the collected teaching on discipleship is finished; 8:1 returns to the narrative of the first phase of Jesus' public ministry begun in 4:17 [TNTC2].

QUESTION—What is the relationship of this section to the following passage?

    This is the first of five formulaic sayings that Matthew uses to end the 5 major discourses of the Gospel. All five begin καὶ ἐγένετο 'and it happened' followed by a finite verb (7:28; 11:1; 13:53; 19:1; 26:1) [EBC, ICC, McN, Mor, NCBC, NIBC, Pl, TH, TNTC2, WBC]. It is a deliberate formal transition, a signpost to the development of Matthew's theme [McN, NCBC, TNTC2], a transition between a long discourse and narrative [NCBC, NIBC]. This expression is common in the Septuagint. This is a self-conscious stylistic device that establishes a structural turning point, introducing the conclusion to a section and introducing a transition to the next section [EBC].

Jesus finished^a these words/sayings^b

LEXICON—a. aorist act. indic. of τελέω (LN 67.67) (BAGD 1. p. 810): 'to finish' [BAGD, NTC, TG, WBC; all versions except KJV, TNT], 'to bring to an end, to complete something' [BAGD, ZG], 'to end' [LN, Mor; KJV, TNT]. Τελέω has connotations of fulfillment [Mor, NAC], perhaps indicating that Jesus had accomplished what he intended to and had said everything he wanted to say [Mor].

b. λόγος (LN 33.98) (BAGD 1.a.δ. p. 477): The phrase τοὺς λόγους τούτους is translated 'these words' [NAB, NASB], 'these sayings' [Mor, NTC; KJV, TNT], 'this discourse' [REB], 'saying these things' [NET, NIV, NRSV, TEV], 'what he wanted to say' [NJB], 'speaking' [CEV, NLT], 'speaking these words' [WBC]. The plural can be used to indicate a discourse [Mor]. See 7:24.

the crowds^a were-astonished^b at^c his teaching;^d

LEXICON—a. ὄχλος (LN 11.1) (BAGD 1. p. 600): 'crowd' [BAGD, LN], 'multitude' [LN]. This plural noun is translated 'the crowds' [NTC, WBC; CEV, NAB, NET, NIV, NLT, NRSV, TNT], 'the multitudes' [Mor; NASB], 'the crowd' [TEV], 'the people' [KJV, NJB, REB]. The disciples were the primary audience, and the crowds were a secondary audience [ICC, TNTC2]. The plural emphasizes that it was not just an isolated few but large numbers of people who were astonished [Mor].

b. imperf. pass. indic. of ἐκπλήσσομαι (LN 25.219) (BAGD 2. p. 244): 'to be astonished' [Mor, NTC, WBC; KJV, NAB], 'to be amazed' [BAGD, TH; NASB, NET, NIV, NLT, REB, TEV, TNT], 'to be greatly astounded' [LN], 'to be astounded' [ZG; NRSV], 'to be surprised' [CEV]. This passive verb is also translated actively: 'his teaching made a deep impression on' [NJB]. This is a very strong word indicating wonder or fear [TH]. The imperfect tense of this verb indicates continuous action [ICC, Mor], perhaps indicating that the people were still being amazed after they left the area [ICC, NTC]. There was an ongoing effect [WBC]. It portrays Jesus' hearers as being spellbound [NIBC].

c. ἐπί (LN **89.27**) (BAGD II.1.b.γ. p. 287): 'at' [BAGD, Mor, NTC, WBC; all versions except NET, NJB], 'by' [NET], not explicit [NJB]; 'because of' [BAGD, LN]. This word marks the cause or reason for an event or state [LN].

d. διδαχή (LN 33.224) (BAGD 3. p. 192): 'teaching' [BAGD, LN, Mor, NTC, TH, WBC, ZG; all versions except KJV, NJB, TEV], 'teachings' [NJB], 'the way he taught' [TEV], 'doctrine' [KJV].

QUESTION—Why were the crowds astonished?

1. They were astonished at Jesus' manner, that is, his authority and power [BSC, McN, NAC, NIBC, Pl, TH, TNTC2, WBC]. The authority is what amazed them [NAC, Pl]. The authority was the consistent and amazing element present whenever Jesus taught [WBC]. Jesus interpreted and went beyond the Law only based on his own authority [TNTC2]. Unlike the

rabbis there was a self-authenticating ring of authority in his words
[NIBC]. It was not because he was teaching something new, but because
he had an innate true knowledge of right and wrong [McN].

2. They were astonished at the content as well as Jesus' manner of teaching
[EBC, Ed, MLJ, Mor, NTC, TG]. It was very different from what the
crowd was accustomed to [Mor]. The content included astonishing things
about himself, particularly that he depicted himself as judge at the final
judgment [Ed (p. 541), MLJ]. There was shock about the judgment
described [Mor]. They were astonished at his authority and power [EBC,
MLJ].

7:29 for[a] he was teaching[b] them as[c] one-having[d] authority[e]

LEXICON—a. γάρ: 'for' [Mor, NTC, WBC; KJV, NAB, NASB, NLT, NRSV,
TNT], 'because' [NET, NIV, NJB], not explicit [CEV, REB, TEV]. It
indicates the reason for the astonishment [Mor].

b. imperf. act. indic. of ειμι + pres. act. participle of διδάσκω (LN 33.224):
'he was teaching them' [Mor, NTC, WBC; NASB], 'he taught them'
[CEV, KJV, NAB, NJB, NRSV, TNT], 'he taught' [NET, NIV, NLT,
REB, TEV]. The periphrastic imperfect construction implies that Jesus
habitually taught in this manner [Pl, WBC].

c. ὡς: 'as' [Mor, NTC, WBC; KJV, NAB, NASB, NIV, NLT, NRSV, TNT],
'like' [CEV, NET], 'with (authority)' [NJB, TEV], 'with a note of
(authority)' [REB].

d. pres. act. participle of ἔχω (LN 57.1): 'to have' [LN]. This participle is
translated 'one having' [Mor, WBC; KJV, NAB, NASB, NRSV], 'having'
[NTC], 'one who had' [NET, NIV, NLT, TNT], 'with (authority)' [NJB,
REB, TEV], 'someone with (authority)' [CEV].

e. ἐξουσία (LN 37.35) (BAGD 2. p. 278): 'authority' [Mor, NTC, WBC; all
versions], 'authority to rule' [LN], 'real authority' [NLT], 'one having
authority himself' [WBC].

QUESTION—What is meant by authority?
He taught as one needing no authority beyond his own, not needing to cite
other authorities as the other rabbis and teachers did [TH]. Jesus is either
being presumptuous and heretical or he is truly speaking for God [NAC].
Jesus' message came from the heart and mind of the Father as well as his
own inner being and from Scripture [NTC]. Although he did appeal to
Scripture, he did not base his teaching on what others had said. He is the
King of the Kingdom of Heaven. [BSC].

and not[a] as their scribes.[b]

LEXICON—a. καὶ οὐχ: 'and not' [Mor, NTC, WBC; CEV, KJV, NAB, NASB,
NET, NIV, NRSV, TNT], 'unlike' [NJB, REB], 'quite unlike' [NLT], 'he
wasn't like' [TEV].

b. γραμματεύς (LN 53.94): 'scribe' [Mor, NTC; KJV, NAB, NASB,
NRSV, REB], 'teacher of the law' [NIV, TEV, TNT], 'teacher of the Law
of Moses' [CEV], 'teacher of religious law' [NLT], 'expert in the law'

[LN; NET], 'their own scribes' [NJB], 'their professional Torah scholars' [WBC]. As teachers and interpreters of Jewish law, their goal was the preservation of tradition and the decisions of past rabbis. By contrast, Jesus was more interested in the plain meaning of Scripture than in preserving the legal system that had been built up [TH]. See this word at 5:20.

QUESTION—How does the teaching differ from the scribes?

Jesus was able to teach from his own authority and did not need to bolster his statements with the previous opinions of rabbis [EBC, McN, Mor, NCBC, Pl, TG, TH, WBC]. Jesus spoke the truth, he spoke systematically, and he spoke about matters of great significance, whereas the scribes often rambled on and on about trivialities. Jesus used illustrations and concrete examples. Moreover, he spoke as someone who truly cared about people, in contrast again with the scribes. He also spoke with authority, not needing to quote fallible sources [NTC]. The whole Sermon on the Mount is not just ethical but messianic, that is, Christological and eschatological. Jesus speaks in the first person and claims OT fulfillment in his teaching. He also claims the prerogative of the divine judge to determine who enters heaven and who will be banished. He says that God's people will be persecuted because of allegiance to him, and claims to know the Father's will fully [EBC]. Jesus' teaching was characterized by originality as well as the claim to be messianic [Mor]. Unlike the scribes, who quoted Scripture and tradition in order to justify their pronouncements [McN, NCBC, Pl], Jesus only quotes Scripture in this Sermon in order to reinterpret it, not to bolster his case; he was his own authority [NAC].